DAMAGED

# DAMAGED

## Musicality and Race in Early American Punk

## EVAN RAPPORT

University Press of Mississippi / Jackson

Publication of this book was supported in part by a grant from
the H. Earle Johnson Fund of the Society for American Music
and a grant from the American Musicological Society.

The University Press of Mississippi is the scholarly publishing agency of
the Mississippi Institutions of Higher Learning: Alcorn State University,
Delta State University, Jackson State University, Mississippi State University,
Mississippi University for Women, Mississippi Valley State University,
University of Mississippi, and University of Southern Mississippi.

www.upress.state.ms.us

The University Press of Mississippi is a member
of the Association of University Presses.

First printing 2020
∞

Library of Congress Cataloging-in-Publication Data available

LCCN 2020032150
ISBN 9781496831217 (hardback)
ISBN 9781496831224 (trade paperback)
ISBN 9781496831231 (epub single)
ISBN 9781496831248 (epub institutional)
ISBN 9781496831255 (pdf single)
ISBN 9781496831262 (pdf institutional)

British Library Cataloging-in-Publication Data available

For Mom and Dad

# CONTENTS

# ACKNOWLEDGMENTS

I have many people to thank for helping me bring this book to completion. First of all, I would like to express my gratitude to the musicians and other members of the punk scene who took the time to speak with me. I am especially thankful for the frank and often challenging conversations that helped me think in new ways about matters I had come to take for granted. In addition to the countless informal conversations I've had with friends and colleagues over the years, for which I am also very grateful, thank you to those who granted me formal interviews: Dennis Anderson, Dug Birdzell, Julian Cashwan, Lawrence Caswell, Joey DeFrancesco, Joe DeGeorge, Bubba Dupree, Eppy Epstein, Lois Kahlert, Jonathan Kane, Wayne Kramer, Chris Kulcsar, Ian MacKaye, Bill Orcutt, Lisa Jane Persky, Lyle Preslar, Mary Regalado, Kira Roessler, Paul Roessler, Victoria Ruiz, Peg Simone, David Soldier, Stew, and Chris Stover.

Working with the University Press of Mississippi has been a great experience, and I would like to thank Craig Gill, the director of the Press, for expressing his initial interest in the project and for supporting the book throughout the writing process. Thank you to the anonymous peer reviewers of the proposal and the manuscript, all of whom helped improve and shape the book with insightful comments. I greatly appreciate their time and serious engagement with the book. Thank you to Will Rigby for his excellent editing, and thanks to Emily Bandy, Katie Keene, and Carlton McGrone for their assistance throughout the publication process.

Thank you to my friends and colleagues who discussed ideas in the book with me, shared their own research, or read and commented on drafts, including Jorge Arévalo Mateus, Mick Barr, Chuck Bettis, Stephen Blum, Alessandra Ciucci, Laina Dawes, David Easley, Yonatan Gat, João Paulo Guimarães, Farzaneh Hemmasi, Ellie Hisama, Travis Jackson, Ben Lapidus, Clara Latham, Jerry Lim, Laura Liu, Steve Lorenz, Maia Lynch, Ian MacKaye, Jordan Musser, Judith Peraino, Benjamin Piekut, David Pier, David Racanelli, Ivan Raykoff, Sergio Sayeg, Gabriel Solis, Alex Stewart, Nick Stoia, and Justina Villanueva. In addition to offering helpful comments on a draft of the manuscript, Daniel London helped me retitle the book. Thank you to Aaron Hill for helping me visualize the chart in the appendix. The initial ideas for *Damaged* came to me in autumn

2004 during my graduate coursework, in Stephen Blum's seminar on "Musical Exchanges of African Americans and European Americans" and Ellie Hisama's course on "New Currents in American Music Studies."

Eugene Lang College at the New School, where I teach, supported this work in several key ways. The book was completed during a sabbatical in 2018, my research trip to the UCLA Library was supported by a Faculty Research Fund award, and permissions fees were partially supported from an award from Lang College. I would like to extend a special thanks to my student research assistants: Emily Fawthrop, Anthony Jillions, Anna Jane Krusell, Will Peil, Eli Recht-Appel, and especially Derek Baron, who helped with many music transcriptions, and Jade Gomez, who transcribed interviews and also put me in touch with many of her friends from the LA punk scene. Thank you to Eli Recht-Appel and Anna Kampfe for creating the final version of the chart in the appendix. I owe a tremendous amount to my thoughtful students in the "Punk and Noise" class, running regularly since 2010. Thank you to those who visited the class and shared their experiences and knowledge with me and the students: Sini Anderson, Esneider Arevalo, Mick Barr, Chuck Bettis, Kathleen Hanna, Jonathan Kane, Ian MacKaye, Carlo McCormick, and Robert Sember.

I am grateful for the support of a research fellowship from the Rock and Roll Hall of Fame Library and Archives and the Center for Popular Music Studies at Case Western Reserve University. My week at the Library in the summer of 2016 truly transformed my thinking about the early punk scene.

I acknowledge the support this book received from the H. Earle Johnson Publication Subvention Award of the Society for American Music, and the General Publications Fund of the American Musicological Society, supported in part by the National Endowment for the Humanities and the Andrew W. Mellon Foundation.

Thank you to Direct Holdings Americas and Global ImageWorks for providing me with access to the archive of unedited interviews for the *Time-Life History of Rock and Roll*. Thanks also to Jonathan Brink, who shared some key live Jonathan Richman recordings.

Chapter 2 began as an article in *Popular Music*, "Hearing Punk as Blues" (2014). Thanks to those who helped bring that article to fruition, and particularly Allan Moore, who was editing the journal at the time.

Thanks to my friends and family for their continual support: Mom, Dad, Wendy, Misha, Liz, Jim, Emily, Shawn, and especially Sarah, Natalie, and Charlie.

# DAMAGED

# 1

## Intro: The Meanings of a Musical Style

On July 19, 2018, Mike Ness was accused of punching a fan during a show in Sacramento.[1] As Social Distortion's frontman for forty years, Ness used his platform from the stage to express his frustrations with Donald Trump and his racist policies. Tim Hildebrand, a fan at the concert, said he yelled, "I paid for your music, not your politics," and protested by giving the middle finger to the band for several songs. Ness eventually left the stage and engaged Hildebrand, resulting in an alleged physical confrontation and Ness repeatedly punching Hildebrand.

Ness's fight with Hildebrand strikes me as a particularly fitting way to begin *Damaged: Musicality and Race in Early American Punk*, a book that attempts to do two related things: (1) present the first full-length portrait of American punk as a musical style, and (2) through this musical study of punk, provide a fresh understanding of American society and ideas of race during the long 1970s (roughly 1968 to 1981), a period that greatly impacts our current moment.[2] Punk is especially useful for thinking about contemporary formations of American whiteness, which during the writing of this book have circulated around Donald Trump and his slogan of "make America great again," but which have been operating in American society for at least fifty years. Since its beginnings, punk musicians have directly confronted ideas of whiteness and have wrestled with America's white supremacist history. And although the punk scene is less white than it has ever been, punk is still considered one of the whitest styles of music, and formations of whiteness are at the core of its history and its critique of American society.

For almost half a century, punk has been a forum for white people to explore, define, debate, and police their own whiteness. How does Mike Ness's idea of a Social Distortion show, after forty years of creating a space to express his opinions (and known since the early days as "always ready for a fight"), and during a time of democratic crisis, differ from Hildebrand's idea of the show as a paying consumer who expects to be entertained, and who decided to display his discontent with Ness in an unfriendly environment?[3] What is the difference between the physical engagement of Ness and Hildebrand at this show, and the physical engagement in the "pit," where one might become similarly injured? Why do some people assume hardcore or punk to be dominated by left-wing politics or anarchist ideas, and others by right-wing politics or even fascism? Is there anything about punk that actually supports Trump's "make America great again" worldview, inviting Hildebrand's presence, even as Ness intends to use punk to criticize xenophobic and racist nationalistic attitudes?

In contrast to most writers, I take the position in *Damaged* that punk's music comes first and foremost. Punk is an extraordinarily powerful style of music, and its power comes from the particular ways in which musicians have approached American popular music resources and their associations. Punk is also an extraordinarily misunderstood music, mostly due to the media's and general public's never-ending thirst for sensationalist stories. Punk is an easy target, unconventional and provocative, and seen as a youth culture and thus manipulable, so it has been frequently scapegoated for society's ills or seen as a symbol of Western civilization's decline. Yet a close look at punk as a musical style and the circumstances out of which it emerged tells a very different story, one that sheds light on American society in the long 1970s much more generally, and one that shows punk to be one of the most meaningful and intense expressions of the race and class tensions at America's core.

*Damaged*, of course, is only *a* story of punk, not *the* story. In this book I focus on race as the central axis around which early punk music revolves, and as the lens most appropriate for considering punk's place in the long 1970s. Race is thoroughly intertwined with formations of class, gender, and sexuality; for example, punk's relationships to queer sexuality are intimately connected to race, traceable to the term *punk*'s complex life in African American slang.[4] Race, and a white/black racial binary in particular, has defined American music from its beginnings as a concept, just as race has defined the United States from its beginnings as a nation. As Haki Madhubuti once wrote: "It is not accurate or, for these times, bold enough to just say that America has a race problem. Without doubt or hesitation, I would say that America *is* a race problem."[5] For American music of the postwar era, the period Omi and Winant referred to as the "great transformation," it should be impossible to avoid analyzing the impact of race on popular music, as well as the ways in which popular music has helped shape American whiteness and blackness.[6]

My analysis of punk music in terms of race, class, gender, and sexuality also differs from many other interpretations in that I am not attempting to describe or reveal how punk is related to "identity," especially white identity, as something like an individual's personality. Nor is *Damaged* solely about how identity relates to representation in punk's self-narrations. I am most interested in the ways in which punk is related to empirical aspects of whiteness and blackness, such as the relationship of racial formations (race understood as formed by sociohistorical processes, neither biological essence nor an illusion) to housing, mobility, wealth, legal rights, and ownership; how gender, sexuality, and class are inseparable from race; and identity as a symptom of historical circumstances and facts.[7] The framework of intersectionality, for example, asks us to look not just at identity, but at how race and gender, or more specifically structural racism and sexism, impact discrimination and inequality. As Kimberlé Crenshaw reminded us two decades after writing her pivotal essay, "intersectionality is not just about identities but about the institutions that use identity to exclude and privilege."[8] In the 1950s, 1960s, and 1970s, race dictated arguably every aspect of daily life in the United States, and race has been literally a matter of life and death in the country. In addition to the immediate examples of racial terrorism and the Great Migration, race determined where black people could perform, where black people could spend the night while touring, who could marry, and what schools black people could attend and the resources provided to and by those schools. Not much earlier, American racism determined who was a free human being and who could be enslaved. American society is still fundamentally connected to the idea and legacy of a white/black racial binary.

Fortunately, many scholars have produced excellent research on American music's relationship to race. Recent books such as *Just Around Midnight*, *The Sonic Color Line*, and *Segregating Sound* continue a long line of publications exploring race in many periods and musical styles.[9] And writing on punk, including scholarship, has frequently tackled issues of race head-on.[10] However, when dealing with the history of white people in the United States (usually treated as racially unmarked), major historical events and social circumstances, especially with respect to race, too often still go unmentioned or unconnected to musical life. And the specific questions I aim to tackle in this book, such as the ways in which aspects of musical style directly relate to racial formations and historical events, remain wide open for future research. These research topics are still largely unexplored even in music that is explicitly engaged with race, and whiteness in particular, such as punk.

As outlined in this introduction, *Damaged* engages, sometimes supporting and sometimes refuting, several premises that are usually taken for granted: punk is a product of the suburbs, punk is white music, punk is simple three-chord music, punk started as a response to the bloated or bland music of the 1970s, and punk is violent. But I also wish to emphasize that *Damaged* is not an attempt at an alternative or "secret" history of punk, as a book such as *Lipstick Traces* purports to be.[11] Revealing overlooked histories is imperative, especially if it amplifies suppressed and marginalized voices, but it can also create new problems if such alternative histories avoid or obscure inconvenient truths that continue to go unaddressed.[12] For example, the essential interventions into restoring the multiracial and multigender history of punk should be considered in relation to the music's complicated history with whiteness and masculinity. In my research, only three African American women musicians, in obscure bands, figured in the American punk scene between the early 1970s and 1981—Amanda Jones of New York's Stilettos (Deborah Harry's group before forming Blondie), Karla "Mad Dog" Duplantier of LA's Controllers, and Toni Young of DC's Red C.[13] This is an astonishingly low number given that African American women have been at the forefront of American popular music styles including blues, jazz, rock and roll, and R&B, and given the importance of African American "girl groups" as punk source material. Certainly, since the 1980s and especially in the past decade, African American women have been key players in many punk bands, but avoiding the remarkable absence of black women in punk's early history runs the risk of obfuscating the structural racism to which punk was originally tied, and also gives a convenient escape route to those who wish to avoid acknowledging that racism.[14] For another example, Asian Americans are similarly underrepresented in early punk, except for a very few exceptions, such as Dianne Chai of LA's Alley Cats and Vale Hamanaka of *Search and Destroy*. In *Damaged* I reexamine punk's well-known stories, myths, truths, and clichés in light of musical analysis and broader historical contexts, which often leads to a divergent, counterintuitive, or uncomfortable reading.

### Punk and Suburban Whiteness

"Starting in the years immediately after World War II, millions of ordinary Americans, flush with the disposable income saved up during the war, longing for more space and, above all, a better life for their kids, began to move to the suburbs," writes David Halberstam in his introduction to the revised edition of Bill Owens's *Suburbia*, a collection of photographs from suburban California at the turn to the 1970s.[15] Halberstam also draws the important connection between the suburbs, home ownership, and class. For many, moving to the suburbs was "the first venture, however tentative, into the great new American middle-class. Many were the children of people who had never owned a home and who had rented cold-water flats in the years before the war. As such, the suburban experience was more often than not an optimistic one."[16]

What Halberstam's language conceals, as is typical when writers describe the suburbs, is that these "ordinary Americans" were overwhelmingly white, due to the racist provisions of the government-subsidized loan system and redlining, as well as white suburbanites' often racist and discriminatory impulses. Ninety-eight percent of federally underwritten home loans between 1933 and 1962 went to white homeowners, and most of the remaining housing was in segregated locations.[17] Even as suburban housing opened up to previously excluded groups, African Americans remained explicitly discriminated against when attempting to buy homes in new developments and majority-white suburbs.[18] The mass migration to suburbia, comprising of literally millions of white Americans, essentially amounted to government-supported segregation. As George Lipsitz reports, "by 1993, 86 percent of suburban whites still lived in places with a black population below 1 percent."[19]

America's racial geography was completely redefined after World War II. In the postwar period to the late 1960s, black Americans became increasingly associated with northern and West Coast cities such as New York, Detroit, Chicago, Cleveland, Washington, DC, Los Angeles, and other sites of relocation during the postwar phase of the Great Migration, also called the Second Great Migration.[20] The black populations of these cities took hold during a rapid and dramatic transformation, the Great Migration constituting more of a forced migration to escape lynchings, white terrorism, and Jim Crow in the South than, as is commonly described, solely or even mainly a pursuit of work opportunities in the North.[21] Into the early twentieth century, African Americans were mostly living in the rural South, and even in 1950, 68 percent of the African American population remained in the South.[22] Meanwhile, Ashkenazic Jewish immigrants and Latin Americans were also newly moving in significant numbers to these northern and West Coast cities beginning in the late nineteenth and early twentieth centuries. Through the nineteenth century in New York, for example, there were only small communities of Sephardic Jews, African Americans, and Latin Americans, and most immigrants were of Irish, Italian, German, and Chinese backgrounds.

It is no coincidence that these cities are also the main sites for punk's beginnings. Punk emerged from the specific situation of those cities that were the main destinations for African Americans during the Great Migration and for European and Hispanic immigrants during the same time, as well as the suburbs surrounding these cities, which grew after World War II in racially discriminatory ways. As African Americans moved to northern and West Coast cities, white people—the category expanding to include European "ethnics" such as Irish, Italians, and Jews—dramatically moved out to the suburbs in what was already commonly referred to as "white flight," and understood by the early 1950s as the "usual pattern" or "the classic response to Negro migration into new residential areas."[23] After World War II, "in a very brief time, the now-familiar image of a black inner-city core surrounded by a white suburban ring emerged as the dominant pattern of American life. Thus did the 'ghetto' become dominant in scholarly and creative literature by the 1960s. The term 'inner city' became a virtual synonym for black people."[24]

Meanwhile, "if black became increasingly synonymous with urban during the war years and thereafter, suburban development after World War II sanctioned the formation of a new 'white' identity."[25] Race was inseparable from class: "To be American had rapidly come to mean being 'middle class' and therefore white, as in the facile equation of 'white' with 'middle-class.' It was as though to be the one was automatically to be the other."[26] The association of the suburbs with white people in contrast to black cities, according to America's racial binary, also created a complex territory to navigate for those with marked ethnicities but historically variable racial status, including Italians, Jews, Latinos, and Asians. Especially for European American "ethnics," the suburbs in many ways "helped turn Euro-Americans into 'whites' . . . but this 'white' unity rested on residential segregation, on shared access to housing and life chances largely unavailable to communities of color."[27]

So-called "white flight" was not a simple matter of black people moving in and white people moving out. White people moved to the suburbs not just for "more space" and a "better life for their kids," but based on fears stoked during the Great Migration period by politicians and real estate developers, who told them that as African Americans moved to their neighborhoods, their quality of life would plummet and, if they owned homes, so would their property values.[28] And despite the pervasive images of America's racial conflicts playing out in the South, the superficially diverse and cosmopolitan northern and West Coast cities were often sites of dramatic confrontation. Northern segregation has long been misconstrued as "de facto" segregation—even during my interviews, I regularly heard white people from northern backgrounds remember segregation as "just the way it was"—rather than a result of intentional discrimination, "deliberate actions taken by white Americans to isolate African Americans spatially, and thus marginalize them socially, economically, and politically."[29] Detroit and Harlem were both sites of intense racial conflicts in 1943, and as Wayne Kramer of the MC5 reflected, "black people who came north for jobs and better living conditions found that Jim Crow's northern cousin was alive and well in Detroit. Motor City racism was institutionalized from the top tiers of industry down to its poorest neighborhoods."[30]

And while segregation mostly took the form of geographic separation—spurred by FHA loans and housing discrimination, the growth of the automobile industry, increased access to cars for the middle class, and the destructive building of the interstate highway system—segregation persisted in institutional divisions in shared urban spaces, such as schools and public transportation.[31] White New Yorkers were at the forefront of protesting school integration efforts in the 1950s and 1960s.[32] White flight was also extremely wide-ranging. Los Angeles, for example, was transformed by the influx of white New Yorkers in the postwar era, represented in the popular imagination by Walter O'Malley moving the Dodgers from Brooklyn to LA in 1957.[33] Discrimination continues to plague ostensibly diverse cities. New York's schools, for example, remain among the country's most segregated, suffering from "a system of segregation that is baked into the system and is just kind of accepted," in the words of Richard Carranza, New York City's schools chancellor in 2018.[34]

The huge population shifts in the first half of the twentieth century can be followed musically. The influx of African Americans, Jewish Americans, and Latin Americans into New York led to the flourishing of Tin Pan Alley and the music of Bessie Smith, George Gershwin, Duke Ellington, and James Reese Europe (leader of the Harlem Hellfighters 369th Infantry Regiment band, for which after 1917 nearly half of whom were recruited from Puerto Rico, including the great Rafael Hernández).[35] Most important for this book, the Great Migration created the circumstances for modern blues and its offshoots, including rhythm and blues and rock and roll, as southern black musicians moved to northern cities during the 1940s and 1950s—John Lee Hooker from Mississippi to Detroit, Sister Rosetta Tharpe from Arkansas to Chicago and then New York, Muddy Waters from Mississippi to Chicago—most adjusting their sounds in collaboration with African American and Jewish songwriters and independent record companies predominantly owned by Jewish immigrants, such as Chess Records in Chicago.[36] Meanwhile, the long-standing musical exchanges between whites and blacks in the South and Midwest continued, exemplified by the styles and careers of Little Richard, Chuck Berry, Elvis Presley, Jerry Lee Lewis, and Buddy Holly. This was a period of great musical exchange and innovation, and the musical life of cities such as Detroit reflected an unprecedented level of diversity. As the radio deejay Dan Carlisle remembered: "In Detroit we had Okies, folks from Tennessee and Kentucky, black people from Georgia and other parts of the Deep South. We had people from Germany and Poland and Jewish people, and so on the radio you had Polish music, German music, gospel on Sundays, hearing all this music in one city. Mitch Ryder made all these records composed of these sounds; the MC5 heard all this and put it together."[37]

By the 1960s the demographic mix of the transitional postwar period was disappearing and also reflected in musical life. As African Americans left the South, the southern vernacular styles played by both black and white songsters gave way to a more fully white-dominated country music, relegating once popular black and mixed-race groups such as the Mississippi Sheiks to obscurity.[38] As white people in the northern and West Coast cities moved to populate the suburbs over the course of the 1950s and 1960s, they continued to create music related to the blues-based styles of the Second Great Migration; however, with increasing segregation, the music played by suburban whites became less connected to actual physical interactions and collaborations with black people. Suburban musical life became increasingly dependent on radio, recordings, and the white imagination. Lou Reed described the scene in "Rock and Roll" (1970), a song described by Lester Bangs as "a perfect distillation of race memory":

"There was nothing goin' down at all" for young Jenny, who says, "My parents are gonna be the death of us all / Two TV sets and two Cadillac cars ain't gonna help us at all" until she hears a "New York station" and "her life was saved by rock and roll."[39] In other cases, new music such as the songs of the Beach Boys emerged as idealizations of the nascent white utopia in southern California.[40]

The suburbs are a cornerstone of punk in myth and reality. Punk rock originally developed as an expression of white people who were raised in these new suburban experiments, largely dissociated from the urban environments of their parents' upbringing and the racial and ethnic intermingling of those cities at the time. This world of early punk rock and the suburbs is intimately connected to the youth years of the baby boomer generation, defined here roughly as those born from 1946 to 1964.[41] One of the key points throughout *Damaged* is that even though punk was youth oriented with respect to lyrics and attitude, the scene of early punk musicians was not entirely, or even mainly, a youth culture or subculture as it is commonly described. For example, nearly all of the musicians in the mid-1970s CBGB scene were adults aged 23 and older when they began participating, some even over 30, and their "youth" refers not to their punk years but rather their time growing up in the suburbs in the 1950s and early 1960s.[42] A typical example is Joey Ramone: born in 1951, his teenage years were from 1964 to 1970, he was 23 when the Ramones formed in 1974, and he was 26 when he sang "Teenage Lobotomy" on *Rocket to Russia*. While some musicians were younger—the Dictators were 19 and 20 when they put the band together—this is a generally unremarkable point, since it is commonplace for musicians to start performing and even recording in their late teenage years and early twenties (first recordings for Miles Davis, 18; Dolly Parton, 21; Smokey Robinson, 19; Bob Marley, 17; Waylon Jennings, 17; Bob Dylan, 21; Jimmy Page, 19; Ronnie Spector, 19; Pinchas Zuckerman, 21; with many examples of much younger starts, such as Anne-Sophie Mutter, 15). With this in mind, the punk scene actually seems unusually old until hardcore bands start forming in the late 1970s. The appendix shows some of these figures and how early punk was created by baby boomers.

Suburban geography and middle-class life is embedded in punk's genealogy and terminology; to play "garage rock" one must have a garage. Memoirs by those figuring in early punk history are filled with references to white suburbia and how rock, and then punk more particularly, served as a way out or as a source of rebellion against this white non-culture associated with their parents.[43] The ideas of suburban boredom and disposable time are omnipresent in American punk, both as themes of punk music and as facilitators of DIY community building, but these factors should also be understood with respect to class and privilege, beyond the world of the baby boomers. "People from working-class cities like mine, where everybody needs a job, they got to pay rent, they gotta do all this stuff. It's important to remember . . . all of those kids were middle- and upper-middle-class kids. . . . Yes, those kids did a whole bunch and they created this whole community and it's not a dis, but if you don't understand the socio-economic situation that allowed them to do that, then you can't see how to use that for yourself," said Lawrence Caswell of Cleveland's This Moment in Black History, remembering the punk scene in the 1990s. Kira Roessler of Black Flag and Dos echoed the sentiment, describing the 1970s and 1980s: "being upper class runaways, we were sort of wasting our time away . . . it's possible in a family that's just trying to get by there's just no time and energy to put into going to shows every night, they have to work [and go to] school [and try to] better their lives."[44] As such, the environment of early punk is not simply white, but located in a particular kind of suburban whiteness rooted in privilege—even if this suburban whiteness is frequently taken as representative of all of white America (or even just America). Other musics, such as country and gospel, continued to be primary styles for white people in the South and rural areas during this period. White people also continued to work in styles such as popular song, jazz, and rhythm and blues in more integrated situations.

My emphasis on the suburbs may seem revisionist or contrarian, since although the suburbs always lurk in the background, early punk is almost synonymous with urban locations such as New York's CBGB & OMFUG in the mid-1970s. But CBGB and the early punk music played there is also inextricable from postwar white suburbia. Stories of CBGB invariably describe the club's location in a bleak and deserted corner of the Bowery, yet these portrayals are rarely connected to the ways in which the desolation of New York was produced by white flight and the policies that enabled it. And even though New York punk was ostensibly urban, the musicians that played CBGB were almost all white and almost all grew up in the suburbs or outer boroughs, and they were making music explicitly linked to those experiences. Although early punk rockers were reacting against their parents and their upbringing in the suburbs, they were also very much products of that environment. And once in New York, participants in the CBGB scene remained mostly separate from the urban black and Latinx musicians surrounding them—and those that did explore New York's other music scenes, such as Blondie, were often later cast out of the punk category for doing so. The myth of New York and the Bowery as an empty blank slate for white pioneers is also quasi-colonialist as it discursively erases the city's active musical life that persisted and even thrived during white flight, such as the loft jazz scene—Sam and Bea Rivers's famed Studio Rivbea, which hosted a steady schedule of concerts from 1972 through the mid-1970s, was one block away from CBGB.[45] Parallel situations can be found in other cities, such as Cleveland, which had a downtown early underground rock scene repopulated by suburbanites: Peter Laughner from Bay Village, David Thomas from Cleveland Heights, Allen Ravenstine from Rocky River, and John D. Morton, Brian McMahon, and Dave McManus from Lakewood. Iggy Pop and the Stooges are linked to Detroit, but their upbringing and formation is inseparable from the area around Ann Arbor. This urban/suburban tension is part of punk's core style and its continual resonance.

As the demographics of the suburbs changed during the 1970s and 1980s—becoming increasingly, and in some cases dramatically, racially and ethnically diverse—so did punk. These changes were experienced by youth born at the end of the baby boomer generation and into Generation X (born circa 1965 to 1980), and the musicians' relationship to the suburbs changed along with shifts in the average age of those in the punk scene, from adults in their twenties to teenagers. This book follows the trajectory of the northern and West Coast suburbs from the 1950s and early 1960s childhood world of most of punk's originators, up to the late 1970s and early 1980s environment of Prince George's County, Maryland, in which Bad Brains, punk's first major all-black band, redefined and reframed the hardcore punk vocabulary.

Throughout the long 1970s, suburban conformity, absence of culture, pressures of capitalism, and links to American whiteness persisted as central issues that punk attempted to address. Punk's ties to suburbia were complex but never subtle. "I want to be a clone / I want a suburban home . . . / I want to be a statistic . . . / I want a house just like mom and dad" sang Milo Aukerman on the Descendents' "Suburban Home"; Aukerman's alternately sarcastic, plaintive, and angry singing style directly conflicting with Tony Lombardo's genuine suburban aspirations when he wrote the song.[46] The differences between the younger Descendents and Lombardo, a full generation older, serve as a microcosm of punk's conflicting and ever-changing relationship to the suburbs.

The paradox and power of punk music cannot be fully understood apart from the specific history of white people in the postwar American suburbs. As mentioned, I am primarily interested in how punk and its musical styles connect to empirical sociohistorical aspects of race, such as how punk and ideas of whiteness and blackness connect to the housing discrimination, geographic separation, governmental policies, and inequalities that created and sustained the suburbs. Issues of identity are symptomatic of these processes, but too often identity is treated apart from structural racism and historical facts, especially with respect to whiteness, which establishes a paradigm in which structural racism can be ignored or dismissed. While whiteness, in the words of Sara Ahmed, "tends to be visible to those who do not inhabit it (though not always, and not only)," whiteness itself operates through an obfuscation of its own relationship to lived experiences.[47] "Whiteness is everywhere in U.S. culture, but it is very hard to see. . . . As the unmarked category against which difference is constructed, whiteness never has to speak its name, never has to acknowledge its role as an organizing principle in social and cultural relations," writes George Lipsitz.[48] The privileges of whiteness can be revealed in moments of rupture and tension, as when Stew (Stew Stewart, later of the Negro Problem, the composer of the Broadway musical *Passing Strange*, and an early fan of punk as a young man growing up in Los Angeles) and the other African American "good kids" being bused to Palms Middle School, west of Culver City, heard a teacher tell another teacher that Governor George Wallace had been shot the afternoon of May 15, 1972. "Involuntarily all the black kids cheered . . . it was like if someone had told us the devil just got shot . . . and then we looked around, and the white kids didn't know of course who Governor Wallace was."[49] American whiteness has always been ultimately about freedom, rights, privileges, and wealth, and questions of identity, at least with respect to white identity, are best understood in relation to this fact.[50]

Punks used whiteness and its privileges to engage, criticize, and reveal whiteness itself, which is what imbues punk's critiques with so much potential, as well as with such severe limitations. Whiteness is supposed to operate covertly, extending privileges and benefits under the guise of opportunity, equality, or entitlement. Punks outwardly and explicitly voiced rejections of their white inheritance and the suburban world they were born into. Yet by using privilege and other tools of whiteness, punks also created a contradictory situation that affirmed whiteness and allowed the hidden processes of whiteness to reclaim or recuperate punk. Histories of punk, even if they point to the suburbs, invariably leave the whiteness of the suburbs' history unmarked and unacknowledged, replicating the deeper processes of whiteness at work.

### "This Is a Chord, This Is Another, This Is a Third, Now Form a Band"

For me, the story is not about the violence. The story is about the people who navigated that violence because they knew that the music was important enough. . . . Not that the chaos isn't a story, but the story is the people that sailed into the chaos because the mission was sound. That's the fucking story.
—Ian MacKaye[51]

The most misunderstood canard about punk is that it is "three chord" music, and by extension, too simple and too amateurish to be worth analyzing. For example, in *Lipstick Traces*, Greil Marcus writes, "If what is interesting about punk is something other than its function as a musical genre, there is no point in treating it as one."[52] Even Dave Laing's *One Chord Wonders*, still one of the only full-length studies of punk to address aspects of musical style, echoes the idea: "'Punk' meant an attitude towards musical performance which emphasised directness and repetition (to use more than three chords was self-indulgence) at the expense of technical virtuosity."[53]

The "three chord" cliché is a good summary of punk's guiding principles: rock music should be accessible, immediate, and a form of expression available to anyone. It also reminds us of punk's basis in the familiar resources of American popular music, such as the I, IV, and V chords heard in the twelve-bar blues. And "three chord punk" is a grassroots formulation as much as an externally applied description; famously, in January 1977 the British fanzine *Sideburns* published a drawing of guitar fingering charts for A, E, and G chords, with the caption "this is a chord, this is another, this is a third, now form a band."[54] Even though these particular three chords don't do enough for the aspiring musician (E, A, and B, or D, G, and A would be more useful, providing the I–IV–V combination needed for most rock songs), the idea of the *Sideburns* illustration was, of course, to encourage punk's core "do-it-yourself" ethos. Unfamiliarity with chords, instruments, or playing music whatsoever need not stand in one's way when using punk as a vehicle of expression.

But while much punk music is based on three chords, just as much is not. Anyone with the ability to distinguish chords can immediately detect that even the most definitive punk bands, such as the Ramones, the Sex Pistols, and the Clash, played many songs with more than three chords. (And a tremendous amount of music is "three chord"—"Free Fallin'" by Tom Petty and "Bad Moon Rising" by Creedence Clearwater Revival are three-chord songs, but I've never heard anyone judge them by their chord count.) Some bands, such as Minor Threat, Bad Brains, X, and Dead Kennedys, wrote extremely varied compositions. And some bands made tremendous use of riff-based music that never moved from one chord to another, and others exploited two-chord patterns; the differences between one-chord, two-chord, and three-chord songs can be enormous. As John Doe of X has written: "Misconceptions about punk-rock songwriting are as wide & flat as the city of Los Angeles itself. . . . Provocative? Yes. Fast? Not necessarily. Simple? Yes. 3 chords? No. Not too serious? Definitely. Culturally significant? Always."[55] Punk has never fallen into a formula, "three chord" or otherwise. Black Flag, Bad Brains, and Dead Kennedys made unique, immediately recognizable music; so did the Damned, the Sex Pistols, the Clash, and the Slits; so did the Ramones, Blondie, the Cramps, and Television; so did the Descendents, the Adolescents, and the Minutemen.

But most importantly, dismissing (or championing) punk as three-chord music generally reflects a misconception of how vernacular or popular musicians compose, and to what end. The modernist conceit of complete originality is diametrically opposed to the ways in which popular musicians generally work with existing resources and models, manipulating them in creative ways and combining them with original material. As Lyle Preslar of Minor Threat explained, "we never thought we were doing anything new. Different, yes, but not new."[56] If popular musicians use three chords, they use them because they are endlessly expressive and meaningful, with deep associations and artistic power. They take these cycles, patterns, and forms (I avoid the term "chord progressions," which implies forward direction rather than cycles, even though other musicians use it) and put them to various new uses. The ways the chords are played; whether the song has two chords, three chords, four, more, or is based on a riff; the rhythmic treatment of the chords (harmonic rhythm); the alignment of the chords to the lyric; the placement of the chords in the larger form—all of these elements affect how we hear the music, move with it, and ultimately understand it.

Furthermore, there is no reason to associate "do it yourself" or informal musical training with unskillful playing. Jazz, one of the world's most technically demanding styles of music, was created almost entirely by informally trained musicians with little financial resources. Those who only think of punk in the clichéd way, that it is about inept kids making amateurish (if expressive) music, will be surprised to learn about musicians such as Kira Roessler, who practiced the bass for six to ten hours a day, seven days a week.[57] Musicians choose what they wish to play and develop skills based on their interests, circumstances, talents, opportunities, and the professional demands they face. Punk's basis in blues resources and I, IV, V chords has everything to do with the affect and creative possibilities of those resources, and relatively little to do with a "do it yourself" impulse.

Although punk musicians regularly explain their distinct sounds as a fortunate by-product of the fact that they "couldn't play" or "couldn't sing"—Richard Hell was inspired by Lou Reed because he "couldn't sing," and Steve Jones said he "couldn't play" while Johnny Rotten "couldn't sing"—these comments should be treated carefully from the perspective of musical analysis.[58] Obviously they all "played" and "sang." Hell, Reed, Jones, and Rotten chose to develop and cultivate styles that emphasized immediacy and authenticity over polished technique because of their aesthetic value, as do many other popular, folk, or vernacular musicians. In some ways, investment in the unmusical image of punk affected the way the music was heard, as Stew explained to me: "I'll never forget a jazz friend of mine came in and said, 'Steve Jones is a good guitar player,' and that was the most offensive thing possible . . . we were confusing it with something that actually wasn't there . . . we were making it more punk than it actually was."[59] Similarly, Pete Townshend said, "When you clear away all the stuff, Steve [Jones] and Paul [Cook] could really play, and John [Rotten] could really scream, and they were a great band." Paul Cook agreed: "We wrote some great songs and we were a good band . . . we've proved that we made great records which have stood well in the test of time."[60]

As outlined in *Damaged*, punk's power and continued resonance directly emanates from punk musicians' bold transformations to familiar popular music resources, especially black music resources and the American vernacular "common stock" shared by white and black musicians. A primary goal of this book is for listeners to hear these resources and transformations in punk, and thus obtain a broader understanding of the music's genealogy and its historical context. I also wanted musicians themselves to recognize the music theory I employ and address.[61] I have compiled some basic requirements based on my perspectives as a musician, an ethnomusicologist, a listener, a reader, and a fan: the book's language should reflect actual musical practice, musicians should be able to hear and see themselves in my representations and analyses (even if they disagree with my ideas), and my writing should position punk rock *within* a broader tradition of American popular music and not as something apart or alone—punk musicians should be seen as one contingent of the "thousands of musicians who have sought to reconcile or coordinate European and African techniques and values" in the creation of American popular music.[62] These many aims raise a number of problems.

There are certain conventions I wanted to avoid. Some writers on punk claim to highlight music but only do so by listing recordings and band names.[63] I also steer clear of the journalistic use of genre terms as *musical* descriptors, since words such as "punk," "post-punk," "new wave," and "rock," are intentionally vague and mutable, useful as industry marketing categories and potentially evocative in criticism and journalism, but far less meaningful as precise characterizations of musical style. That is not to say that these words have no meaning at all, or that musical characteristics approaching a true "genre" might not be applicable to these terms. However, these terms cannot be used as if everyone immediately understands what they mean musically. I am especially resistant to hybrid "-punk" formulations such as "cow-punk," "pop-punk," "ska-punk," and "horror punk," which have proliferated on the internet. These terms incorrectly and ahistorically separate bands and the music they created, making it difficult to understand how musical elements connect under a broader umbrella of American music, and they misrepresent how people actually made music in the 1970s.

For my purposes, I found the scholarly and critical discourse on blues and other common stock resources to be the most useful, in that American vernacular music is the overall vocabulary and grammar for punk as well as rock music in general.[64] These writers also established productive ways of analyzing musical exchanges between African Americans and European Americans, and ways in which these exchanges have been in constant tension with the binary categories of racialized "black" and "white" music. Following this theoretical underpinning, reading this book requires accepting a few basic premises from the start:

(1) punk is a form of rock music, and like almost all forms of rock music, it is primarily based on African American musical resources; (2) cycles are at the core of American popular music, not linear forms; (3) the blues can encompass a wide range of forms and harmonic cycles, including but hardly limited to the familiar twelve-bar blues; and (4) the coordination of musical techniques to terminology (e.g., genres, song types, and dances) is in constant flux. Throughout *Damaged* I focus on meaningful musical trends and characteristics that I hope can be understood regardless of one's fluency in music theory terminology: Do cycles get shorter or longer? Do forms have multiple parts? How similar or different are those parts from each other? What are the instruments and how are their voices coordinated?

The final introductory point about punk as music is that it ultimately becomes more of a guitar-based than a keyboard-based music, following its connections to the blues as interpreted by rock musicians in the 1960s (discussed in the following chapter). The European harmonic cycles that were adapted and transformed by people of African descent throughout the Americas and the Caribbean—such as the cycles used for the quadrille and schottische—are still based on the mechanics of the keyboard, even when transformed into styles such as jazz and American popular song.[65] One of the main characteristics of punk, and some other forms such as heavy metal, is the competing musical theory stemming from the guitar's physical characteristics.

### Was Punk Really a Response to the Bloated or Bland 1970s? And Is Punk Violent?

To read the usual history of punk, or to see one of the many punk documentaries, one would think that Emerson, Lake, and Palmer was the most popular group in the world in the 1970s, in heavy rotation on every radio station and long multi-movement pieces such as "Karn Evil 9" playing in living rooms all over the United States. Punk was supposedly created in opposition to this kind of progressive rock. Or to disco, or to arena rock. Or to the Eagles, Captain and Tennille, or Fleetwood Mac. Or to concept albums, jazz fusion, or rock bands playing with orchestras.

The facts tell a different story. More than anything else, "prog rock" and the Eagles are convenient scapegoats and symbols for the problems of the 1970s, just as punk is. Classic bare-bones rock was played in the United States before, during, and after the British Invasion, and remained popular through the 1970s— Bruce Springsteen, Bob Seger, Aerosmith—not to mention the continued success of British and Canadian musicians who were popular in the 1960s, such as the Rolling Stones, the Band, Neil Young, and Led Zeppelin. Most early punk musicians profess listening to mainstream hard rock such as AC/DC, Cheap Trick, and Jimi Hendrix more than other punk bands, even during the late 1970s and early 1980s, when there were plenty of punk recordings available to listen to. Punks also maintain their admiration and love for musicians who created long, difficult, high-concept compositions, such as Frank Zappa, Captain Beefheart, and the Residents. Punks or musicians in the punk universe made long, difficult, high-concept recordings themselves: "We Will Fall" on the first Stooges record is over ten minutes long, and Half Japanese's first full-length was a triple album loaded with experiments. Paul Roessler of the Screamers, Nervous Gender, and other early LA punk bands is a classically trained pianist who in 1975 composed a forty-seven-minute rock opera, "The Ark," and who has consistently loved Jethro Tull and Emerson, Lake, and Palmer; he also mentioned to me that Don Bolles (Germs), Keith Morris (Black Flag, Circle Jerks, Off!), and Jack Grisham (T.S.O.L.) were all big fans of progressive rock.[66] Jazz, improvisational music, even the long jams of the Grateful Dead are regularly mentioned as favorites.[67] So why do these myths have such staying power?

If punk was created in opposition, its targeted opposites remain varied and unclear. In *Damaged* I suggest punk was not opposed to the music of these divergent bands, but to the social environments associated with them. The white American suburban environments in which punks grew up were lacking culture, for the most part by design, symptomatic of the ways houses were built apart from cities and their cultural institutions, with only modest replacements for the human experiences of the cities. In many ways, separation from direct experience and urban culture was seen as the price of a suburban middle-class existence, as white suburbanites aimed to remove themselves from what they considered unpleasant experiences associated with poor people, foreigners, old people, black people, and others. (Allen Ravenstine of Pere Ubu: "In those days, people didn't use things like garlic and if your house smelled like fish, it was because there was something not right! . . . And I hated it—it was so sterile."[68] Chrissie Hynde: "No one wanted to share their space with strangers. Heaven forbid they might not even be white. . . . American households had no room for Grandma, but the car's needs were paramount."[69]) As such, the suburbs manifested a century-old process equating whiteness with civilization, civility, and the mind, and blackness with the natural, the primal, and the body.[70] By the early 1960s, opinions about suburbia as cultureless and contributing to the demise of healthy communities had become widespread, formulated in widely read critiques such as Jane Jacobs's *The Death and Life of Great American Cities*, and not at all limited to young adults or rebellious teenagers.[71]

In the suburbs, schools and athletics became the main sites for youth to satisfy human needs and experiences, such as romantic contact, fun, and physical activity. Those young people who were unable to fully thrive in those social environments, "misfits," sought other avenues to experience their humanity. Folk music provided an early outlet for a way out of suburban alienation; in words reminiscent of later punk culture, "it was so darn easy to play, anybody could do it."[72] So did garage rock–type bands, which started the musical careers of individuals such as Iggy Pop in the 1960s. Drugs provided some alternatives, as did returning to the city. Arena rock culture in the 1970s, growing out of rock festivals, generated powerful experiences but presented new problems for some—even as one could experience the music, the band was far away in more ways than one.[73] As opposed to the communal experience of the rock festival, arena rock involved driving to a suburban arena; getting wasted before, during, and after the concert; and driving back to other suburbs.

This 1970s culture, as many punks have described, made the experience of *playing* music feel unattainable. This idea, that the experiences of playing in— and not only listening to—a rock band were unattainable, is a common thread that runs through arena rock, lite rock, prog rock, symphonic rock, and all the other opposites punks have described. Even disco can fit this bill. Disco provided physical, human experiences, but the music culture centered on dancing to music played by a DJ, and could not provide the distinct pleasures of playing in a loud rock band. By extension, playing in a rock band also reinstated suburban youth with a sense of their own agency, and this broader idea of agency is where the issue of "DIY" is best addressed. Musical experiences in the suburbs could be accessed through private lessons and school bands, but these methods are limited to a small subset of people with an aptitude for these particular approaches. Those with regular and immediate access to fun, immersive, physical, pleasurable musical experiences, such as singing or playing in church, or playing in a family band with siblings and parents, have little relation to the problems that DIY punk rock musical life originally tried to solve for some suburbanites.[74] Punk, like its garage band precedent, provided one avenue for young suburbanites to access the expressive, physical, and cathartic pleasures of playing music, and an extremely loud, fast, and visceral version of those pleasures. Punk audiences tended to overlap with punk performers because audience members thought, "I can do that, and it looks like fun," not because they thought they could do it and make money or have a career.

Punk's immediate access to physical experience and pleasure also provides some answers to the question of punk's "violence." Certain activities sometimes conflated with violence, such as body piercings and the use of offensive imagery, are ways to access strong sensations and physical reactions. Most of all and most controversial, the pit provides fun, visceral, and physical experiences.[75] The suburbs only provided limited access to the pleasures of moving one's body, crashing into other people, and engaging in physical contact, mainly from athletics (compare football or hockey). For young men in particular across a range of sexualities, and living in repressed environments with severely restricted ideas of masculinity, the pit was also "the gateway for many boys to touch other boys without having to wear a helmet and catch or throw balls in the air."[76] Punk gave "misfits" in general an opportunity to experience these many pleasures, and the internal battle over conduct in the pit after "jocks" started participating is more than a question of violence, as it directly connected to suburban power relations, gender dynamics, and access to experiences. Ray Farrell of SST Records remarked, "Hardcore made it more like a sporting event than music—with like the worst jocks you've ever seen. It excluded women. It became exclusionary only because it was violent—people couldn't handle the physicality."[77]

This is not to belittle or dismiss the very real presence of violence in punk, especially concerning unequal power relationships: men abusing women, police abusing civilians, and able-bodied people abusing people with disabilities. The high rate of violence by men against women overshadows the "fun" element of violence. I explore these serious issues throughout *Damaged*, especially in chapter 6. However, these acts of violence are in no way limited to punk. Unfortunately, every situation in American life is rife with these forms of violence: athletics, religious institutions, workplaces, marriages and other romantic relationships, fraternities and sororities, K-12 schools and higher education. Alcohol and drug abuse are also found in all of these places and circumstances. Punk has been wrongly singled out for sensationalist treatment. Punk is inherently about physical and social experiences, but I reject any argument supporting punk's inherent violence, and I do my best to avoid any sensationalist storytelling in *Damaged*. I am basically in agreement with D.O.A.'s Joey Shithead: "But out of respect for people's privacy, and because stories about people being drunk and stoned are a waste of time, I'm not going into detail about it in this book."[78]

### Reconstructing Punk

If punk is at least partly a "culture of deconstruction," *Damaged: Musicality and Race in Early American Punk* can be summarized as a project of reconstruction, identifying the stylistic currents at play in punk and placing them within their historical context.[79] The stylistic history outlined in *Damaged* is based first and foremost on musical features and the ways in which musicians speak about those features in interviews and as documented in primary sources. Punk is defined here in terms of specific approaches to common resources of American popular music—specifically, blues and other common stock vernacular resources—with shared (even if debated) ideas about those approaches among a network of performers and listeners. Looking first at music and musicians helped me address two difficult concerns: (1) the thorny relationships between criticism, history, reception, and performance in punk, and (2) the selection of the book's corpus, given punks' general resistance to agreeing upon musical characteristics and even the term *punk* as a musical style or genre.

The history presented in *Damaged* is a narrative of musical style informed by the assessments of critics rather than the other way around, which is my approach to dealing with the problems of criticism and history in punk. For an example of one major issue, writing on punk often falls into the phenomenon sometimes called "rockism," which refers to critics, mostly white men, arguing among themselves over the artistic value and rankings of recordings.[80] Rockism has especially become a problem in the writing of punk history, as the historical record can be revised according to whatever the critic deems exceptionally worthy, often resulting in the erasure of women and people of color. In fact, this historiographical problem is not just rockism, but a dilemma that runs throughout all writing of music history.[81]

This historiographical issue in *Damaged* largely concerns the blurring of the "essential divide between history and criticism."[82] I am tracing history through general and typical musical trends, but I am also studying a self-consciously underground music with its musical development immediately and continually analyzed, especially in the form of fanzines, and with histories written by the same critics who previously assessed the music.[83] Rock criticism dominates histories that cover the early punk era, including recent scholarship that engages rock criticism itself, and punk is sometimes even considered to be primarily an invention of critics such as Lester Bangs, Dave Marsh, and Caroline Coon.[84] I don't take that approach, and in highlighting musical style and the words of musicians, the writings of these prominent critics ended up playing a minor role in my analysis. Those of us who are invested in writing and reading about music can easily forget that musicians develop and create in rehearsal and performance, in collaboration with other musicians, and in response to their audiences, and quite often they reject or pay scant attention to the things that are written about them in magazines and books.

One of the most serious problems with punk rockism is the difference, often completely contradictory, between critics' interpretations of punk and what musicians actually say and do. For one striking example, early punk musicians regularly referred to their music's connections to the blues, while critics frequently promoted a story of punk as coming "from nothing" or as stripping rock of its blues features. (Interviewer: "what you were doing stood on the shoulders of nothing"; Joe Strummer replies: "you gotta make the point in your *History of Rock and Roll* that the blues is the root of everything."[85]) Musicians are also regularly misquoted, and sensationalist storytelling (e.g., obsessing over the deaths of Sid Vicious and Nancy Spungen, or the chronicle of sex, drugs, and violence rather than music which makes up the nearly 500 pages of Legs McNeil and

Gillian McCain's *Please Kill Me*) have too often overshadowed the music's real resonances and meanings for the vast majority of those who care about it. Musicians also contradict themselves, intentionally and unintentionally. But rather than discard critical writings because they are in tension with musicians' words or actions, my approach has been to investigate these tensions and contradictions for the meanings they generate. Why do these contradictions exist in the first place? Throughout the book, I return to these historiographical problems and try to analyze them with respect to the primary questions of musical style and the ways in which musicians articulate their own work and experiences.

Another concern is my method for developing the corpus for *Damaged*. One common type of question I have been asked when describing my book is, "Is Blondie (or DEVO, or the Go-Go's, etc.) really punk?!?" I start with the music which seemed to be universally accepted as "punk," such as the Ramones, the Dead Boys, Patti Smith, Black Flag, and British groups such as the Sex Pistols, the Clash, and the Slits, as well as the groups these musicians most often referred to as antecedents, such as the Stooges and the Velvet Underground, and the venues and scenes most often discussed in punk history, such as CBGB and the Masque. (For example, Phast Phreddie wrote in 1977, "When this current 'Punk Rock' or 'New Wave' stuff is over, the Stooges will turn out as the Chuck Berry of that era," and Brian Gregory of the Cramps "grew up in Detroit [and] must have seen the Stooges 500 times."[86]) I've extended the corpus using this music and the words of these musicians as starting points, and have tried not to include or reject bands based on how well I think they fit into my own ideas of "punk," or what I imagine to be the generally accepted boundaries of the style. Instead, I consider bands based on how their approaches to popular music resources coalesced, and how productive those approaches were for subsequent bands. This means that some bands may have an unexpectedly prominent place, such as the Flamin' Groovies or the Damned, while some exceptional bands, such as Television, are less illustrative for the particular musical narrative that emerged from my research (although I believe the analysis in *Damaged* can be usefully applied to most of those exceptional groups as well). I hope that my focus on stylistic trends and illustrative examples, rather than unique masterworks, will make it possible to relate and apply my analyses to music created by the countless artists I have not included, from the long 1970s and beyond.

I use a combination of musical style and musicians' words to tell the story of punk in *Damaged*. In order to get a wide and varied perspective, I consulted hundreds of recordings and oral histories, conducted over twenty formal interviews myself with musicians of varied backgrounds and experiences, studied several important archival collections, and drew on my experiences as a performer of many different styles of music including jazz and punk (for example, three years as part of the revolving cast of characters in Washington DC's All

Scars).[87] I place all of this varied information in relation to a range of historical, musicological, and sociological research, aiming to portray a "life and times" of early punk music. And while *Damaged* is not an ethnography, the questions I seek to answer and my foregrounding of music and musicians come from my primary disciplinary focus of ethnomusicology. I want to explore punk's musical styles in relation to musical life, and to highlight the typical aspects of punk as much as the exceptional and the innovative. My analyses are geared toward a broad understanding of punk with an in-depth view of the music; I do not ultimately aim to demonstrate the "greatness" of punk music (although I love punk, justifying its musical worth is a pointless and uninteresting assignment). In the words of Ruth Finnegan, I tried to think and write ". . . not about 'the best' but about what people actually *do*—about 'is' not 'ought' . . ."[88] Nor are the musical discussions only there to support conclusions concerning society. Like most ethnomusicologists, I consider music and society to be inseparable, and I believe they are best understood in relation to each other.

The historical period, type of music, nature of a musician's career, and my own experiences all had a considerable impact on the different methods I have used in writing *Damaged*. For extremely famous or dead people, such as Lou Reed, Iggy Pop, and the Ramones, I relied on published interviews, archival materials, and sometimes interviews with their acquaintances. On the other hand, the time I spent in the DC–area music scene meant that section could be much more ethnographic and based on my own interviews and experiences. Growing up in suburban Columbia, Maryland, as an Ashkenazic Jewish male during the 1970s and 1980s, living and working for two decades in New York City and Long Island, and my family's strong connections to Cleveland, means the portraits of those areas are probably richer and more complex than those of places I do not know as well, such as Los Angeles, in which cases I had to depend more on interviews and secondary sources. Throughout the book, I have tried to include a range of methods for each chapter while using the most appropriate tools for each analysis. As always, I look forward to future research and corrective work by other scholars.

Recordings and oral histories form the backbone of *Damaged*, but this corpus is very limited. Recordings present only a small piece of reality, as many bands never record (such as the seminal LA band the Screamers), and those that do may record or have their recordings released long after they began playing (such as Suicide and the Modern Lovers). As Kira Roessler commented, even into the late 1970s, "A bunch of the early punk rock was never recorded, period . . . very few bands were recording, very few bands were being documented . . . [many bands] were together for a while before they recorded [and] it was difficult to get the opportunity to record."[89] Recordings are by definition mediated, and they document culminating moments although they are often later understood as beginnings. Conversely, many musicians and serious fans during the 1970s were also heavily involved with tape trading and bootlegging, so commercially available recordings often only represent a sliver of what was being heard.

Oral histories and autobiographies also present a number of problems. Published interviews are heavily edited and responses can be easily guided by questions; for example, in the unedited interview with Don Letts for the *Time-Life History of Rock and Roll*, he concludes his answer to a question about reggae and punk by saying, "Do you want me to elaborate any more on that? Is that sort of it? I mean, I'll make up some more bullshit if you want."[90] And memories are notoriously unreliable, an issue especially pertinent with punk, since oral histories such as *Please Kill Me* and autobiographies such as Johnny Ramone's *Commando* depend on individuals remembering years far in the past, often including one's childhood, a period typically of limited perspective with respect to how one's reality relates to broader historical and social circumstances.[91] Memory is particularly open to question when it comes to issues of race. For example, in *Commando*, Johnny Ramone remembers Westbury, Long Island as "half black" when he lived there in the 1950s, when the number was no more than 6 percent, and Johnny is not unusual in making this type of mistake (a common phenomenon known as innumeracy).[92] He also admits, "my world was very small. I basically didn't leave my block or two."[93]

This is not at all to disparage punk recordings and oral histories, only to acknowledge the issues associated with them. Actually, despite these considerations, today's historians and researchers have the intensely good fortune of a seemingly endless trove of recordings and oral histories, as well as unprecedented access to living individuals. The voices of marginalized people in punk such as women, people of color, and LGBTQ individuals are louder and clearer than ever, with new memoirs, histories, recordings, and documentaries being constantly released on the internet and in traditional media.[94] In fact, while punks often talk about the ephemerality of their culture, it is hard to imagine a group of people more concerned with documenting themselves. Punks were almost immediately convinced of the importance of their own activities. There are countless interviews and record reviews in hundreds of books and fanzines, and there is no end to bootlegs and live recordings. Punks saved thousands of fliers and set lists. Recently there has been a mushrooming of punk archives at libraries, indicating not only that Johan Kugelberg, Kathleen Hanna, V. Vale (Vale Hamanaka), Greg Shaw, and many others collected all of these materials, but that they saved them and deemed them—as do the librarians—important enough to be deposited at archives where they will be potentially stored in perpetuity.[95]

What emerges through this varied research is a particular view of American punk in the long 1970s, beginning with punk's ambiguous origins in the 1960s as a way of playing rock, and ending at the turn to the 1980s, by which time hardcore punk had developed into a fully formed set of musical approaches. As I explain in *Damaged*, conventional understandings of punk as beginning in the mid- to late 1970s, such as the marking of punk's "big bang" with the Sex Pistols in 1976, create a strong narrative but can lead to misunderstanding punk's timeline and many of its meanings.[96] Again, punk music was originally created by baby boomers in response to the 1960s and even the 1950s, and this includes the activity in the United Kingdom.

To tell this wide-ranging and ambitious narrative, I have loosely connected stylistic trends to time periods and regions, although many individuals and groups will appear in many places throughout the book. Most of the musicians I include belong in more than one chapter, but their particular stylistic influence led me to emphasize their music in one area. For example, Captain Beefheart certainly could have been a major player in the chapter on protopunk transformations of blues resources, but the distinct experimental techniques he introduced on *Trout Mask Replica*, which ended up being so important to punk, make his work more intensely addressed in the chapter on the American avant-garde.

The first half of the book constitutes Part One, *punk (adj.)*: punk as a set of possible ways to play rock music. The three musical approaches described in this part are stylistic currents that punk musicians later modified for their own purposes. Chapter 2, "Raw Power," addresses the late 1960s to the early 1970s, focusing on the transformation of blues resources by the Stooges, MC5, and others. These musicians participated in the 1960s counterculture, and they were directly engaged in the changing musical expressions of blackness and whiteness during a period of intense social upheaval. Chapter 3, "Ignorance of Your Culture Is Not Considered Cool," revisits the avant-garde impulse in punk with a discussion of Captain Beefheart, the Residents, and others in the early to mid-1970s who were wrestling with the counterculture's limitations and failures. Chapter 4, "Pure Rock and Roll with No Blues or Folk or Any of That Stuff in It," focuses on the Ramones and other groups, especially in mid-1970s New York and Boston, who looked back to rock and roll and R&B styles associated with the late 1950s and early 1960s, including musical schemes intended to be heard in contradistinction to blues-based music. Although this scene was ostensibly urban, the music harked back to childhoods in postwar white suburbs imagined as removed from the racial turbulence and Vietnam War chaos of the mid- to late 1960s, reflecting both nostalgia and repudiation.

Part Two of the book, *punk (n.)*, treats the formation of punk as a defined if extremely varied style. Chapter 5, "Punk and the White Atlantic," looks at how transatlantic relationships between white Americans and Britons forged punk in the mid-1970s, recycling the 1960s British Invasion processes that paradoxically disconnected American rock from its black American heritage despite a discourse of indebtedness. As a reminder, *Damaged* is focused on American punk, so British punk is primarily analyzed here in relation to the broader American narrative.[97] Chapter 6, "Less Art and More Machine," focuses on Los Angeles, its suburbs, and San Francisco, the "California Crucible" in which a distinctly American punk was formed in the late 1970s by bands with widely varying sounds and intentions, such as X, the Screamers, Germs, Black Flag, Circle Jerks, Fear, and Descendents. This chapter also covers a seismic and schismatic change in punk from being considered a heavily female, queer, and arty scene to a prevailingly white, male, heterosexual, and aggressive one, as well as the beginning of generational shifts from baby boomers to Generation X, and from adults to teenagers. "Less Art and More Machine" also examines changing issues of race and ethnicity through the case study of Latinx participation in LA punk. Chapter 7, "Decisions with Precisions," turns to the late 1970s and early 1980s with a focus on hardcore punk in Washington, DC, and the expanded possibilities and directions for punk presented by Bad Brains and Minor Threat in particular. The conclusion, "A New Way to Pay Old Debts," is a reflection on the book's narrative and further questions I believe it generates, via the work of some contemporary musicians.

# PART ONE

## *punk (adj.)*

Punk music started mainly as an adjective, as a way of approaching rock, the term in use since the early 1970s. The main figures who developed the early punk rock style came from a variety of backgrounds, but they generally shared the characteristics of being white American baby boomers from rapidly expanding suburban middle-class environments in the North and the West Coast. By and large, they were born during the 1940s or early 1950s, their musical habits were shaped during the 1950s or early 1960s, and they began performing and recording in the 1960s or early 1970s. And the music they made during punk's mid-1970s heyday strongly reflected their experiences living through the 1950s and 1960s, the scene skewing older than it is usually portrayed. Many of them were on the fringes of the suburbs in one way or another, perhaps from poorer families, not cissexual or heterosexual, or members of ethnic groups newly but still tenuously able to access the privileges of whiteness. They borrowed extensively from black music resources but were also determined to avoid imitation and pursue authenticity. They were part of the 1960s counterculture but were also seriously concerned with its limits and failures, and by the end of the 1960s, these musicians were making music that spoke to their discontent and the varied crises facing Americans into the 1970s.

To create their music, they focused on several stylistic approaches. Part One of *Damaged* considers three of these musical styles, flourishing between 1968 and 1976 and roughly mapping onto different American locations: (1) transformations of the blues, especially in and around the Midwest; (2) experimental reworkings of rock and American music of the past, especially in California; and (3) nostalgic expressions of classic rock and roll from the 1950s and early 1960s, particularly in the Northeast. This introduction to the first part of *Damaged* sets the scene in which these various approaches to rock music took place.

The architects of early punk grew up during the 1950s and 1960s as the United States was undergoing paradigmatic changes redefining race, class, and geography. The main sites of punk's development were, uncoincidentally, similar environments: major northern and West Coast cities to which black people were moving in large numbers and from which white people were moving away. These twin migrations of millions of people, the Second Great Migration of African Americans and mass "white flight" to the suburbs, were heavily determined by discrimination and eventually linked white, suburbia, and middle-class in the white American racial imagination, as opposed to black, urban, and poor. White flight thwarted the aims of *Brown v. Board of Education* (1954) in areas such as New York, where by 1964 "white flight to the suburbs and suburban school districts and long-standing white protest meant that there were over two hundred segregated schools in New York, compared to fifty-two in 1954."[1]

During this period, African Americans were excluded from buying homes in the new suburbs through practices such as redlining, resulting in segregation and extraordinary wealth disparities that remain to this day.[2] African Americans were the target of most housing discrimination until the Fair Housing Act of 1968, when "levels of black residential segregation were extreme, higher than any group had ever experienced before or since."[3] Meanwhile, specific groups of European immigrants and European Americans such as Ashkenazic Jews and Italians, as well as Mexican Americans and Asian Americans, were increasingly granted access to these suburban opportunities, expanding definitions of whiteness and the middle class.[4] As children or teenagers, many of the early creators of the punk style were part of this migration during the 1950s; for example, Tommy Ramone moved from Hungary to the South Bronx and then the suburban environment of Forest Hills, which was being newly populated by significant numbers of Jews, and Lenny Kaye lived in Washington Heights until high school, when the family moved to North Brunswick, New Jersey.

Suburban whiteness was intentionally separated from the culture of the cities. A desire of the silent generation veterans and others who first moved to the suburbs, the lack of culture became a concern and liability for their children. White baby boomers included the first cohort of bored suburban youth, trying to create their own culture, entertainment, and musical life. Yet the 1940s and 1950s were also extremely transitional decades, as many white people, especially the nascent white Jews and other so-called "ethnics," still lived close to or in the urban centers, before or at the beginning of the expansion of the interstate system and consequent dependency on cars, and often still facing discrimination. As one of Ray Suarez's interviewees cynically said, integration "is the period of time between the arrival of the first blacks, and the departure of the last whites."[5]

With suburban sterility and segregation in the 1950s and early 1960s, "rock and roll," originally understood as black music, became the primary mode for young white people to access the pleasures, emotions, and notions of authenticity that they attached to blackness and black people.[6] The blues repertoire was the basis of this music, as is common knowledge, and white "rock and roll" was meant to be heard as a kind of black music. James Brown said, "Rock 'n' roll is a white man trying to play the blues. He can't play the blues, so he plays rock 'n' roll."[7] As I have argued elsewhere, white rock and roll was supposed to be heard as a form of appropriation—"a white man trying to play the blues"—and much of rock's effect on white audiences depended on the ways in which white musicians took black music and repurposed it while retaining the music's associations with its black roots, breaking down societal barriers but reinforcing racial hierarchies.[8]

Despite a racialized terminology distinguishing them, white "rock and roll" and black "rhythm and blues" musicians in the 1950s and early 1960s played a similar repertoire, adopted corresponding performance styles, and often had the same figures working behind the scenes.[9] And although racial economic inequalities persisted in early rock and roll, the musical exchanges and personal interactions of black and white people during this time served as a counternarrative of racism and a resolution of racial tension for white people. This early rock and roll, including early British Invasion bands, "girl groups" and doo-wop groups, and California beach and surf records, took on a renewed importance for punk musicians in the mid-1970s as they revisited the music of their childhood. In retrospect, the music of this period captured a lost world of optimism and promise, articulated even by those early punks who were ostensibly parodying or rejecting the past.

Also important to punk's development, in the 1950s and 1960s white countercultural musicians also began seriously investigating early twentieth-century recordings in their search for identity and authenticity. One of the most significant collections of American vernacular music in terms of its effect on the white counterculture, and rock musicians generally, was the *Anthology of American Folk Music* compiled by Harry Smith (Folkways, 1952).[10] Smith's *Anthology* reintroduced much of the common stock (blues, country, folk) repertoire that would be studied by popular musicians in the 1960s. It should be added that while these interests were widespread among white musicians in the 1960s, some young black musicians at the time were also deep into this repertoire, such as Taj Mahal, who explored a wide range of blues styles as part of the Rising Sons with Ry Cooder and Jesse Lee Kincaid. But most of the major figures creating early punk or the music that would become punk, such as Iggy Pop and Peter Laughner, were white people who took a strong interest in the kind of blues and country music documented in the *Anthology*, emphasizing punk's connections to broader musical trends.

Over the course of the 1960s, many white rock bands began exploring new ways to remain committed to countercultural goals of social change, but increasingly separate from the efforts of African American musicians. This was directly in response to the voices of younger African American activists, such as the Student Nonviolent Coordinating Committee (SNCC) under the Black Power direction of Stokely Carmichael (Kwame Ture) and the Black Panther Party's formation in 1966. With continuous violence against African American citizens, activists, and political leaders—from the Ku Klux Klan's bombing of the 16th Street Baptist Church in 1963, killing the young girls Addie Mae Collins, Cynthia Wesley, Carole Robertson, and Carol Denise McNair, to the assassination of Martin Luther King Jr. in 1968—many key figures began calling for new civil rights strategies. Huey Newton called for "parallel but separate" work by white allies, and similarly, black writers such as Amiri Baraka became more vocal in their criticisms of white appropriation, urging white musicians to stop profiting from playing black music and instead find their own path to musical authenticity.[11] "In the late 1960s, blackness was a confrontational identification that stood in clear opposition to whiteness," and the shifting musical styles of Nina Simone, Curtis Mayfield, and James Brown reflected the changes in the outlook of many African Americans.[12]

Treatments of the blues took on a heightened significance during this time, and the white rock musicians laying the groundwork for punk began exploring blues transformations as "parallel but separate" to black musicians' creative endeavors. White rock musicians' efforts in this respect could be explicit, as with the MC5's relationship with John Sinclair and the White Panther Party in Detroit, or they could be musically implicit.[13] But this "parallel but separate" work took on a different tone and quality from the music of black and interracial rock bands at the time, including those who were directly engaging civil rights issues in their music such as War (*Eric Burdon Declares "War,"* 1970) and Sly and the Family Stone (*Stand*, 1969), the first mainstream rock group to have black and white members and men and women.[14]

More racial separation occurred in the 1970s in the wake of the uprisings expressing the frustrations of African Americans with persistent racism and inequality, some of the most famous being those in Watts (1965), Newark (1967), Detroit (1967), Washington, DC (1968), and Attica Prison (1971). The uprisings were already linked to the mass migration of white Americans from urban centers to the suburbs, which had disproportionately affected the infrastructures of cities, and this segregated landscape meant that most white suburban Americans saw these volatile turning points from a distance. The uprisings would have a serious effect on punk, as white people perceived more reasons to segregate themselves and ossify boundaries between the suburbs and the so-called "inner cities" or "ghettos." Bill Harkleroad (Zoot Horn Rollo of Captain Beefheart's Magic Band), who grew up in Hawthorne, outside of Los Angeles, vividly remembered the Watts uprisings, noting "when the riots happened there was a complete division between black and white."[15] Regarding Detroit, Wayne Kramer wrote, "After the uprising, whites fled to

the suburbs in increasing numbers, leaving people of color behind in a smol-
dering and shattered city."[16]

Racial segregation between the cities and the suburbs continued through the
1970s. By 1980 Cleveland had lost 37 percent and Detroit 35 percent of their 1950
population numbers; meanwhile, although the percentage of African Americans nationwide remained at around 12 percent, the black population of Cleveland went from 16.2 percent to 43.8 percent, and Detroit from 16.2 percent to
63.1 percent, during that same period.[17] Yet such statistics can miss the layered
and uneven transformation of these cities. Wayne Kramer (b. 1948) explained to
me, "In particular for me growing up in Detroit I lived with people of color all
my life; my earliest boyhood childhood memories were kids up the street were
Mexican and African American . . . and I never really knew how racist America
was until I started touring in the MC5 . . . I mean Detroit certainly had almost
exclusively black communities, but it all overlapped. The glue that holds everything together of course is *jobs*. Everyone had good union jobs working in the
automobile industry."[18]

By the 1970s many of those jobs were gone, the white population had almost
completely deserted the city borders, and union laborers were striking repeatedly, as with the United Rubber Workers and Teamsters strikes in 1967, 1970,
and a 130-day strike against Goodyear in 1976. Slightly younger boomers who
were involved in creating the punk style remember factories not as agents of
social cohesion and drivers of the economy, but as polluters of a ruined landscape, symbolized in the collective imagination by the Cuyahoga River catching
fire on June 22, 1969.[19] As young people they viewed the cities' transformations
from the perspectives of white "middle-class or upper-middle-class" suburban homes.[20] When these musicians were moving back to the "inner cities" in
the early 1970s, their perception was of decline, decay, and racial antagonism.
Compare Wayne Kramer's recollections of Detroit in the 1950s and early 1960s,
above, with Allen Ravenstine's (Pere Ubu) memories of Cleveland in the early
1970s: "But it was really very depressed. Nobody lived downtown. Pretty much
roll up the streets after dark and everybody was afraid to be down there 'cause it
was all black people and everyone was terrified 'cause they'd get killed. I'm not
saying that these fears were realistic but that's what they were 'cause race was a
huge problem in Cleveland."[21]

Finally, punk emerged in relation to the disillusionment of white American
countercultural youth with hippie idealism and values. This disillusionment
largely surrounded efforts to end the war on Vietnam, which, especially early
on, disproportionately affected the poor and people of color who were unable
or less equipped to avoid the war than wealthy and middle-class whites.[22] The
reality for white American youth changed significantly in the late 1960s as the
Vietnam War increasingly affected them directly. The antiwar movement built in

the mid-1960s up to the large March on the Pentagon in October 1967, but Nixon introduced a new Vietnam draft lottery in December 1969 ending student defer-ments, and he extended American involvement in the conflict to Cambodia. Iggy Pop, Johnny Ramone, Wayne Kramer, and many of punk's early protagonists were deeply enmeshed in this politics of this time simply by having draft numbers. However, it should be emphasized that despite the counterculture's strong legacy on American culture, through the 1960s antiwar protests by African Americans such as Muhammad Ali's refusal to fight or Martin Luther King's speech against the war were widely decried by white Americans as unpatriotic, as were the kinds of strategies to avoid the war taken by Iggy Pop and others.[23]

The turn to the seventies brought the realities of American imperialism and the limits of the counterculture into sharp relief for the baby boomers. As Lisa Jane Persky remembered:

> We knew we had moved the ball but we thought it moved a lot farther than it did, and of course it was followed immediately by one of the worst periods in music and in the country. It was just so dark, it became so dark. I think whether we realized intellectually what had happened or not—which I don't think we did because you need distance to see it—we felt it. We felt it go down.[24]

A decisive moment for many was the killing at Kent State of Jeffrey Miller, Allison Krause, William Schroeder, and Sandra Scheuer by the Ohio National Guard on May 4, 1970, as they opened fire on Americans protesting Vietnam and the Cambodia surge. This gruesome event occurred while Chrissie Hynde (Pretenders), Chris Butler (Waitresses, Tin Huey), and Gerald Casale and Mark Mothersbaugh (DEVO) were students at Kent State, and it directly led to DEVO's formation.[25] Underscoring the significance for white countercultural youth, this deadly encounter with state power happened at a suburban uni-versity outside of Akron, unlike the violent altercations in the "inner cities" of Watts, Detroit, and DC. As Casale remembered, "it completely changed me from some kind of free love, pot-smoking hippie into a very politicized person that had a new agenda and a new well-founded anger...."[26] Furthermore, World War II and the Holocaust were still recent history, giving particular resonance to the many references to fascism and Nazism in early punk. For artists such as Casale and Mothersbaugh, the atmosphere of war in the early 1970s harked back to the interwar and World War II years in Europe.

More events at the turn of the 1970s contributed to a general feeling of rage, hopelessness, and disillusionment: Meredith Hunter's death at the chaotic Altamont Free Concert and the Manson Family murders in 1969, and the deaths of Jimi Hendrix and Janis Joplin within one month of each other in 1970 and Jim Morrison less than one year later. Chrissie Hynde remembered, "The Beatles were breaking up. It was like a nightmare. It seemed like everything was on the brink of collapse. It was over for Janis and Jimi. Brian Jones was gone. Jim Morrison was losing it, getting his cock out onstage, a drunken, belligerent mess like the rest of us. He wasn't long for this life either."[27] The next few years would add the Watergate scandal, Patty Hearst's capture by the Symbionese Liberation Army, and the beginning of production on the neutron bomb.

Many rock musicians expressed disillusionment during this time. Albums by hugely successful rock groups of the period, including *The Beatles* (the "White Album"), the Rolling Stones' *Let it Bleed*, and the Doors' *L.A. Woman*, contained songs depicting nightmarish or unsettling visions of this turbulent period: "Revolution 1," "Midnight Rambler," and "Riders on the Storm." Edwin Starr's "War" (1970) hit #1 on the *Billboard* Top 100. Black Sabbath, newly emerging but quickly rising in popularity, were creating tormented blues-based scenarios that set the stage for heavy metal, offering their own antiwar perspectives in the iconic "War Pigs" (1970). Given this climate, groups widely referenced as "protopunk" bands, including the Stooges and the Velvet Underground, were hardly alone in their bleak outlook, although they are often singled out for it.

The social history of the suburbs and the vicissitudes of the 1960s and 1970s counterculture help explain the environments in which punk developed. As teenagers, early punk rockers resented their cookie-cutter, heavily white suburban experience, but many later came to embrace it or feel nostalgic toward it. Similarly, when they moved to the cities in the early 1970s, they saw an abandoned tabula rasa marked by racial segregation, and in many ways they replicated the segregated environment of the suburbs within urban environments. Suburban childhoods and deserted cities are widely understood as cornerstones of punk's aesthetic and music, yet few of early punk's protagonists directly confronted the discriminatory practices and racist policies that created the suburban experiences of their childhood and the formative years of urban punk, and the full significance of these historical factors still needs to be reckoned with. The intertwined relationship of white flight and the Second Great Migration is especially key to understanding the racial landscape of the 1960s in the northern and West Coast metropolitan regions where the style of punk began to take shape.

# "Raw Power":
# Protopunk Transformations of the Blues

Iggy was Detroit. He was north. He was industrial.
He was more black than black in a sense man.
—Alan Vega[1]

This story of punk's musical style begins with the blues, especially uses of blues resources in the American Midwest during the 1960s. The blues-oriented musicians who set the stage for punk rock, such as Iggy Pop and the MC5, were white baby boomers deep into the sixties counterculture, trying to find ways to play rock music that were up to the social and political demands of the times. Specifically, these musicians joined many others at the time who were newly looking to the blues as resources, and who were reshaping the blues in connection with changing ideas of musical blackness and whiteness. They were also part of a wider group of white artists searching for authenticity in the wake of social programs that separated whiteness from authenticity as the price of privilege, and who were becoming increasingly concerned with the issues of theft and appropriation surrounding the familiar practice of white people playing black music.

The stakes of playing the blues were arguably never higher than they were in the 1960s, and the blues, in its various forms, took on an unprecedented intensity. Early punk musicians drew on approaches to the blues that they heard as the most powerful and the most unrestrained, the sounds that would later be named "raw power" by the Stooges. Yet at the same time, the blues has had a paradoxical and ambiguous relationship to punk. While the blues remains at the core of punk's musical style, it has disappeared as punk's acknowledged foundation. It is even common to claim that punk music is devoid of the blues rather than rooted in it (e.g., Sasha Frere-Jones: "The first wave of punk rock erased the rules and tendencies of blues—those standard melodies and harmonic intervals").[2] The complicated relationship between punk and the blues is fundamental for grasping the many paradoxes at the heart of the punk aesthetic, such as the dissonance between punk's musical blackness and its discourse of whiteness.[3]

## Blues and White Counterculture

Among the white counterculture in the 1950s and early 1960s, the blues was put to renewed use as a racial symbol. For African Americans, the Second Great Migration proliferated a variety of blues styles expressing a complex mix of northern urban realities and rural southern experiences, but for many white rock musicians in the US and UK, the rural and southern associations of the blues overshadowed other meanings. For these musicians, ideas of authenticity increasingly settled on a particular kind of black male country blues musician. Following the work of American folklorists, journalists, and folk musicians in the 1950s and early 1960s, rock musicians looked to Robert Johnson and others as representatives of essentialist and primitivist ideas of authentic blackness.[4] Young American musicians in and beyond the rock world, such as John Fahey, became particularly interested in "discovering" the old southern blues masters who might still be alive (and these efforts to find and record musicians such as John Hurt and Skip James predated and spurred interest in blues among British rock musicians).[5]

American whiteness has often depended on trading a sense of an authentic identity for privilege and power. Just as they were in the past, black music and the idea of blackness were especially important resources for countercultural white people struggling to recover a meaningful identity in the postwar era. These hipsters followed the lead of earlier examples, often directly. Mezz Mezzrow's autobiography *Really the Blues*, published in 1946 with a Signet reprint in 1964, describes the role of early jazz and blues in a Jewish Chicagoan's self-identity transformation into a black person, rejecting his white and Jewish background but, in articulating this rejection and journey, still tied to it.[6] Norman Mailer's essay "The White Negro" is another well-known (and strange and disturbing) meditation on the ways in which ideas of blackness inform white counterculture or hipster identity.[7] Key to the white Negro subjectivity in these writings is the white hipster's idea of the black man's relationship to violence (Mailer: ". . . no Negro can saunter down a street with any real certainty that violence will not visit him on his walk"), drugs (especially tied to marijuana), black music, and authority, especially the police (Mezzrow's imprisonment in a black prison cell at Riker's Island is the culmination of his memoir).[8] This white hipster mode of wrestling with identity without fully questioning institutional and structural racism greatly impacted punk, especially as punks in the mid-1970s ostensibly rejected earlier white hipsters' uses of blackness.

The blues had particular resonance in the northern midwestern cities such as Detroit, Chicago, and Cleveland, which were the primary Great Migration destinations for African Americans from Mississippi and Alabama.[9] The new northern residents included several of the architects of the blues styles that would become the basis for punk, such as John Lee Hooker, Muddy Waters, Bo Diddley, and Howlin' Wolf. "To learn that John Lee Hooker was actually from Detroit and he was singing about Detroit streets in some of his songs made me identify with him even more," said Wayne Kramer.[10] These musicians cultivated an amplified, urban style of blues that spoke to both their southern roots and new northern homes. Their commercial recordings were largely produced by the European Jewish immigrants who were also transforming these cities, such as Leonard and Phil Chess in Chicago. These black musicians and Jewish record men and women (e.g., Evelyn Aron of Aristocrat) were living in close proximity, both groups having fled discrimination and pursuing new opportunities within the narrow range of occupations to which they had been historically limited, and in which they also thrived.

Los Angeles, New York, and other northeastern and West Coast cities were undergoing similar transformations that created similar conditions, and many of these sites would also become central to early punk. However, the music of the postwar Midwest was distinctive. It was different from the popular music of 1960s New York, for example, which was connected to its durable music industry historically based around Tin Pan Alley and created to a large extent by earlier African American and Jewish migrants. Crucially, the midwestern cities were also hubs of black unionization, including the Brotherhood of Sleeping Car Porters primarily in Chicago, and at the Ford Motor Company with the United Automobile Workers in Detroit, Ford serving as a model for Berry Gordy's enormously successful Motown label.[11]

The prominence of black music in Detroit, Chicago, and other midwestern cities contributed to the environment in which white musicians developed a strong interest in the blues and blues-based music. Mitch Ryder, Iggy Pop, Alice Cooper, Bob Seger, Wayne Kramer, Ted Nugent, Terry Knight, the Woolies (who supported Chuck Berry starting in 1969), Corky Seigel, Jim Schwall, Jim McCarty, Mike Bloomfield, and Paul Butterfield were some of these musicians.[12] Detroit "was the key to my musical education," said Iggy Pop, along with the "Chicago blues players."[13] Wayne Kramer "would hear things like 'Honky Tonk' by Bill Doggett or 'Hideaway' by Freddie King, these songs and the blues, growing up in Detroit it was all kind of in the ether, it was just always there," especially on the radio.[14] Broadly speaking, their repertoire included the blues as played by the prominent black blues musicians in their cities, as well as blues-based rock music, often accessed through British Invasion bands during the 1960s. At the time the discourse of this music was highly racialized, very clearly defined as white people playing black music, with the terms "blue-eyed soul" and "white soul" coming into use. Iggy Pop was inspired by the "greaser bands"—the groups that would later be described as "garage" or even "punk" bands—who had "a certain animal vigor in the way [they] could play and enunciate a beat, and it was the nearest thing to black that white ever got."[15] But these white musicians were also part of a midwestern world in which both white and black people played blues-based rock music—an environment that would also produce Funkadelic and later Death (for more on Death, see chapter 8). Mitch Ryder was a particularly important musician at the time, his style of straight-ahead rock becoming essential to the punk aesthetic. Chrissie Hynde's desire to play rock was ignited by seeing the Detroit Wheels at Chippewa Lake in 1965.[16]

Iggy Pop was one of the musicians of this period who became a blues enthusiast in search of authentic blues musicians. In 1965, while still based in Ann Arbor, Iggy became the drummer for the Prime Movers, a group that "would only play the real, true, Blackaspossible Chicago Blues."[17] He went to Chicago and played with Sam Lay, the drummer for the original Paul Butterfield Blues Band, and stayed in the basement of Bob Koester's Delmark store; Koester "loved the blues, knew his shit, and was very involved in the black Chi-town scene." He historicized and romanticized black musicians:

> I started getting gigs playing with these black guys. I was still very young and raggedy at this time, but I started getting gigs. The first thing I noticed about playing with these black guys—older guys—their music was like honey off their fingers— real childlike and charming in its simplicity and lack of any real arrangement, not like any Chicago blues played by the white groups, who really misinterpret.[18]

Such ideas of black blues musicians were becoming common among white people in the 1960s.[19] Earlier black Southern musical life became a preoccupation of white musicians and audiences in the 1960s looking for "access to the emotionally sincere, masculine, rebellious, darkly exotic world of the 1920s Mississippi Delta."[20] Charles Keil identified the emerging widespread idea of the authentic bluesman in the early to mid-1960s as old, obscure, taught by a legendary figure, and rural, "uncontaminated by city influences."[21] As Hamilton writes with respect to 1960s white folk musicians, they developed "a profoundly imaginative relationship to black music . . . that held black music and musicians to be engines of raw and unknowable power that existed almost exclusively in the past."[22]

White people reinforced this version of the archetypal authentic black blues musician by selecting and magnifying aspects of a far more complex reality. Rock musicians' ideas, along with the writings of Amiri Baraka and others, resulted in a recasting of the blues' place in the history of African American popular music, and the de-emphasis or ignoring of those who in fact dominated the earlier blues market, such as women, songsters, hokum players, and vaudevillians.[23] The blues musicians cast as the most authentic were generally older, but often still contemporaries of these rock musicians (in the early 1960s John

Lee Hooker was only in his forties, while Sam Lay was twelve years older than Iggy Pop), with their formative commercial recordings released in the recent past. Even the musicians who seemed archaic, such as Blind Willie Johnson and Blind Lemon Jefferson, were recording in the relatively recent past; for comparison, the time between the first Stooges record (1969) and Blind Willie McTell's "Statesboro Blues" (1929) is forty years, the same time elapsed between me writing now in 2018 and the release of the first Black Flag EP, *Nervous Breakdown*.

Blues performers through the 1950s and 1960s also typically had a wide range of musical approaches at their disposal, a trait they shared with most professional musicians. Howlin' Wolf and Muddy Waters had diverse repertoires filled with assorted song forms and harmonic schemes, as would be expected from professional musicians who lived and worked in so many different locales and contexts.[24] When describing his repertoire to Alan Lomax and John Work, Muddy Waters listed hits by Gene Autry, "Corrina," "Deep in the Heart of Texas," and other pop tunes, "not at all what one would expect from hearing his recordings."[25] As their image and the market changed in the 1960s, Muddy Waters and others stopped performing songs and styles that ran counter to the archetypal image and sound. For example, Howlin' Wolf, who released commercial singles for Chess Records to black audiences in the 1950s, became an authentic "folk" musician in the early 1960s, appearing on the American Folk Blues Festival in Europe in 1964 and releasing *The Real Folk Blues* in 1965.[26] John Lee Hooker "had been relatively successful as a 'city blues' musician, but was recast as a down home folk-bluesman to fit the revival circuit."[27] Lightnin' Hopkins, in collaboration with Samuel Charters—the author of *The Country Blues* (1959) and Hopkins's record producer—switched to acoustic guitar in 1959; and although he remained based in Texas, he toured widely on the blues and folk revival circuit.[28]

Meanings of the blues, and the stakes of white people playing the blues, changed dramatically over the course of the 1960s. Amiri Baraka's writings captured some of the tensions surrounding the blues, and although he was far from the only writer to investigate the meanings of the blues at the time, his writings are illustrative of many wider issues. In *Blues People* (1963) Baraka articulates the blues's importance to a revised narrative of African American history and definition of African American identity.[29] For Baraka, the further African American expression was from his idea of the blues, beginning with what he called "primitive blues," the less authentic it was and the more it reflected assimilation and whiteness; for example, ragtime was a "pitiful popular debasement," and Hazel Scott playing Grieg was akin to the "pitiful spectacle of Carnegie Hall boogie woogie."[30] Baraka also directly connected race to class, equating assimilation and whiteness with a facile portrait of the black middle class.[31]

Ralph Ellison at the time understood Baraka as actively reframing and reshaping African American expressive history. Ellison (twenty years older than

Baraka) interpreted Baraka as speaking directly to the massive social changes taking place, writing: "read as a record of an earnest young man's attempt to come to grips with his predicament as Negro American during a most turbulent period of our history *Blues People* may be worth the reader's time. Taken as a theory of American Negro culture, it can only contribute more confusion than clarity."[32] Ellison's assessment of Baraka's view of history as a reflection of the 1960s was borne out as the ideas expressed in Baraka's writings became much more commonplace.

One central point of contention was the consistent appropriation by white people of black musical resources.[33] Although Baraka was scathingly critical of white rock musicians, the historical narrative and the spectrum of musical blackness to whiteness he describes in *Blues People* and later essays (e.g., those collected in *Black Music*) dovetailed with the attitudes of many white blues revivalists and rock musicians in the 1960s and their idea of the authentic natural folk blues musician. For white rock musicians also—including those from the United Kingdom such as Eric Clapton, Jimmy Page, and the Rolling Stones—the effectiveness of their music depended on the idea that the closer music was to "primitive" blues models, the more authentic it was.[34]

Meanwhile, although black audiences in the 1960s continued to support blues musicians, and even as elements of southern styles remained key to black music, over the course of the 1960s the northern black audience for the urban blues musicians who were popular in the 1950s began to ebb as white audiences became more interested in the music. African Americans were increasingly invested in rhythm-and-blues artists such as Aretha Franklin, Sam Cooke, and the artists on Motown, as well as the concept of soul music, driven later by James Brown's innovations.[35] In Washington, DC, black middle-class audiences were generally uninterested in the "revival" performances of John Hurt, as Dick Spottswood told Stephen Lorenz: "they would have been very conspicuously black in that white audience, listening to a black performer playing music they had never heard before, from some kind of archaic, downhome, Mississippi cotton plantation, and they didn't relate to that shit either."[36] In the mid- to late 1960s James Brown led the way to a new musical performance of blackness, a sound that became increasingly politicized with respect to the Black Power movement. Brown and his arrangers, such as Alfred "Pee Wee" Ellis, were transforming blues resources, but they did so without employing a discourse of romanticizing the Delta blues musicians and their environment, as white rock musicians did. Like his blues contemporaries, Brown had a diverse repertoire, but by 1967 he was focusing heavily on vamps, straight-eighth rhythms and syncopation, and riff-based compositions—"I Can't Stand Myself," "Cold Sweat," "Let Yourself Go," and "There Was a Time" charted that year—laying the groundwork for funk and soul music. As Rob Bowman described, Brown's "drastic reduction in harmonic movement influenced virtually all black music at the time."[37] Curtis Mayfield's "(Don't Worry) If There's a Hell Below, We're All Going to Go" (1970), the Chi-Lites' "(For God's Sake) Give More Power to the People" (1971), and Rahsaan Roland Kirk's "Blacknuss" (1972) can be heard as similar extensions of blues resources, demonstrating the direct line between riff-based music and Black Power politics by the early 1970s.[38]

White musicians who directly aligned themselves with Black Power politics, such as the MC5, also contributed to the association of riff-based blues resources with blackness, revolution, and soul.[39] Richard Goldstein, "arguably the most influential" rock critic of the late 1960s, considered the blues to be inherently revolutionary.[40] Together, white rock musicians' mythologizing and appropriation of particular blues resources, the associated recordings and collaborations with African American blues musicians themselves, the writings about black music's essential qualities by black and white critics, the soul music breakthroughs of James Brown and his contemporaries, and the inspired music of the new rhythm-and-blues artists collectively revolutionized the concept of black music and blackness in the 1960s.

As the stakes intensified for white people using blues resources, some musicians who were previously deeply committed to the blues, such as Iggy Pop, altered their style. Iggy Pop "needed to go back [from Chicago to Michigan] and create his own blues," as Wayne Kramer put it.[41] However, the music of these artists remained rooted in the blues and black music. Iggy Pop himself has always maintained that the blues was the essence of the rock musical language in all its forms, saying in 2009: "Stuff like [Bukka White and John Lee Hooker], that's the basis. That's the Rolling Stones, that's every—that's Cream, that's even Sonic Youth. In fact, it's very close to Sonic Youth. It's everything that's happened in . . . rock, right up from Chuck Berry through alternative. . . . That's the vocabulary there."[42] He has always been clear about his debt to the riff-based music of James Brown, and he said "Down on the Street" was his version of "Let Yourself Go."[43] To create this distinctive blues, Iggy Pop and others emphasized open-ended, riff-based, compositions with limited harmonic movement, supporting monophonic minor melodies. These particular approaches, creating an effect of "raw power," eventually became a cornerstone of punk and one of the most consistently productive styles for punk musicians.

### Raw Power Musical Style

Many of the musicians who punks refer to as their stylistic antecedents, such as the MC5, Velvet Underground, the Stooges, and the Kinks, are often now retrospectively grouped together as "protopunks," although they may have had little to do with each other while active, and also despite the fact that members of these groups may not—and often did not—hear themselves in the punk music they inspired. For example, when Wayne Kramer returned from prison in 1979 and joined Gang War with Johnny Thunders, he felt out of step with the punk scene. "I was shocked . . . [Thunders] would abuse them and call them names and everything, call them douchebags . . . we used to call them brothers and sisters, you know."[44] This is the paradoxical nature of a category such as *protopunk*: unlike a "prototype," in music writing *proto-* is only applied retrospectively. *Protopunk*, for instance, unsurprisingly began appearing in general usage around 1978 along with the twin term *postpunk*.[45] Saying protopunks "influenced" later punk groups results in a similar sort of historical misdirection, as the verb "influence" wrongly places agency with the "influencer" and not the "influenced," who are in fact the actors. But despite the easily misleading term, *protopunk* can be useful for understanding punk musicians' active interpretations of the music they found generative and meaningful. From this perspective, a musical analysis of white North American and British protopunk bands' music reveals particular approaches to blues resources that were especially distinctive in the climate of the 1960s and early 1970s, even when compared to the styles of other contemporaneous white rock musicians.

Collectively (and to avoid too much misdirection with the term *protopunk*), I refer to the blues styles with the most significant impact on later punk musicians as the "raw power" style, from the title of the pivotal third album by the Stooges. "Raw power" musicians' approaches to blues resources are best heard as distinct from the many widespread treatments of the blues in circulation at the time, with the twelve-bar blues as a standard point of reference. For both "rock and roll" and "rhythm and blues" musicians in the 1950s, the twelve-bar, three-line blues with a strophic AAB lyric, simply known as the "twelve-bar blues," became the dominant blues form. Twelve-bar blues songs usually employ minor pentatonic–based melodies sung with a flexible rhythm, with the naturally stressed syllables of the lyrics coordinated with the downbeats of each four-bar group. The harmonic pattern generally follows I (4 bars); IV (2 bars) I (2 bars); V (1 bar) IV (1 bar) I (2 bars, often with V "turnaround" in the last bar). Yet the twelve-bar blues is only one of many blues schemes, and blues musicians subjected even this scheme to countless variations, such as changing lengths of phrases, altering lyric patterns, and adding and subtracting chords.

By the 1960s, approaches to the blues had come to loosely signify different interpretations of African American experiences, and in turn, various blues styles were used in different ways by white musicians. When treated as a tight compositional structure for ensemble playing, with or without harmonic additions or substitutions (such as 9ths, 11ths, and 13ths), the twelve-bar blues had become a primary resource for communicating an urbane sound of African

American life in the northern cities. On the other hand, riff-based performances and three-part structures with unequal phrase lengths, usually played by solo artists or very small ensembles such as duos or trios, signaled the South and the rural backdrop of the Great Migration. Some musicians, such as the southern artists who themselves migrated or worked in northern cities, were especially adept at combining these two—the "classic blues" legends Ma Rainey and Bessie Smith; Muddy Waters, Howlin' Wolf, Hubert Sumlin, and other originators of the Chicago blues sound; and John Lee Hooker, who left Mississippi and became popular in Detroit.

The many forms of a classic such as "See See Rider" illustrate some of the various meanings and uses of blues resources. The earliest example, recorded by Ma Rainey in New York in 1924, is a "classic blues" twelve-bar version with collective jazz improvisation accompaniment by Fletcher Henderson, Louis Armstrong, Charlie Green, Charlie Dixon, and Buster Bailey.[46] This particular "See See Rider" is a good example of blues as an expression of early Great Migration exchanges, featuring Ma Rainey's southern blues singing style in combination with the instrumental voices of other southern jazz musicians, taking place in a New York studio. Later jazz versions such as Red Garland's recording of 1959 also stick to the twelve-bar form, but use notable harmonic substitutions. This connecting thread seems to support Gerhard Kubik's assertion that by the 1950s, the twelve-bar blues had flourished as a common resource among jazz musicians; having acquired associations of urban sophistication for several decades, it was "promoted by those blues musicians and their clients who had come to perceive the use of these chords as status-enhancing."[47] In contrast, the versions of "See See Rider" associated with the "country blues" or "folk blues" tradition, such as those by Big Bill Broonzy (1934) or Lead Belly (recorded in 1935 and released in 1951 by Folkways) reflect uneven phrase lengths and significant chord variation.[48] LaVern Baker's hit rhythm-and-blues version for Atlantic in 1962 is an example of a popular 1960s performance, tightly sticking to the twelve-bar form and introducing backup singers. The appropriation of the song into the rock repertoire is probably best represented by the twelve-bar, riff-heavy British Invasion version by Eric Burdon and the Animals (1966), which hit the US Top Ten.

White rock musicians in the 1960s generally capitalized on associations of the blues with either urban sophistication or rural primitive authenticity as they adopted the music for their own purposes. Those aiming for a more mainstream sound followed the course of R&B and rock and roll antecedents, using the straightforward twelve-bar blues as a compositional framework, whereas those who wished to express a primitive aesthetic favored riff-based music with looser frameworks and less harmonic movement. To Iggy Pop, for example, the Rolling Stones were a "band of Chuck Berrys" while Led Zeppelin was "a band of Howlin' Wolfs."[49]

The Doors' version of Willie Dixon's "Back Door Man" demonstrates a middle-of-the-road rock approach popular in the mid- to late 1960s, and includes illustrative aspects of rock's racial codes. The original performed by Howlin' Wolf and his band (1962) is an open-ended, harmonically static performance, with various approaches to the riff and which never leaves the I chord. Howlin' Wolf's unique voice carries the song through a wide expressive range, his distinctive rasp not an affectation but a product of his childhood in the sharecropper South, "subslavery levels of health care resulted in chronic throat and teeth infections, the musical yield on which was Wolf's claim to fame. . . ."[50] In the Doors' version, the lyric is recast in a twelve-bar AAB, I–IV–V form with a simplified repetitive unchanging treatment of the riff, and the original shuffle beat turned into a straight-eighth feel. Jim Morrison sings differently than he does elsewhere on their debut album, impersonating a composite Chicago bluesman with some overtures to Howlin' Wolf specifically, even cringingly singing in a pseudo-black dialect ("eat yo' po'k and beans," "de men don't know"). As mentioned, I posit that this audible appropriation—probably almost as awkward then as it is now—is part of a certain rock aesthetic that can be traced as far back as the minstrel tradition, separating musicians such as the Doors from white musicians who tried to position themselves more squarely in the blues lineage and to take on blues voices without using stereotypical dialect, such as Mitch Ryder, Canned Heat, Johnny Winter, the Allman Brothers, and Paul Butterfield. In this performance Jim Morrison is trying to sound like a white man putting on a "black" voice, just as minstrels before him were visually and audibly white men faking blackness.

While many rock and roll and R&B musicians were adhering to a tight twelve-bar blues structure with little variation and improvisation, raw power musicians were focusing on "country" riff-based models, with a high degree of variation and improvisation, and associated to a large extent with Mississippi-born and Chicago-based bluesmen. Some groups, such as the MC5 and Stooges, took this particular blues aesthetic to extremes. Other groups took elements of this style but adjusted their vocal performance styles and the alignment of vocal syllables to the underlying beat. These groups, such as the Velvet Underground, adopted blues resources as a musical foundation while separating their music from the most racially marked qualities of American blues styles, in effect "whitening" their sound, a strategy they enacted for authenticity. Meanwhile, all of the raw power musicians cultivated harmonic and melodic approaches that retained the powerful affect of black musical resources even when obscured, such as blues-based riffs and vamps.

Musicians who paved the way for punk had a particular interest in raw power blues treatments, but for many of them, an interest in deep authentic blues also led many of them to other blues styles found on the *Anthology of American*

*Folk Music* and early twentieth-century commercial recordings. For example, as shown in figures 2.1 and 2.2, Peter Laughner, the driving force behind Cleveland's Rocket from the Tombs and Pere Ubu, was a serious student of the blues. The 1969 recordings of his group Mr. Charlie—the name of a Lightnin' Hopkins song—feature the Howlin' Wolf songs "Evil" and "How Many More Years" in quintessential riff-based one-chord raw power style.[51] The variety of blues styles in Laughner's repertoire is also on display on a recently surfaced recording of his group the Original Wolverines playing on Cleveland's WMMS in 1972, featuring songs by Blind Blake, Blind Willie McTell, and Jimmie Rodgers, as well as contemporaneous songs with old-fashioned characteristics, such as Lowell George's "Willin'."[52] Following a performance of Bob Dylan's "Please, Mrs. Henry," a sixteen-bar medium tempo country blues, a telling exchange between Laughner and deejay Shauna Zurbrugg points to some of the different meanings of the blues in the early 1970s:

ZURBRUGG: Pete, how 'bout some blues?
LAUGHNER: I just did a blues. (laughter)
ZURBRUGG: Some *down* blues. *Down* blues.
LAUGHNER: I don't know, we could do one, sure. Let me think of one. I
    got all these lyrics floating around in my head and I just gotta set 'em
    together. I wish I had my harp [harmonica] . . .
ZURBRUGG: It's a double request. Lightnin' Hopkins?
LAUGHNER: Well, yeah, something on that level. I'd like to do an up-tempo
    one if you wouldn't mind. [Plays Arthur Crudup's "Mean Ole Frisco."]

Early punk musicians were also interested in the rock bands of the mid-1960s comprised of young white Americans such as the Shadows of Knight, the Standells, the Blues Magoos, the other groups collected on Lenny Kaye's *Nuggets* compilation, and Iggy Pop's early group the Iguanas. These groups also based much of their music on blues forms. The Standells' "Dirty Water" (1965), for example, is a twelve-bar blues played with a distinct intensity, and the Sonics' "The Witch" (1964) is also based on a twelve-bar form. The musicians in the 1970s New York punk scene, discussed in chapter 4, regenerated interest in these inspirational bands, often retrospectively categorized as "garage rock" or even punk rock, and during that time the *Nuggets*-style bands took on symbolic associations of an earlier time than the "raw power" groups profiled here. The two uses of blues resources often had different meanings; the garage rock approach reflecting a simpler mode of appropriation typical of white groups in the 1950s and early 1960s, and the Stooges and the MC5 responding to the heightened complexities of white appropriation in the mid- to late 1960s and into the early 1970s.

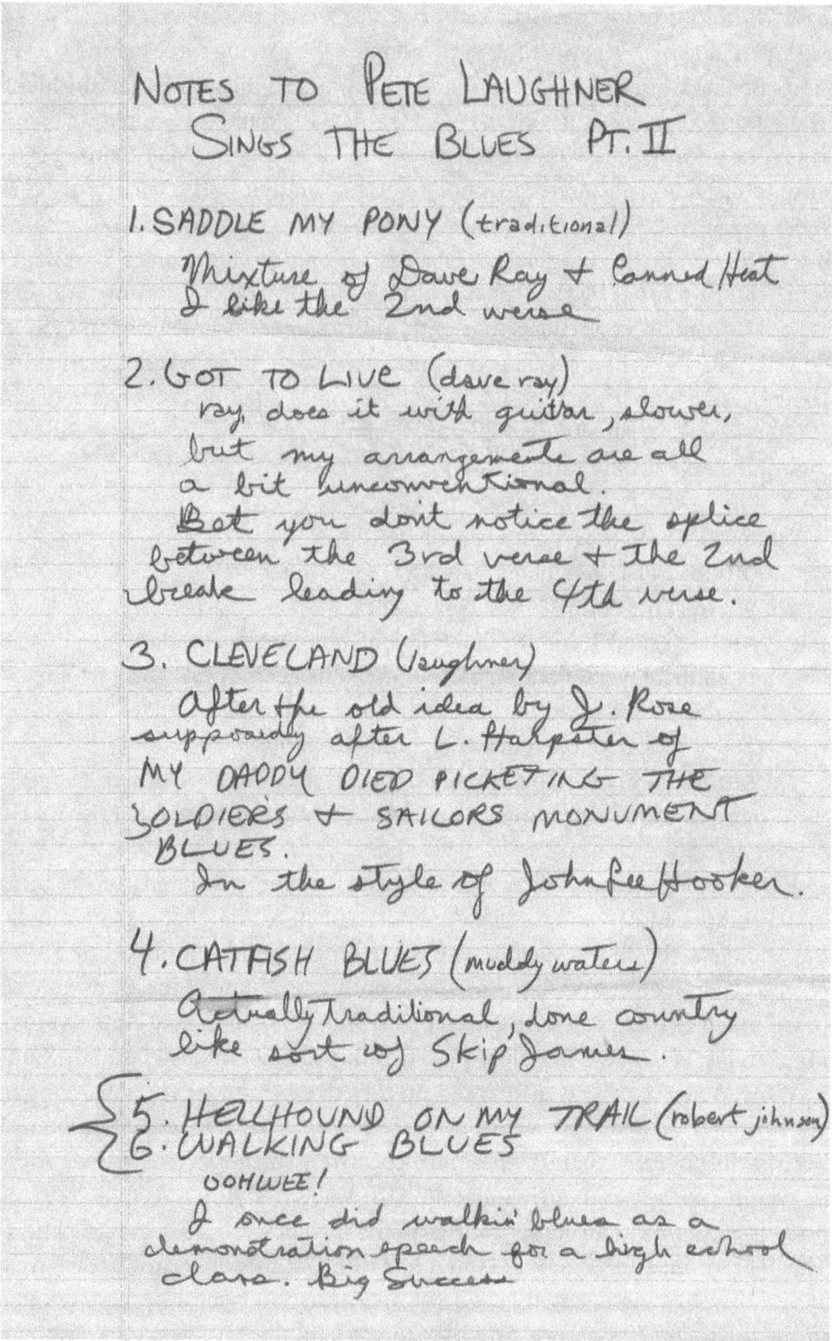

NOTES TO PETE LAUGHNER
SINGS THE BLUES PT. II

1. SADDLE MY PONY (traditional)
   Mixture of Dave Ray + Canned Heat
   I like the 2nd verse

2. GOT TO LIVE (dave ray)
   ray, does it with guitar, slower,
   but my arrangements are all
   a bit unconventional.
   But you don't notice the splice
   between the 3rd verse + the 2nd
   break leading to the 4th verse.

3. CLEVELAND (Laughner)
   After the old idea by J. Rose
   supposedly after L. Halpern of
   MY DADDY DIED PICKETING THE
   SOLDIERS + SAILORS MONUMENT
   BLUES.
   In the style of John Lee Hooker.

4. CATFISH BLUES (muddy waters)
   Actually traditional, done country
   like sort of Skip James.

5. HELLHOUND ON MY TRAIL (robert johnson)
6. WALKING BLUES
   OOHWEE!
   I once did walkin' blues as a
   demonstration speech for a high school
   class. Big Success

Figure 2.1a and 2.1b. Peter Laughner's personal notes to "Pete Laughner Sings the Blues Pt. II." Photo courtesy of Smog Veil Records, LLC on behalf of the estate of Peter Laughner.

7. ONE KIND FAVOR (jefferson)
   Bob Dylan, sort of Van Ronk, sort of
   my own!
   I like the lonely d tuning and
   <u>eternal</u> feeling. MOAN.

8. WINDOW RAG (laughter)
   self explanatory.
   Also made up spontaneously
   with no forethought. Basic
   tune is "Special Delivery Blues"
   by Tampa Red.

9. Streetcorner Man (laughter
   also spontaneous and
   open to vague interpretation

The raw power groups discussed in this chapter were not "ahead of their time" (implied by "proto-") nor some kind of heretical fringe rock subculture. Rather, they were enmeshed in the racial and cultural conversations of the 1960s. They heavily based their music on the riff-based country blues increasingly considered authentic, while they toyed with a range of approaches to the voice, harmony, rhythm, and production values. They strategically set themselves apart from other white rock groups in the 1960s, as they viewed their peers as too imitative and thus inauthentic. And their intense study of blues and country styles indicates that the stylistic choices they made were indeed deliberate choices culled from a wide range of possible options. Their treatments of the blues set the stage for a potentially radical and, in hindsight, schismatic scene that would be paradoxically read as a "white" opposite to the blues and explicitly blues-based rock music.

### Raw Power Harmony and Form

The musicians I group together as playing in a raw power style are distinguished by the extent to which they drew upon short riffs, one-chord vamps, and limited harmonic movement—especially oscillations between two chords or two harmonic centers—instead of the twelve-bar blues form. Whereas the Animals, the Doors, and many other rock musicians in the 1960s were using short riffs in their blues treatments, protopunks took these approaches to extremes and based their sound even more explicitly on the country or folk models established by Big Joe Williams, John Lee Hooker, Howlin' Wolf, and Bukka White. Instead of standardizing the blues of Big Bill Broonzy or Lightnin' Hopkins, these musicians took their songs and made them even more riff-based and cyclical.

For example, Them's version of "Baby Please Don't Go" uses riffs and vocal improvisations and sticks to one harmonic center, removing the subdominant (IV chord) and dominant (V chord) elements in versions by Lightnin' Hopkins, Big Bill Broonzy, even John Lee Hooker, and harking all the way back to the earliest recording by Big Joe Williams, which stays on the I chord, a notable aspect of his style. This transformation from a blues often played with I, IV, and V chords, as Lightnin' Hopkins usually played it, to a static one-chord version is a protopunk reversal of the Doors' taking "Back Door Man" from a one-chord version to a twelve-bar I–IV–V version, described above. The Amboy Dukes' treatment of the song, immortalized on *Nuggets*, resembles Them's performance, using the same riff, but emphasizing Ted Nugent's delirious soloing over an open-ended whole-step alternation.[53]

The Stooges were directly inspired by Them's open-ended one- and two-chord take on the blues, beginning with the opening track on *The "Angry" Young Them* (1965), "Mystic Eyes":

And you had cuts on this album like "Mystic Eyes" where the entire song threw out any semblance of verse. No verse, no chorus, no normal chord pattern, it's just the guys pounding and not even a backbeat, just guys pounding on two chords back and forth, and he's singing a lyric . . . there's no melody exactly, he just sings, "One Sunday morning I went walking down by the graveyard. The morning sun, I looked at you, wow, your mystic eyes." And that's the whole lyric, that's it, it just repeats over and over . . . within that simple two chord pounding, the way the music was arranged was, it was very bluesy. And there was really great slide guitar playing, great blues harp, great drumming, the stuff had a roots to it, too. And, of course, what I didn't know then and found out later is Van Morrison knew his blues very, very well, which is what I started to learn after I investigated well, where does this rock come from? And, and he was taking blues idioms and just redoing them, recycling them and making them fresher and he did this again and again in some of his best work.[54]

The Stooges' seminal albums include entirely riff-based, one-chord (or one–harmonic center) songs without any nod to twelve-bar-type patterns, such as "T.V. Eye." The riff-based one-chord approach was key to the styles of musicians such as Howlin' Wolf ("Moanin' at Midnight") and generally ascendant in the 1960s: one of Captain Beefheart's first recordings is a cover of Bo Diddley's "Diddy Wah Diddy," a riff-based blues mostly on the I chord. Canned Heat's "On the Road Again" (1968) is a classic reworking of the style. These musicians were close to early punk: Lydia Lunch's band 8-Eyed Spy (1980) later covered "Diddy Wah Diddy" again, while Bob Hite of Canned Heat introduced Exene Cervenka and the other members of X to many 78 RPM blues and country music recordings.[55] Another important element of the raw power approach is the use of riff-based sections or two-chord oscillations as extended sections in compositions that employed twelve-bar or multipart forms. In the Stooges' "No Fun" and the Velvet Underground's "Foggy Notion," extended sections provided places for musicians to improvise, dance, and enter or simulate trance.[56]

These deceptively simple structures encouraged social interaction and do-it-yourself aesthetics, later staples of the punk aesthetic. According to Wayne Kramer, open forms challenge musicians to "pay complete attention to the other people that you're playing with so that you're actually playing together and all working together on a musical idea, a unified thought."[57] Open-ended forms and improvisations also had strong spiritual and transcendent qualities, exemplified by African American "New Thing" or "free jazz" musicians such as John Coltrane, Albert Ayler, and Sun Ra; rock and jazz inspired by Indian classical music; and the excursions of the Grateful Dead.[58] Interpretations of free jazz included the Stooges' "L.A. Blues," MC5's "Starship" (interpreting a poem by Sun Ra), and the Velvet Underground's "Sister Ray," about which Lou Reed reportedly told Lester Bangs, "I had been listening to a lot of Cecil Taylor and Ornette Coleman, and wanted to get something like that with a rock 'n' roll feeling."[59] Although sometimes based on primitivist misunderstandings, these performances speak to transcendence and expression as key factors in the later punk aesthetic. As Television's Tom Verlaine remembered, "I used to have these jam sessions with a friend. We couldn't play at all; we just used to like to make noise; fantastic noise, this raw expression . . . I was especially into saxophone players then . . . guys like John Coltrane and Albert Ayler. I played sax for maybe two years, but I never really played it well, because I was eager for expression before I'd got the technique right."[60] Patti Smith intensely explored the spiritual possibilities of open-ended forms in early punk through her poetry.

A closer look at some key songs, beginning with the Stooges' "No Fun," reveals quite a bit about the approaches to the blues that punk musicians found so inspiring. The Stooges perhaps more than any other group laid a blueprint for punk, with Stooges records continually serving as vehicles for social outcasts assembling into bands. In his memoir, John Lydon recalled the Sex Pistols' cover of the Stooges' "No Fun": "'No Fun' is a song I love. We made up our version on the spot. I always wanted to do it. I asked Steve [Jones] to learn the riff, which he did very quickly. Paul [Cook] filled in, and it went on from there."[61]

As shown in musical example 2.1, the first part of "No Fun" is based on a blues form that moves to different harmonic areas: an eight-bar A section (I–V–I–I twice) and a twelve-bar B section (IV–I–V–I / IV–I–V–V / I–I–I–I), anchored throughout by a whole-step riff played together by the guitar, bass, and hand claps. But the real "No Fun" does not appear until this multipart blues scheme is over, set up after the second time through the cycle by an expanded four-bar V chord ("Maybe go out, maybe stay home, maybe call Mom on the telephone"). The multipart section gives way to an extended improvisation built on the riff oscillating between I and IV every measure while Iggy Pop repeats "well come on!" While the composed "No Fun" song lasts 1:45, the extended vamp goes on for over twice as long, another 3:30 on the record, fading out to demonstrate that it should continue for much longer. The vamping two-chord I–IV section is a place for Iggy Pop to improvise lyrics, exploit the blue notes that are touched on in the verse, and add screams and growls, while Ron Asheton plays increasingly wild blues guitar solos. This trend of minimizing multipart blues cycles and maximizing riffs, vamps, and limited harmonic movement became a cornerstone of the raw power style.

The Velvet Underground also effectively combined multipart blues forms with extended riff-based sections. Although more than a few writers have pointed to the gloomy and bleak aesthetic of "Heroin" and "Venus in Furs" as the Velvet Underground's punk legacy, the most direct and far-reaching musical impact of the group in punk is found in the (also gloomy) blues-based

Musical example 2.1. "No Fun," Stooges, *The Stooges*, 1969. Transcription by the author.

songs that later groups adapted or interpreted, such as "Sister Ray" and "Foggy Notion," and classic rock and rollers such as "We're Gonna Have a Real Good Time Together" and "Sweet Jane." Iggy Pop heard "Sister Ray" as an example of the Velvet Underground "also rewriting blues idioms," like he was.[62] Lester Bangs recognized that the Velvet Underground's approach was an extreme manifestation of the style of other blues-based rock bands: the Velvet Underground "seemed to have carried the Yardbirds/Who project to its ultimate extension."[63] In his 1970 review of *Loaded*, Lenny Kaye writes: "Lou Reed has always steadfastly maintained that the Velvet Underground were just another Long Island rock 'n' roll band, but in the past, he really couldn't be blamed much if people didn't care to take him seriously. . . . Well, it now turns out that Reed was right all along, and the most surprising thing about the change in the group is that there has been no real change at all."[64] Rhythm and blues runs deep in the Velvet Underground's music; before forming the Velvet Underground, the members were immersed "in the wildest black music of the late fifties and early sixties," in Lou Reed's words.[65] For example, "Rock and Roll" is clearly in the rhythm and blues vein when interpreted by Mitch Ryder on *Detroit* (1971), that particular version assessed by Reed as "the way it was supposed to sound."[66]

Like "No Fun," "Foggy Notion" combines multipart blues cycles with riffs and two-chord oscillations. "Foggy Notion" is constructed mostly on a repeating two-bar riff, but with a twelve-bar blues section ("Sally Mae") dropped into the overall structure. Live versions of "Foggy Notion" extended the vamps and minimized the twelve-bar sections, demonstrating a general move away from the twelve-bar patterns toward more open-ended forms. Some interpreters amplified the song's blues aspects, such as Rocket from the Tombs' 1975 cover with blues guitar solos and retention of the "Sally Mae" twelve-bar blues section. This version makes sense in light of Peter Laughner's extensive blues background, the blues-drenched atmosphere of the northern Midwest, and the consistent visits of the Velvet Underground to Cleveland's La Cave. On the other hand, a Modern Lovers performance from 1972 completely avoids the twelve-bar blues section.[67]

The Velvet Underground was one of the most prominent rock groups to go even further and transform the one-chord or one–harmonic center blues approach into drones used for improvisations, as in the long open-ended section of "Sister Ray." But while the midwestern and Californian musicians such as Iggy Pop, the MC5, and Captain Beefheart retained some associations with the blues, the Velvet Underground became more generally linked with a mostly white avant-garde art scene rather than blues-based rock. The Velvet Underground's use of one-chord drones is central to a non-blues interpretation of their music, with drones linked to avant-garde musicians such as La Monte Young or Indian classical music, long understood as an inspiration for rock musicians in the 1960s, and rarely traced back to blues roots. Young's approach to the drone did find its way into the Velvet Underground's music and on to the Stooges and others, and Indian classical music was equally if not more influential.[68] However, the blues is also the original source for La Monte Young's drones and thus those he inspired, and as such bears special consideration with respect to rock drones.

La Monte Young is particularly germane to punk history in that his colleagues in the 1960s included the Velvet Underground's John Cale and original member Angus MacLise. Because of these connections, La Monte Young is considered a secret or unrecognized source of underground rock and punk. For example, in an essay by Alan Licht, Young is considered "the *birth* of NYC drone" (emphasis mine), tracing a lineage of white men beginning with Arnold Schoenberg and Igor Stravinsky and then proceeding from John Cage to Young to Steve Reich and Philip Glass to Cale, MacLise, Reed, and Tony Conrad, and on to so-called "krautrock" and bands such as Sonic Youth, as well as more classically oriented composers such as Glenn Branca and Rhys Chatham.[69]

Yet Young himself pointed to the blues and jazz as the original source of his inspiration for repetitive forms based on one harmonic center. In addition to becoming "a devotee of the cutting-edge jazz of Charlie Parker, Lee Konitz, and John Coltrane," "the blues became a particular obsession for Young, and he explored blues harmonies and adapted blues structure in ways that foreshadowed his later work."[70] Young "eventually . . . abandoned the twelve-bar blues structure altogether in order to spend much longer periods of time in what he described as 'modal drone' improvisations over each chord," and "this type of static-harmony, single-mode improvisation" runs through Young's work from the 1950s up to later career work with his Forever Bad Blues Band.[71] Young has been consistently open about his music's basis in the blues: in 1993 he wrote that the blues was "one of the ancestral lineages of my music . . . It may come as a surprise to some to find that I consider much of my music either to be blues-based or to have a strong relationship to blues."[72] The early rehearsals with Angus MacLise and John Cale were "to provide this sustained accompaniment for these sopranino sax improvisations" on sustained harmony blues inspired by John Coltrane.[73] But even without these clear connections to Young, if we "draw a straight line" from the many one-chord rock songs underpinning minor and minor-pentatonic melodies in the 1960s, the closest stylistic point of reference is not Stravinsky, Cage, or Ravi Shankar, but rock's basis in blues harmony and the blues' extensive one-chord manifestations. The drummer for the Forever Bad Blues Band, Jonathan Kane, has created the strongest link between the blues rock and "NYC drone" in his contemporary group February, as they explicitly stretch out harmonic centers of blues compositions into rich droning textures.

By the early 1970s, musicians in the northeastern United States had adopted the vamps and cyclical aspects of the Velvet Underground's methods and turned them into a foundation of the emerging punk style. The two most significant groups in this regard are Boston's Modern Lovers and the first group known to designate their own music as "punk," New York's Suicide (both groups formed in 1970, although their debut albums weren't released until 1976 and 1977, respectively).[74] The Modern Lovers played droning one-chord vamps via the Velvet Underground on "Pablo Picasso," which like their version of "Foggy Notion," has no reference to the twelve-bar blues. All of Suicide's music through 1977 is based on open-ended short harmonic cycles, and they particularly cultivated the open-ended riff-based drone on songs such as "Ghost Rider," which additionally included vocal gestures and stylistic elements reminiscent of Iggy Pop.[75] The Velvet Underground's drone and limited harmonic movement approaches had remarkable staying power and can be traced to a wide variety of later rock styles. The Feelies, for example, are usually associated with 1980s indie rock, due to the quirky and introspective quality of their first two recordings *Crazy Rhythms* (1980) and *The Good Earth* (1986). Yet the group was performing in 1977 as part of the punk scene at CBGB and other underground venues, and especially during that time, were using Velvet Underground–inspired one-chord and two-chord songs such as "Slipping (into Something)" and "Forces at Work" as vehicles for ecstatic improvisations.[76] Contemporary punk groups such as Pissed Jeans ("Boring Girls") continue to have songs directly in this mode.

Emphasis on blues riffs and short cycles run throughout the raw power repertoire, with musicians taking a variety of related approaches. The Flamin' Groovies' "Teenage Head" (1971) retains three-part blues movement but with a strong emphasis on a I-chord blues riff, the Groovies' harder-edged style inspired by their playing with the Stooges in Cincinnati in 1969. Short cycles that conveyed a "blues-like effect," such as the four-chord "Steppin' Stone" pattern (I–♭III–IV–♭VI) also became central to the punk style.[77] Several songs on *Nuggets* also fall into this category of "blues-like" short cycles, such as the Seeds' "Pushin' Too Hard," the Castaways' "Liar, Liar," and the 13th Floor Elevators' "You're Gonna Miss Me," as do Stooges songs such as "Real Cool Time" and "I Wanna Be Your Dog." Overall, these musicians explored repetitive short cycles and extended sections of patterns built on one-chord riffs or two-chord oscillations, while they minimized the twelve-bar cycles that had become almost synonymous with "the blues" by the 1960s. And as is typical of American popular musicians, they explored short cycles and extended sections at the ends of performances, presented as a contrast to the earlier parts of a song. The Patti Smith Band's version of "Gloria," for example, starts with the famous three-chord I–♭VII–IV pattern (a rotation of I–IV–V) but quickly goes into a two-chord oscillation (I–♭VII) for the verse—the important two-chord section is often ignored in descriptions and transcriptions—until returning to the short three-chord cycle for the extended build at the end.

As already noted, the raw power emphasis on riff-based blues picked up by early punk musicians was not unique but part of a wider trend among musicians in the 1960s, both black and white, in linking short-cycle blues resources to an authentic, rural, natural idea of blackness. Those musicians now considered to be antecedents of heavy metal, such as Black Sabbath and Led Zeppelin, emphasized the same blues features and could also be considered raw power examples. Like Them's and the Amboy Dukes' treatments of "Baby Please Don't Go," Led Zeppelin's version of "When the Levee Breaks" replaces the twelve-bar form and intricate countermelodies of Memphis Minnie and Kansas Joe's original (1929) with a one–harmonic center riff. Although the three-part AAB form of the verse remains ("If it keeps on raining, levee's going to break / If it keeps on raining, levee's going to break / And the water's gonna come in, have no place to stay"), it has become completely disassociated from any I–IV–V harmonic movement.[78]

### Raw Power Rhythm

Raw power bands often increased tempos and moved toward a straighter subdivision of the beat in further transformations of blues resources, and these rhythmic treatments could be an important point of distinction from blues antecedents and their more straight-ahead rock contemporaries. Johnny Winter's version of "Rollin' and Tumblin'" (1969) is a strong example of this approach to the blues, with the main adjustments from Muddy Waters's famous version being John "Red" Turner's drumming: the slightly faster tempo (about 128 beats per minute, up from about 120 bpm), and the straighter subdivision of the beat, along with a drastically increased volume. The sound of Ernest "Big" Crawford's upright bass strings against the fingerboard on Muddy Waters's drummerless version accents the syncopated upbeats, while Red Turner emphasizes beats two and four in a heavy backbeat that approaches an "oom-pah" rhythm. Similarly, the transformations of "Baby Please Don't Go" follow an even more striking rhythmic path, with Big Joe Williams's original in a triplet shuffle subdivision without a strong backbeat, Them's version retaining some triplet feel and adding a strong backbeat, and the Amboy Dukes' version with a clear equal eighth-note subdivision along with the backbeat.

The Stooges also went from including more swing (if not quite triplet subdivisions) and syncopation on their first album to much more prominent straight-eighth subdivisions on *Fun House*. *The Stooges* features a variety of rhythmic approaches, including the straight-eighth subdivision of "I Wanna Be Your Dog," but much of the album contains rhythmic feel with a great deal of swing, as heard on "1969," "No Fun," "Real Cool Time," and "Little Doll." "1969" features the syncopated hambone rhythm (the "Bo Diddley" beat, close to a Latin music clave) over mostly "two-chord pounding," as Iggy Pop described the similar "Mystic Eyes," which also uses the hambone pattern. The following year's *Fun House*, while also containing syncopation and swing elements, leans more heavily toward equal eighth-note subdivisions of the beat, as heard on "Loose," "T.V. Eye," and "1970."

These raw power bands, while incorporating straight-eighth rock subdivisions, also retained strong backbeat feels on beats two and four at tempos suitable for rock and roll or rhythm and blues dancing. Maureen Tucker of the Velvet Underground established an essential drumming style for punk by emphasizing a chugging eighth note subdivision with a relentless accent on two and four. Many groups in punk's lineage following the Velvet Underground, such as the Modern Lovers and the Feelies, directly adapted her rhythmic approach.

The shift from swing and triplet subdivisions to straight-eighth rhythms may seem to imply a shift in racial associations from the approaches of earlier black blues musicians to those of white rock musicians. However, the racial associations were not so clear-cut. Maureen Tucker connected her style to the drumming of Olatunji, whose albums for Columbia beginning with *Drums of Passion* (1959) were extremely popular with white and black American listeners.[79] As with other aspects of the raw power style, Tucker's drumming was designed to communicate musical blackness and its power—here African and tribal rather than African American and the South—without explicit appropriation, as Tucker explained: "I wanted a deeper sound . . . and I was not really trying to sound African but sort of in a way trying to." Lou Reed added, "what she was doing was very tribal, an incredible amount of unrelenting energy pushing at the thing."[80]

Furthermore, the blues musicians referenced by raw power musicians also often used a straight-eighth feel. Both Robert Pete Williams's "Grown So Ugly" and Captain Beefheart's version use a straight-eighth equal subdivision with syncopation. And at the same time, raw power rock musicians used shuffle, swing, or triplet-subdivision rhythms. Captain Beefheart's "Diddy Wah Diddy," like Bo Diddley's version, has a shuffle blues feel. But perhaps most of all, the shift to a straight-eighth feel was already being led by African American musicians, culminating in the new soul and funk styles of rhythm and blues, supporting the stances of the civil rights and black liberation movements. More equal subdivisions and oom-pah backbeats were a staple of rock and roll early on, in such prominent examples as Chuck Berry's "Maybellene" (1955) and "Johnny B. Goode" (1957) although such rhythms at the time still had strong country and bluegrass associations. As Alexander Stewart points out, "what seems clear is that, though early rock 'n' roll often maintained the 12/8 metre along with other things it borrowed from R&B, by the early 1960s an even-ing of the basic subdivision of the beat linked to new styles of dance movement had become emblematic of modern youth, while jazz, swing and shuffles were largely relegated to the previous generation."[81] Stewart further traces the move to straighter feels in rhythm and blues over the course of the 1960s, via innovations introduced by drummers from New Orleans, such as James Brown's drummer Clayton Fillyau. Ray Charles's "What'd I Say" (1959), James Brown's "I've Got Money" (1962), and Wilson Pickett's "In the Midnight Hour" (1965) are all examples of rhythm and blues songs with a straight rather than shuffle rhythm, and by the late 1960s songs such as James Brown's "Cold Sweat" (1967) had firmly established the equal subdivision approach as a major way forward for contemporary African American musicians, as well as African musicians such as Fela Kuti, in light of black liberation struggles.[82]

In this sense, the transformation of blues standards from shuffle rhythms to straight-eighth subdivisions by rock musicians may have been less a transformation or stylistic change across racial lines than, as with the use of limited harmonic movement, an adoption of the kinds of rhythmic changes already taking place in rock and roll and rhythm and blues on a large scale, initiated and developed by African American musicians. In other words, these rhythmic changes were originally attempts by white musicians to make their music sound more in line with black music of the time, not less. Later in the 1970s, however, faster tempos and more oom-pah rhythms would be racially distinguishing factors in hardcore punk, especially as backbeats and syncopation became less prominent.

## Raw Power Melody and Vocal Style

Punk's musical lineage reflects a remarkable adherence to melodic approaches to the blues, especially the minor pentatonic scale and neutral "blue notes" such as the neutral third that falls between the minor and major third. The riffs that form the basis of most songs hang on the minor pentatonic scale or "blues scale" (minor pentatonic with an added flatted fifth), and improvisations invariably follow the lick-based, pentatonic guitar soloing styles of Albert King, Buddy Guy, Albert Collins, and other bluesmen, even if they are buried in added noise. Remembering Robert Quine, the guitarist for the Voidoids, Lou Reed, and many others, Alan Licht wrote, "besides the fact that I don't think he much liked punk, he should really be ranked with people like Ike Turner or Otis Rush—that violent take on the blues—or Pete Cosey."[83]

A less apparent blues feature that remained an essential element of punk is monophony: one melody sung and played simultaneously by the voice and instruments. Rather than follow the lead of most rock and roll songs, in which chords played on accompanying instruments support one clear overarching vocal melody, raw power musicians followed the monophonic approach heard on recordings such as Muddy Waters's "Rollin' and Tumblin'," in which voices and melodic instruments perform the same lines simultaneously with only minor expressive variations. The voices and instruments are also often in call-and-response dialogue with each other. The Stooges' "T.V. Eye" (1970) is a blueprint for this approach: a riff-based song built on the blues scale with Iggy Pop's voice in a monophonic relationship to the guitar and bass lines. Iggy also exploits blue notes such as the neutral third between the natural and flattened pitches, and the vocal and instruments are in a call-and-response dialogue.

Raw power musicians made the most significant transformations in the area of the voice and lyrics. As in most rock music, the connection of blues resources to stereotyped notions of black masculinity and sexuality is evident in the shift away from the diverse range of themes in blues poetry, such as migration, work, religion (including retentions of African religious elements), personal concerns, and social problems—themes heavily explored by female blues singers—to lyrics primarily dealing with sex and machismo.[84] Some raw power groups differed from other rock groups to the extent that they pushed these associations, such as the Stooges in "Loose" and "Penetration." The MC5 pushed at the limits of convention, employing profanity ("Kick out the jams, motherfucker!") rather than the metaphor and allusion used by blues and R&B singers (the watershed moment of Ronald Isley singing "all this bullshit going down" on "Fight the Power" did not happen until 1975). As described by Steve Waksman, the MC5 traded heavily in the merging of blues resources, blackness, and masculinity.[85]

However, vocal performance styles—the *ways* in which these lyrics were sung—are just as important to consider as the lyrical themes. Iggy Pop and Rob Tyner often emulated the vocal timbres and styles typical of many blues musicians, in the same vein as other white male rock singers, such as Mick Jagger and Van Morrison, who were looking to American blues men as models of sexual potency and societal rebellion. Iggy Pop loosely imitated the voices of Howlin' Wolf and Bukka White (Pop's "personal favorite blues singer"), and fellow musicians heard this. Alan Vega of Suicide commented, "Iggy has a great voice, a great blues voice."[86] Pop also rhythmically sang in a blues style, as part of an overall rhythmic approach which reflected the elasticity typically heard in blues and jazz. The styles of these vocalists were explicitly coded as black, and in some ways understood to be an artificial or exaggerated "black," "more black than black" to repeat Alan Vega's characterization of Iggy Pop.

Early punk singers continued to manipulate blues vocal styles for racial associations. One of the most indicative white "raw power" uses of blues singing techniques is the Patti Smith Group's "Rock N Roll Nigger," in which Smith incorporated growls and howls into a vocal style that moved from one approach to another, supporting a lyric that directly (if extremely ill-advisedly) engaged

America's racist history with respect to what she understood to be social limitations on freedom and expression.[87] Her use of the racist epithet, even in the song title, is the most blatant possible way to reference America's racial troubles, and although "Rock N Roll Nigger" did not appear on vinyl until *Easter* (1978), her attempt to reclaim the word as anyone "outside of society" was the culmination of a consistent trajectory and something she had been publicly doubling down on for years. The song had been in the band's live repertoire since at least 1976, following her poem "Nigger Book," which she had been performing live since 1975.[88] She herself was a "nigger of the universe," completely free, and Satan was "the first absolute artist-the first true nigger . . . one graced in high beauty w/ a fine position in the social order but he saw another" in the liner notes to *Radio Ethiopia* (1976).[89]

Smith's endeavors to redeem or reclaim "nigger" were very much of her time, following a long trend of manipulations of the word by bohemian poets and performers who were not African American, including Lenny Bruce, Norman Mailer, John Lennon and Yoko Ono, and John Sinclair.[90] Yet Smith's attempt to take this word and reframe it in the context of a straight-ahead hard rock song is distinctive, and her use of vocal timbres racially coded as black and masculine over blues riffs creates an unusual cognitive dissonance representative of early punk's raw power style. Especially at the time, Smith's uses of the word were directly in conflict with Sly and the Family Stone's pointed "Don't Call Me Nigger, Whitey" (1969) and Curtis Mayfield's "(Don't Worry) If There's a Hell Below, We're All Going to Go" (1970). In addition to singing in a blues style, she names Jimi Hendrix, Jesus Christ, "grandma," and Jackson Pollock as deliberately disconcerting examples of "niggers," Hendrix and Pollock invoked as ultimate embodiments of artistic freedom. Jackson Pollock was Smith's favorite artist: "His paintings don't represent intellectual energy so much, they represent a very strong merging of intellectual and physical energy which to me is like guitar playing. Looking at a Jackson Pollock or listening to Jimi Hendrix—it's a very similar experience."[91]

Although Patti Smith was intentionally creating jarring dissonances in an early punk mode, today her choices are nearly impossible to reconcile with what she says she wanted to communicate. It is extremely unsettling to hear the name of the recently deceased Hendrix, as a black man the historical target of this word in its most virulent usage by white people, invoked right away, and despite Pollock's artistic nonconformity, he jumps out today as a quintessential example of art institutions and a problematic canon of white males. Yet these tensions also reveal how punk musicians zoomed in on the most controversial and provocative aspects of the raw power style. The punk qualities of the song are even more apparent in Smith's use of the record industry apparatus, as the song appeared on her popular album featuring the hit song "Because the

Night," and also representative of punk, her adoption of the racist epithet took place in an almost entirely white environment (as opposed to, for example, the word's use by the integrated Sly and the Family Stone). The process of appropriating the word is, in this way, an extreme linguistic analogue to the taking on of black musical codes by white musicians, a "verbalizing" of "the white attraction to blackness," in an effort to reclaim, reuse, and eventually take ownership of those styles.[92]

Iggy Pop, Rob Tyner, and Patti Smith adopted blues voices for the power and unsettled qualities the sound gave their music. However, some took an opposite approach as they wrestled with the augmented stakes of singing the blues. These musicians strongly differentiated their vocal styles from typical blues voices. This approach has a long historical precedent, as white musicians effectively combined "white" country vocal styles with shared blues melodies and harmonic resources: for example, Jimmie Rodgers's blue yodels, Bill Monroe's "Rocky Road Blues," Dock Boggs's "Country Blues," and Hank Williams's "Long Gone Lonesome Blues."[93] Lou Reed emphasized the limitations of his range, cultivating a vocal style that worked in tension with his blues-based music, and which conveyed authenticity rather than imitation. Jonathan Richman modeled his vocal style after Reed's. For both Reed and Richman, this meant highlighting talky, nasal, white northeastern accents. The Velvet Underground also made use of John Cale's Welsh accent on "The Gift" (1968), with Cale narrating the absurdly macabre tale in a matter-of-fact tone of voice over a riff-based groove and blues guitar jamming. In Cleveland's Pere Ubu, David Thomas's unique combination of warbling and screaming was juxtaposed intriguingly with blues-based riffs on songs such as "Life Stinks." By highlighting "white" voices, these musicians allowed their music to be heard as white, regardless of how blues-based the melodic and harmonic resources were.

### "A Legit, Pure Thing"

The raw power musical style began as part of a broader effort among white rock musicians to engage with the formidable blues styles played by African American musicians especially in the North and Midwest during the period of the Second Great Migration. Simultaneously, raw power music was supposed to sound different from black blues *and* white rock imitations of the blues. In the early 1960s, young white baby boomer musicians' fascination with, and appropriation of, recent and contemporary black music was generally in line with the old "love and theft" processes traceable all the way back to blackface minstrelsy, reflecting entrenched racial hierarchies and inequalities but from the new perspective of expanding segregated suburbs.[94] Since the mid-eighteenth century, white people had used black music and the idea of blackness freely and unapologetically, and they often even viewed this process as progressive and sympathetic.[95] There was nothing subtle or secretive about this business. In fact, even after the general (but never complete) disappearance of blackface minstrelsy, the racial dynamics of American popular music were on full display.

But over the course of the 1960s, the "Great Transformation" of American society owing to the civil rights and Black Power movements, denunciations of white appropriation by black critics such as Amiri Baraka, and the musical innovations of James Brown, Nina Simone, and others created a newly charged atmosphere surrounding the old process of white people adopting and imitating black musical styles. Blues resources became especially fraught and meaningful. Some white musicians in the late 1960s and early 1970s responded to the new circumstances by doubling down on the blues and its heightened associations with authenticity, expanding their purview to older, southern, and country blues styles. The resulting raw power music, emphasizing riffs and limited harmonic movement, became a cornerstone of punk, especially as it carries so many complex and contradictory racial associations.

At the same time, some white musicians responded by retaining elements of the blues, especially melodic and harmonic elements, but changing other aspects, especially vocal styles. As racial identity is heavily connected to vocal style in American popular music, the use of "white" and non-blues vocal styles supported an idea of these particular performances as separate from rock's black music roots. This trend especially took hold in the Northeast, in more segregated social environments than those in the Midwest, and apart from the strong blues presence in Chicago and Detroit. Again, this approach was not hidden or subtle, but an explicit and self-conscious response to the changing stakes of musical blackness during this period of social upheaval. Even more intensely, these musicians wanted to separate themselves from other white musicians who were blatantly using the blues and imitating black music.

By the mid-1970s, these particular discursive and musical arguments over the meanings of the blues and the uses of black music resources had become primarily a debate about whiteness among white people. For example, Lou Reed maintained that "under the surface," all of his songs were in the rhythm and blues tradition in which he got his start as a songwriter. Yet he also claimed that the Velvet Underground did everything they could to avoid recognizable blues licks: "We used to have a thing in the Velvet Underground because, you know we knew all this [R&B], was that, it was like a ten-dollar fine if you play a blues lick. It was like *not allowed*. Because it was not legit. They had all these white guys out there playing blues; we didn't want anything to do with that. We wanted to create our own, own legit, pure thing."[96]

Rock music relies on associations of blackness with particular kinds of blues resources, as well as the audible processes of white appropriation and transformation of those resources. The raw power style is an extreme manifestation of this approach to rock. Without hearing white appropriation of a strongly defined black music (as in rock versions of European classical music), rock has little tension, power, or spirit of rebellion. Raw power music was especially effective in the late 1960s and early 1970s, as musicians drew on layered meanings of the blues during a period of extreme social and political upheaval, with major revisions of the ways race and class categories governed American society. The tension between blues resources and efforts to mask those very same resources, at once reinforcing ideas of "white" and "black" *and* unsettling these categories, became a key element of punk's core aesthetic.

# 3

## "Ignorance of Your Culture Is Not Considered Cool": Reconsidering the Avant-Garde Impulse in American Punk

"Ignorance of Your Culture Is Not Considered Cool!" announced an insert in the Residents album *Duck Stab/Buster and Glen* (1978). Along with an image of four silhouetted Klansmen with blank glowing eyes, the flier advertised the first Residents Official Fan Club: W.E.I.R.D. (We Endorse Immediate Residents Deification).[1] Often referenced but increasingly misunderstood or marginalized in punk histories, the music of the Residents and other American experimentalists such as Captain Beefheart (Don Van Vliet), DEVO, Chrome, Pere Ubu, the Los Angeles Free Music Society (L.A.F.M.S.), and Destroy All Monsters in the early and mid-1970s is reconsidered here as essential to punk's stylistic formation.[2] These musicians paved paths for punk through interrogations of the narratives and myths of American popular music, the techniques they introduced for deconstructing popular music materials, their sense of humor, and their independence from the record industry. In the case of the Residents, for example, the listener is confronted with familiar elements of punk: signaling the intertwined features of capitalism and racism in popular music, fascist iconography, racially coded voices, blatant appropriations of heavily loaded symbols, and deliberate mythmaking. Most of all, this chapter introduces a rethinking of punk's relationship to avant-garde treatments of American popular music that were originally intended to tackle its unacknowledged or whitewashed racist history, including the practice of blackface minstrelsy, and also meant to reveal the grim aspects of white suburbia. Avant-garde approaches enabled these artists to engage some of the most difficult aspects of American music, but like other modes of critique informing punk, their reception and efficacy was ultimately circumscribed by whiteness.

Early American punk used avant-garde techniques to criticize and satirize racism and suburbia, part of a homegrown experimentalism directly responding to the war in Vietnam, the failures of hippie idealism, the inescapable transformations to American life wrought by industrialization and suburbification, and

Figure 3.1. Leaflet for the Residents' W.E.I.R.D. fan club.

the battle-scarred civil rights movement. The musicians profiled here expressed a tangible dissatisfaction with both mainstream American culture and its counterculture, serving as missing pieces in American punk's stylistic development, connecting and overlapping with blues transformations that thrived in the late 1960s (described in chapter 2) and the return to classic rock and roll by many punks in the mid-1970s (described in chapter 4). Although the groups described in this chapter are generally associated with the late 1970s and 1980s, including the Residents, DEVO, and Chrome, their music and their experiences are properly placed considerably earlier, in the 1960s and early 1970s. For example, the Residents had been making music as a band since 1972, with earlier incarnations dating back as far as 1969, and they had been independently releasing albums on their own label since *Meet the Residents* in 1974.[3] The ideas and approaches of the various musicians discussed here relate to others in the 1960s, such as the experimental commentaries on American society by Frank Zappa with the Mothers of Invention and by Joseph Byrd and Dorothy Moskowitz's group the United States of America.

Musicians highlighted in this chapter had various relationships to avant-garde art and music both historical and contemporary, from DEVO encountering Dada in college at Kent State to Destroy All Monsters' interest in the intermedia sound explorations of the Art Ensemble of Chicago.[4] They can each be considered part of a broader vernacular avant-garde, as described by Benjamin Piekut, with their strong connections to the market and "taking shape with and across myriad genre formations, which meet and mutate by means of recording, not writing."[5] Musically, a group such as Half Japanese combined the many varied approaches described in this chapter, including noise, eccentric covers of pop songs, avant-garde visual art, improvisations, affected voices, and ambitious conceptual recording projects.[6] For the history of musical style presented in *Damaged*, I focus on the musicians with direct stylistic links to later punk musicians, especially those groups who related avant-garde impulses and techniques to blues-based rock, and those who came from the same white American suburban baby boomer background as other early punk musicians.

Captain Beefheart is a lodestar for these groups who made music that was "experimental but accessible," as Viv Albertine of the Slits described Captain Beefheart's first record: "it sounds like pop music, all the songs are short with strong choruses and melodies but they're undermined by Beefheart's deranged singing."[7] Captain Beefheart was a direct inspiration for DEVO: Mark Mothersbaugh said, "I copped a couple of licks from 'The Blimp' for one of our songs. Beefheart was a major influence on DEVO as far as direction goes."[8] Casale later posited that DEVO belonged "somewhere between Muddy Waters and Captain Beefheart" in the history of rock, and indeed, much of the group's aesthetic derived from juxtaposing blues-based rock with exaggerated, heavily articulated "white" voices (e.g., "Auto Modown," DEVO's depiction of an actual car accident in Youngstown in 1971, in which a driver ran over and killed six pedestrians in extremely gruesome fashion).[9]

These experimental musicians on the edges of early punk were often linked by invoking Captain Beefheart as an inspiration, and they coalesced around regional scenes in California, Ohio, and Michigan.[10] These geographically dispersed musicians originally created similar art out of shared concerns but without awareness of each other; however, they soon connected with each other through the mail and through touring. This network included British artists such as Throbbing Gristle and Cabaret Voltaire, and eventually fully associated with the punk scenes of the late 1970s and early 1980s.[11] The seminal punk zine *Search & Destroy* featured articles on DEVO, the Residents, Chrome, and other experimentalists, and musicians such as Half Japanese's Jad Fair were in regular correspondence with V. Vale, the magazine's creator—one letter from Fair to Vale includes the postscript, "Please run articles on L.A.F.M.S."[12]

Today these American connections call for an assertive reconsideration, especially since the publication of Greil Marcus's *Lipstick Traces* (1989) and to a lesser extent Jon Savage's *England's Dreaming* (1991) attributed avant-garde techniques in punk almost exclusively to the Situationist Internationale and a European lineage traced back to Dada.[13] Marcus marvels at the intensity and excitement of British punk around 1975: "I knew a lot about rock 'n' roll, but I didn't know about this. Did the voice and the gestures come out of nowhere, or were they sparked? If they were sparked, what sparked them?"[14] He finds his answer in the European avant-garde, poetically elaborating almost stream-of-consciousness connections while mystifying historical and musical processes.

Casually dismissing punk's musical genealogy (Chuck Berry, Kinks, Stooges, Velvet Underground, etc.) and absurdly asserting that Fairport Convention could easily be argued as punk's origin point, Marcus clears the way for a "history" that says whatever he wants it to say—such as a bizarre diversion connecting John Lydon to a "John of Leyden" in 1534 ("serendipity is where you find it").[15] Meanwhile, although historical events are everywhere in *Lipstick Traces*, historical context is hardly anywhere; e.g., one never in fact learns what May 1968 in Paris was actually about, what really motivated the protests, how the upheaval was connected to the US, Vietnam, and other world events, and the effect this social revolution had on the women's liberation and gay rights movements. Strangely, Marcus (although not Jon Savage) also neglects the radical groups in the US such as the Motherfuckers, who had connections, even if strained, to the Situationist Internationale. Anarchist and anticapitalist political thought was already pervasive in the American counterculture scene during the 1950s, and firmly entrenched by the end of the 1960s, especially in and around San Francisco, Los Angeles, Chicago, and New York.[16]

Situationist ideas contributed to the punk style as it developed in the UK in the mid- to late 1970s. It is well known that Malcolm McLaren and Jamie Reid, both heavily involved with developing the Sex Pistols' style, were inspired by the Situationists' call to resignify and transform capitalist symbols.[17] But even with respect to the United Kingdom, the "links both conscious and unconscious between situationism and punk are very tenuous, much more than they are presented in the English-language literature. . . ."[18] And most relevant for the musical narrative outlined in *Damaged*, in the process of revealing this "secret history" and in exaggerating the extent of British punk's engagement with Situationist ideas, the direct line from earlier American rock experiments to punk has become blurred or even erased, along with the ways in which this music was specifically meant to comment on the social upheaval and changing racial landscape in 1960s America. The effect of *Lipstick Traces* is especially problematic in the case of punk's connections to Dada, with which American rock musicians had been engaging well before British punk surfaced.

This brief response to *Lipstick Traces* suggest that, as with the rest of *Damaged*, the familiar timeline needs to be adjusted. Many of the groups covered in this chapter started releasing recordings in the mid- or late 1970s, placing them in the popular imagination after punk's mainstream emergence in 1976 and 1977 Britain. But like others in Part One, these groups were mostly made up of white baby boomers who grew up in newly populated American suburbs during the 1950s and 1960s and who developed their musical style in the late 1960s and early 1970s. Their primary contact with the United Kingdom's music was the Beatles, the Rolling Stones, the Kinks, and Them—not the Sex Pistols or the Clash. For example, despite DEVO's association with the late 1970s and early 1980s—their first album was released in 1978 and their breakout hit "Whip It" made them a household name in 1980—Mark Mothersbaugh graduated high school in 1968 and attended Kent State during the 1970 massacre, and the group is more appropriately placed in the early to mid-1970s alongside Beefheart and the Residents as experimentalists responding to the sixties.[19] Each of these groups pointed directly to American antecedents; Captain Beefheart, for example, was David Thomas of Pere Ubu's "of course my all-time favorite."[20] Later punk groups also established this American lineage. Dead Kennedys saw themselves in line with Captain Beefheart, the New York Dolls, DEVO, the Ramones, and Iggy Pop, "the Sex Pistols and the MC5 to a much lesser degree."[21] Furthermore, the experimental elements generally attributed to Britain's punk revolution, including visual collage techniques, can be found in the work of the artists profiled in this chapter. And still in need of more research are the ways in which these American avant-garde interrogations of suburbia, American history, and capitalism, dating back to the 1960s, had an impact on the celebrated British punk political critiques of the late 1970s.[22]

Timeline issues are also prominent for many of the groups somewhat misleadingly described as "post-punk." Chrome is an excellent example: they are most known for their groundbreaking "post-punk" recordings *Alien Soundtracks* (1977) and *Half Machine Lip Moves* (1979), yet Damon Edge had already begun his rock experiments when he formed the group in 1975. It is only the conceit of a British punk "big bang" around 1976 that makes these two Chrome records "post-punk" rather than a product of Damon Edge and Helios Creed's longstanding interests and development. Edge's particular vision grew out of his studies with Allan Kaprow at CalArts (Kaprow also taught members of the L.A.F.M.S.), his antagonistic relationship to the film and music studio culture of Los Angeles, and his American childhood diet of monster movies, while his partner Helios Creed directly connected Chrome's music to that of the Stooges (the opening track to *Half Machine Lip Moves*, "TV as Eyes," is an homage to "T.V. Eye").

My emphasis on an American genealogy is neither nationalistic nor intended to dismiss crucial European avant-garde connections, but an attempt to establish the American contexts in which these particular avant-garde rock musicians worked. By tracing this direct musical lineage, I hope to revisit the meanings of techniques such as noise, collage, play with vocal timbres, and layered references in American punk, and to reconnect punk's avant-garde impulses directly to the social circumstances in the United States out of which they emerged.

## Punk's Avant-Garde Genealogy and the End of the Sixties Dream

By the late 1960s, the fear of being sent to die in Vietnam was widespread and palpable among young white Americans, with a major effect on experimental art and rock music. As Bill Harkleroad (Zoot Horn Rollo) of Captain Beefheart's Magic Band noted, "Vietnam was raging by then [around 1965] and all I was thinking about was not coming home in a body bag."[23] The revolutionary music of Beefheart's *Trout Mask Replica* (1969) was created in a collective house where the group endlessly rehearsed while being kept hungry, penniless, and sleep-deprived by Beefheart, a situation made possible by the increasing fear and limited options felt by white American youth during that time:

> Life in the Magic Band seemed to consist of these gruelling marathon practice sessions—sometimes for up to 16 or 17 hours a day. Then I'd curl up in a corner on the floor and sleep, just to get up and practise some more.
>
> But it was very difficult for me to complain about the situation. You have to remember that at the time Don was my hero, and when I joined the band he was doing the coolest music ever. I was living in such fear of going to Vietnam and dying. Instead I was not going to Vietnam, I was in a band, I was going to be famous,

I was going to make money, I was going to get laid—all these wonderful things were doing to happen. And as it turned out the main guy was just kicking my ass up and down the street.[24]

The changes in rock music paralleled or followed artistic interventions happening more broadly. The Diggers in San Francisco expressed the anarchist politics, performance art techniques, and dissatisfaction with American hippie idealism picked up by early punk.[25] For example, the October 1967 "Death of Hippie" parade "tried to reclaim the counterculture's spirit of personal freedom from the commodified and 'stereotyped hippie artifacts' that many young people donned as a superficial badge of a media-generated phenomenon."[26] The Diggers criticized countercultural rock groups that had made commercials and otherwise sold out.[27] Early punk musicians were also paying attention to the Living Theatre, which was established in the early 1950s and became tied to the Situationist Internationale, and Up Against The Wall Motherfucker (also the Motherfuckers, originally Black Mask) in New York, a homegrown anarchist and Dada-inspired organization who conflicted with the MC5 over accusations of the group selling out, presaging later punk arguments.[28] Judith Malina and Julian Beck of the Living Theatre participated in the May 1968 Paris student riots and drew on those experiences for their theatrical work *Paradise Now*.[29]

For the early architects of the punk rock style specifically discussed in this chapter, the decline of sixties idealism presented a problem. They still rejected mainstream culture, represented by their parents' quick embrace of suburban life, and still understood the dreams and possibilities of counterculture, but they also saw the counterculture's limits and failures. As Charlotte Pressler described the underground scene in Cleveland:

> Most of them were from middle or upper-middle class families. Most were very intelligent. Many of them could have been anything they chose to be. . . . There was no reason why they should not have effected an entry into the world of their parents. Yet all of them turned their backs on this world, and that meant making a number of very painful choices. First, there was the decision not to go to college, at a time when the draft was still in effect and the Vietnam War was still going on: and several of these people were drafted. Most of these people did not marry; those that did generally did not have children; few of them worked jobs for very long; and the jobs they did hold were low-paying and dull, a long ways away from a "career." Yet they were not drop-outs in the Sixties sense; they felt, if anything, a certain affection for consumerist society, and a total contempt for the so-called counterculture.[30]

These musicians were also fascinated by the dilapidated urban landscapes caused by white flight. They saw a potential for new creation in these environments and they were attracted to the city's grittiness, but they also had generally internalized a fear of the "ghetto" from their upbringings in the geographically and racially segregated suburbs. For example, with respect to the Plaza (3206 Prospect Avenue), the "artist colony" where several members of the experimental Cleveland scene lived, Allen Ravenstine of Pere Ubu remembered, "I spent a lot of the time that I lived in Cleveland just absolutely terrified because that the building I had was right on the edge of a ghetto. I had guns pointed at me more than once when I was there. And that building would get broken into almost every night. And some people got robbed at gunpoint. I was scared a lot of the time. So I'm sure that was in there. With the sounds I made, some of those sirens and things . . . that was the level of intensity to that place that was frightening."[31] These were the sounds of suburbia's twin, the black urban "ghetto" viewed as dangerous, empty, and gritty by white suburbanites and the young artists moving back to the cities.

The stories of this neglected cohort of musicians add a great deal to the larger story of punk's contradictory nature. They were caught between the groups still embedded in a 1960s ethos (MC5, Stooges, the Velvet Underground) and a rejection of late-1960s ideals that would find its most prominent expression in the mid-1970s New York scene. This "avant-garage" network (a term coined by David Thomas) embraced rock and roll and its mythologies while recognizing its artifice and complicity in the problems of America they perceived. They were attracted and repelled by both the suburbs and urban decay, as well as African American culture, with which they had limited direct contact due to increased segregation over the course of the 1960s. Seen through the analytical lens of musical style, for several of those transitional figures in the Cleveland, Akron, Detroit/Ann Arbor, Los Angeles, and San Francisco scenes avant-garde techniques and approaches drawn from Dada spoke to the wartime world they inhabited. Musicians in the late 1970s and early 1980s continued to use this musical language to express the contradictions presented by the failures of the 1960s, heard in music as wide-ranging as early American punk groups such as the Dead Kennedys, the experiments of Half Japanese, and throughout the burgeoning British punk scene.

## Experimental Visions of American Music in Black and White

For Captain Beefheart, the Residents, and others, the failures of the 1960s counterculture resulted in a skepticism about rock's power and its ability to affect social change, as well as a renewed interest in the uncomfortable aspects of American popular music history. These interests included American music's long-standing relationship to a binary racial division of white and black, associated with different musical styles. While still rooted in rock, their experimental music treated American music, its narratives and histories, and rock and roll itself as topics. Their use of rock to deconstruct and comment on rock itself had a significant impact on the way American punks eventually formulated their stance.

In the 1960s many rock musicians began seriously exploring early twentieth-century recorded blues and country music as a key to American national identity and its complex links to race. Bob Dylan, the Grateful Dead, the Allman Brothers, and others in the mid- to late 1960s were working with varied repertoires that covered the American common stock heard in blues and country music. A primary source for these musicians was Harry Smith's *Anthology of American Folk Music* (1952), "the founding document of the American folk revival."[32] The *Anthology* promoted the idea of a shared common stock, as Smith included white and black artists, originally presented on racialized "race" and "hillbilly" (or "old familiar tunes") catalogs, without delineating race.[33] The impact of the *Anthology* went beyond the recordings to the quality of the packaging, which went a long way in categorizing these popular recordings as "American folk music," rather than commercial records, and then associating that folk with a certain mysterious weirdness and low-fidelity aesthetic.[34] As Greil Marcus reflected, "the whole bizarre package" of the *Anthology* "made the familiar strange, the never known into the forgotten, and the forgotten into a collective memory that teased any single listener's conscious mind."[35] In most cases, these recordings were only a few decades old, but they became heard as arcane remnants of a lost America.[36]

Captain Beefheart also engaged the American popular music past and ideas of blues, country, and folk music, but via experimentation. Beefheart was originally a devoted blues musician, and in 1964 his group the Magic Band was "a pretty straightforward blues band doing Howlin' Wolf, Muddy Waters, Jimmy Reed, John Lee Hooker stuff. They were 'the band' in the little town just north of Los Angeles called Lancaster."[37] By 1969—as Dylan and other musicians had done—Beefheart turned toward a wider variety of common stock blues and country resources as musical inspiration and as a way of understanding American identity. But whereas Dylan and others interpreted and inhabited their American "folk" ancestors, with the unique *Trout Mask Replica* (1969) Beefheart created a distance from American popular music resources, using techniques that opened up avenues for punk as they spoke to a particular segment of white Americans responding to both an empty mainstream and a failing counterculture. The embrace of artifice was central to his approach. While other musicians were striving for authenticity, Beefheart spun unverifiable stories, especially for the press: "Since virtually no one has ever seen him play, stories about his life and art have taken on the character of legend, that is, of endless tall tales."[38] Artifice is explicit on *Trout Mask Replica* in the front-and-center manner of punk, from the album's name (a replica of a mask), the cover (Beefheart in aforementioned trout mask), and the band members' pseudonyms.

Beefheart musically communicated his experimental vision of America. In general, melodic motives and riffs are disengaged from an underlying groove on *Trout Mask Replica*, with repetitions that often operate as self-contained rhythmic patterns in the manner of tape loops, a crucial experimental technique of the time. Most significantly, John French (Drumbo, who also transcribed and taught the parts to the band) played melodic patterns on the drums in the same style as the other instrumentalists. Bill Harkleroad described the music as "both polyphonic and polyrhythmic—with some repeated shapes. We would play in various time signatures, often at the same time. For instance, one part might be in 3/4 time while another was in 4/4 time. . . . You'd hold on to your part for dear life against the thrust of what everybody else was doing."[39] Without an underlying groove, Beefheart's listeners are compelled to step back and puzzle through this complex mixture of sounds.

In contrast to Beefheart's earlier recordings, blues resources appear infrequently throughout *Trout Mask Replica*, abstracted as elements alongside the other musical gestures rather than the compositional foundation. Ry Cooder described the approach coming out of *Safe as Milk*, as Beefheart left behind conventional grooves and 4/4 time: "Somehow the concept seemed to be that you take the raw blues elements, like the sound of the John Lee Hooker idea, the Howlin' Wolf, down to its purest element which is just sound, a grunt maybe, and something abstract, and then you take your John Coltrane crazy time-signature free-jazz Ornette Coleman thing, and sort of hybridize them together, and this is what you come up with."[40] When blues riffs appear on "Sweet Sweet Bulbs," non-blues patterns and melodies in other tonalities and time signatures are played simultaneously. Beefheart's strategy of detaching blues riffs from their usual harmonic contexts and structures, and his method of repeating layered melodies, were soon picked up by early punk rock musicians, such as Cleveland's X__X ("X Blank X"), with John D. Morton of the Electric Eels.[41] The only song on *Trout Mask Replica* truly reminiscent of Beefheart's older blues style is the improvisation "China Pig," which appears as a low-fidelity recording evoking early country blues field recordings.

On *Trout Mask Replica* Beefheart broadened his sense of the blues from the riff-based and one-chord models that informed his earlier albums. Mike Barnes notes, "Van Vliet's interest in the blues encompassed all points from country blues to urban R&B, but the blues that informs *Trout Mask* is the older, almost 'songster' style."[42] By "songster," Barnes is referring to the role that would still accurately describe most "bluesmen," especially from the 1920s to the 1940s: a musician who would sing various modes of American blues, country, and popular tunes. Beefheart also found inspiration in the music of his older counterpart,

Harry Partch, who was living in California and enjoying a resurgence of interest among young composers.[43] Partch set hobo speech to music in an attempt
to capture the quintessential individualistic and independent American figure,
wanting to "help free American music from its inherited European past by
applying speech-song to the vernacular, natural speech of American people."[44]
These various American music references are treated as gestures and signals,
Beefheart making "the familiar strange" as he combined these elements in layers, reminiscent of the ways in which Charles Ives layered snippets of Americana a half-century earlier. The amalgam of references in *Trout Mask Replica*
adds up to an impression of America, not a secret code.

The technique of layering music references was even more explicit in the
music of the Residents, who first started performing in San Francisco in the
early 1970s. Although the Residents' recordings became known in the mid- to
late 1970s, their use of avant-garde techniques is clearly connected to Captain
Beefheart and other California-based experimentalists of the late 1960s and
early 1970s. In their origin story, they may have made hidden references to Captain Beefheart as a mentor in referring to a Bavarian avant-gardist known as
"the Mysterious N. Senada who had developed a complex musical system based
on phonetics"—N. Senada, as some have pointed out, may be a nod to the house
on Ensenada Drive in Woodland Hills where the Magic Band was sequestered
while preparing *Trout Mask Replica*.[45] They also covered Frank Zappa's "King
Kong" as early as 1971 and invoked Harry Partch with the music on *Fingerprince*
(1976) and "Death in Barstow" (*Babyfingers*, 1979). They specifically adapted collage, layering, and manipulation of records and tapes to draw attention to the
mediated aspects of pop music, parodying and satirizing the earnestness and
dependence on "authenticity" in rock and roll culture of the time. They made
the "familiar strange," for example, with "N-ER-GEE (Crisis Blues)" on *Meet the
Residents* (1974), which begins with the Residents playing along to the Human
Beinz' version of "Nobody But Me" (1967), the record itself skipping on the word
"Boogaloo" and the repetition of the word rendering it nonsensical, a psycho-
logical effect called semantic satiation. Semantic satiation surfaced again as a
technique for rendering absurd the clichés of pop music in DEVO's well-known
cover of "Satisfaction" (1977), when Mark Mothersbaugh repeats the hackneyed
word "baby" thirty-four times.

Experimental music and avant-garde approaches seemed to empower
both Captain Beefheart and the Residents to tackle blackface minstrelsy, the
most forbidden and forbidding intersection of American popular music and
race. Blackface minstrelsy is simultaneously the most important and the most
neglected tradition of American popular music ("ubiquitous, cultural common
coin; it has been so central to the lives of North Americans that we are hardly
aware of its extraordinary influence").[46] This too is "Americana." By engaging

minstrelsy in particular, Beefheart and other experimentalists began to reveal the irony and masquerade at the core of the sources being fetishized by their contemporaries. For example, the black Texas songster Henry Thomas, included on the *Anthology of American Folk Music* and a favorite of Bob Dylan, Canned Heat, and others in the sixties, played repertoire such as "Fishin' Blues" by the African American vaudeville composer Chris Smith, as well as "Bully of the Town" (on his medley of songs recorded under the title "Bob McKinney"), originally made famous by the white "coon shouter" May Irwin in the 1895 show *The Widow Jones*, and a song based on the minstrel show's pervasive stereotypes of violent black men. Mississippi John Hurt also played songs such as "Hot Time in the Old Town Tonight," composed by Theodore August Metz in 1896.[47] Such back and forth was typical, not exceptional, often missed when the music of these performers was repackaged as authentic folk music or blues in the 1960s.

Captain Beefheart used "black" and "white" voices as aural characters to engage minstrelsy and its legacy. In this way, *Trout Mask Replica* is immediately set apart from earlier recordings where Beefheart mostly attempted to become a bluesman. One of the most striking segments on *Trout Mask Replica* is during "Moonlight On Vermont," when Beefheart quotes both the Negro Spiritual "Old Time Religion" and Steve Reich's manipulation of Daniel Hamm's testimony regarding the Harlem Six in *Come Out* (1966). When repeating "come out to show them" he references Reich's piece, which repeats "come out to show them" for nearly thirteen minutes, phasing the repetitions to the point of unintelligibility. Reich's piece was originally associated with the Harlem Six trial, but has been questioned for the way in which Hamm's natural speaking voice, a black voice speaking directly to an experience of a traumatic incident, was distorted beyond recognition by Reich through layered phasing and semantic satiation into an abstract experimental composition, deracinating the recording.[48] Beefheart went in the opposite direction, turning Hamm's words—and Reich's manipulation of those words—into a highly racialized lyric, performed in a Howlin' Wolf style with yelps and an overwrought dialect ("Come out . . . to show dem," with a very hard emphasis on the *d* in *dem*) amid the "Old Time Religion" verses. Beefheart's minstrelization of Reich's abstraction demonstrate a different kind of avant-garde approach than Reich's, one which seeks to parody and draw attention to musical attempts at reconciling America's racial binaries. Beefheart does not try to rise above the morass; he digs it up and pushes the boundaries of acceptability. However, as will be seen again and again, this boundary pushing is determined and constrained by whiteness, both in its creation and its reception.

Beefheart's manipulations of "white" and "black" voices can be heard by comparing the solo vocal songs on the album, "The Dust Blows Forward 'n the Dust Blows Back," "Orange Claw Hammer," and "Well." These vocal solos are low-fidelity recordings, part of the presentation of *Trout Mask Replica* as a found object or collection of obscure field recordings (a "bush recording," as Beefheart tells some unnamed listeners at the end of "Hair Pie Bake 1").[49] "The Dust Blows Forward" and "Orange Claw Hammer" are delivered in a "white" voice with a country or "hillbilly" twang. With one exception ("Beatle Bones 'n' Smokin' Stones," on *Strictly Personal*), Beefheart had not used this particular vocal approach before on record. These two poems conjure white country ballads as well as the hobo speech set by Harry Partch, reminiscent of the songs of dust bowl "Okies" and the internal immigrants living in the California FSA (Farm Security Administration) camps.[50] On their Library of Congress ethnographic trip to the FSA camps, Todd and Sonkin identified "traditional English ballads, songs of the American Southwest (cowboy songs), and newly composed songs in the ballad style about the migration."[51]

"Dust" consists mostly of rhymed couplets; lines of seven, eight, or nine syllables; and heavy use of iambs. Beefheart seems to draw attention to the balladic scansion in lines such as "hung on a pointed forked twig" as he pronounces "forked" like "point-ed," keeping the same rhythm. "Orange Claw Hammer" is even more reminiscent of a standard ballad form, with the long story it tells, alternating rhymes (evoking ABCB form) and a quasi-iambic meter ("I'm on the bum where the hobos run / The air breaks with filthy chatter / Oh I don't care, there's no place there / I don't think it matters"). "Dust" paints country life—a riverboat, worms and pole fishin', "one red bean stuck in the bottom of a tin bowl"—and the protagonist of "Orange Claw Hammer" is "on the bum where the hobos run," singing of "clothes in tatters," "a gingham girl," and a "soft brown lass." Like the other songs on *Trout Mask Replica*, Beefheart takes a style that was romanticized and reverentially treated by his contemporaries and replaces it with imagery that is somehow both surreal and raw: "I was shanghaied by a high hat beaver moustache man and his pirate friend / I woke up in vomit and beer in a banana bin."

"Well" is the opposite of "Dust," delivered in a "black" voice, with dialect consonants ("night blocks out de heaven"), a deeper vocal timbre, and recurring cadence of "Well" in the manner of an African American sermon, also a popular genre of early American recordings. The poem evokes apocalyptic visions, reminiscent of such recordings: "I sensed the thickest silence scream / then I began to dream / My mind cracked like custard / Ran red until it sealed / Turn to wood and rolled like a wheel, well well." Unlike the major scalar scaffolding of "Dust" and "Orange," the melody of "Well" is a recurring minor third, evoking sermons by Rev. J. M. Gates (who appeared on the *Anthology of American Folk Music*), Rev. H. C. Gatewood, and Rev. J. C. Burnett, which often featured minor pentatonic melodies and ♭3–1 cadences.[52]

*Trout Mask Replica* also contains direct parodies of American minstrelsy in "Ella Guru" and "Hobo Chang Ba." "Ella Guru" is about a young "high yellow" girl of loose sexuality who "comes lookin' like a zoo." Beefheart plays on "high Ella" and "high yella," and "high blue" she "blew," with the verses delivered in his affected blues-voice dialect. Critics regularly acknowledge Beefheart's racial reference to "high yellow" but without delving into his tricky usage of the term.[53] In the context of *Trout Mask Replica*, "Ella Guru" engages a well-established genre of American minstrelsy, the song about the "high yellow gal," the light-skinned or "mulatto" "yellow girl" ("Lucy Long," "Lucy Neale," etc.), one of the broader "wench" characters caricatured as young and promiscuous.[54] Jeff Cotton's peculiar high vocals are also in line with this type of "female impersonator" genre.[55] In other words, "Ella Guru" is less a weird rock song about a girl than it is an avant-garde deconstruction of a minstrel song type. Similarly, "Hobo Chang Ba" seems to be about a Chinese hobo, "Oriental immigrants who came over to America looking for work, but ended up becoming hobos, riding the trains into uncertainty," which Beefheart sings "in a ridiculous voice that was apparently his approximation of an Oriental accent."[56] Given the importance of Beefheart's various vocal approaches, the strange style he brings to "Hobo Chang Ba" evokes songs about Chinese immigrants, again dating from nineteenth-century minstrelsy, and which flourished especially around California.[57] These songs featured characters with names like "Gee Sing" and "Ching Chong," and after 1870 began incorporating outrageous pseudo-Chinese dialect.[58] The reductive and absurdist "Chang Ba," with its sleigh bells and an odd flute moment, fits right in. "Hobo Chang Ba" arguably engages yellowface minstrelsy more than it engages the plight of a Chinese immigrant, just as "Ella Guru" parodies songs about the "yellow gal."

However, the concealed history of minstrelsy means that such parodies of minstrel tropes and song types were virtually certain to be lost on the average listener. *Trout Mask Replica* evokes historicity as part of a mysterious vision of America, but given that Beefheart's music trades in stereotypes, it also has the effect of reinforcing those tropes as part of the American music vocabulary. And to be historically accurate, the early minstrels and their audiences, both black and white, had an awareness of minstrelsy as a performance of race and gender, the artifice of the practice foregrounded in a way that became lost during the twentieth century as popular musicians increasingly emphasized the commercial and aesthetic value of authenticity. The reinforcement of minstrel types in avant-garde rock seemed to be especially strong with yellowface characters such as the one evoked in "Hobo Chang Ba," which fell outside the white/black binary. Later, DEVO also walked the fine line between parodying racist Americana and reinforcing offensive Asian stereotypes with Gerald Casale's "Chinaman" character, created with kitsch "Oriental" glasses of offensively slanted eyes, appearing in performances as early as 1974 and very briefly in their early short film *In the Beginning Was the End: The Truth about De-Evolution*, directed by

Chuck Statler.[59] Casale enacted the "Chinaman" with a derogatory accent, supported by stereotypical Chinese music tropes (parallel fifths and a koto-esque synthesizer sound) on the rare "Somewhere With Devo." DEVO similarly satirized and strengthened the Asian "Dragon Lady" stereotype with "Soo Bawls" and "Bamboo Bimbo" ("He caught his first whiff / In the jungles of 'Nam / That slant-eyed catfish / Tasted better than Mom").

The Residents continued to explore the territory mined by Beefheart, extending the use of stereotypical white and black vocal styles from historical American popular music (reframed as American folk music), manipulation of low fidelity in imitation of field recordings to evoke the "authentic," and deliberate use of pseudonyms and myth. While the members of the Magic Band were given pseudonyms, the Residents remained completely anonymous. While Captain Beefheart spun fanciful stories about himself, his biography and the person of Don Van Vliet remained intact; the Residents presented only myths. While Beefheart evoked the aesthetic of field recordings, the Residents satirized the fetishization of the authentic field recording, such as the sealed bottle of pure arctic air brought to them by N. Senada after his travels in search of "some musical link . . . hidden among the Eskimos of the frozen North."[60] The Residents pursued their project, they said, according to N. Senada's "Theory of Obscurity": "The only valid art can be done truly in obscurity."[61]

The Residents "populated their work with 'characters,' closer by far to acting than singing," and their racial characters or caricatures were created through vocal approaches, like Captain Beefheart, supported by musical binaries such as major (white) and minor (black) modes.[62] On *Meet the Residents*, the "black" male voice is manipulated to be low, growly, and guttural, mapped with minor pentatonic riffs, wah-wah guitar, and funky disco patterns on "Infant Tango" and their timely take on the 1970s energy crisis, "N-ER-GEE (Crisis Blues)." By contrast, a "natural," unmanipulated white southern voice, matched with major tonalities, is used in "Skratz" to sing lyrics resembling Beefheart's: "The sheets still showed the yellow spot / Ann ran her tongue along the ridges by the Gulf / Thoughts slipped into valleys / Concealed by dense Mexicali underbush hair." An aural white/black binary is most apparent on "Seasoned Greetings," as a corny 1950s white suburban voice (rather than a southern or country voice) says "Merry Christmas Mom, Merry Christmas Dad, and Merry Christmas Sis, I love you" over a major triad. This is immediately answered by an exaggerated caricature minstrel "black" voice: "Uh . . . it's Christmas . . . but there ain't nobody raisin' much of a fuss!"

The Residents' costumes and visual iconography support the hypothesis that they consistently drew on the codes of American minstrelsy, albeit in ways that could be variously interpreted. First seen on the cover of *Eskimo* (1979), their most famous costume is a tuxedo with tails, top hat, cane, and white gloves, immediately identifiable as a formal tap dance outfit but also a minstrel's costume connected to the character of Zip Coon, to those familiar with the tradition. In the place of blackface the Residents wear eyeball masks, seemingly saying that the minstrels are looking back at us, the audience. They also employ a white character in blackface makeup (who was apparently singing Al Jolson's hit "Mammy") in their early avant-garde film *Vileness Fats*.[63] Other songs, such as "Flight of the Bumbleroach" (1979), directly and satirically invoke "coon songs" in a manner evoking Beefheart's earlier "Ella Guru" experiment.

The Residents' interrogation of racial stereotypes and characters in American popular music is central to their project, especially when considering the full range of their output. They reserved the deep guttural voice for black and "ethnic" characters, most dramatically beginning with the Shaman in *Eskimo*. In *The Mole Trilogy* (1981–85), their multipart story of a struggle between two races—the Moles, a mistreated race of laborers, and the Chubs, who enslaved and exploited them—the "black" voice appears in the role of the Moles' leader.[64] The Residents employed this heavily manipulated voice on *George and James* (1984) to represent James Brown in their 1984 interpretation of *Live at the Apollo*, particularly striking as Brown famously sung in a tenor range and falsetto on that album. On the other hand, the Residents continually represented white characters with an unmanipulated voice and a white Southern accent. Their treatment of James Brown is directly opposed to their interpretation of Hank Williams on *Stars and Hank Forever!* (1986), whose songs are delivered in a naked, intimate, almost conversational voice—also very different from Williams's actual singing style.

Through the "Theory of Obscurity" and deliberate artifice, these racial characters are unmoored from taken-for-granted notions of authenticity, asking listeners to instead broadly consider the importance of authenticity itself, as well as the role of race in the reception of American popular music. In many different ways the Residents have told the story of American popular music as a combination of white + black. But their embrace of myth and stereotype reveals the artifice of the narrative: rock and roll is not white + black but "white" + "black," with whiteness and blackness being socially and musically constructed performance styles linked primarily to country music ("white") and the blues ("black"). And yet, as with the dilemmas that surface in Captain Beefheart's approach to the messy raw materials of American popular music, the ways in which the Residents engage with race and American music reveal how these explorations are themselves deeply embedded in American formations of whiteness. At what point, in other words, does a self-conscious critique of minstrelsy using masking techniques become a form of minstrelsy, given that minstrelsy was already a self-conscious performance of race using masking techniques?

The Residents pushed Beefheart's ideas to a certain extreme, but in doing so, they also revealed the limits of a critique of whiteness based simultaneously on a white subjectivity and conceits such as anonymity. The identities of the Residents remained "unknown" (for the most part), or more accurately, "the Residents" existed as anonymous artistic avatars apart from the humans who used them for creative expressions. Yet their own whiteness, transformation through black music, and story as relocated Southerners has always been central to their presentation. The Residents situated themselves as white Louisianans growing up in the 1950s, with an origin myth describing a typical narrative of disaffected youth rejecting the fake quality of their suburban lives: "Let your mind drift back to simpler, more pathetic times . . . to an age when American teenagers jitterbugged in plastic hula hoops to the savage jungle rhythm of payola'd rock 'n' roll, and spent their parents' hard earned pay on Jughead comics and Slinkys. . . . The Residents themselves grew up in all this, but their early memories are clouded by small-town Louisiana swamp gas, where they spent their formative years like normal white American Southern children on a diet of Jello, Skippy peanut butter, and Kool-Aid."[65] They bonded over *The Catcher in the Rye*, James Brown, and Bo Diddley, and in 1966 they relocated to San Mateo, outside of San Francisco, "licking their chops, ready and willing to participate" in the psychedelic revolution.[66] Their vocal manipulations reinforce a white subjectivity, as black and "ethnic" characters are always manipulated and very strongly "othered," whereas white southern country voices are not. And the minstrelizing vocal techniques they use ("Uh . . . it's Christmas . . . but there ain't nobody raisin' much of a fuss!") are among the most extreme practices used historically to reinforce whiteness through a stereotyping of "blackness."

The paradox of the Residents' anonymity and their whiteness comes together most blatantly and most problematically in their use of the Klansman's hood. The Klansman, of course, is both "anonymous" (masked, hooded, robed) and immediately identifiable as white, southern, and male. Obviously, the pointed hoods are only effective in the Residents' repertoire of masks because of the aura of racial violence and fear they communicate, as well as the questions about racism and subjectivity that they raise. Yet the Residents' representatives and their fans denied that this costume contained Klan references, stating the group's outfits were simply "newspaper costumes . . . the tall, conical hoods . . . were made that way because that was the simplest way to make a head-covering out of newspaper."[67] This strange explanation elides the fact that the entire enterprise is Residents-driven, with complete creative independence (no one asked them to make newspaper costumes in the first place), as well as the obvious point that nothing the Residents did was simple, including the extremely elaborate homemade films featuring said newspaper costumes, with sets and costumes created from scratch. The early LA punk band the Bags achieved this effect with paper bags quite easily and without evoking the KKK. The silhouetted conical hoods, worn by southern white men (and also used in a film to complement *The Third*

*Reich 'n Roll*, an album decorated with swastikas), cannot but evoke America's white supremacy iconography.

But if this iconography is meant to be evoked, or even flirted with, why do listeners explain it away, and how are they able to do so effectively? Whiteness itself empowers the Residents' listeners to avoid the symbolism and consider these gestures as pure art or as transcending race when the stakes or ramifications get too intense. Their fans' denial of front-and-center racial references, and the Residents' resistance to fully confronting the issues they raise, demonstrate the limits of white people parodying and interrogating whiteness's symbols and narratives. This ultimately ambiguous critique of whiteness, with the privileges of whiteness remaining at the core and ready to be accessed when deemed necessary, has a strong legacy in punk.

### Paradoxical Criticisms of the Music Industry

In addition to looking back at America's musical past, the Residents and other avant-gardists used experimental techniques to criticize the contemporaneous popular music industry and rock's self-aggrandizing myths. This particular area of engagement stemmed chiefly from their experiences as listeners and consumers. For as they dismantled popular music and its myths, they also expressed love for the industry that shaped their subjectivities as young white rock and roll fans growing up in the postwar suburbs. Earlier 1950s and 1960s rock and roll was their sound of their youth and their escape from the meaningless, boring, inauthentic lives they believed they were born into, but as they looked back on that music from the standpoint of the mid-1970s, they also saw the nefarious aspects of the music that meant so much to them. Their stance was fundamental for punk, especially as a balance to the less critical and more nostalgic views of the early rock and roll era that were becoming commonplace among white people in the 1970s, as I describe in detail in chapter 4.

The Residents were especially concerned with the culture of popular music in the 1960s. To explore the meanings of these songs, they manipulated and played along with the consumer object of the recording itself, challenging American copyright law as well as the sacred authenticity of musicians' creative output. Although the topic of 1960s popular music runs through their catalog (e.g., "The Beatles Play the Residents and the Residents Play the Beatles" sound collage of 1977), their boldest statement was *The Residents Present the Third Reich 'n Roll*, with Dick Clark holding a carrot in a Nazi uniform on the cover, and couples of male and female Hitlers in various outfits. The two suites of dismembered songs, "Hitler was a Vegetarian" and "Swastikas on Parade," include "The Land of 1,000 Dances," "Hanky Panky," and "Double Shot (Of My Baby's Love)" interspersed with German voices and the sounds of gunfire. The Nazi imagery in *Third Reich 'n Roll* is part of a Dada-inspired critique of the popular music industry that is scathing, humorous, and ambiguous, as well as an homage.

The Residents preemptively signaled the ambiguity of their attack on "bubblegum pop" and the uncertain reception of their own listeners and consumers. The back cover announces, "Already, people are speculating whether The Residents are hinting that rock and roll has brain-washed the youth of the world. When confronted with this possible philosophy, they replied, 'Well, it may be true or it may not, but we wanted to kick out the jams and get it on.'" The Residents' critique of popular music attempted to simultaneously support and dismantle popular music structures, and they implicated themselves as the very "brain-washed" youth they wanted to expose: "The Nazi imagery of the cover, with its Dick Hitler on a sort of American Bandstand surrounded by dancing Hitlers, reflects some cultural deficiencies THE RESIDENTS see in Rock and Roll Culture, although they realize that they are a product of the same culture they both support and denounce," as explained in the Ralph Records catalog of August 1977.[68] And Ralph Records itself is an independent record label that both satirizes and uses the corporate model—it is "Ralph Records, Uninc."—and the company's advertisements caricatured capitalism, exhorting consumers to "Buy or Die!" On the back cover of the album, the Residents admit their embrace of the popular music industry's methods even as they confront it: "[Ralph Records], as the parent company, support The Residents in their tribute to the thousands of little power-mad minds of the music industry who have helped make us what we are today, with an open eye on what we can make them tomorrow." The system of popular music demands that the Residents' fans and record buyers listen to the music based on the blatantly mythologized origin narratives, and imagine and construct identities for the anonymous four out of the clues they are given.

DEVO similarly satirized, embraced, and deconstructed the commercial aspects of popular music, but more directly connected the record industry to factories, corporate culture, and mechanized labor. Even more specifically, they linked these industrial elements to the dreams of the suburban white middle class and their own midwestern experiences. In Akron the rubber industry built up the white middle class, but by the early 1970s was also tearing it down, another element of a fundamentally pessimistic and disillusioned worldview that shaped DEVO in the wake of the Kent State massacre. DEVO, like the Residents, created their self-parodying critique of American whiteness through Dada techniques, racialized voices, and corporate structures, musically expressed in compositions such as the "DEVO Corporate Anthem." As their fame grew and they became an integral part of the pop music industry they parodied, DEVO doubled down on the commercial aspects of their art project. In the visual aspects of their music, especially in the 1980s, they drew on the kinds of advertising in comic books, magazines, and fan clubs, selling "action vests," "energy dome" pins, yellow suits, and 3D glasses alongside t-shirts and posters.

DEVO, like the Residents, captures a fundamental aspect of the broader punk paradox as the band "implicates itself in the very processes of socialization and conditioning, commercialization and corporatization, that they critique."[69] Punk experimentalism and the punk project overall depends on taking the established consumer products that shape the individual subject and then explicitly destroying or obscuring these products while retaining their auras: a ripped Pink Floyd t-shirt, a skipping Human Beinz record, or a pop song so filled with profanity it cannot be played on the radio. *The Third Reich 'n Roll* and DEVO's hit songs are both complicit in the structures that prop up the popular music industry because they exist within the same economic network and they depend on the same equation of listener and consumer.

### American Connections of Dada and Punk

The American avant-garde rock musicians discussed here looked to Dada for inspiration but did so as part of an American art tradition, and they specifically used Dada's ideas to comment on the conflict between the veneer of utopian white suburbia and the realities of Vietnam's horrors and urban decay. These musicians also invoked direct connections to the European avant-garde beyond Dada, as with Pere Ubu's band name, drawn from Alfred Jarry's Symbolist play *Ubu Roi*, widely understood as an inspiration for Dada.[70]

The Residents situated their "rock band" as a kind of performance art with masks and costumes. A direct line can be drawn from these masking techniques to Dada performances such as those by Hugo Ball and Emmy Hennings at Zürich's Cabaret Voltaire in 1916.[71] In their film *Whatever Happened to Vileness Fats?* (started in 1972, revised and released in 1984) and their short film for *The Third Reich 'n Roll* (1976), exaggerated characters and images of Hitler play out absurdist stories in surreal black-and-white scenarios drawn from the Dada universe. They created these films as art pieces, and their records and films were heard and viewed by a small audience interested in experimentalism and extreme countercultural art.

DEVO, formed in the wake of the Kent State shootings, saw Dada's responses to capitalism, utopianism, and bourgeois society as useful for satirizing a false idealization of white American suburbia, and they related to the primitivist aesthetic and the war-torn world out of which Dada emerged. Their home of Ohio "fit in with the early-20th century art movements—Expressionism, Dada and others that were influenced by those kinds of environments in Germany and England. We had our very own backyard version of it."[72] They became aware of Dada and experimental art as students as Kent State, where Mark Mothersbaugh and Gerald Casale were exposed to the on-site art works *Graft*, Allan Kaprow's attaching of dollar bills to trees on campus, and *Partially Buried Woodshed*, for which Robert Smithson dumped "twenty truckloads of earth on an abandoned woodshed" on campus.[73] Mothersbaugh noted in his journals who among his acquaintances was "DADA" and who was "non-DADA," and at Kent State Mothersbaugh and Casale were also introduced to Bauhaus, Futurism, and Surrealism.[74] Casale explained that he and Mothersbaugh were "mixing Dada ideas with Ronald McDonald and doing performance art, although there was no word for performance art and we didn't know what we were doing then."[75]

DEVO's experiences at Kent State at the end of the 1960s and the beginning of the 1970s, along with their particular backgrounds, make them a quintessential group for understanding this missing or at least misunderstood generation of 1970s avant-garde punk inspirations and American uses of Dada at the time. Mothersbaugh in particular had an insider/outsider relationship to the underground art and music scene, reflected in a multifaceted, freewheeling approach in DEVO's artistic analysis of American society. Unlike most of the suburbanites of Cleveland, New York, and Los Angeles in the punk scene, Mothersbaugh came from a family of coal miners and was the first in his family to attend college.[76] And Mothersbaugh's uses of Dada and experimental art were directly geared toward an understanding of "the conditions of American society," like the work of his friend the artist Bruce Conner.[77]

In Dada, Mothersbaugh saw a movement responding to a time analogous to his own. "Dada's founders resembled Mothersbaugh's generation of draft dodgers, deserters, and pacifists who had experienced not the heroics and high-tech destruction that futurist writing and art had promised them, but the realities of the muddy trenches where soldiers were all too human."[78] Collage, montage, and décollage became crucial techniques drawn from Dada, applied visually and aurally. John Heartfield, the German-Jewish artist of the World War II period who satirized Hitler and the Nazis in his photomontages, particularly resonated with Mothersbaugh: "humans are a pretty scary species. John Heartfield manages to capture that in his collages. Although I love all Dada art, I think Heartfield's collages are my favorite for that reason."[79] Heartfield remained an important touchstone for punk artists; his collage *Hurrah, die Butter ist alle!* resurfaced as the cover art for the Siouxsie and the Banshees single "Mittageisen," the song inspired by his work.

DEVO used Dada's ideas primarily to satirize white American suburban society, which they saw as a façade masking the grim realities of war, industrialization, and the ruins of American cities—society's "de-evolution." As early as 1971 or 1972, Mark Mothersbaugh used the character of Booji Boy (pronounced "boogie") as a strange character who, like the Residents' eyeballs did later,

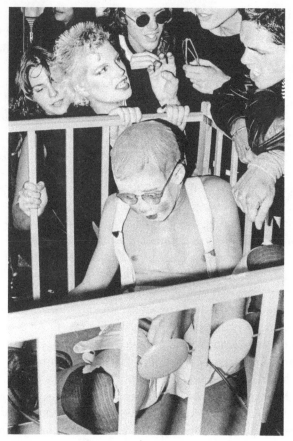

Figure 3.2. Booji Boy performing at Mabuhay Gardens, San
Francisco, 1978. Photograph by Richard Alden Peterson.

reflected white audiences' fears and fantasies back to the viewer. Booji Boy is a
pale-white, rosy-cheeked "all-American" 1950s kid and "an absurdist, Dada-like
character who can pretend to be an innocent child. At the same time, he can be
confrontational and make people uptight."[80] As shown in figure 3.2, Booji Boy
could later be found performing at punk shows, continuing to bewilder a scene
that had also started to embrace a kind of conformity.

Booji Boy is also the pseudonymous author of Mark Mothersbaugh's col-
lage-based book, *My Struggle*, invoking Hitler's manifesto.[81] As with other artists in this chapter, alter egos, masks, characters, and pseudonyms helped DEVO
explore controversial ideas, in this case the concept of "de-evolution." Rather than
rendering a simple judgment on society, de-evolution conjured America's racist and apocalyptic ideologies, and with masks and characters, DEVO explored
those ideas from the inside. De-evolution came directly from B. H. Shadduck's

Figure 3.3. Chrome, *Alien Soundtracks*, 1977.

evangelical tract *Jocko-Homo Heavenbound*, a "big rant against evolution, how evolution was bullshit, science was bullshit" by an Ohio preacher, given to Mothersbaugh by Ian Short.[82] Shadduck also authored the racist minstrelsy-inspired *Rastus Agustus Explains Evolution*.[83] Ultimately, de-evolution targeted DEVO's American surroundings and the ignorance they saw contributing to the violence around them, but it did so through cryptic methods that sought to raise questions.

Other artists who impacted punk, especially those who studied art, used Dada's aesthetic to comment on suburbia and the youth of white American baby boomers. For example, Destroy All Monsters, the University of Michigan/Ann Arbor–based anti-band and art collective formed in 1973 and which included Mike Kelley, Niagara, Cary Loren, and Jim Shaw, as well as eventually ex-Stooge Ron Asheton, Ben Miller, Larry Miller, and Rob King, created magazines with avant-garde deconstructions of Americana: e.g., Superman, monster movies, monopoly money, and Yogi Bear.[84] Chrome, also like DEVO and Destroy All Monsters, targeted white suburbia, Americana, and rock conventions with their experiments. Damon Edge of Chrome studied at CalArts and also worked with Allan Kaprow. As shown in figure 3.3, the cover of Chrome's *Alien Soundtracks* (1977) features a collage of a white woman lounging on the floor of a suburban 1950s scene with a deconstructed face hovering around her, and the back cover replaces her face with an eyeball. American punk collage artists such as Winston Smith, who created art for Dead Kennedys, continued the visual work of these American experimental bands alongside that of British artists Jamie Reid, Gee Vaucher (in her collaborations with Crass), and Linder (in her collaborations with Buzzcocks).

Although many members of these groups were connected to art schools and the art world, they also distinguished themselves from contemporaneous artists by their irreverent approach to Dada (which is in itself in the spirit of Dada), but also Surrealism, Symbolism, Futurism, Expressionism, and other "isms" in their quest for understanding the American society they inhabited. They freely disregarded or negated "influences." This was especially true beyond the world of art schools and for the musicians who picked up on these approaches through the 1970s. The Electric Eels developed "Artist's Rules" which included "Artists can be self-contradictory."[85] They extended this attitude to nearly everything they encountered, from Stockhausen, Subotnick, and avant-garde jazz recordings to "low art" monster movies. John D. Morton remembered Dave E. (Dave McManus) buying Ornette Coleman's *Free Jazz*: "We thought it was great/top shelf/ primo, but after 7 minutes of it (well, maybe 5) our collective attention span was spent and we quickly put on [Fleetwood Mac's] *English Rose*."[86] Their relationships to these recordings, musicians, and art movements are best considered with respect to their suburban circumstances and networks, which continued into their urban lives. They were attracted to avant-garde art as misfits and for the visceral sensory experiences such art generated, but their primary way of accessing this art was through mass media, and they were removed from the original meanings, social contexts, and in many cases, the academic environments in which avant-garde art traditions thrived and persisted.

### Noise Experiments and Suburbia

Another key element in the punk style with a strong debt to the avant-garde rock musicians of the early and mid-1970s is the incorporation of noise elements, especially synthesizer-generated white noise and saxophone improvisations appropriated from "new thing" or "free jazz" playing of the 1960s. Bands featured in other chapters, such as the Stooges, also figure here. The noise elements of the Stooges can be directly related to Robert Ashley's experimental work (*The*

*Wolfman,* 1964) and Antonin Artaud's "Theater of Cruelty," in addition to Iggy Pop's experience as a fourteen-year-old audience member at a Michigan barn dance seeing Jerry Lee Lewis kicking a piano and leaving the stage.[87]

Saxophone improvisations became the most direct connection of the "avant-garage" to contemporaneous experimental jazz and "Great Black Music" such as the intermedia explorations of AACM (Association for the Advancement of Creative Musicians) composers and the Art Ensemble of Chicago, which, like blues, was deeply connected to the Great Migration and the urban spaces affected by white flight.[88] Early punk musicians and their antecedents, including Captain Beefheart and the Stooges, tended to use the saxophone for unbridled expressions of freedom or "freak outs," imitating, approximating, and often misinterpreting the abstract modernist experiments of Ornette Coleman and Cecil Taylor, the historical Afrocentricity of the Art Ensemble of Chicago, and the spiritual journeys of Albert Ayler.[89] The saxophone also became a signifier of funk and soul music in a complex web of racial associations most dramatically picked up by James Chance with his "No Wave" bands the Contortions and James White and the Blacks.[90] But beyond these associations, as with collage, masks, and voice caricatures, noise experiments were primarily aspects of a larger critique of white American suburbia.

The British group Roxy Music popularized the use of noise in a postmodern reimagining of early rock and roll's heyday, with Brian Eno an integral part of the ensemble next to Bryan Ferry's affected croon. The visual aesthetic of *Roxy Music* (1972) borders on John Waters's, as a heavily made-up model in a 1950s-style dress lays on a bed and grimaces at the camera. Throughout the blues-based "Re-Make/Re-Model" Eno's noisy squeals combine with Phil Manzanera's minor pentatonic guitar improvisations and Andy Mackey's blasting saxophone. Collage and synthesizer noise are also central to "Ladytron" and "The Bob (Medley)." The original Roxy Music instrumentation of oboe, saxophone, and synthesizer added to the standard vocals, guitar, bass, and drums (similar to the instrumentation of late-1960s Soft Machine) also became an important format for punk, new wave, and other rock bands using experimental and avant-garde techniques, especially Ohio bands such as Pere Ubu and Akron's Tin Huey. Other groups incorporated either woodwinds (e.g., clarinet on the Electric Eels' "Bunnies") or synthesizers and electronic manipulations (DEVO, Cleveland's Home & Garden), but not together.[91] Key to Roxy Music's impact on punk, Eno's noise, Mackey's freestyle saxophone, and Manzanera's occasional atonal madness (as on "Sea Breezes") are subsumed within larger rock structures. For example, Jerry Casale pointed to the experimental style of Roxy Music and David Bowie circa *Diamond Dogs* (1974) as giving "me hope that the ideas that DEVO had could be put together in some formal way and get a voice in the marketplace."[92]

In the United States, synthesizer and noise experiments were often directly connected to critiques of white American suburbia of the 1950s and 1960s. The United States of America's "I Won't Leave My Wooden Wife for You, Sugar" (1968) is a relatively early example. In 1975, members of the Los Angeles Free Music Society created "Suburban Magic" to be performed at CalArts, a "flight of fancy thru the kitchens and yards of Suburban L.A."[93] The instrumentation of shears, radios (playing "easy listening" music, the news, and Biblical sermonizing), blenders, ice crushers, rake, eggbeater, and can opener accompanied banal parental statements and directives such as "wash your hands," "who used all the shampoo?" "Mommy went through a red light," "get your shoes on," "hang up your clothes," "hamburgers again?" "say please," "you'll be late for school," and "let's go to McDonalds."[94] "Suburban Magic" could be performed straight, or manipulated through the "Electric Music Box" (Buchla 200 Series), resulting in a distorted harsh noise composition.

Pere Ubu's "Sentimental Journey" (1977) similarly featured synthesizer noise and harsh everyday sounds—in this case, breaking bottles—with oboe, arhythmic drumming, and guitar improvisations. Over this commotion, David Thomas murmured about the privileged confines of suburbia that this cohort of musicians was actively rejecting: "table and chairs and TVs and books and a lamp and other stuff . . . it's home it's a rug it's a home it's a rug it's a window a pbbblblblblbl a pluh a pluh I'll go home, it's home, it's home . . ." Allen Ravenstine, Pere Ubu's synthesist, remembered:

> What was the one where we're breaking the bottles? In my mind, it was a take on a Doris Day ditty.[95] . . . OK, where I grew up, which I could not wait to get away from, was a place called Rocky River in Ohio. It's a suburb on the west side of Cleveland. And we moved there in 1955 from Canton, Ohio for a couple of reasons. [ . . . ] But it was the epitome of American suburbia in the '50s and '60s. And what that means in my mind is that it was ALL about appearances—who had the nicest car, the prettiest wife, the nicest house . . . and I hated it. And what I was aware of was an undercurrent that inside this façade that looked so good, there was all this turmoil. There was a lot of drinking, a lot of fighting, a lot of stuff that was always swept under the rug. When you go into somebody's house, it was nice and quiet and clean. In those days, people didn't use things like garlic and if your house smelled like fish, it was because there was something not right! That was all blue collar stuff, you know? And I hated it—it was so sterile. And it was a lie in my opinion. And I couldn't wait to get out of there. And that song that I can't think of the name of . . . "Sentimental Journey," that's it! "Gonna take a sentimental journey . . ." That's that period of time. And the whole breaking of the bottles and all that stuff, that's what I think. I wanted that undercurrent—there's chaos here.[96]

Synthesizer noise, used as an undercurrent in Pere Ubu and other groups such as DEVO, Chrome, and Throbbing Gristle, could also indicate darkness, sinister energy, and fear of suburbia's opposite, neglected urban spaces. Allen Raven-stine's *Terminal Drive* (recorded 1975), a legendary piece of electronic music from the Cleveland scene, was "not only a reflection of The Plaza [3206 Prospect Ave.] but in many ways also a reflection of Cleveland in the mid-1970s, an audio document of urban decay in real time and a soundtrack to the beginning of the slow decline in the dwindling cities of industry within the Midwest American rust belt."[97] For members of those groups rejecting the suburbs and returning to the cities, ideas of urban decay often circulated around race-based fears accom-panying white flight and the growth of the so-called urban "ghetto." For example, as mentioned above, *Terminal Drive* contained "sirens and things" reflecting the "frightening" sounds Ravenstine heard living "on the edge of a ghetto."

Martin Rev of Suicide is a consummate example of an early punk figure who used electronically generated noise to comment on white American suburbia of the 1950s and the accompanying search to escape boredom. Whereas in "Ghost Rider" and "Rocket U.S.A." Rev matched simple blues-based, minor pentatonic, or whole-step riffs to the simple pulsation created by his Rhythm Prince drum machine, on songs such as "Cherie" and "Frankie Teardrop," Rev created a dense thicket of pulsation unrelated to the melodic riffs and Alan Vega's eerie vocal-izing about the dark, exciting, and seductive side of American teenage life (the 1950s world when Vega was a teenager—he was almost forty when *Suicide* was released). Vega's screams, howls, and whispers were manipulated into noise and disembodied echoes throughout the Suicide catalog. "Frankie Teardrop" is Sui-cide's magnum opus in this regard, concluding with five minutes of noise exper-imentation and barely discernable recorded samples. Suicide's music matched Alan Vega's summary of the images he assembled for *Art-Rite* 13 (1977):

> We dedicate this issue to the average American in search of excitement. These images, distilled from the ambient culture, are the touchstones of a new sensibil-ity, icons of the dissipations and strengths of the modern spirit. Let the way of life idealized in these pages by the To Lose lo Track of the punk scene bring into your home the romance of the underculture—horse racing, white-trash smut, greasy rock 'n' roll, muscles, motorcycles and the end of civilization.[98]

## Whiteness and Avant-Garde Critique

The experimental bands following in the footsteps of Captain Beefheart pre-sented an important path for punk musicians incorporating avant-garde techniques for the purpose of critique and commentary. Their pointed uses of collage and noise were not generally abstract investigations into sound but part of a wider critique of the 1950s white suburban world they grew up in, the

failures of 1960s counterculture, and the 1970s urban landscape they had reen-
tered, and they located these critiques mostly within the structures of American
popular music they were engaging. Captain Beefheart, the Residents, DEVO,
and Chrome asked the listener to reevaluate their ideas about popular music
and its relationship to American mythologies, the culture (or lack thereof) of
white suburban environments, and the ways in which capitalism and consum-
erism create white subjectivities.

Avant-garde engagement with American ideas of race lie underneath these
various critiques, and the approaches of these musicians persisted in punk.
While punk musicians rarely inhabited racial caricatures and stereotypes in the
specific ways that the Residents and Captain Beefheart did, the flirtation with
ambiguous racist iconography and symbolism continued, as did the idea of a
humorous, Dada-inspired self-reflexive critique of racial formations. Elements
of these absurdist interpretations of race can be found in the ironic self-impli-
cations of punk songs such as the Urinals' "I'm White and Middle Class." These
groups also continued to explore ideas of race as their careers continued in and
around the punk scene of the late 1970s, such as DEVO's productive exploita-
tions of parodic "white" voices, the most well-known example being their angu-
lar cover of the Rolling Stones' "(I Can't Get No) Satisfaction," transforming
Mick Jagger's exaggerated imitation of American blues singers.

And in a cycle that continued with punk, these avant-garde critiques of
whiteness have been implicated as heavily dependent on whiteness and ultimately reinforcing it. Revealing the whiteness of these avant-garde expressions,
many of those engaging in these critiques eventually invoked the privileges of
whiteness to undermine the ambiguity and ambivalence of their original artistic statements. The Residents themselves (or more likely, remaining members),
for example, shifted away from the uncertain reflexivity of their earlier work
and instead attempted to establish a place as important figures in the American
music and modern art canons. In the performance of "Life Would be Wonderful" in the *Demons Dance Alone* tour (2004), the "singing Resident" sang, "Life
would be wonderful / If we had a major label / And a nice four-figure deal / And
a promo guy able / To make you think that we are real / Or if we got a nomina-
tion / For a Grammy maybe we / Could start a comeback and an agent / Could
get us back on MTV . . . If our good friend Snakefinger / Hadn't had a heart
attack / Or if we had a Negro singer / Who could do some mellow rap."[99] After
generating discomfort with these lines ("Negro singer"), the "singing Resident"
then attempts to dispel his audience's potential unease with an authenticating
narrative, delivered in a natural speaking voice, about how he met James Brown
in 1965 after seeing him live in Lafayette, Louisiana, and it was "absolutely one
of the most amazing moments of my entire life." The impulse to create one's
own marginalization and then lament injustice and inequalities, followed by an

embrace of privilege (implicitly revealing the impossibility of true self-marginalization), is one of the greatest ironies of the punk paradox and perhaps the most revealing aspect of punk's strong relationship to white privilege.

Most of the experimentalists considered in this chapter eventually did find their place in the mostly white and European world of art history and art museums. The Residents' early films are included in the Museum of Modern Art collection, a fact often invoked by the group's representatives; in a foreshadowing of punks' institutional archiving impulses, the group originally donated these films to this ultimate legitimizer of modern art. The finale of the Residents documentary *Theory of Obscurity* is the accession of the group's $100,000 *Ultimate Box Set* to MoMA's permanent collection.[100] The Residents, DEVO, and Captain Beefheart were featured alongside Steve Reich, John Cage, Robert Wilson, Bruce Nauman, Ray Johnson, and others in the overwhelmingly white and male (with the exception of Yoko Ono and Nam June Paik) MoMA exhibition *Looking at Music* (2008).[101] As Don Van Vliet, Captain Beefheart had a stellar career as a visual artist, as did Mike Kelley of Destroy All Monsters. Mark Mothersbaugh's visual art has also been celebrated by the mainstream art world, culminating most recently in the major retrospective *Myopia*.

The lives of these artists and their work suggest a return to analyzing American racial formations and how they play out in historical narratives, reception, and critical assessments. George E. Lewis's analysis of the Eurological and Afrological approaches to improvisational styles after 1950 still provides one of the most useful ways into understanding the complicated racial dynamics at the core of experimental work like the Residents' and Captain Beefheart's.[102] According to Lewis, one of the key differences between Afrological and Eurological approaches is the attitude toward the past: Eurological artists tend to "deemphas[ize] memory and history" and establish their work in a supposedly objective space, whereas Afrological artists, "coming from a legacy of slavery and oppression, cannot countenance the erasure of history" and emphasize personal narrative.[103] The Residents, for example, enact Eurological strategies by "othering" black voices through distortion and exaggeration against a blank slate of whiteness, as well as committing to the "Theory of Obscurity" and its conceit of creating a space where "pure" art and innovation can take place, and from which their art can be interpreted as transcending race. Paradoxically, this conceit is primarily accessible to white people and thus heavily racialized.

But despite the many ways in which the Residents and others described in this chapter fit into Lewis's constructions, their deep engagement with American history and ideas of race ultimately makes them an awkward fit with a Eurological interpretation. This is especially true during the period of the late 1960s and early 1970s, when their critiques were the most forceful. Their explorations of history and race are of the utmost importance when thinking through the strategies of American punk musicians who picked up elements from these avant-garde approaches. Despite some moves in the direction of transcendence, Captain Beefheart and the Residents never really attempted to go beyond the idea of race, although the avant-garde techniques they used opened the door for that interpretation, and audiences ultimately seized on it. Actually, as I have attempted to show in this chapter, they explicitly critiqued and wrestled with American ideas of whiteness and blackness, American history, and the complex relationship of American society to its popular music. Their experimental work paradoxically undermined and reinforced racial categories, rock and roll narratives, and popular music myths. The punk musicians they inspired extended these contradictions: humorous and serious, artificial and authentic, popular and obscure, tethered to the past and devoted to the vanguard.

# 4

## "Pure Rock and Roll with No Blues or Folk or Any of That Stuff in It"

In an interview with *Rolling Stone* published in 1979, Timothy White asked the Ramones, "How would you describe your own music?" Johnny Ramone responded: "We're playing pure rock and roll with no blues or folk or any of that stuff in it. And we try to be entertaining and bring back the feeling of kids coming and having a good time—united with us. But we never considered the whole local new-band scene here or in England. We never had the weird pointy haircuts. These are our regular haircuts."[1]

Johnny Ramone's response sets the stage for this chapter, raising a number of questions related to punk history, historiography, musical style, and ideas of race. What does it mean, *musically*, to play "pure" rock and roll? What did he mean by "blues," "folk," or "any of that stuff" at that time? What is the musical expression of the feeling, located in the imaginary or real past, that Johnny says the Ramones are trying to "bring back"? And at that point in 1979, how and why did Johnny consider his music in relation to the punk scene in the United States and England, which he refers to as the "local new-band scene"?

This quote is a starting point for understanding the Ramones in relation to their contemporaries, the musical conversations in which they all participated, and the ways others represented the Ramones in particular as the originators of "punk." Like other early figures connected to the punk scene, the Ramones were ambivalent toward the category of punk and the other bands grouped with them under that term; in the words of one journalist, "It's punk-rock, an appellation disdained by most of its practitioners but zealously adopted by others."[2] Intensely ambitious as a band, they attempted to capitalize on the term and the scene's explosion, even as they distanced themselves from what was going on around them. Between 1975 and 1976, the Ramones went from being an "original Rock and Roll group," with no mention of "punk," to "a hard-hitting rock and roll band . . . punk rock 'n' rollers" and "so punky you're gonna have to react!" in their press releases.[3]

Five years after the first Ramones show at CBGB, these contradictory attitudes were already a hallmark of punk, as were the tensions between musicians' own words and the ways their words were represented or interpreted by others. In the Ramones' case, punk's contradictory culture came to the fore. Looking back, John Felice, an original Modern Lover and founder of the Real Kids, articulated the lack of context surrounding the categorizations of "punk," explaining: "we play our rock and roll aggressively. . . . And because of that it's been confused with punk rock. But being aggressive doesn't make you punk rock. . . . I don't think the Ramones are a punk rock band. I think the Ramones were a rock and roll band. *Period*. I think if any one of them were alive to agree with me, I think they would. I knew them all personally and I'll tell you right now: None of them bought into that fucking punk rock crap. Joey and Dee Dee, who were writing all the songs, their favorite things were the Beatles and Girl Groups and Phil Spector. What does that have to do with punk rock? *Nothing*."[4]

The Ramones' complex relationship to punk, the style they in many ways invented, carried over into other contradictions and misrepresentations. By "pure rock and roll," Johnny meant concentrated and undiluted. Joe Strummer echoed this usage of "pure" in a later interview, calling the Ramones and Motörhead "pure": "The Ramones are obviously pure. They play Ramones. And they're going to be the Ramones forever. . . . the Ramones and Motörhead, they will never jump on the next trend."[5] But in a striking twist, Johnny's words— "pure rock and roll with no blues or folk or any of that stuff in it"—have been continually misquoted and given racial overtones. "Mr. Ramone once described his guitar style as 'pure, *white* rock 'n' roll, with no blues influence,'" wrote Ben Sisario in Johnny's *New York Times* obituary (emphasis added).[6] This version of the quote circulates widely (I have repeated it in a previous publication) yet this is most certainly a misquoting or fabrication following White's original article.[7] However, the fact that the mistake exists and that it has had such staying power means that something deeper than a simple error is at work.

By the late 1970s, the Ramones' "pure rock and roll" musical models had been described as opposed to riff-based blues music for a decade, symbolizing an implicitly white perspective on the American past even when combined with an ambivalent, outsider, punk point of view. This pure rock and roll music was based on particular common-stock American schemes played extensively by both white and black vernacular musicians in the first half of the twentieth century, but which had become attached to a new racial binary after the 1960s. For rock musicians in the 1970s, these various schemes retained some of their older shared common stock legacy, and were also put to new uses according to changing ideas of musical whiteness and blackness.

## The New York and Boston Scenes

The Ramones' music stands in direct contrast to the open-ended, one- and two-chord, riff-based blues models exploited most dramatically by the Stooges in the late 1960s and early 1970s—the "raw power" approaches discussed in chapter 2. However, like the music of all the groups appearing in this book, the Ramones' music was not sui generis but a particular expression of a widespread cultural conversation in the United States regarding rock's essence, function, and relationship to racial formations. The Ramones composed with particular approaches to popular music that, despite some revisionist historical claims, were consistent throughout the 1960s. In other words, the Ramones' style and their innovative approaches should be seen as both a culminating end point and a trendsetting starting point.

Significant facets of the Ramones' style can be heard in most of the music made by their contemporaries in New York and the closely related Boston scene in the early to mid-1970s. And similar stylistic approaches can be found in the music of certain early and mid-1960s groups, such as those collected on *Nuggets* and later classified as garage rock or even punk, due to the ways some groups in the 1970s were explicitly drawing on those recordings. This music, what I call here "pure rock and roll" following Johnny Ramone, strongly evoked the late 1950s and early 1960s. Much of the source material for these bands is variously described by the musicians as rock and roll, bubblegum, and girl group, and less commonly as doo-wop or rhythm and blues. These sources added up to a historically oriented repertoire for a scene often portrayed as uninterested in the past.

The standard punk chronology, beginning with the Ramones and other CBGB bands in 1976 or the British "graduating class" of 1977, misses how punk emerged to a great extent by musicians looking back to a romanticized America which was startlingly different from the world they and their audiences inhabited. And an overall shift in emphasis at this time from "raw power" ("proto-punk" of the mid- to late 1960s) to "pure rock and roll" (punk rock of the early to mid-1970s) seemed to echo the changing attitudes and concerns of white baby boomers from the late 1960s to the mid-1970s, echoed in the repertoires over the course of the varied careers of bands such as San Francisco's Flamin' Groovies and Boston's Modern Lovers. These groups were exploring questions of musical style in relation to each other in small underground scenes, especially in the early 1970s, playing out specific manifestations of broader mainstream trends. For example, one journalist wrote "lately, however, rock has been returning to its basic roots with bands like J. Geils and the Flamin' Groovies" in a 1971 review of Mitch Ryder's *Detroit*.[8]

Specifically, this chapter focuses on aspects of the musical style played by some of the key bands on the New York and Boston scenes from 1972 to 1976. Among those associated with New York are the New York Dolls (formed in 1971 and performing at the Mercer Arts Center in 1972), Blondie (emerging out of the Stilletos, who began performing at CBGB in 1974), and the Dictators (performing at the Coventry in Queens and recording their debut album in 1974);

and among those associated with Boston are the Modern Lovers (performing around Boston in 1970 and New York in 1972) and the Real Kids (performing in Boston in 1972). I have linked Boston and New York because these bands frequently heard each other and played on shared bills, although Boston's scene is virtually unknown today.[9] This is not to exclude bands on these scenes discussed elsewhere in the book, such as Suicide and Patti Smith, or contemporaneous bands in other scenes, such as Minneapolis's Suicide Commandos (formed 1974). This chapter only aims to look closely at one important aspect of punk rock's musical style, culminating in the most influential of all these bands for punk, the Ramones.

This chapter may require even more reorientation than others for those readers familiar with the records made by these bands and the standard telling of punk rock history. As with the rest of this book, I am most concerned with musical style and punk's place in the larger context of American popular music, meaning that I link bands with similar approaches and who performed at the same venues, even if they have been separated by forty years of retrospective division into various "genres" ("glam," "new wave," etc.) and debates over who is and isn't "punk." One prime example is Blondie, whose popular success in the late 1970s and early 1980s as a "new wave" or "disco" band led to their being devalued in relation to the early punk rock scene.[10] Such divisions often come down to punk's later associations with young white heterosexual men, despite the fact that punk had much different, and in many ways diametrically opposite, connections in its early days.

If these bands are known today, they are known almost entirely from their recordings, many of which came out years after they began performing live. And some of those musicians had been writing songs and working on their style for years before they started performing. Albums by the Modern Lovers and the Real Kids (1976 and 1977; Suicide and the Real Kids were labelmates on Marty Thau's Red Star label) were released five to seven years after these bands had been performing live. In many cases, the band that was performing live at CBGB in 1975 or 1976 was different from the band we know from records, especially with respect to the covers they played—always a clue into how groups compose their original material. Many of the New York bands, for example, regularly played songs from the 1960s: in 1975 Blondie's repertoire included the Velvet Underground's "Femme Fatale" (1967), the Marvelettes' "Heat Wave" (1963), and the Shangri-Las' "Out in the Streets" (1965); Television's included the Count Five's "Psychotic Reaction" (1966, included on *Nuggets*) and the 13th Floor Elevators' "Fire Engine" (1966); and in 1976 Talking Heads played the 1910 Fruitgum Co.'s "1, 2, 3, Red Light" (1968) the Troggs' "Love Is All Around" (1967), and covered the Ramones' "I Wanna Be Your Boyfriend," a song in an early 1960s style.

The formative music for many of the artists analyzed in this chapter constitute the same repertoire that many of their so-called "influences" heard, as many of these early punks were not at all "youth" in the mid-1970s. In other words, what appeared to be harking back to music made by individuals of an earlier era actually reflected shared experiences. Deborah Harry was thirty-one when the first Blondie record was released, her teenage years from 1959 to 1964. Harry is actually several years older than Mary Weiss and the other members of the Shangri-Las, as they were teenagers when "Leader of the Pack" was released in 1964. We may think of Talking Heads as starting with *Talking Heads: 77*, but members of the Talking Heads had been playing in bands since 1967 (including Jerry Harrison's tenure with the Modern Lovers from 1971 to 1974); Harrison was already twenty-eight years old when he started playing with the band. Boston mainstay Willie Alexander, featured on 1976's *Live at the Rat*, filled in for Tony Williams as a jazz drummer in 1962, and toured with the Reed-less and Morrison-less Velvet Underground in 1971.[11]

Focusing on scenes and musical life rather than discography not only moves the timeline further toward the early 1970s, it also changes the stylistic portrait of the period. Many of the groups that broke out of the CBGB scene were innovative critic's darlings, unusually fortunate in personnel and management, or otherwise exceptional. But the local scenes out of which these bands emerged were filled with now-obscure bands that played music stylistically applicable to this chapter. They include scores of bands that played CBGB, including some who performed there as early as 1975, such as the Mumps, Shirts, Tuff Darts, Marbles, and Planets; other bands in the New York metro area such as the Good Rats and Blue Öyster Cult; transplants such as Cleveland's Dead Boys; and most of the Boston bands, such as Mickey Clean and the Mezz, the Lost, the Boom Boom Band, Fox Pass, DMZ, and Third Rail.[12] Local scenes also play a huge role in the sphere of so-called "influences," even if the references are relatively unknown. Jonathan Richman, John Felice, and other Boston musicians were inspired by the Rockin' Ramrods, the house band at the Surf in Nantasket from 1963 to 1967, and who toured with the Rolling Stones in 1965.[13] As the Real Kids sang on "Better Be Good": "Everywhere I go I hear kids talkin' / there's nothin' goin' on, the town ain't rockin' like it did before, hey back in '64 / we were rockin' with the Ramrods, we were shakin' with the Pandas / and it just don't seem the same, without the Remains."

Members of local New York and Boston bands were often right to criticize the retrospective categorization of "punk" as early as 1976, when they saw new and younger bands receiving record deals and radio support. In 1976 Peppi Marchello of the Good Rats told an interviewer, "Punk rock? The Ramones? Man, fuck the Ramones. We've been doing punk rock since before they were born. Like we were the original punk rockers ten years ago . . . they do better public relations."[14] The Good Rats had been playing since 1964, and what Marchello meant by "punk rock" was aggressive rock and roll, the music Felice said had been "confused with punk rock." The typical night at CBGB, Max's Kansas City, or Boston's Rat in the early or mid-1970s would feature aggressive rock in the "pure rock and roll" mode described in this chapter, although a contingent remained more committed to the riff-based models of the Stooges.

The picture and sound of the early 1970s New York scene in particular also changes when considering that many of the early New York bands had openly LGBTQ members (e.g., Jayne County, the Fast, Leather Secrets, the Mumps featuring Lance Loud after his appearance on PBS's *An American Family*), and women (e.g., Shirts featuring Annie Golden, now in *Orange is the New Black*, Erasers, Sic Fucks featuring Tish and Snooky, who later founded Manic Panic).[15] African Americans were not well represented, but they were not completely absent either; Ivan Julian of the Voidoids and Tally Taliaferrow of the Planets were two prominent black musicians on the scene. Most of these groups are now obscure but were prominent at the time. Many expected the Planets, for example, to be a breakout band from the CBGB scene.

The diverse reality of the scene, both stylistically and demographically, has been obscured in retrospect by a later stereotype of punk as loud, fast, white, hetero, and male, a particular conception of punk beginning to take hold with the relatively late arrival of *Punk* magazine, which "specialized in a fanatically narrow canon of hard core punk bands," and then became fully entrenched by the emergence of hardcore at the turn to the 1980s.[16] When bands from these scenes do not fit the punk stereotype, they are retrospectively excluded through categorization, such as "glam" for bands with LGBTQ members. A similar semantic switch is at work when terms such as "girl groups" and "rockabilly" are retrospectively considered distinct genres rather than as part of a larger rhythm and blues scene. At the same time, bands with women and openly LGBTQ members were often resistant to the musical style that was coming to define "punk" and the perceived limitations of the category, adding to the later separation.

Another area of misapprehension is the extent to which the musical style of these bands is a product of these musicians' upbringing in segregated suburbs, especially with respect to the New York scene. These bands are associated with New York City and even understood as quintessentially urban groups, although they are acknowledged to have roots in the suburbs. But the deep relationship between New York City and the suburbs goes far beyond the suburbs' effect on rockers' identities and their desire to move to the city to participate in alternative communities and cultural activities. The development of the punk rock scene goes hand in hand with the massive waves of white flight from the cities to the suburbs, directly shaped by governmental policy and redlining, and populated by early punk rockers' parents, a trend which would repeat in the late

1970s and early 1980s but with different demographics.[17] Later, punk also had a significant impact on gentrification.

Most (although not all) of the first wave of New York and Boston punks, such as those in the early CBGB scene, grew up in the suburbs during the 1950s and 1960s.[18] At the time, the suburbs would include neighborhoods that are now considered diverse parts of New York City but which were almost entirely white through most of the 1940s and had only begun to be populated by people who had been excluded by language such as "non-Caucasians" (e.g., Jews, Irish, Asians, Latinos, Italians, and Greeks) in the postwar era, limited by restrictive covenants that were only ruled unconstitutional in 1948.[19] These neighborhoods include Forest Hills (home to the Ramones), Jackson Heights/Elmhurst (home to Sylvain Sylvain, Billy Murcia, and Johnny Thunders of the New York Dolls, and Andy Shernoff of the Dictators), Borough Park (home to the Fast), and the Gun Hill Road area of the Bronx (home to Handsome Dick Manitoba of the Dictators). Furthermore, many early punk rockers and their immediate predecessors spent some of their childhoods in Brooklyn, the Bronx, or Queens but then moved further from New York to Long Island and other suburbs, a typical pattern for white families during the 1950s. Maureen Tucker was born in Jackson Heights and raised in Levittown; Lou Reed was born in Brooklyn and moved to Freeport at age nine; Lenny Kaye lived in Washington Heights until high school, when the family moved to North Brunswick, New Jersey; and Tommy Ramone's family emigrated from Hungary to the South Bronx before they moved to Forest Hills.

The suburbs dominate the landscape of underground rock musician's childhoods. CBGB regulars and Ramones associates Dennis Anderson and Lois Kahlert, now living near Lou Reed's hometown of Freeport, Long Island, told me, "When I pass his house, I think, 'I understand Lou.'"[20] Deborah Harry grew up in "the cloying suburbia of Hawthorne" in New Jersey, "a typical suburban commuter kind of town."[21] Jonathan Richman and John Felice grew up in the 1950s and 1960s in Natick, Massachusetts: "Strictly middle class, tract housing . . . as suburban an environment as you can imagine. Fifteen miles west of Boston. Shopping malls and all that kind of shit."[22] Throughout early punk the suburbs remained crucial to the scene. Besides generating new punk rockers, more music happened outside of the city than is typically acknowledged, such as the many important shows at My Father's Place in Roslyn, Long Island, which also hosted several CBGB nights, and WLIR, the Long Island radio station that was the first to play punk records; as My Father's Place owner "Eppy" Epstein explained: "the reason CB's broke was because 'LIR was playing their records; there were no New York City stations of *any* kind. . . . It was a phenomen[on] of the Bowery but 'LIR took it on."[23] Whether or not early punk musicians rejected or embraced their suburban upbringing, their songs were understood to be "the expression of a suburban kid's *weltenschauung*."[24]

The downtown New York City punk scene did not emerge organically from urban New York's musical life, as boogaloo and hip-hop did.[25] Early punk consisted mainly of white suburbanites who first started exploring the city and then reversed the paths of their parents and moved back, taking advantage of cheap rents and the decay of the city's infrastructure. Legs McNeil explained, "New York was empty. It was a free-for-all and especially the Bowery . . . the ruins of the urban decay . . . all our parents had run from so that they could move to the suburbs and live these idyllic lives. We were all rushing back into the city to the urban nightmare and loving it."[27] Or as Andy Shernoff remembered with respect to the year 1973, "Meanwhile, New York was fraying at the edges. The middle class was evacuating the city for safer options in the suburbs. This meant cheap rents for artists and musicians who were willing to put up with the dirt, drugs and crime of a desolate downtown."[28]

These remembrances and portraits of 1970s New York contain thinly veiled racial language referring to a black ghetto ringed by white suburbs, and the downtown punk scene often seemed to replicate the segregated environments from which the musicians came. As Clem Burke of Blondie remembered, "There weren't many black folks around, and it was a very white middle class scene."[29] Lisa Jane Persky similarly told me, "honestly, no one [no people of color] came, Neon Leon was the only person . . . I honestly think that some of the people in the punk scene would've been super uncomfortable if there had been a black person there."[30] The narrative of CBGB as a blank slate—only "bums" on the Bowery—also undermines the active cultural life that was already happening in these neighborhoods in spite of economic collapse, such as the downtown underground and queer theater scene, straight-ahead jazz, the folk scene (Tom Verlaine occasionally played West Village hootenannys before forming the Neon Boys and Television), the poetry scene (frequented by Patti Smith), the performances of the Living Theatre and the Fugs, and the avant-garde jazz loft scene.[31] Rashied Ali played Hilly's on the Bowery (315 Bowery, before it became CBGB) at least twenty times in 1973.[32]

The suburbs were also linked to New York as a social and cultural home for LGBTQ people. For LGBTQ white people, being "outside of society" or "punk" (the term itself emerging from black queer culture) was not a choice but a fact of life in the suburbs, and antithetical to the suburban project of whiteness as a product of assimilation and conformity. Sexual orientation cannot be considered a matter of "identity" apart from discrimination, the law, and the state: sexual activity between two people of the same sex was a felony crime in all fifty states until 1962, and so-called "sodomy laws" persisted until *Lawrence v. Texas* in 2003. In migration terms, moving to downtown New York was both "pull" (the attraction of a strong openly LGBTQ community) and "push" (leaving the hostile environment of suburbs and small towns) for musicians such as the Fast (the Zone brothers).[33] As Lisa Jane Persky explained, "They wanted to be part of a scene . . . but also the hate drives you away [from the suburbs]."[34]

Punk grew directly out of the diverse queer culture in late 1960s and early 1970s Greenwich Village, and despite overtures to David Bowie's popularizing of "gender-bending" and Andy Warhol's relationship with the Velvet Underground and Max's Kansas City, the importance of this relationship has been diminished.[35] Drag ("cross-dressing," in the common parlance of the 1970s), for instance, is too often dismissed as a fad of the time, an aspect of 1970s "glam," represented by figures such as the New York Dolls, who became famous for dressing in drag but were stereotypical "cock rockers." Drag contrasted with their being "guy-guys . . . very confident in their heterosexuality": "I think they made [drag] even more okay by being privileged white guys who would put on dresses."[36] It is helpful to remember at this point how drag operated in the early minstrel show, as white men enacted stereotypes of black male and female sexuality in the formation of nineteenth-century American white masculinity.[37] As Eric Lott writes, "Unlike gay cross-dressers, they wear women's clothes as a fetish substitute for the (hetero)sexual object, never losing sight of the fact that they are male: on the contrary, they do it to preserve male potency."[38]

An objective look at New York punk in the early to mid-1970s indicates a scene heavily populated with queer musicians such as Jayne County (known as Wayne County before 1979) playing familiar rock and roll styles with explicit and double-entendre lyrics. Two blocks from CBGB at the Truck and Warehouse Theater, Divine and Lisa Jane Persky performed Tom Eyen's *Women Behind Bars* in 1976. New York punk overlapped with a queer view of the past: an embrace of the 1950s and early 1960s but with camp, humor, and irony.[39] Patti Smith's play with gender is well established, as is her relationship with Robert Mapplethorpe.[40] Deborah Harry "was heavily influenced by something much more queer: the trashy [*sic*] downtown drag queens she hung out with."[41] Camp was an essential aspect of Greenwich Village culture and the alternative New York aesthetic, especially with respect to underground theater: "it exploded those things [racism and sexism] to a ridiculous degree so that we were able to laugh at the things we were really uncomfortable about. . . . [We would] exaggerate every single thing about it, which would shed light on the ridiculous stereotypes."[42] The Ramones' leather-and-denim, classic-fifties rock and roll style can be seen in relation to the queer background of the scene and in the fashion mode of the New York gay underground.[43] The Ramones' image was developed by gay men (Danny Fields, their manager; Arturo Vega, who designed their logo) and women (the photographer Roberta Bayley). Blondie engaged what might be considered a queer aesthetic, such as Chris Stein's pink "Rhythm Kings" jacket on the back cover of their debut album.

The history of the suburbs also helps explain the relationship between punk and the ethnicity of many of its early participants, especially the high representation of Jews. As Jews, Joey Ramone, Tommy Ramone, Lou Reed, Jonathan Richman, Handsome Dick Manitoba, and many others were from a historically discriminated-against ethnic group that had just survived genocide, but whose status meanwhile was quickly changing in postwar America. Their parents moved as suburban housing was newly available to European Jews, helping facilitate assimilation into whiteness and its social privileges.[44]

Assimilation among Ashkenazic Jewish Americans during the postwar period was so rapid and intense that their prewar status among the world's most discriminated-against and poorest populations became largely overlooked, a phenomenon affecting even more recent historical analyses.[45] Yet antisemitism remained potent in the United States, and even escalated along with Jewish assimilation; such is the nature of antisemitic logic, which is partly based on Jews' perceived ability to "pass" as white people.[46] Jewish suburbanites in the 1950s and early 1960s were navigating this shifting landscape, in between whiteness and the marked otherness that externally defined Jewish ethnicity, racial status, and access to citizenship and freedoms for centuries.[47] As teenagers, some Jews who became early punk rockers resented the cookie-cutter, white suburban experiences envisioned by their parents, finding common ground as "misfits." Others embraced their suburban backgrounds, as in the case of Jonathan Richman, or maintained multiple, perhaps conflicting ideas about their suburban upbringings. But in all cases, their lives in the suburbs were determined by shifts in the intersections of Jewish ethnicity and whiteness, as well as significant changes in the racist policies that had governed the suburbs.

Finally, the music created by this mostly white scene of the early to mid-1970s captured the beginnings of a shift away from the pressures of wrestling with rock's relationship to black music and the blues, as well as away from avant-garde critiques of American society, and toward nostalgic reworkings of the music of suburban 1950s and early-1960s childhoods, an idealized innocence mediated by some early British Invasion bands, the romantic golden age of "girl groups" and doo-wop groups, and the fantasy of California beach and surf records. To engage this musical period, these groups explored a diverse repertoire that mirrored that of early rock and rollers, such as Elvis Presley ("That's Alright, Mama," "Blue Moon," "Hound Dog") and the early Beatles ("Twist and Shout," "Roll Over Beethoven," "Baby It's You"), who employed a wide assortment of rhythm and blues forms.

### Pure Rock and Roll Musical Style

Pure rock and roll music manipulated an assortment of styles that were originally designed to exploit associations of whiteness and blackness in a kind of idealized synthesis. Over the course of the 1960s and 1970s, these styles became increasingly heard as white, although some retained the associations of racial integration; however, as musical blackness became tied to particular treatments of blues resources, all of these other styles became "whiter." This was especially true in the world of early punk, as these sounds became increasingly opposed to the types of blues played by the raw power musicians. So although the musical sources of pure rock and roll combined white and black tropes, their treatment by punk groups in the mid-1970s were part of a larger remapping of the racial landscape, contributing to the "whitening" of the particular source material described in this chapter, and in turn, punk in general.

But what about this music explicitly sounded nostalgic; white, racially ambiguous, or not black; and like the 1950s and early 1960s? The reference points for these "pure rock and roll" bands have been variously categorized as bubblegum, girl group, surf rock, and just rock and roll; sometimes doo-wop, Tin Pan Alley, and Brill Building; and less frequently, rhythm and blues.[48] These terms are gendered; "bubblegum," for example, a term mentioned by Clem Burke and Joey Ramone as influences, evokes teenage girls and their buying habits and suggests music opposed to "cock rock," characterized by blues-based songs and guitar solos (early punk's embrace of "bubblegum" is another striking contrast to punk's later associations with young white heterosexual men).[49] "Bubblegum" was generally used pejoratively and dismissively, "throwaway" hits as opposed to artistic, serious, heavy, virtuosic rock. Jimmy Page, for instance, did not play "bubblegum" because he was a "musician," deriding the "teeneys" who came out to see Cream at Madison Square Garden. "They hadn't really come to listen to the Cream's music had they?"[50]

These terms referring to pure rock and roll's source material at the same time suggested music that was white—"country"—and not "black," which was primarily mapped onto "blues."[51] In Johnny Ramone's words:

> The songs were just pure rock and roll. I never liked blues music, and I really didn't like jazz. I liked Chuck Berry as far as that went, but he was rock and roll, not blues. I liked rock and roll music the way the Stones played it. They made it more interesting. They made it in a way I could relate to, which was what our music was intended to be like. The early rock and roll came from more of a country influence anyway, not a black influence. The Everly Brothers, Eddie Cochran, and Buddy Holly were all more country influenced.[52]

"Girl groups" were especially germane to the pure rock and roll sound. Clem Burke "had already liked girl group stuff, Shangri-Las, Ronettes."[53] The "girl groups" in many ways best represent the complex web of associations involved in pure rock and roll. The style of female harmonizers singing rhythm and blues was synonymous with African American women through the 1950s; however, although the "girl group" references by punks in the 1970s vaguely reached back to those early associations, they more strongly invoked the white groups that followed, such as the Shangri-Las, during the period between 1960 and 1964 when both white and black groups were having commercial successes.[54] Futhermore, when played by all-male groups such as the Ramones (as opposed to Blondie), the "girl" associations—white or black—became obscured even more.

The term "doo-wop" is closely related to the sound of the girl groups, also characterized by group harmonizing and originally dominated by African Americans, and then later by both black and white groups. Many of the doo-wop songs informing pure rock and roll music were written by Brill Building writers, such as Jerry Leiber and Mike Stoller, who wrote hits for the Coasters.[55] The Brill Building (1619 Broadway) and nearby hit-making offices around Times Square in New York are well known for the strong Jewish and female presence in its formidable stable of young songwriters, which included Leiber, Stoller, Carole King, Gerry Goffin, Jeff Barry, Ellie Greenwich, Burt Bacharach, and Hal David (and Lou Reed, briefly).[56] The Brill Building sound is often compared or conflated with Tin Pan Alley, the offices for popular music songwriters and publishers along New York's 28th Street in the early twentieth century, most of which relocated to the Brill Building area after 1919. "Girl groups," "doo-wop," "Brill Building," and "Tin Pan Alley" share a commercial purpose, but there are complicated racial dynamics and stylistic differences within this large repertoire that are masked by lumping them together.

At the time of its release, all of this music was generally called "rock and roll" or "rhythm and blues," increasingly falling along racial lines over the course of the 1960s: "rock and roll" among white audiences or when associated with white performers, and "rhythm and blues" among black audiences or black performers.[57] Johnny Ramone referred to this wide repertoire as "rock and roll," rarely qualifying it except to distinguish it from "blues." And for musicians in the 1970s, this music all referred back to the late 1950s and early 1960s. For Richard Nolan of Boston's Third Rail, his music was "city music, very primitive East Coast rock and roll developed from styles set in New York City in the early '60s."[58] Jonathan Richman's favorite songs centered on "old rock and roll" from 1962, when he was in sixth grade.[59] Lenny Kaye's first music was doo-wop.[60] Deborah Harry said, "The first rock stuff I got into was Frankie Lymon doo-wop during the fifties," and she referred to the Shangri-Las as "aggressive rock": "I wanted [the Stilettos to be] a combination of the aggressive Shangri-Las rock and the round, solid vocals of an R&B girl group, and the overall idea was to be both entertaining and danceable."[61] (Harry is also one of the only artists to explicitly use the term "R&B" with respect to her inspirations, reflecting her longstanding interest in black music.) The treatments of this music by punk bands drew out the energy of those songs, as Stew remembered: "I never understood the fifties until punk happened. Lennon and Dylan went crazy telling you how great all these guys were, how this music fired them up. Chuck Berry, Bo Diddley, I just heard it immediately."[62] Similarly, Dennis Anderson commented about recently listening to a "compilation of Sun Records stuff, rockabilly from the late fifties, and I swore I was listening to a Cramps record. It was exactly that feel."[63]

The music most relevant to the pure rock and roll style originally captured an ambiguous racial quality and reflected the shifting circumstances for vast numbers of white Americans in the 1950s and early 1960s. Much of the specific music referenced by those in the pure rock and roll mode was already a product of white performers working with black styles, or who combined white and black elements in exciting ways, such as Buddy Holly, Eddie Cochran, and Gene Vincent. Many of these earlier white performers and composers came from social backgrounds that drew them into close contact and business arrangements with African American musicians, such as Italian and Jewish immigrants, and working-class southerners. Especially during the 1950s, New York and Los Angeles became key centers for the creation of ethnically multivalent R&B and rock and roll, the product of collaborations between African Americans, moving to these cities in large numbers in a new phase of the Great Migration, and Jews, Italians, Latinos, and poor white southerners who were also living in these cities and increasing in numbers due to other migrations. The music industry, long extant in New York and emerging in Los Angeles, shaped these exchanges in particular ways. Collaborations such as Leiber and Stoller's work with Willie Mae "Big Mama" Thornton and the Coasters on Ahmet Ertegun's Atlantic label are emblematic of this music.[64] Although such relationships continued through the 1960s and 1970s, the rapid white flight and movement of Jews, Italians, and the earlier German and Irish population out of the cities also created an aura of nostalgia among those groups for this music.

For white people who grew up in the newly populated and expanded suburbs of the 1950s and early 1960s, the rock and roll or R&B of the period harked back to a time of less racial division than the turbulent mid- to late 1960s. White youth in the suburbs primarily heard this music through AM radio—such as in New York, the shows of the "Good Guys" on WMCA, Bruce "Cousin Brucie" Morrow on WABC, Murray "the K" Kaufman on WINS—later romanticized in the 1970s as stations switched to FM frequencies and AOR (album-oriented radio) formats.[65] "[In 1957] I was listening to Ricky Nelson, the Everly Brothers, and was a big Jerry Lee Lewis fan. And Little Richard . . . it was easy to be a kid back then. All this good music was played on the radio, not like now," wrote Johnny Ramone.[66] Deborah Harry remembered, "1959–1965 was a great time to be a rock 'n' roll teenager. . . . Radio was at its peak."[67] Multi-act shows at the Brooklyn Paramount Theater and the Fox Theater also featured racially diverse lineups.[68]

In many ways, the diverse AM radio repertoire of the baby boomers' youth did represent a certain ideal or at least momentum toward exchange. However, this sentiment, like the romanticization of the deep South in the early twentieth century, was mostly a white phenomenon. Collaborations such as Leiber and Stoller's songs for the Coasters were idealized and simplified by white people who heard this music when they were young, rather than understood as products of intense, complicated, and unequal racial dynamics.[69] "California Sun," for example, was not "written by music industry professionals Henry Glover and Morris Levy," but rather written by the prolific African American songwriter Glover, with the mob-connected Levy adding himself as a songwriter to generate publishing revenue.[70] The "surf rock" coming out of California during the 1960s was similarly correlated to the white suburban utopias created in the postwar era, but again obscuring the racial discrimination that led to both the suburbs and the music.

In contrast, my interviews with African Americans reflected fond memories of that AM radio period but with a lack of romanticization. For example, Stew remembered the tail end of the AM radio era as "pretty ideal," but added, "let me be clear, those people had an *idea* of what the fifties were; to black people, we just thought that's when everybody was catching hell."[71] Similarly, not all white people naïvely remember the past, even if they favorably remember the music of those days, especially as the shift to television brought visual racial factors into a larger role. When Dennis Anderson worked in the 1960s for *The Clay Cole Show*, a New York television program featuring live performances, the show was put on notice for booking too many black acts. Cole and his team were dumbfounded, as "we were a *rock and roll* show," which at that time would have still implied African American practitioners; nevertheless, the station starting demanding photos in order to assess how black the musicians looked and whether or not they could be featured on the show.[72]

The R&B or doo-wop that informed pure rock and roll music was heard in the 1970s in opposition to the blues, mapped as black, but in fact this "non-blues" music had followed a trajectory of racial appropriation similar to that of blues-based rock and roll in the 1950s and 1960s.[73] Using terms such as "Brill Building" generically also obscures black producers, writers, and performers such as the Marvelettes and the Supremes, who were making similar music as part of the Motown hit factory, but classified as rhythm and blues or soul.[74] With respect to doo-wop, "before 1958, more than ninety percent of the participants in the doo-wop movement were African-American. In 1958, that changed, as white groups entered the arena in large numbers."[75] Through the 1950s, the commercial strategy was for white producers and songwriters to work with black performers, but most of the doo-wop marketed to white suburbanites in the late 1950s and early 1960s—meaning the many baby boomers who were teenagers between

1958 and 1965—were white artists such as Randy and the Rainbows, who were a product of New York's song factory. The most prominent example is perhaps the Shangri-Las, a group of white teenage girls from Cambria Heights, Queens, produced by Shadow Morton, a young songwriter who grew up in the suburb of Hicksville, Long Island. White suburban youth such as Deborah Harry saw themselves in the Shangri-Las "tough girls" who lived a similar life to theirs.[76] (On the other hand, about girl groups Judy Nylon said, "They were supposed to be singin' to people like me and I didn't give a *shit* if my fucking boyfriend was back or what!"[77])

The romanticization of this music, embraced by 1970s punks, was part of a general trend among white Americans in response to social upheaval, a trend that had already begun during baby boomers' childhoods. Songs in these styles had been nostalgically repackaged as music of a simpler time as early as the late 1950s, beginning with Art Leboe's *Oldies But Goodies* compilation series. The popular first volume (*Oldies But Goodies in Hi-Fi*, 1959) recast songs such as "In the Still of the Night" (1956), "Let the Good Times Roll" (1956), and "Tonite Tonite" (1957) as "oldies" only two or three years after their release.[78] From a 1970s perspective, this music skipped over the racial uprisings of the 1960s (Watts, Newark, Detroit, DC), and the assassinations of John F. Kennedy, Robert Kennedy, and Martin Luther King Jr., and for white people, often naïvely signaled a time of racial harmony. Johnny Ramone remembered, for instance, "Westbury [Long Island] was half black when we lived there, but it was a different country then, where everybody got along—you know, the 1950s." It is hard to imagine then or now an African American person describing the 1950s, an era with segregated schools, the Little Rock Nine crisis, and the Montgomery Bus Boycott, as a time when "everybody got along." And in fact, Westbury was hardly "half black" in the 1950s—it was nearly all white through the 1950s and even the 1960s, with almost the entire African American population confined to buying homes in the historically black community of New Cassel.[79] White America's nostalgic fascination with the 1950s and early 1960s became fully mainstream in the 1970s, with Gus Gossert's broadcasting of early rock and roll and doo-wop "oldies" on FM radio stations, beginning in 1969 on New York's powerful WCBS-FM, and culminating in mainstream (and extremely white) 1970s products such as *American Graffiti* (1973), *Happy Days* (1974–84), and *Grease* (1978, which played on double bills with the Ramones' B-movie feature *Rock 'n' Roll High School* in 1979).[80]

A major distinguishing stylistic issue surrounding the pure rock and roll groups of the early 1970s is the use of specific rhythmic-harmonic cycles heard in opposition to blues forms, including both twelve-bar and riff-based blues. As I discuss in chapter 2, the twelve-bar blues is rock and roll's musical base against which punk rock and all other rock innovations and transformations can be compared and contrasted. The twelve-bar blues was the most consistent resource for rock musicians, and its ubiquity thus signaled a middle-of-the-road approach; for groups that mostly played riff-based songs, the twelve-bar blues also took on throwback characteristics, as in Led Zeppelin's "Rock and Roll" (1971). These rhythm and blues or rock and roll songs remained standard repertoire for a huge range of rock bands through the 1960s and 1970s, and even those I discussed as raw power bands often played these songs. The MC5, for example, covered "Back in the U.S.A." (Chuck Berry, 1959) and "Tutti Frutti" (Little Richard, 1955) in 1970, and "Ramblin' Rose" (Jerry Lee Lewis, 1962), which draws heavily on twelve-bar blues conventions, was their concert opener.

In the case of the Stooges, MC5, and other raw power groups discussed in chapter 2, musicians moved away from the twelve-bar form in favor of riff-based blues models that tapped into, and amplified, stereotyped notions of black masculinity. These groups were directly in conversation with the contemporaneous riff-based innovations of black musicians exploring the concept of soul, funk, and other newly framed conceptions of musical blackness. James Brown was the key stylistic trailblazer, but rock musicians' fetishization of Robert Johnson and other Delta bluesmen also played a major role in these stylistic shifts. But just as the Stooges and the MC5 moved away from twelve-bar schemes in favor of one- and two-chord riff-based blues, groups such as the New York Dolls, Modern Lovers, Ramones, and Blondie audibly moved in the other direction, away from both the riff-based and twelve-bar blues models. Sometimes, as in the case of the Modern Lovers, this was a very audible transition. Instead of riffs and little or no harmonic movement, these musicians drew on longer sixteen- and twenty-four-bar forms and common-stock schemes that were especially used to support melodies in major tonalities and equally divided binary question-and-answer phrases. Emphasizing these models and then reworking them in transformative ways, the Ramones in particular brought together multiple stylistic currents and laid the blueprint for a fully formed punk style.

By the early 1970s, interpretations of rock's relationships to the blues and common-stock musical schemes constituted a conversation dominated by white people with respect to American identity, blackness and whiteness, and class distinctions. Ignoring, bypassing, or rejecting integrative efforts of the 1960s, these white rock musicians in the 1970s rarely collaborated with African American blues musicians and seldom discussed black music or the blues as intimately connected to rock in the ways the MC5, the Stooges, or the Rolling Stones did in the previous decade. As a result, the point of reference for early punk bands in the 1970s was other white rock musicians and bands. Clem Burke did not know too many people "who really liked The Shangri-Las or The Velvet Underground. They were all in their bedrooms trying to be the next Jimmy Page."[81] When in 1979 Johnny Ramone emphasized that the Ramones played

| 1 | 2 | 3 | 4 | 5 | 6 | 7 | 8 | | 9 | 10 | 11 | 12 | 13 | 14 | 15 | 16 |
|---|---|---|---|---|---|---|---|---|---|----|----|----|----|----|----|----|
| I | – | IV | – | I | – | V | – | | I | – | IV | – | I | V | I | – |

or

| 1 | | 2 | | 3 | | 4 | | 5 | | 6 | | 7 | | 8 |
|---|---|---|---|---|---|---|---|---|---|---|---|---|---|---|
| I | | IV | | I | | V | | I | | IV | | I V | | I |

Musical example 4.1. The passamezzo moderno harmonic pattern.

pure rock and roll with no blues or folk, he was referring to other white rock bands; "no blues" meant "no white bands playing blues," just as "no folk" meant "no middle-class white people imitating poor white folks from Appalachia." Legs McNeil said punks rejected "blues" and "the black experience," but primarily rejected white fascination with black culture: "in the sixties hippies always wanted to be black."[82] John Holmstrom echoed his partner McNeil's words in even more problematic language: ". . . we weren't racists. But we were unashamedly saying, 'We're white, and we're proud.' Like they're black and they're proud. That's fine."[83] The Boston bands that "hail from middle-class suburbs like Arlington, Watertown, and Auburndale [do] not musically genuflect to the black tradition and, therefore, one hears no tedious, if proficient, writhing guitar solos on a twelve-bar blues, no horn sections or irksome exhortations to 'put yo hands together an' git funky'"—a criticism of white "genuflectors," not black bands.[84] In this sense, punk helped establish a new kind of hipster who not only defined him or herself in contrast to bourgeois whites, but also in contrast to white bohemians in the familiar "white Negro" mode.

For most of these groups, "pure rock and roll" still partially meant using the familiar twelve-bar blues form and other tightly arranged forms heard in rhythm and blues and early rock and roll. But the major difference between these groups and their rock and roll contemporaries in the 1970s was the use of major melodies, binary equal-length question-and-answer phrases, regular and frequent harmonic movement, and short closed-form cycles. In pure rock and roll models, the most remarkable manifestation of these elements appeared in the use of harmonic cycles and forms closely related to the eight-bar scheme (supporting one couplet) or sixteen-bar scheme (supporting two couplets) that scholars have connected to the sixteenth-century passamezzo moderno (musical example 4.1).[85] The passamezzo moderno pattern was enormously productive in British music as the basis for a huge number of tunes in what John M. Ward identified as the "*Buffons* family of tune families" (such as "John Come Kiss Me Now," "O'er the Hills and Far Away," and "Shepherd's Hey") and continued to be useful in the United States as part of the common stock shared by white and black musicians.[86]

The music historian Otto Gombosi first recognized this scheme, which he inexactly referred to as Gregory Walker, in many of Stephen Foster's minstrel songs such as "My Old Kentucky Home" and "Old Folks at Home," compositions which already produced complex mixtures of European American and African American associations, stereotypes, and fantasies.[87] The passamezzo moderno pattern and its many variations became essential to country, gospel music, and American popular song in the early twentieth century, as one of many I–IV–V schemes, including blues cycles, collectively called the common stock by later scholars since they were used by both black and white vernacular musicians especially before World War II.[88] The pattern (which did not acquire a common name among American popular musicians) is the basis for many common stock melodies recorded during the first half of the twentieth century, including "Wreck of the Old 97" and "Bury Me Under the Weeping Willow," as well as songs named as blues, such as "Titanic Blues" and "Fare Thee Blues," and gospel melodies, such as "Saviour Don't Pass Me By."[89] Some songs using the scheme, such as "Bile Them Cabbage Down," are associated with both white and black populations.[90] The passamezzo moderno pattern was especially used for supporting major melodies, using I, IV, and V chords in different ways from the twelve-bar blues; the I–IV–I–V sequence, for example, often supported major mi-fa-mi-re melodies. The early American applications of the common stock cycles employing I, IV, and V chords should be broadly understood as "useful resources for the thousands of musicians who have sought to reconcile or coordinate European and African techniques and values," an apt description of quintessential American popular musicians germane to this discussion, such as Chuck Berry and Buddy Holly.[91]

Black and white musicians originally used a wide variety of common stock schemes to create compositions supporting multiple lyrical forms and dances, and which were not especially racialized. Even after record companies began effectively selling in black (race) and white (hillbilly or old-time) catalogs after the 1920s, common stock schemes such as the passamezzo moderno remained useful to both black and white musicians.[92] Blues musicians broadly speaking— including "rock and roll" or "rhythm and blues" musicians—continued to use the passamezzo moderno and its variations during the 1950s and 1960s. Even the full scheme could be used for the blues in the 1950s and early 1960s, as in Bo Diddley's "Pills" (1961), covered by the New York Dolls (1973), as shown in musical example 4.2.

But after the 1960s, musicians used common stock schemes for their racial and historical associations as much as for their compositional utility. For white musicians during the 1970s, passamezzo moderno patterns had lost most of their associations with black music and had become a sort of white "country" opposite to the blues.[93] (When the New York Dolls played "Pills," they made it a

Musical example 4.2. "Pills," Bo Diddley, 1961. Transcription by the author.

little closer to the blues by ending the cycle with a turnaround on V rather than the I–V–I ending as played by Bo Diddley.) The use of this pattern in its many variations is an important part of what Johnny Ramone was referring to when he said, "early rock and roll came from more of a country influence."[94]

For one prominent example, connoisseurs of American music the Rolling Stones used the scheme in its unaltered form in one of their takes on country music, "Honky Tonk Women" (released as a single in 1969). In case the average listener wasn't able to make the connection, the Rolling Stones made the racial associations as obvious as possible on *Let it Bleed* (1969) with the "Country Honk" version, featuring Mick Jagger doing his best hillbilly impression and Byron Berline playing fiddle—a historically shared instrument once strongly associated with black people but which had become almost entirely associated with white people by the end of the 1960s. The Rolling Stones meant to emphasize the country and white associations of "Country Honk" on the album, contrasting it with songs exploiting blues riffs and one-chord vamps, such as "Midnight Rambler" and "Gimme Shelter." Popular music composers pick schemes through imitating other songs and adjusting them, often without being named as such by musicians. Keith Richards and Mick Jagger wrote "Country Honk" while "kicking around old country songs" while traveling in Brazil in 1968, "and saying, 'this sounds like Jimmie Rodgers or Hank Williams' . . . it's a damn old good country song, and a damn good country song quite often is a damn good rock and roll song."[95]

The changing race and class associations of the schemes based on the passamezzo moderno are easily identified by comparing the outlier quality of "Country Honk" on *Let It Bleed* to the scheme's use in the Beatles' 1963 hit "I Saw Her Standing There," where it stands unremarkably alongside the many other schemes the Beatles used at that time.[96] Bo Diddley himself avoided it, as well as other common-stock schemes, once his one- and two-chord riff-based blues ("I'm a Man") and his recycling of the vernacular hambone rhythm ("Bo Diddley") became widely known among a younger white audience. The country and rural white associations of the scheme continued and intensified past the 1970s, as evidenced by Bruce Springsteen's evocative uses of the pattern on *Nebraska* ("My Father's House," "Reason to Believe," 1982), Violent Femmes' "Jesus Walking on the Water" (1984), or, in 2018, Anderson East's country cover of Bob Dylan's "Forever Young" underpinning a truck commercial.[97]

This backdrop should underscore the significance of the resurgence of passamezzo moderno schemes among early punk rock groups. By the early 1970s, it was relatively rare for rock musicians to use this pattern due to its loss of cultural currency and forgotten ties to the blues. The New York Dolls' choice to cover "Pills" in particular on their debut album in 1973 should be seen in this context of a rock scene dominated by white musicians playing covers or recycled versions of particular sorts of American blues, usually via British Invasion bands. Rock musicians regularly covered Bo Diddley through the 1960s, but invariably chose his one- or two-chord songs such as "I'm a Man" (Yardbirds), "Mona" (Rolling Stones, Troggs, also the Iguanas with Iggy Pop on drums), and "Bo Diddley" (Shadows, Animals). By comparison, "Pills" was an obscure Bo Diddley track of a completely different tenor.[98] Bo Diddley's name could mislead listeners, as for example when Robert Christgau criticized Arthur Kane's playing on the track, writing "If he doesn't sink a blues line under Johnny's force field on (Bo Diddley's) 'Pills' on the first album, it's only because he doesn't know one that fits; by the time of (Sonny Boy Williamson's) 'Don't Start Me Talkin'' on the second he is double-timing an utterly conventional Willie Dixon part as Johnny sows discord all around him."[99] In fact, Kane's bass lines must be different because the two songs are completely different types of compositions, despite both being originally recorded by "bluesmen." Kane's playing on "Pills" fits the passamezzo moderno pattern of the original, fundamentally different from the twelve-bar blues "Don't Start Me Talkin.'"

As noted, the proper passamezzo moderno scheme as heard in "Pills" is unusual in punk rock of the early to mid-1970s, but versions are heard throughout early punk, including traditional or straightforward iterations in songs such as the Electric Eels' "Jaguar Ride," remembered by John D. Morton this way: "Brian [McMahon] brought his chunky rock guitar style and R&B writing styles such as the very traditional 'Jaguar Ride.'"[100] More broadly, certain elements found in the passamezzo moderno pattern took on a remarkable salience for punk groups, especially as ultimately transformed by the Ramones and then adopted by a wide variety of punk groups in the late 1970s and early 1980s. These elements could also be found in many other common-stock schemes, especially those that became linked to country and early rock and roll music, and they help define the pure rock and roll model:

- melodies in a major mode, often with stepwise movement,
- eight- and sixteen-bar sections divided into binary phrases of equal lengths,
- a question-and-answer quality between phrases, usually indicated at least with a first ending on a half-cadence (the V, or dominant chord) and a second ending on the full cadence (V–I), and increased harmonic rhythm in the answer phrase, and
- harmonic rhythm of frequent and regularly spaced chord movement, e.g., chord changes on every measure, every other measure, or twice in a measure.

These elements are opposed to those I described as the raw power style: major melodies instead of minor melodies or blues scaffolding, binary phrases instead of open-ended riffs, and frequent chord changes instead of minimal harmonic movement. Eight-bar and sixteen-bar blues schemes supporting major melodies, also found throughout the common stock, also conform to these guidelines, as will be discussed below in this chapter.

Pure rock and roll music often contained at least one contrasting-strain phrase used in various ways (contrasting strains also appeared in common-stock songs generated by the passamezzo moderno).[101] The most common element in the contrasting strain was the appearance of IV in the first position and each chord lasting double the length of the harmonic rhythm in the primary strain. One very typical contrasting strain is IV–I–IV–V (two measures per chord), which can be considered a rotation of the first half of the passamezzo moderno cycle, beginning on IV (IV–I–V) and adding a IV between I and V. In pure rock and roll songs, contrasting strains were usually couched as B phrases within short forms, such as the extremely popular twenty-four-bar AAB form, which ambiguously sat between the shorter blues and common-stock cycles and the longer American popular songbook or Tin Pan Alley thirty-two-bar forms. Songs such as the Ramones' "Blitzkrieg Bop" and Jonathan Richman's "Government Center" are good examples of these major and binary-phrase pure rock and roll compositions with a contrasting strain. As shown in musical example 4.3, Blondie's 1977 cover of Randy and the Rainbows' doo-wop hit "Denise" (1963) (as "Denis," seemingly to keep the conventional gender roles straight) illustrates several of these elements as they appeared in pure rock and roll songs. The introduction is a short cycle repetition of the first half of the passamezzo moderno scheme: I–IV–I–V. The verse consists of two major binary phrases, one ending on a half cadence (V) and the second on a full cadence (I), and the contrasting B phrase or bridge starts on IV, slows the harmonic movement, and ends on V.

Shorter and medium-length cycles such as those heard in "Denis" and "Blitzkrieg Bop" are crucial to understanding pure rock and roll's racial associations

| | 1 | 2 | 3 | 4 | 5 | 6 | 7 | 8 | 9 | 10 | 11 | 12 | 13 | 14 | 15 | 16 |
|---|---|---|---|---|---|---|---|---|---|---|---|---|---|---|---|---|
| Intro: | I | IV | I | V | I | IV | I | V | (first half of passamezzo moderno) | | | | | | | |
| A phrases: | I | | IV | V | I | | IV | V | I | | IV | V | I | IV | I | V |
| | I | | IV | V | I | | IV | V | I | | IV | V | I | IV | I | |
| B phrase: | IV | | | | I | | | | IV | | | | II | | V | |

Musical example 4.3a. "Denis" chords, Blondie, *Plastic Letters*, 1977.

and the style's connections to early rock and roll, especially as compared to longer American songbook forms such as a full thirty-two-bar AABA. The full thirty-two-bar AABA form connected to early Tin Pan Alley is more conditional in rock music than is generally taken for granted, and it declined heavily over the course of the 1960s.[102] For the purposes of this book, one AABA form that takes the entire three- or four-minute duration of a song (as in the Coasters' "Charlie Brown") is not the same as an AABA song in the Tin Pan Alley mode, in which the pattern audibly repeats at least once in a manner that feels cyclical.[103] A persistent issue is that these songs are often analyzed as unvarying compositions, or as if musicians primarily perceive "length in bars and harmonic progression . . . as characteristic and defining," when popular musicians are more likely to treat songs and harmonic schemes as resources to be modified and put to multiple uses; and furthermore, the "musical components that performers regard as fixed and stable vary from scheme to scheme."[104] Condensing the longer AABA forms typical of American songbook Tin Pan Alley songs was a key factor in early rock and roll; although doo-wop and rock and roll standards did often use a true AABA ("Earth Angel," "Everyday"), rhythm and blues and rock and roll musicians frequently extracted A and B sections and used them as short cycles of their own. For example, Elvis Presley's version of the thirty-two-bar AABA standard "Blue Moon" (1956, Rodgers and Hart, 1934) consists solely of repetitions of the eight-bar A section. The Marcels' well-known version of "Blue Moon" (1961) follows an AABABA pattern, but most audibly exploits fast short repetitions of the opening I-vi-IV-V cycle—the archetypal doo-wop "Ice Cream Changes"—which constitute the first two bars of the A section (and in a customary substitution, IV-V replaces the ii-V of the original composition).[105] Popular musicians typically find the most exciting and accessible aspects of a composition and repeat them, and American musicians have long treated chord sequences as "over-and-over strains that seem to have no very clear beginning and certainly no ending at all," in the words of W. C. Handy.[106] Compare the breakbeat in hip hop, which is a short cycle taken from a longer form and turned into the basis of a new composition, and which in performance can be further manipulated by DJs into even shorter cycles (in contrast, early British punk musicians tended to use longer forms, as explored in chapter 5).

In the 1960s rock and roll compositions often did not return to the A form after a contrasting section to form a full thirty-two bars. Instead, the end of the bridge, chorus, or refrain indicated a return to the beginning of the cycle, as with the Ronettes' "Be My Baby" (1963), in which the "Be My Baby" chorus is followed by a return to the A-section melody ("I'll make you happy baby, just wait and see"), which functions as the beginning of a new twenty-four-bar cycle, and not the end of the previous one to complete a thirty-two-bar form. Interludes amid repetitions of those cycles operate differently from B sections in a thirty-two-bar AABA form, as they typically occur only once. In my experience, these habits have come into play when musicians trained to improvise in the jazz tradition over thirty-two-bar AABA cycle American songbook standards play with musicians more familiar with twenty-four-bar rock cycles that return to the beginning of the cycle after a contrasting section; often the rock-oriented musicians "drop" the last A section as if it were an AAB pattern.

The shorter, medium-length forms (i.e., not the long thirty-two-bar forms, but not the riff-based songs, either) lay at the evocative space of racially ambiguous or integrated 1950s and early 1960s rock and roll. Pure rock and roll groups exploited these forms and continued the trend of shortening longer multipart songs. Blondie's "Denis" is also a strong example of this development: the original "Denise" follows the bridge with a return to the opening chorus, akin to a thirty-two-bar AABC pattern, while Blondie skips the return to the chorus and instead goes right back to the verse, akin to a twenty-four-bar song.

| "Denise" (Randy and the Rainbows) | "Denis" (Blondie) |
|---|---|
| intro | intro |
| chorus | chorus |
| | |
| verse | verse |
| verse | verse |
| **bridge** | **bridge** |
| **chorus** | |
| | |
| **verse** | **verse** |
| chorus | chorus |
| outro | outro |

Musical example 4.3b. "Denis" form, Blondie, *Plastic Letters*, 1977.

The ending also shows the trend of extending short-cycle "over and over" vamps. The original "Denise" hints at a vamp, with the I–vi–IV–V from the chorus turned into a short cycle with a fadeout. Blondie changed this section by emphasizing the ending vamp with a short breakdown and using a simpler

I–I–IV–V pattern. Blondie would exploit this vamp in live performances, although such vamps were generally confined to a short span of time, especially when compared to the long and ecstatic explorations heard in riff-based vamps in the raw power style.[107]

The racially ambiguous qualities of the AAB cycle in pure rock and roll is especially important in songs that combined major melody and binary phrases with the three-part blues form, a typical feature of the common stock. These songs evoke elements of the twelve-bar blues structures but do so within eight-, sixteen-, and twenty-four-bar forms, and they almost always support major melodies rather than minor pentatonic ones.[108] Chris Montez's "Let's Dance" (1962), covered by the Ramones in 1976, is an excellent example of this type of composition, often associated with California and surf or beach music of the early 1960s. The main quality of the eight-bar cycle is the alternation of equal-length phrases, the first four bars or question phrase ("Hey baby won't you take a chance? Say that you'll let me have this dance / Well Let's Dance, well Let's Dance") and the concluding four bars or answer phrase ("We'll do the twist, the stomp, the mashed potato too / Any old thing that you want to do / But Let's Dance, well Let's Dance"). At the same time, as shown in musical example 4.4, "Let's Dance" contains elements of a I–IV–V / AAB three-part blues form. "California Sun," made famous by the Rivieras in 1964 and covered by the Dictators in 1975 and the Ramones in 1977, is a similar song, following a three-part I–IV–V / AAB structure, but with major melodies, an ending on an authentic cadence with more rapid harmonic rhythm, and in this case, a twenty-bar form (8+8+4). "California Sun" and "Let's Dance" also follow a model heard in many compositions favored by early pure rock and roll punk rock groups, in which these major-melody, binary phrase songs begin with a stop-time or no-chord section for the first A, continue with another A in a dance mode (around the I chord or IV chord), and then end with a cadential B turnaround. Other songs of the late 1950s and early 1960s with a similar approach to "California Sun" and "Let's Dance" are those songs that use contrasting sections (usually beginning on the IV chord) to complement twelve-bar blues forms supporting major-mode melodies, such as Buddy Holly's "Rave On" (1958), covered by the Real Kids (1977).[109]

Early punk rock adoptions of these songs, whether covers or new compositions in the style, employed additional conventions of 1950s and 1960s doo-wop, rhythm and blues, and rock and roll to signal the time period. Bands used background vocals in call-and-response format (e.g., "ah-ha," "oh yeah" in "Back in the U.S.A.") and doo-wop style vocables (e.g., "do-be-do" in "Denis"). Subject matter followed the precedent of 1950s and 1960s rock and roll and doo-wop hits: teenage love ("Denis," "Looking for a Kiss," "Goin' Steady"), cars ("[I Live for] Cars and Girls"), monsters ("Frankenstein," "The Attack of the Giant Ants"),

| | 1 | 2 | 3 | 4 | 5 | 6 | 7 | 8 |
|---|---|---|---|---|---|---|---|---|
| blues comparison (form): | A | | A | | B | | | |
| chords: | (I) | | IV | I | V | IV | V | IV | I |

Musical example 4.4. "Let's Dance" chords, Chris Montez, 1962.

dancing ("Let's Dance"), going to the beach ("California Sun"), debauched use of free time ("Weekend," "Babylon"), and the jungle ("Stranded in the Jungle").[110] Early punk rockers sometimes portrayed these 1950s utopias with irony and sarcasm in relation to their lived experiences, but they still retained fantasies about the images, such as Andy Shernoff's description of "Brian [Wilson's depiction of] Southern California as a teenage paradise of cars, girls, surfing, and beer."[111] This repertoire of 1950s and early 1960s surf music, R&B, and rock and roll continued to have exponents in punk. Lux Interior and Poison Ivy of the Cramps, who started playing CBGB in 1976, emerged as two of the most dedicated advocates and students of this style.

"Rave On," "Let's Dance," "Surfin' Bird," "California Sun," and other songs of the late 1950s and early 1960s covered by the Ramones and their contemporaries are effective because of the many ways they combined white and black musical signifiers. These songs are designed to be heard in different ways, following the songs of Chuck Berry, Buddy Holly, and the countless other American musicians "who have sought to reconcile or coordinate European and African techniques and values."[112] But by the 1970s, and especially with pure rock and roll punk, these songs became imbued with a nostalgic overtone of white suburban baby boomer youth. They conjured the idea of a simpler time in which black and white music came together in productive ways; however, in the context of the 1970s, following the upheaval of the 1960s and the changes in expressions of musical blackness during that decade, the emphasis on rock and roll of the 1950s and early 1960s served to "whiten" the source material. And in the early 1970s, even though they were sometimes less than ten years old, these songs sounded like the distant past when compared to the music of the late 1960s, especially the music that drew heavily on riff-based blues models.

### Perspectives on the Past and Changing Repertoires: The Modern Lovers at Town Hall

Jonathan Richman is an iconic figure, sometimes characterized as an inventor of punk rock, and known today for his commitment to the musical style of the early 1960s and the world of his suburban Massachusetts upbringing.[113] His journey also sheds a light on the changing styles and shifting sensibilities of white baby boomer musicians on the New York and Boston scenes in the 1970s,

Figure 4.1a. Flamin' Groovies, *Teenage Head*, 1971. Courtesy of Sony Music Entertainment.

and the ways in which these shifts reflected changes in American society. When he performed with his band the Modern Lovers at New York's Town Hall on October 9, 1976, their music seemed out of time, out of place, and incongruous with *The Modern Lovers* album then recently released on Beserkley. The music on that album was heavily inspired by the Velvet Underground, as discussed in chapter 2. Songs like "Roadrunner," "Pablo Picasso," and "Astral Plane" exploited chugging one-chord harmonies or two-chord oscillations as springboards for meditations on loneliness and love. Recorded in 1972 as demos, *The Modern Lovers* was released in 1976 by Beserkley and is now considered one of the most important "protopunk" documents.[114]

In the years since those 1972 recordings, Richman had switched the Modern Lovers' style to a quieter, 1950s and early-1960s style of rock and roll. But by 1973 the Modern Lovers already had at least one song firmly in this pure rock and roll style: "Government Center." Beserkley released four tracks in Richman's

Figure 4.1b. Flamin' Groovies, *Shake Some Action*, 1976. Courtesy of Rhino Entertainment Company.

new style on 1975's *Beserkley Chartbusters* compilation, including "Government Center" and a lighter version of "Roadrunner," before fully introducing *Jonathan Richman and the Modern Lovers* in 1976, soon after the demos. Still, these examples of Richman's "second career" (which is now going on for over fifty years) had yet to make a significant impact on Richman's New York audience.

Retrospectively, the "old" Modern Lovers demos of 1972 were completely of their time, as were the "new" Modern Lovers of 1976, a definitive expression of the "pure rock and roll" nostalgic impulse that many members of Richman's generation had been exploring in earnest for several years. As discussed throughout this chapter, Richman was not the only one who had moved in this direction, although his music was perhaps the most extreme manifestation. Groups often went back and forth or maintained both styles. The Velvet Underground had the extended harshness of "Sister Ray" on *White Light/White Heat* in 1968 and the singles-oriented *Loaded* in 1970. The Flamin' Groovies, another band of

Richman's era, went to harder edged, blues-based music after playing with the Stooges in Cincinnati in 1969 (e.g., *Teenage Head* [1971], "Slow Death" [1972], also covered by the Dictators) but returned to a nostalgic pure rock and roll mode on *Shake Some Action* (1976), produced by Dave Edmunds, with a cover modeled on early British Invasion records, as shown in figure 4.1 (compare also the moody cover for *The Modern Lovers* with the playful follow-up *Rock 'n' Roll with the Modern Lovers*). According to a 1976 Sire advertisement, *Shake Some Action* was "pure rock 'n' roll as you haven't heard it in years . . . tough, raw and uncompromising, the way the Stones used to be. Bright, melodic and exhilarating, the way the Beatles used to be. . . . Rock & Roll the way it used to be; the way it was meant to be; the way it will be."[115]

The main stylistic differences between songs such as "Government Center" and the Modern Lovers' 1972 recordings are the pure rock and roll formal structures and major melodies, which Richman supported with quieter instrumentation and the inclusion of background vocals and other hallmarks of 1950s and early 1960s rock and roll and rhythm and blues. Very different from the open-ended, one- and two-chord compositions that Richman emphasized in 1971 and 1972, "Government Center" is instead an original pure rock and roll song in a major mode with equal-length binary question-and-answer phrases marked by cadences, and a contrasting strain beginning on the IV chord. Richman includes I–IV oscillations, but as an introduction, an interlude, and as an up-tempo coda, in the style of early rock and roll. The form is tightly arranged without extended improvisations.

By 1976, as represented on *Jonathan Richman and the Modern Lovers* and the Town Hall concert, Richman's repertoire was dominated by nostalgic pure rock and roll songs, including "Ice Cream Man," "New England," and covers of rock and roll chestnuts such as Chuck Berry's "Back in the U.S.A." (a twelve-bar blues also covered by MC5 and many others) and Richie Valens's "La Bamba" (1958). Richman explicitly embraced his suburban experience on songs such as "Rockin' Shopping Center," continuing a theme already heard on his earlier songs such as "Roadrunner," with its lyrics reminiscing about the "spirit of 1956" the heavenly smell of "suburban trees," and AM radio.

When Richman brought his current version of the Modern Lovers to Town Hall in 1976, he began with "Back in the U.S.A.," prompting exchanges with the vocal audience. In one of the few points in the concert with a long improvisation, he played a long version of "Roadrunner," using the I–IV oscillation to recount his time at age eighteen (in 1969), trying to make it New York, alone with his guitar and his "big Vox Super Beatle amplifier," in a nod to the Velvet Underground's amp of choice.[116] In Richman's case, even the New York of the Velvet Underground's heyday, conventionally portrayed as hard-edged and depraved, is turned into a wistful reminiscence.

After "Roadrunner," the audience continued to exhort Richman to turn it up. Finally Richman responded, "No! I don't care what you think," to audience applause. Such back-and-forth continued during the concert, with the audience urging Richman to perform in his "old" style as heard on *The Modern Lovers*, which was familiar to those who knew the album or had seen Richman perform in New York years before, perhaps at the 1972 New Year's Eve show at the Mercer Arts Center with the Modern Lovers, Suicide, Wayne County, and the New York Dolls.[117] As Lisa Jane Persky remembered, "We played [the first album] a lot . . . then we saw him [at Town Hall]. It was completely another thing, but we didn't really think about, 'Oh, it's been some years.'"[118]

Before "Ice Cream Man," Richman stopped and evoked his childhood, directly connecting the song to a simpler life in the 1950s and early 1960s:

. . . Remember when the ice cream man first came down the street. [applause and laughter]

I remember the truck, I remember how great it was in my neighborhood when the ice cream man came by. [audience member calls out]

[Richman responds:] No, I'm not being metaphorical! I'm telling you right about this—[audience applause]

—There's no symbolism here at all. I'm talking about the ice cream man, and his ice cream truck, and nothing else but! And I'm talking about how this really had an effect. And when we sing this song, and when I sing it, and the Modern Lovers help, and we all help and sing this song, well I don't care. It makes me feel real good because it reminds me of the way I felt when I was real little and it's time to start the song.

The multiple-way conversation continued throughout the show. To start the encore, one audience member yelled "Route 66" (the rhythm and blues standard famously played by Chuck Berry) and another responded "Heroin!" (the Velvet Underground song); Richman played "Abominable Snowman in the Market" (an original pure rock and roll song). Already a veteran at twenty-five, Richman performed the concert on his own terms and won over the Town Hall audience, but the back-and-forth represented a confusion over the expectations in musical style surrounding the belated release of *The Modern Lovers* and the changing sense of "punk rock" as emblematic of a particular new kind of culture, with CBGB and New York at the center. Many heard Richman's quiet and rose-colored music in opposition to punk, but in retrospect, his music at the Town Hall concert can be heard as part of a broader punk style that was prevalent in the early 1970s scene, and which very much included the CBGB bands, hinging on new approaches to familiar early 1960s rock and roll.[119]

Jonathan Richman's pure rock and roll songs have much in common with other punk songs of the early to mid-1970s. He is often deemed exceptional

because of his naïve and unironic stance, but Blondie, the Real Kids, the Flamin' Groovies, and other bands on those scenes also sang their songs without
irony. Even the New York Dolls, renowned for their defiantly punk attitude, sang
songs like "Frankenstein" and "Lonely Planet Boy" without sarcasm; these songs
were instead throwbacks to a slightly earlier era of rock and roll, as were their
covers of jocular hits like "Stranded in the Jungle" (1956). On the other hand,
songs like Richman's "Dodge Veg-O-Matic"—his take on the classic rock and
roll muscle-car song—are at least as comical as the Dictators' attempts at humor.
Irony, camp, and irreverence are hallmarks of this pure rock and roll style and
emblematic of rock and roll as a symbol of teenage or youth culture.

### A Fast Drill on a Rear Molar: The Ramones Blueprint

The Ramones took the pure rock and roll impulses of the early to mid-1970s and
transformed them into punk as the term is currently understood. The Ramones
quickly developed a substantial repertoire containing compact, tightly arranged
songs based on common-stock models, and they drew liberally on traditional
rock and roll lyrical themes and images. Even more important than their widely
discussed speed and volume, they wrote original material that was innovative at
the structural level, altering the familiar models and schemes, and they presented
new guitar-based harmony with Johnny Ramone's uses of the barre chord. They
combined diverse rock and roll elements in unusual ways and reemphasized
the short pop song format as a primary mode of expression. In essence, they
raised the standard for composition as a component of the punk style, and the
emerging British and American punk musicians almost immediately put the
original Ramones models to use for their own creative expressions.[120] Through
their transformations and innovations, the Ramones fully established ways in
which the whiter, "non-blues" rock and roll materials could be used as the basis
of an aggressive punk style that addressed the contemporary world of the 1970s,
and that did not primarily look back with nostalgia.

Like the Modern Lovers, Blondie, and others in Part One of *Damaged*, the
Ramones were baby boomer musicians who had been enmeshed in the politics
of the Vietnam War and the musical life of the late 1960s. Johnny Ramone was
born in 1948, graduated Forest Hills High School in 1966 with a high draft number, was ambivalent about the war, "hated hippies," and didn't form the Ramones
for almost a full decade after high school, including five years working construction with his father.[121] Joey Ramone and Dee Dee Ramone were born in
1951, just missing the cutoff for the draft but culturally experiencing Altamont,
Kent State, and the deaths of Jimi Hendrix, Janis Joplin, and Jim Morrison as
much as the culminating spirit of Woodstock in high school and immediately

after. The Ramones also had an international perspective: Tommy Ramone was born in 1949 in Budapest, immigrating to New York in 1957 with his parents, who were Holocaust survivors, and Dee Dee Ramone spent much of his childhood in Germany as an "army brat." This diversity helped make them who they were, expressed in their adopted Ramones personas and their wide range of musical models.

They also grew up in the middle of rapidly transforming urban and suburban environs. Every account of the Ramones begins with their childhood in Forest Hills, taking it for granted as a "middle-class," "mostly Jewish" neighborhood.[122] Yet Forest Hills has never been "mostly Jewish." As with Johnny Ramone's memories of Westbury as "half black," remembrances of neighborhoods as "Jewish," "black," or "Latino" must be taken with a more than a grain of salt, as "Americans vastly overestimate the sizes of their minority populations."[123] Forest Hills, like other suburbs, was undergoing a huge expansion and demographic shift during the 1950s, especially regarding the neighborhood's ethnic makeup. According to the 1943 *New York City Market Analysis*, Forest Hills was almost entirely "native-born white" and "a good segment of the world's wealthiest market," with a small but significant population (8,098, or 18.7 percent) of "foreign-born white" led by Germans ("foreign-born white" included immigrant populations such as Jews, Italians, Irish, and Germans).[124] By contrast, the Lower East Side in 1943 had a "foreign-born white" population of mostly Eastern and Central European Jews and Italians numbering 100,566 (42.8 percent, over twelve times the size of the mostly German "foreign-born white" population of Forest Hills). Jews had been slowly moving out to Forest Hills and other neighborhoods in the boroughs for decades, especially Brooklyn, but it was not until the postwar era that significant numbers of Jews (but still much smaller numbers than usually believed) migrated to these near suburbs. Families such as the Hymans (Joey Ramone) and the Erde-lyis (Tommy Ramone) were part of the larger move for many New York Jews into suburbs that were newly available to them. This substantial portion of the city's Jewish population was mostly made up of the children of the immigrants who made the Lower East Side the most densely populated area in the country in the late nineteenth and early twentieth centuries, or immigrants themselves.[125] Importantly, the suburban "American dream" especially as it concerned home ownership remained largely inaccessible to African Americans at this time, and the suburbs remained heavily divided according to race and ethnicity.[126]

This is the Forest Hills landscape in which the Ramones and their parents lived, and which shaped their sound. From the outset, the Ramones self-consciously highlighted their music as a fresh take on classic rock and roll, emanating from a particular New York–area suburban experience. In Tommy's original press release, the Ramones defined themselves in distinction from other rock bands in 1975, in the same manner as the "pure rock and roll with no blues or folk" quote from Johnny Ramone that opened the chapter. The press release is still one of the great descriptions of the band:

> The Ramones are not an oldies group, they are not a glitter group, they don't play boogie music and they don't play the blues. The Ramones are an original Rock and Roll group of 1975, and their songs are brief, to the point and every one a potential hit single.
>
> The quartette consists of Johnny, Joey, Dee Dee and Tommy Ramone. Johnny, the guitarist, plays with such force that his sound has been compared to a hundred howitzers going off. Joey, the lead singer, is an arch villain whose lanky frame stands threatening center stage. Dee Dee is Bass guitar and the acknowledged handsome one of the group, and Tommy is the drummer whose pulsating playing launches the throbbing sound of the band.
>
> The Ramones all originate from Forest Hills and kids who grew up there either became musicians, degenerates or dentists. The Ramones are a little of each. Their sound is not unlike a fast drill on a rear molar.

Combined with their formation in the near New York suburbs and use of classic American rock and roll style from the 1950s such as leather jackets and jeans, the Ramones took the pure rock and roll look and sound to an extreme. As mentioned, the Ramones represented one expression of a widespread aesthetic of the New York and Boston scenes. For example, Blondie's genesis and aesthetic mirrored the Ramones; in many ways, these two groups were the eventual extensions of the Shangri-Las project, tough yet vulnerable teenager personas, suburban-made in relation to a changing New York City, and delivered through pure rock and roll structures that absorbed black and white common-stock musical sources into mostly white containers. The opening song on *Blondie*, "X-Offender," is as iconic and archetypal as "Blitzkrieg Bop," a tightly arranged major melody song based on binary I–IV–V patterns with variations (twelve-bar B section, IV–V–III–IV–I–V), a middle eight (VI–IV–V), and a short-cycle vamp coda (I–IV–V). The punk impulse that these two groups brought to the equation added a bundle of contradictory associations. The Ramones and Blondie combined sincerity with artifice and irony, and they played with ambiguity along social constructions of ethnicity, race, gender, sexuality, class, and even political orientation (Joey was left-wing, Johnny leaned right-wing). Unlike the Dictators, the Ramones and Blondie were not tongue-in-cheek about the past they conjured, but they were not completely nostalgic either in the manner of some mainstream hits, such as Bob Seger's "Old Time Rock and Roll" (1978). But the Ramones in particular distinguished themselves among their contemporaries with a highly distilled pure rock and roll repertoire, without any overtures to the riff-based blues excursions so characteristic of the late 1960s and early 1970s.

The Ramones' songwriting production was extraordinary. By 1975 they were regularly performing all thirteen original songs on the debut album (*Ramones*, 1976) as well as some songs from 1977's *Leave Home* ("Swallow My Pride," "Glad to See You Go") and *Rocket to Russia* ("I Don't Care," their first song, written by Joey using the chords from Alice Cooper's "Eighteen") and B-sides ("Baby-sitter").[127] By the end of 1977 the Ramones had released thirty-eight original compositions on the LPs alone. Including their covers—"California Sun," "Let's Dance," "Surfin' Bird," and "Do You Wanna Dance"—the Ramones laid the groundwork for a new approach to rock and roll.

The most recognizable Ramones song and the first song on the first album, "Blitzkrieg Bop," set the stage as a classic twenty-four-bar AAB song with a major melody, binary phrases, and a contrasting B section beginning on IV. "Blitzkrieg Bop" also incorporated familiar tropes of the 1950s and early 1960s style, including a no-chord section ("Hey! Ho! Let's go!") and background vocals. Other songs in this pure rock and roll corpus used I–IV–V patterns in two equal-length phrases in a question-and-answer relationship and a contrast-ing B section beginning in another harmonic area (usually IV). These songs include "I Wanna Be Your Boyfriend" (built on such a conventional model that it sounds like a cover of an oldie), "Rockaway Beach," "I Love Her So," "Suzy Is a Headbanger," "Swallow My Pride," "You're Gonna Kill That Girl," "Babysitter," and "Sheena Is a Punk Rocker." In many of these songs, especially as developed by the Ramones and other pure rock and roll punk groups, the B section is not really a chorus (since it is the A section of "Rockaway Beach," "Blitzkrieg Bop," or "You're Gonna Kill That Girl" that sticks in your memory) and it is not a bridge that takes you back to the A section to finish the cycle—it operates as a "bridge" in an AABA song but the last A is dropped, and this mode of dropping of sections in order to shorten the cycles is a key element in the pure rock and roll style.

A 1976 Sire press release credits Joey Ramone with a "surprisingly supple voice reminiscent of the best mid-60's English pop singers" (not necessarily implying an English accent, as many of those singers imitated American accents), and he had also clearly listened a lot to the "girl group" singers, especially Ronnie Spector. Most of all, Joey's voice distinguished by what it *was not*—his was not a "blues voice" in the style of Iggy Pop, not an "authentic" white northeastern voice in the style of Lou Reed, and not a falsetto voice in the style of Robert Plant.[128] Joey's voice was a quintessential example of this norm in punk, as Paul Roessler put it more generally, "It's what you're not allowed to do, what was no longer acceptable, and Robert Plant's voice was no longer acceptable."[129]

Several Ramones songs include background vocals ("Suzy," "You're Gonna Kill That Girl," "Rockaway Beach," "Sheena"), classic teenage-style rock and roll themes, and references to old rock and roll songs ("Second verse, same as the first" in "Judy" refers to Herman's Hermits' "I'm Henry the Eighth, I Am"). Even Dee Dee's famous count-off can be heard throughout their models, such as Chris Montez's "Let's Dance." In this group, we also find sections broken out from the form and used as short cycles, as in "Suzy" and "Boyfriend" (I–IV–V in the outro), "You're Gonna Kill That Girl" (I–IV–IV–V in the outro), and "Rockaway Beach" (I–IV–I–V bridge as an outro).

The Ramones definitively established their repertoire's basis in 1950s/early 1960s rock and roll, doo-wop, and "girl group" music. Notably, the Ramones not only avoided riff-based blues, they even refrained from playing the twelve-bar blues. The covers with connections to blues forms, such as "Let's Dance" and "California Sun" are instead of the eight- or sixteen-bar type with binary divisions of the phrases and major melodies, the whitened and racially ambiguous versions of the blues reminiscent of the 1950s and early 1960s. They fully committed to this style, and later songs such as "Do You Remember Rock 'n' Roll Radio?" (1980) are in the same format. Johnny Ramone never played guitar solos (with the possible slight exception of the one note solo on "Today Your Love, Tomorrow Your World," and one solo on *Road to Ruin* on "Go Mental"), and the short cycles that they occasionally used as outros never exceeded a few repetitions.

Johnny Ramone's approach to the guitar produced remarkable new possibilities for composing with familiar pure rock and roll structures. Johnny played mainly with barre chords, in downstrokes, on his Mosrite guitar. Combined with high volume and Johnny's particular rig and playing style, the shape of the barring yielded a heavy emphasis on the root and fifth, reminiscent of (but not exactly) a "power chord."[130] Dee Dee Ramone supported the effect by doubling Johnny's lines. The end result obscures the chords' functional harmony, giving the chords a quality of moving unmoored from root to root.

The Ramones' cover of "Let's Dance" demonstrates this transformation in action. Chris Montez's original features an instrumental section with a bluesy organ solo. In the first half of the solo, the organ arpeggiates a dominant 7th chord ($\hat{1}$–$\hat{3}$–$\hat{5}$–$\flat\hat{7}$) over a no-chord space implying the I chord, followed by a blues riff played along with the full band (IV–V). The second half of the solo answers the first half in the expected fashion of two equal-length phrases, with an instrumental performance of the vocal line (V–IV–V–IV–I). In the Ramones version, Johnny and Dee Dee perform that arpeggiated dominant 7th as four separate chords: I–III–V–$\flat$VII.

In this subtle change over the course of two measures, the Ramones stripped the song of its most recognizable nod to blues styles, moving this already racially ambiguous song closer to "white." (They did keep the organ riff, though.) Even more, they took a harmonic language that was still rooted in functional piano-based harmony and turned it into a guitar-based language. The song remains based on functional tonal harmony but intrinsically tied to physical movement up and down the fretboard. The Ramones used this technique throughout their repertoire, taking functional harmonic progressions and replacing them with simultaneous barre chord and bass root movement, and these new models took hold in later punk compositions. In the verse for "Loudmouth," the common vi–IV–V–I pattern found throughout early rock and roll becomes VI–IV–V–I. In "Chain Saw," a IV–ii–V–I cycle becomes IV–II–V–I, and then expanded from the short cycle for a middle eight (IV–I–IV–II).[131] But besides these harmonic changes, "Chain Saw" is very much a song with pure rock and roll qualities. The song begins with "wa-oo wa-oo" vocables, and the middle eight has an instance of background harmonies on "ooh, la la." The horror movie theme ("Texas Chainsaw Massacre") is also typical, rather than exceptional, as the early rock and roll and doo-wop repertoire is filled with songs about movies and monsters. As Lux Interior of the Cramps explained, "Some songs we write are based on [horror movies], but it has to do with American culture and we're not trying for that image."[132]

The Ramones also applied the barre chord/bass root transformation technique to the whole-step oscillations that flourished in the raw power approaches, disconnecting from a blues context. "I Don't Wanna Go Down to the Basement" revolves around an alternating whole-step oscillation, but instead of a riff-based movement, fifths are added to become a new V–II–V to IV–I–IV oscillation. This pattern would become a cornerstone of hardcore punk (the Germs' "Forming," Black Flag's "Nervous Breakdown"), as shown in chapters 6 and 7. The verse of "Now I Wanna Sniff Some Glue" is built on a whole-step ♭VII–I oscillation, as is the B section of "Today Your Love, Tomorrow Your World." And rather than using one cycle for an entire song, as was typical in many pure rock and roll throwbacks, the Ramones combined patterns in new and unexpected ways. For example, "Today Your Love" combines the whole-step oscillation with an A section barre chord/bass root transformation of a minor chord arpeggiation, VI–III–I, and the song ends on a I–IV–V short cycle. Another feature of the Ramones' barre chord/bass root movement is the presence of melodic interludes that shift the harmonic rhythm in unanticipated ways, as in the 6/4 intro and interlude in "We're a Happy Family," the 6/4 turnaround in "Loudmouth," the 6/4 intro in "Gimme Gimme Shock Treatment," the 5/4 intro and 6/4 interlude in "You Should Have Never Opened That Door."

Barre chord/bass root techniques also altered minor-pentatonic blues riffs in the Ramones' music. For example, they used ♭VII–I–♭III–IV, a pattern which first appears in their repertoire as a small instrumental aside in "Havana Affair," dating back to 1975. This pattern was also the basis for one of their signature songs, "Pinhead" (*Leave Home*), with Joey singing monophonically with the riff in a whole-step transposition. "Pinhead" is one of the clearest examples of their placing blues riffs and blues melodic scaffolding within their idiosyncratic compositional style, which mitigated the blues effect. The tight arrangement also includes a question-and-answer section with a no-chord refrain ("D-U-M-B, everyone's accusing me"), a brief interlude on IV and a short-cycle outro on the pattern I–♭III–♭VII–V ("gabba gabba hey"). The riff also appears in the verse of "Commando," "Go Mental," and "Chinese Rocks," the Heartbreakers song written by Dee Dee. Another Ramones song built on transformed minor pentatonic riffs is "We're a Happy Family" (*Rocket to Russia*), the same chords and with a monophonic vocal line but this time arranged I–♭III–I–IV–I–♭III–♭VII. "Pinhead," showing misfit solidarity with the titular characters of Tod Browning's *Freaks*, and "We're a Happy Family," about a seriously dysfunctional situation ("Daddy's telling lies / baby's eating flies / mommy's on pills / baby's got the chills"), are as close to Stooges-style blues-based rock as the Ramones ever got. However, while these transformations "whitened" the blues sources, like most pure rock and roll, they retain qualities of the blues elements that are necessary for the music to effectively sound like rock music.

To end this section and set up the second half of the book, I focus on "Rockaway Beach" (*Rocket to Russia*) and "Bad Brain" (*Road to Ruin*, 1978, with Marky Ramone on drums instead of Tommy). "Rockaway Beach" represents one of the fullest expressions of the Ramones' pure rock and roll impulse, an adaptation of the California beach song from a Queens perspective. "Bad Brain" is a more enigmatic lyric about becoming unable to function in society, with a composition built on three distinct harmonic schemes and pointing toward the emerging hardcore style.

After Dee Dee's customary count-off, "Rockaway Beach" begins with a four-bar instrumental introduction based on IV, with Johnny playing a whole-step riff beginning with the lower note on the first beat and delaying the main note to the second beat (an appoggiatura). This whole-step melodic riff, heard also in "Commando," "Sheena is a Punk Rocker," and "Carbona Not Glue," is also a staple of later punk and hardcore.

As shown in musical example 4.5, "Rockaway Beach" starts in a very simple fashion. The verse resembles an eight-bar blues moving from I to IV and V (more "Let's Dance" than "Denise"). The chorus, supported with background vocals and harmonies, is an eight-bar repetition of the first half of the passamezzo moderno cycle (I–IV–I–V).

|         | 1 | 2 | 3 | 4 | 5 | 6 | 7 | 8 |
|---------|---|---|---|---|---|---|---|---|
| verse:  | I |   |   |   | IV |   | V |   |
|         | I |   |   |   | IV |   | V |   |
| chorus: | I |   | IV |  | I |   | V |   |
|         | I |   | IV |  | I |   | V |   |

Musical example 4.5. "Rockaway Beach" chords, Ramones, *Rocket to Russia*, 1977.

Then "Rockaway Beach" immediately gets more recognizably in the distinct Ramones style, with a 10/4 instrumental interlude based on a barre chord/bass root whole-step pattern transformation:

| 1 | x | x | x | x | x | x | x | x | x |
|---|---|---|---|---|---|---|---|---|---|
| ♭VII | IV | | | | ♭VI | ♭III | | | |
| ♭VII | IV | | | | ♭VI | ♭III | | | |

And then back in 4/4 time, a middle eight with background vocals, following more barre chord/bass root transformations of rock and roll patterns, especially the opening VI–I pattern:

| 1 | 2 | 3 | 4 | 5 | 6 | 7 | 8 |
|---|---|---|---|---|---|---|---|
| VI | | I | | VI | | IV | V |

The song continues with a repetition of the verse and chorus pattern, the 10/4 instrumental interlude sounding like a coda. But instead, after a brief pause and four hits from Tommy on the drums, the song finishes with the chorus treated in the manner of a short cycle vamp. The ending short cycle is only repeated twice on the recording in the customary mode of early rock and roll songs.

The lyrics about Queens' Rockaway Beach (a New York adaptation of the endless California summer utopias of those early-1960s songs), the background vocals, the barre-chord interlude with off-kilter harmonic rhythm, and the slightly odd-sounding middle eight (because of the barre-chord/bass root movement) combine to make "Rockaway Beach" a paradigm of the Ramones' punk take on 1950s and early 1960s pure rock and roll.

As discussed in this chapter, most Ramones songs rely heavily on references to existing models from the 1950s and early 1960s. "Bad Brain," on the other hand, is a Ramones composition that takes these models in a different direction. "Bad Brain" was not one of the Ramones' popular songs, and they did not play it live nearly as often as they did songs such as "I Wanna Be Sedated" or "Sheena is a Punk Rocker," or even lesser known songs such as "Cretin Hop" or "Commando." However, it leveraged the harmonic possibilities the Ramones had already started exploring with "Loudmouth," "Pinhead," and other songs, in a manner that was crucial for hardcore punk (the 1978 date of the recording places it at the beginning of a generally transitional period).

"Bad Brain" is faster than most Ramones songs (200 beats per minute, as opposed to 188 for "Rockaway Beach" and 176 for "Sheena is a Punk Rocker"), and relevant for hardcore, the song stays in 4/4, not cut time, despite the fast tempo. Instead of connected verses and choruses, with or without intros, outros, interludes, and middle eights, "Bad Brain" consists of three original schemes, arranged in different ways throughout the song. And rather than outlining conventional I–IV–V rock and roll patterns, the harmonic schemes are mono-phonic and melodic, as with the barre-chord/bass root transformations heard in other songs. "Bad Brain" moves from conventional functional harmony toward the guitar-based movement of hardcore. To show the unusual harmonic rhythm, this chart shows the quarter-note level (each pattern is played twice):

|  | 1 | x | x | x | 2 | x | x | x |  |
|---|---|---|---|---|---|---|---|---|---|
| scheme A: | E |  | A |  | D |  | A | D |  |
|  | IV |  | bVII |  | bIII |  | bVII | bIII | (2x) |
| scheme B: | A |  | E |  | B |  | E | D |  |
|  | bVII |  | IV |  | I |  | IV | bIII | (2x) |
| scheme C: | D |  | B |  | F# |  |  |  |  |
|  | bIII |  | I |  | V |  |  |  | (2x) |

Musical example 4.6a. "Bad Brain" chords, Ramones, *Road to Ruin*, 1978.

Also unusual for Ramones songs, the "chorus" is just the lyric refrain "bad, bad brain," and not linked to a particular harmonic scheme. In the form chart below, the refrain appears as a superscript "ref." Except for the end vamp, lyrics only appear on the B scheme; patterns with lyrics are boldfaced. The form follows:

| Instrumental: | A A B B C |
|---|---|
| Verse 1: | **B B B**ref C |
| Verse 2: | **B B**ref A A C  [note: refrain only second half of pattern] |
| Verse 3: | **B B B**ref C |
| Verse 4: | **B B**ref |
|  | percussion breakdown |
| Refrain: | over percussion (no chord) |
| Refrain over C: | Cref (vamp) |

Musical example 4.6b. "Bad Brain" form, Ramones, *Road to Ruin*, 1978.

The form of "Bad Brain" is most unexpected given the conventional verse-chorus patterns of most Ramones songs. Here, verses can take two cycles or one, and no overarching cycle such as AAB can be easily heard. It is especially unusual for the Ramones to treat a refrain in this fashion, not tied to a particular harmonic scheme, and to base so much of the song on one short cycle.

The Ramones had experimented with these compositional techniques on earlier songs, but "Bad Brain" and some other songs on *Road to Ruin* such as "I'm Against It" and "Go Mental" presaged a complete guitar-based punk lan-guage based on barre-chord/bass root movement, unusual harmonic rhythm based on these resulting schemes, and the combination of schemes into longer forms regardless of the overall songform conventions. This fully developed application of the Ramones style grew out of the pure rock and roll approach but it no longer looked only toward the past for meaning—ironic, nostalgic, or otherwise. Hardcore punk composers would also develop elements of this style in their language.

Yet "Bad Brain" did not at all represent a wholesale transformation of the Ramones' style. For the most part, the Ramones continued to compose in and perform pure rock and roll, even as they took this particular approach to its most punk rock expression, meaning its most ambiguous, contradictory, and aggressive manifestations. In some ways, they moved even closer to pure rock and roll nostalgia. *Road to Ruin* features both "Bad Brain" and an extremely respectful cover of Jackie DeShannon's "Needles and Pins" (1963), "a song that already fits our style," with strumming on an acoustic guitar.[133] Songs such as "Do You Remember Rock 'n' Roll Radio?" (1980), underscored that their use of pure rock and roll "non-blues" schemes evoking the early 1960s was never ironic or sarcastic, but a genuine response to their lives in the 1970s and what they saw as a lost energy and spirit in the music of their youth. As Joey Ramone remembered,

"Do You Remember Rock and Roll Radio" was about the demise of radio basically in America. And then really, not just America, but I mean radio used to be great when we were kids. I mean we got turned on to all this great music, the Beatles, the Stones, and all that. And nowadays, and even by the '80s it was a big business and it was all mediocrity and bullshit. And it was upsetting to someone who really is a real lover of music, really, that was important. A lot of people don't care about stuff like that. So to them it's just kind of trivial.[134]

The Ramones' punk legacy lies in how they harnessed the nostalgic turn toward the late 1950s and early 1960s among their contemporaries, predominantly the white baby boomers who grew up in the newly expanded suburbs during the 1950s and 1960s, and used these musical resources to form an original repertoire that effectively spoke to the spirit of the mid-1970s and looked forward. Their original music was not merely nostalgic, it captured an ambivalence about life for white suburban teenage youth, from the perspective of adults looking back on that period of life. They loved the perceived innocence and simplicity of that era, captured by "pure rock and roll," but the transformations, mostly through Johnny and Dee Dee's approach to harmonic language, also communicated their reactionary 1970s moment, and a sense of being out of place then as well as when they were kids. By 1976 their original repertoire had established a model for punk as a distinct musical style, punk as a noun, rather than as one particularly aggressive way of playing old time rock and roll.

# PART TWO

## *punk (n.)*

Out of these various approaches to playing rock music, punk became widely recognized as a noun—a named set of styles and approaches—around 1976. The particular ways in which musicians combined, altered, and manipulated aspects of earlier punk rock styles created distinctions between the music punks were making and the music that inspired them. Whereas Part One of *Damaged* focuses on three important musical approaches for punk between 1968 and 1976, Part Two describes some of the major styles musicians created out of those approaches from 1976 to 1981, focusing on the products of inventive exchanges between musicians in the US and UK, and the various manifestations of punk and hardcore punk in Los Angeles and Washington, DC. Underscoring the shift to punk as a named style were significant changes in the American suburbs and who was growing up in them and living there.

Punk emerged as a recognizable style in the United Kingdom primarily in London, and in the United States primarily in New York and Los Angeles. Musically, punks in the US and the UK put together currents such as the riff-based blues of the Stooges, the experimental metamusic of Captain Beefheart, and the original back-to-basics rock and roll songs of the Ramones. In retrospect this so-called protopunk and early punk music makes sense together, but they only cohere because of the innovative ways in which punk musicians synthesized them. In the early and mid-1970s, these musical approaches were often divergent or even in conflict. In punk, the clash of styles and their meanings became an asset and eventually an essential feature of the music.

The appearance of more clearly defined punk music, along with an upsurge in the use of the word "punk" by musicians, journalists, and fanzine creators, created enough of a division for many to consider 1976 punk's origin point despite the clear evidence of punk rock before that year. After the explosion of punk in the UK in 1976, people started asking when and where punk began. Who was first? Where was punk invented? Like ranking bands, such questions might be interesting conversation starters, but they misrepresent musical and historical processes. The punk style is a consummate product of *exchanges* between musicians in the United States and the United Kingdom. And these exchanges circulated around formations of race and class, as they had for decades. For punk, although black musical resources served as the vocabulary, British–American exchanges took place mostly among white people concerned with whiteness, replicating earlier "British Invasion" exchanges and much earlier interactions as well. As musical and journalistic discourse converged on the definition of "punk" and the relationships between (white people in) the US and the UK, punk became obscured from its roots in black American music and removed from the complex racial dynamics that characterized the world of musicians such as the MC5.

Debates over punk's style and its meanings were also taking place in local scenes in the United States. Los Angeles had an especially vibrant and unsettled punk scene, and the music that came from there effectively defined American punk. In the United States, punk continued to be primarily an expression of the suburbs, whiteness, and the middle class through the 1970s, as younger musicians inherited the legacy of the music's ties to white, suburban, middle-class America in the 1950s and early 1960s. But the music being played in Los Angeles—and soon Washington, DC, and many other cities and towns around the country—reflected the increasing diversity of those suburbs, new migrations and the changing demographics of the country, shifting definitions of "white," and the economic fluctuations of the 1970s.

Perhaps most of all, punk changed as a younger generation of musicians became its main participants. Whereas earlier punk was led by baby boomers, the distinct American style of punk that emerged around 1976 and 1977 was steered by the incipient cohort of Generation X, or more accurately, as Jello Biafra described himself: "people like me . . . who are *between* 'baby boomers' and 'Generation X-ers.' Even though we were very young, my generation felt the real impact of the '60s."[1] The generational differences become more salient when considering that musicians such as Deborah Harry and Johnny Ramone were around thirty years old in 1977, while Bill Stevenson and Frank Navetta were about fifteen years old when they formed the Descendents around the same time. Although punk is almost always analyzed as a "youth subculture," in fact, early punk in New York and even later was really a scene of adults, at least as far as the bands are concerned, and it was not until the teenagers around Los Angeles started forming their own bands that American punk truly became a music for kids by kids, rather than music by adults about being kids. At this point in punk history, it had also become standard for bands to release their own recordings independently, meaning that the span of time between early shows and a band's first releases became much shorter. (The graph in the appendix shows these age and generational issues.)

The young American punks followed the lead of the British punks who established punk as a style for a younger cohort. However, it is still an exaggeration to fully characterize even early British punk as a "youth subculture." Although in 1976 the Sex Pistols were 19 and 20 and Ari Up was a young 16, Joe Strummer was 24, and many on the scene were even older: that same early year, Eve Libertine of Crass was 27, Ana de Silva of the Raincoats was 28, Penny Rimbaud was 33, Jet Black of the Stranglers was 38, and Vi Subversa of Poison Girls was 41.[2] (And as mentioned in chapter 1, it is typical for musicians to begin their careers in their late teens and early twenties.) And while the teenagers in Los Angeles strongly changed the orientation of punk toward younger participants, even into the late 1970s and early 1980s American punk could skew older than most people may realize: V. Vale was 32 or 33 when he produced the first issue of *Search and Destroy*, Ted Falconi of Flipper was a Vietnam veteran (served 1967–69), and Tony Lombardo was in his thirties when he joined the Descendents.

From the late 1960s to the late 1970s, the period in which the younger punk generation came of age, the suburbs were rapidly becoming more diverse in terms of race and class, while the cities were becoming defined by increasing segregation and wealth disparity. In the northern cities, white flight and the loss of smokestack industry and union jobs had hit African American people the hardest. After *Brown v. Board of Education* (1954) and the Fair Housing Act (Title VIII of the Civil Rights Act of 1968), intense segregation, housing discrimination, and acute inequalities in wealth and education remained between white people and black people. In response to discrimination lawsuits, and noting the lack of on-the-ground improvement, courts began ordering cities and school boards to actively make their communities more integrated and equal. In the 1970s the most concerted efforts were in the area of education, such as the landmark 1974 court order for Boston to desegregate its public schools, with busing (almost always black city children bused to majority white suburban schools) the most immediate and controversial method for changing schools' demographics.[3] Civil rights advocates also started winning some court cases to desegregate housing, but given the wording of the Fair Housing Act (e.g., "fair" rather than "integrated"), the court rulings often upheld discrimination; *United States v. City of Yonkers*, filed in 1980 and decided in 1985, was a later case linking housing and school desegregation.[4] Even with these significant challenges, which still remain—"residential integration declined steadily from 1880 to the mid-twentieth century, and it has mostly stalled since then"—through the 1970s the suburbs and suburban schools became increasingly populated with African Americans, a major change from the almost entirely white and segregated suburbs of the 1950s.[5]

One thing that remained the same from baby boomer punk rock to Generation X punk was the overall context of superficially cosmopolitan and diverse

metropolitan areas that were actually sites of severe discrimination. But as edu-
cational and housing policies were changed to combat these persistent problems in these locations, young people were left to navigate and negotiate the
battles being waged by adults. In their neighborhoods and schools, white and
black youth newly came together or recreated racist patterns. Class divisions
were also palpable, for example between middle-class and working-class black
people, and between middle-class and working-class white people.[6] The locales
of punk's strongest and most dynamic scenes, such as the Los Angeles and
Washington, DC areas profiled in *Damaged*, were also the sites of exceptional
changes in these respects, even as desegregation efforts were ultimately unsuc-
cessful in most areas around the country, and remain so.

Los Angeles was particularly volatile as a region of extremes. Of all the major
US cities, LA experienced perhaps the most substantial change in the postwar
era, with much of the area newly built as migration to the city skyrocketed.
LA was home to a significant black middle class as well as some of the country's most severe geographical segregation and a police force notoriously beset
by racist behavior and leadership. When ordering desegregation in 1970, LA
County Superior Court Judge Alfred Gitelson found the Los Angeles Unified
School District to have been racially segregated "at least since May of 1963," the
year litigation began in *Crawford v. Los Angeles Board of Education*.[7] The ethnic landscape of LA was extremely varied and rapidly shifting, with sizeable
Mexican American, Asian American, and Jewish American populations, each
facing their own forms of discrimination and unsettled racial status. But while
many members of these groups populated the LA suburbs over the course of
the 1970s, African Americans for the most part could not, reflecting the reality
that "as the twentieth century progressed, property and residency restrictions
mostly faded away for all except African Americans."[8] Added to this potent mix
was LA's role as a white utopia and a fantasy dreamland for glamorous stars of
the film, TV, and music industries, and the fact that LA had some of the most
acute wealth disparities in the country.[9] In this environment, early punk had its
most explicit identity crisis, with generally older punk rockers within the city
limits in tension with the younger punks from the suburbs.

The DC area had a similar combination of a segregated city population,
diverse suburbs, a strong black middle class, and conservative, even outwardly
racist, surroundings. Both DC and LA experienced major uprisings in black
communities in the 1960s, and both cities were facing challenges in neglected
areas of the city. But the city of DC, unlike LA, was majority black with a significant black presence in the suburbs. In this environment, a watershed in
punk history came in the form of Bad Brains, an all-black punk quartet that
sounded different from any group before them. They changed punk with their
technically masterful music, but also with their particular attitudes regarding

their blackness and the mostly white punk rock scene. It is not an exaggeration to say that Bad Brains, despite consistent controversy surrounding them, almost singlehandedly demonstrated how punk could be an authentic form of expression for African Americans and other people of color in the late 1970s and early 1980s, and also renewed punk's possibilities for white people of different backgrounds. While some singular black musicians played earlier forms of punk, and with time the mid-1970s all-black bands Death and Pure Hell have become increasingly visible and acknowledged, Bad Brains was remarkable in that they were all black *and* extremely influential during their prime. With the hardcore style that Bad Brains developed along with Black Flag, Circle Jerks, Minor Threat, and others, punk categorically transformed from an expression of white baby boomers who grew up in the 1960s into a voice for Generation X in the 1980s.

# 5

## Punk and the White Atlantic

Q: I think that they also had to stand on the shoulders of punk and what you were doing stood on the shoulders of nothing.

JOE STRUMMER: Well, I dunno, yeah, I suppose, I mean, I am rooted in the blues. You know . . . you gotta make the point in your *History of Rock and Roll* that the blues is the root of everything. Everything that I've heard in my life is rooted in the blues. Except Johann Sebastian Bach.

—From unedited interviews for the *Time-Life History of Rock and Roll* (May 17, 1994)

By 1976, mainly due to the stylistic directions opened up by the Ramones, punk was primed to become a distinct branch of the rock family tree. However, it was the exchanges between the United States and the United Kingdom, especially between 1976 and 1981, that led to punk's full-fledged emergence as a set of musical styles. Reevaluating these exchanges, and the transatlantic interactions that have characterized popular music efforts by white Europeans and white Americans more generally, is key to understanding the music of punk and how its musical features support or contradict punk's discourse.

As Jack Hamilton did in his study of race in rock and roll, *Just Around Midnight*, I refer to these US–UK exchanges as the "White Atlantic," invoking Paul Gilroy's important formulation of the Black Atlantic, with its essential disaporic circulations and exchanges that lie at the heart of black music.[1] However, my use of the term is more explicitly intended to invoke similar diasporic associations, as white Americans problematically constructed Great Britain as a quasi-homeland and origin point in "white Atlantic" exchanges.[2] I also want to restore the colonial history of the exchanges, as the uses of black musical resources by white Americans and white Europeans enacts a kind of colonization in economic terms. Marking the musical exchanges of white people across the Atlantic as explicitly white, and in fact a process through which whiteness has been formed, draws attention to the racialized nature of the ways in which early punk turned into something quite different from 1976 forward.

European–American exchanges based on manipulating ideas of blackness have long served as ways for white people to consider their own histories and identities, although they are rarely articulated as such. This tangled knot of performance, racial and national identity, and transatlantic musical life begins at least as far back as the first "type of music recognized abroad as characteristically American," and the first international American popular music hit song: T. D. Rice's blackface minstrelsy act "Jim Crow," which he performed in England "with great success" in 1836.[3] The term "British Invasion" itself, of course, describes a phenomenon of exchange, and many songs at the heart of punk rock, such as "Gloria," are songs based on black American resources with versions and transformations that can be traced through European–American relationships. In the 1970s, as in earlier periods, black American music served as the primary vocabulary for this discourse among white people across the Atlantic. Blues-based music such as rhythm and blues and rock and roll dominated this discussion, but other African diasporic musics such as reggae played an important part as well.

My goals here are the same as those that run throughout *Damaged*: to outline history through musical analysis, emphasizing the core issues of race, and to reconcile the musical story with the often contradictory narratives that dominate discourse. In the case of the "white Atlantic," one key underlying contradiction is British musicians' acknowledgment of their black American sources, and the avoidance of recognizing those black American sources by white Americans in favor of placing Britain as an origin point. Furthermore, the conversation surrounding rock's origins and sources often falsely pigeonholes the eclectic, transnational, and exchange-based nature of the black styles being invoked, such as reggae and blues. But rather than simply try to correct the historical record, I want to go a step further to examine the *purpose* of the dominant narrative, which often flies in the face of the evidence. Since it is primarily white Americans—not Britons—who advance the narrative of British origins, what is gained from them placing Britain rather than black America at the center of their story, and specifically the story of punk rock?

I argue that the impulse to emphasize Great Britain as an origin point for the American developments in rock following the so-called British Invasion (e.g., the Beatles' performance on the *Ed Sullivan Show* on February 9, 1964), rather than highlighting the murkier history of exchange, comes from its potential to remove popular music from its uncomfortable connections to American racism and the obvious inequalities that persisted and even intensified in the postwar era. Black liberation efforts during this period illuminated the stark racism in popular music, intensifying the perceived need among many white Americans for an alternative narrative and approach, whether they were sympathetic to the struggles articulated by African Americans (and thus wanting a "parallel but separate" musical form of solidarity that didn't only imitate or steal from black sources) or whether they were ambivalent about, or even against, equality and integration (and thus wanting a musical genealogy that established a separate European lineage).

The idea of a British Invasion provided one solution, although it too came with its own complications. As Britons appropriated and interpreted the blues, the process made the same music newly available for white Americans to appropriate and interpret; e.g., a white American band playing Led Zeppelin covers became something fundamentally different from that same band attempting to cover Memphis Minnie and Joe McCoy, even when the song in both cases is "When the Levee Breaks." In a conversation, my colleague David Racanelli likened the process to money laundering—an effective metaphor given black music's value as a monetary resource and the economic language (theft, borrowing, appropriation) that governs discourse about popular music. Laundered through the offshore account of Great Britain, the ostensible homeland and origin of American whiteness, black music returns to the United States as something whiter, ready to be "spent" again, and removed far enough from its roots to avoid direct allegations of theft and appropriation.

This metaphor of money laundering is not to cast the whole enterprise as nefarious and intentionally criminal, although record label executives were certainly well aware of the financial implications of selling to the white market. But the segregated conditions of America in the 1960s and 1970s were reflected in—and also shaped by—the marketing and categorization of popular music. Young white people in the 1960s and 1970s came to view the music they consumed as white rock music and thus their own property as white people, largely—and paradoxically—due to the British Invasion phenomenon. At this point, in the white imagination, rock had become unconnected to an idea that it was a product of racist historical circumstances, even if questions of individual appropriation remained salient—just as the suburbs were read as white, "vanilla," American dream, middle class, and the like, without any connection to the racist policies that generated them, "just the way it was." Northern and West Coast white people seemed especially drawn to this subtle form of revisionist history, which denied any nefarious large-scale racism, such as Nixon's insistence on pervasive *de facto* segregation (no one's fault, and thus permissible, even defensible) versus *de jure* segregation.[4] Undeniably useful for white Americans' attitudes about their society and privilege, the narrative was recycled with punk rock.

## The Language of the White Atlantic

Jack Hamilton and others have effectively debunked the "myth of the British Invasion," noting its historical inaccuracies, and the fact that it did not "happen 'to' America": the "British Invasion wasn't so much a way for Americans to understand a transatlantic musical movement as it was a way to understand something they perceived as happening *to them.* . . ."[5] The British Invasion is indeed a sort of myth, containing "a deeply American bias," but my analysis extends Hamilton's in that I aim to understand why Americans, and white Americans in particular, invented and embraced this myth.[6] What purpose does it serve?

The British Invasion established a formula for white Americans looking to Europe as the source of blues-based rock music. In 2009 Iggy Pop remembered:

> I read in an interview once [when Pete Townshend] said, "You know, we were nervous when we first went to America about, were we going to be able to sell them their own music?" And that's what they did. That's what they all did. They sold us our own music because we rejected it. We rejected it. Unwisely. They did a nice job, it's ok, it sounded good, and you know it came back in another way, but still, it was rejected.[7]

John Lennon, in conversation with Jann Wenner in 1971, presented a similar perspective from the British side: "I'm a bit self-conscious—we all were a bit self-conscious and the Beatles were super self-conscious people about parody of Americans which we do and have done. . . . I know we developed our own style but we still in a way parodied American music [ . . . ] Yes, there was a self-consciousness about singing blues."[8]

The narrative of white Americans rejecting and forgetting black music, only to be reintroduced to it by British musicians, quickly took hold in the 1960s. British musicians such as Joe Strummer had fully internalized this narrative as a point of pride: "I'd spent my whole life listening to music that came really from America. The Stones and the Beatles were very quick to tell us where they were getting this influence from, I mean they didn't pretend they'd made it up at all. In fact, they brought it back to America and redisplayed American roots to Americans who'd forgotten it, and for us, to be big enough to actually make it over to America, and tour, I mean, we just loved it."[9]

However, it is not true that Americans forgot or rejected the blues until the British Invasion. The resurgence of blues musicians such as Mississippi John Hurt and Skip James in the late 1950s and early 1960s came in tandem with the general "folk revival" in the United States, and it was through these American efforts that the "country blues" reached Cream, the Rolling Stones, and Led Zeppelin.[10] Also, white American bands had been consistently playing black rhythm and blues through the 1950s and 1960s. Especially in the Midwest, groups such as the McCoys, Bob Seger's early bands, Mitch Ryder and the Detroit Wheels, and Tommy James and the Shondells were playing rock and roll in a classic R&B vein. The groups retrospectively termed "garage rock" of the early and mid-1960s, such as the Sonics, the Trashmen, the Iguanas, the Standells, and ? and the Mysterians, played unpretentious blues-based music alongside and sometimes even before their counterparts in England such as the Troggs.[11] American baby boomer musicians knew the records in this style, such as those compiled by Lenny Kaye on *Nuggets* (1972). Although these songs are often described now as having been forgotten until the release of *Nuggets*, Kaye served as a compiler and not a discoverer or even reframer in the vein of Harry Smith. Richard Hell later explained that he didn't know how Legs McNeil and John Holmstrom came up with their definition of *punk*, as "there already was a punk rock" that meant a lot to him and his circle. "It was really in the same stream, '60s garage band music . . . like the Kingsmen, the Seeds, the Shadows of Knight, those kinds of groups that Lenny put on the *Nuggets* records. That was punk rock. And then it started being applied to us."[12]

Futhermore, many of the earlier rhythm and blues records, such as the hits produced by Atlantic, were products of interracial collaboration. However, racism and the record industry's strategy of selling to separate black and white markets set the stage for people to lose track of this (intentionally obscured) history. In fact, the "de facto segregation of American culture was in some ways growing stronger" over the course of the sixties, supported by industry moves such as *Billboard*'s reinstitution of the R&B chart.[13]

As the idea of the British Invasion took hold, American musicians turned to emulating British bands rather than black American sources, while self-consciously voicing the "white Atlantic" exchanges at stake. Jim Sohns, of the mid-1960s garage rock band the Shadows of Knight, explained, "The Rolling Stones, Animals, and Yardbirds took the Chicago blues and gave it an English interpretation. We've taken the English versions of the blues and added a Chicago touch."[14] But although American blues musicians were often invoked in these assessments, this back-and-forth across the Atlantic historicized black American blues and R&B musicians, even when they were roughly contemporaneous, positioning black music as a music of the past that British musicians were bringing back to the United States. About the British Invasion, Willie Alexander explained, "Everybody tried to affect British accents and grow long hair. The local bands [in Boston] really liked a lot of the English bands because they were bringing that sort of music back here, the same songs [1950s R&B]."[15] Such historicizing resonated with the rapid changes in American society at the beginning of the 1960s, making the late 1950s seem much further in the past than it really was.

As the 1960s progressed and turned into the 1970s, the recent past seemed remote. In the 1970s, the British Invasion stood alongside 1950s and early 1960s American rock and roll for its nostalgic meanings, as shown in chapter 4 with respect to groups like the Flamin' Groovies, or the Ramones' nod to Herman's

Hermits on "Judy Is a Punk." Meanwhile, British punk bands had their own analogue to the American pure rock and roll stance, with the British Invasion and
the 1960s as reference points. The Jam, for instance, began wearing early 1960s
mod-style hairstyles in 1977, accompanying their past-oriented music.[16] British
bands looked to earlier local rock bands for inspiration, or in the words of Joe
Strummer, "white rock and roll out of London."[17] In March 1977, one fanzine
writer reviewed Buzzcocks as "decked out in what could be described as 3rd rate
pop-art shirts '65. The 'Who' wouldn't of been seen dead in them . . . even then!"[18]

British Invasion discourse detached rock and roll from its black American
roots and from the murky racial undertones of the folk and blues revivals.[19]
While the separation of white and black American bands in the 1950s directly
stemmed from social segregation and the pervasive limitations on integration
during Jim Crow (such as touring the American South), as the United States
attempted to desegregate in the 1960s, persistent racial segregation in music—as
in housing, education, and other aspects of society—needed another logic to
support it. One solution was to recast rhythm and blues as rock and roll, based
in the British bands and the ways in which those groups interpreted American
music. Before the British Invasion, the term "rock and roll" was equivalent to
black music and rhythm and blues in the United States.

The language that characterized white Atlantic exchanges continued through
the 1970s and into the mainstream emergence of punk, with 1976 or 1977 serving as a new historical cusp rather than 1963 or 1964. The continuity of white
Atlantic language is not an accident or a coincidence, for the actors engaged
in the earlier British Invasion discourse were often the same as those involved
in the latter a mere decade later. Early punk rockers in the UK, just like their
counterparts in the United States, were of a similar postwar baby boomer generation. Patti Smith covered "Gloria" a decade after Them released it, but Smith
is only one year younger than Van Morrison. The slightly younger generation
of musicians who integrated punk into a defineable style tended to be born in
the early to mid-1950s on both sides of the Atlantic: for example, Captain Sensible (Damned) and Viv Albertine (Slits) were born in 1954, as were Handsome
Dick Manitoba (Dictators) and John Doe (X). However, they were still all baby
boomers growing up in a postwar environment.

And as in the United States, the punk recordings released at the end of the
1970s often documented musicians who had been playing for years. The debut
album *The Undertones* (1979) captured a group formed in 1974. Joe Strummer,
born in 1952, cut his teeth in the English pub scene of bands directly imitating American rhythm and blues, first joining Tyman Dogg's group around 1971
and then, as is more widely known, the 101ers. Contemporaneous bands such as
the Hammersmith Gorillas, Dr. Feelgood, and Eddie and the Hot Rods played
rhythm and blues in the footsteps of Them and the Kinks, aggressive rock and roll

in the same punk-as-an-adjective mode as American bands such as the Real Kids and the New York Dolls.[20] Strummer's youth in the 1950s and 1960s, as well as his experience in pub rock bands, can be heard in certain songs in the Clash's repertoire, such as "Brand New Cadillac," the (British) Vince Taylor minor-blues tune from 1959, and "I Fought the Law," made famous by the Bobby Fuller Four in 1965.

For these groups in the UK, punk in the new style, such as the music of the Sex Pistols, was schismatic. Joe Strummer remembered the time: "And about [the time the 101ers released "Keys to Your Heart" on Chiswick in 1976], we'd been running maybe eighteen months, two years, and the R&B scene had kind of run its course with Dr. Feelgood and Eddie and the Hot Rods, us, the Hammersmith Gorillas, various other groups. And then the Pistols came out and changed the face of the whole scene. And it wasn't entirely welcome. For example, I think I was the only person in my group who said, 'That is the future.' And it destroyed my group because we couldn't agree anymore."[21]

Dick Hebdige's *Subculture: The Meaning of Style*, a groundbreaking work of the new cultural studies written while the author was still in his twenties, bolstered the broader white Atlantic language around punk even as it highlighted issues of race. Written during British punk's explosion and published in 1979, Hebdige immediately recognized the significance of punks' attachment to reggae and West Indian culture, and he also astutely analyzed the broader meanings of punk fashion statements with respect to British youth subcultures, both aspects I discuss further below. Hebdige also cast punk as a British-born phenomenon, created out of a disparate "dubious parentage" of musics equated with various subcultures, including American rock; the Ramones and Richard Hell, for example, became "proto-punk."[22] In this particular sense of describing punk as something newly put together in the United Kingdom, *Subculture* added to the general language breaking punk away from its American background and the changing American racial context that originally fueled the music. Similarly, Hebdige's emphasis on reggae helped establish Jamaican musical styles as the singular black component in punk culture, replacing African American music such as the blues, which receives no attention in his book. Furthermore, his descriptions of reggae confuse that style's inseparable links to African American popular musical styles and its multifaceted commercial history. These issues continued in his monograph on Caribbean music, *Cut 'n' Mix*, which incorporates some analysis of African American music but which also recycles simplistic tropes such as dividing Caribbean music's parentage into African rhythm and European melody and harmony.[23]

"White Atlantic" language is directly related to the real transatlantic collaborations, migrations, and travels that were central to the emergence of the new punk styles out of the older "aggressive rock" vein, just as the older punk rock grew in part out of the British Invasion (and a special nod to groups such as the Velvet

Underground and the Pretenders, with mixed European and American personnel). Malcolm McLaren visited New York in 1973, where he encountered the New York Dolls and the Max's Kansas City scene, inspiring him with ideas he brought back to London.[24] Chrissie Hynde left Akron for London in the same year, where she wrote for *New Music Express*, worked for Malcolm McLaren and Vivienne Westwood at Let It Rock, and played with Mick Jones, Rat Scabies, and Keith Levene.[25] Dave Edmunds and Nick Lowe created throwback American-style rock and roll in their groups, culminating in Rockpile (the name taken from that of a Long Island club), and in turn, Edmunds produced the Flamin' Groovies *Shake Some Action*, with its British Invasion style. The US–UK axis is also represented in the mix of bands covered in fanzines or underground press on both sides of the Atlantic, beyond the fanzines that have become the best known, such as *Sniffin' Glue* and *Punk*. Zines covering underground music generally also included early punk bands amid a wide assortment of US and UK groups. Wrapping up 1974 in San Francisco's *The Record Rag* 11 (Winter 1974/1975), Michael Wright put Patti Smith together with Paul Revere and the Raiders, Roxy Music, Montrose, Badfinger, the Kinks, and ELO. Los Angeles' *Back Door Man* 7 (June/July 1976) is another representative assortment of Ted Nugent, the Rolling Stones, Blue Öyster Cult, Led Zeppelin, Elliott Murphy, Kiss, Dr. Feelgood, Aerosmith, and the Ramones. Similarly, London's *Zig Zag* 65 (October 1976) covered the Beach Boys, Linda Ronstadt, Ted Nugent, and the Ramones.[26]

The standard narrative of punk follows a British Invasion storyline: neglected or underappreciated American music travels to England where it is extraordinarily successful and influential, transformed and "packaged" (probably the most common word for Americans to describe what the British did with their music) into something new, and returned to the United States to spark the movement on the other side of the Atlantic. According to Joe Strummer, the New York Dolls' performance on British television in 1972 "planted the seed": "that was something we'd never seen before . . . and it was wild and young and crazy and these people were having fun."[27] Patti Smith's performance at the Roundhouse in London in May 1976 has been considered the beginning of the Raincoats and the Slits, as the Slits' Palmolive (Paloma Romero) and Ari Up (Ariane Forster) decided to form an all-female band at the show, and the Raincoats' Ana de Silva and Shirley O'Loughlin left the show "feeling baptized."[28] The Ramones, Flamin' Groovies, and the Stranglers at the Roundhouse on July 4, 1976, with members of the Clash and the Sex Pistols in the audience, is described as another catalyst, or even the primary spark, for the British punk scene.[29] Like earlier Americans in British Invasion stories, the Ramones were continually struck and frustrated by their success in Europe and lack of success at home. Johnny Ramone told KROQ's Stereo Steve: "We were playing for two hundred, maybe four hundred people on the Bowery. There [in London], two thousand seats, all full, they had all bought our record, and we met all the kids starting their bands, the Sex Pistols, the Damned, the Clash."[30] The Ramones' longtime friends Dennis Anderson and Lois Kahlert told me, "In England they were playing theaters, and they always had a thing about how much bigger they were there."[31]

An impression quickly formed in the United States that punk returned to the United States a changed or new music. Reminiscent of language about the British Invasion and the blues, the British punk bands generated excitement in places such as LA, where they "arrived to sell American punk rock back to the Yanks."[32] Later, the idea of British musicians introducing or reintroducing white Americans to black American music was also recycled, as in the case of the Clash, who brought Lee Dorsey and Bo Diddley on the road with them.[33] As Strummer said, "we would always try and bring somebody on the bill that was part of the culture that had fed us."[34]

A few British Invasion–esque moments have taken on a starring role, such as the 1977/78 Sex Pistols tour mostly through the American South and culminating in their breakup in San Francisco. But for Binky Philips of the Planets, the Damned's performance at CBGB in April 1977 was "the night punk was officially born in the USA."[35] His reminiscence of this show captures many of the important facets of the US–UK narrative described in this chapter. As he describes it: ". . . I was down at CBGB to check out The Damned as 'competition,' as opposed to being a fan boy. In fact, I was there with a chip on my shoulder. The Velvet Underground, The New York Dolls, The Ramones, were all New York City bands. *My* town was Punk Ground Zero. . . . I was, in fact, without a struggle, reduced to fan boy within 30 seconds. . . . It was as if the entire evening proceeding them had been in black and white and suddenly we were thrust into Technicolor Oz."

This particular show is also considered as one of the sparks for New York hardcore. Denise Mercedes, the influential guitarist for New York's Stimulators (and Harley Flanagan's aunt) and the woman who "set down the rules that governed NYHC," said:

> I was very fortunate to have a friend who worked for the label that put out the first Damned album, *Damned Damned Damned*. We went down to CBGB to the first Damned show. Literally the second they started to play, my life changed. When I saw the Damned bust out, that was it. I went insane for punk rock. I felt this was what I wanted to be doing.[36]

An important running theme in both the US- and UK-centered narratives is that genres' beginnings are often ascribed to visits across the Atlantic. The establishment of rock genres as something separate from black American genres seems to be dependent on the perceived travel of that music across the Atlantic, to be transformed by the white musicians there, and then return as something new. Consistent exchange furthermore has the benefit of creating a network of white bohemians supporting exploratory travel as well as touring. White Americans have been consistently invested in these British imitations and transformations of black American music, which they see as revealing something about themselves.

## Developing Punk in Britain out of American Sources

British musicians were explicitly and self-consciously developing punk out of American sources around 1976, just as bands such as the Beatles and Rolling Stones were explicitly working with American sources to create their versions of rock music a decade earlier. The opposite is less accurate: while white American musicians drew on British inspirations, the genealogy of early American punk is much more in line with its American sources, especially its black American sources, than has been generally acknowledged. What I have already tried to do in this chapter is show the purpose and significance of white Americans positioning Great Britain as the starting point for punk, and for rock more broadly, despite the music's consistent and demonstrable roots in black American music. But also, as is appropriate to the scope and thesis of this book, I am not focusing on British punk in general. Instead, I concentrate on the British bands who were widely interpreted by Americans as changing punk and returning it to America in one way or another, and the groups that were most vocal about their debt to, rejection of, or relationship with American punk, and as such were central to the white Atlantic exchanges that solidified the punk style in America.[37]

Echoing John Lennon's words quoted above, "We developed our own style but we still in a way parodied American music," punk in the United Kingdom followed a similar path of developing a British style through imitating and then adjusting American music. British punk bands ran a stylistic gamut, from bands who continued to make music based on American models but with different vocal and rhythmic approaches to bands who extended the new possibilities opened up by the Ramones. The British bands also expanded the repertoire of covered material, especially with respect to the incorporation of reggae. Finally, British bands introduced an intense element of fashion which went beyond "packaging" to shift punk's discourse from race to class.

Many of the early British punk bands played fast, aggressive rock and roll in standard song forms, drawing heavily on the Ramones blueprint. The extensive distribution of some American punk music in 1975 and 1976, especially Patti Smith's *Horses* (Arista) and *Ramones* (Sire), enabled the music to travel quickly and to be studied. For Viv Albertine of the Slits, *Horses* was "emancipating" in terms of self-expression, sexuality, and style.[38] In the words of Kris Needs, the

Ramones' "glorious three-chord barrage" became "the template" for many bands in the United Kingdom (although the Ramones' music was not really "three-chord," even on the first album).[39] Joe Strummer explained, remembering 1976, *Ramones* was "almost the only piece of vinyl that we had that we could say was punk." He said Sid Vicious, Paul Simonon, and others used the album when learning to play, because "it was obviously simple and you could kind of follow the chords even if you had only just picked up the instrument. So they gave us a lot of fuel, the Ramones."[40]

It bears repeating: in no way did every British punk band model themselves anew after hearing the Ramones debut record, and *Ramones* did not magically create the British punk scene from scratch. On the contrary, as noted above, there were parallel developments in the UK of bands drawing on 1960s and early 1970s punk and R&B inspired by the Stooges, the Velvet Underground, the Kinks, Captain Beefheart, Them, the New York Dolls, and others. But *Ramones* gave the British scene "a lot of fuel," providing a catalyst for innovation among a significant cohort.

From this point on, there was also a new relationship between punk and major-label full-length albums, with wider distribution and drastically increased accessibility for the music, but also fraught with commercialism and "selling out." And the speed at which musicians developed punk became more rapid. Styles that took several years to take hold in local scenes were now spreading over the course of a few months, creating a more condensed timeline. For example, the Ramones released their second album, *Leave Home*, before *The Clash*, and had already released their third, *Rocket to Russia*, before *Never Mind the Bollocks*. Meanwhile, the music discussed in the next chapter on the burgeoning LA scene was roughly contemporaneous with what was happening in Great Britain. The narrative placing 1976 or 1977 England as punk's starting point obscures the fact that Panic (Black Flag) also formed in 1976, Greg Ginn inspired by his interest in New York punk such as Television and the Ramones, as well as Black Sabbath, the Stooges, and the MC5.[41]

Many of the early documents of British punk that had an immediate impact in the US, including *Damned Damned Damned*, *Never Mind the Bollocks Here's the Sex Pistols*, and *The Clash* (all released in 1977) or *Generation X* (1978), capture a range of approaches to the Ramones blueprint.[42] The major stylistic innovations of these groups all supported the white Atlantic process of unmooring punk from the backdrop of race in America, and resolving stylistic tensions found in earlier American punk—including in the New York scene—into a new music that could be interpreted as white and British in origin. British punks increased tempos and minimized backbeats, emphasizing straight rhythms over swing, separating the music from its rock and roll dance background; they amplified white working-class British vocal accents; and they expanded song forms to the longer AABA cycles associated with Tin Pan Alley and British precedents. Part of the overall racial remapping also involved a heavier emphasis on reggae as a signifier of blackness, placed in relation to white punk as complementary expressions of British's black and white working classes.

The British bands started to increase tempos, but not as much as is generally taken for granted. Fast songs such as "Neat Neat Neat" and "New Rose" (the Damned) and "Boredom" (Buzzcocks) hover around 180 beats per minute, roughly the same tempo as the Ramones' fast songs such as "Blitzkrieg Bop," and "Chain Saw." The Clash played faster—"White Riot" and "Janie Jones" are played at about 210 bpm—and the Sex Pistols tended to play slower—"Anarchy in the UK" is only about 142 bpm. But a different rhythmic approach and drumming style made British punk sound quicker. Songs such as "Blitzkrieg Bop," although faster than typical rock and roll dance songs, still have a strong backbeat on beats two and four, making the song sound slower, more danceable, and like it has a certain swing. It is still in the vein of "pure rock and roll." On the other hand, "White Riot," "Janie Jones," and "New Rose" often emphasize beats one and three as much as beats two and four. Even the Sex Pistols, the most musically traditional of the new British punk bands, used a backbeat but moved toward this straight-four drumming style on songs like "God Save the Queen." A comparison of the Stooges'"1970" and the cover version by the Damned (renamed "I Feel Alright") brings this transformation into sharp focus. They are only a few beats per minute different—the Stooges' original is much faster than it sounds at 225 bpm, while the Damned's version is a little faster at 236 bpm—but they sound very different. In the Stooges' version the bass and guitar riff emphasizes the backbeat, and the hi-hat/snare pattern is interspersed with a snare/tom-tom pattern giving the song a strong swing and danceability, as expected from the group that produced "1969" and "No Fun." The Damned keep the riff, but the accents on two and four, which are so important to the original, are downplayed within Rat Scabies' barrage of steady cymbals on every beat.

The most obvious and drastic change in British punk was the overt use of British accents rather than imitations of black American blues voices, which was the standard approach of earlier British rock singers. This was a break with American models that had the effect of seriously undermining punk's connections to its black American and common-stock sources. Johnny Rotten's lyrics and his voice, using exaggerated theatrical inflections taken from Laurence Olivier's performance as Richard III, are arguably the only aspects of the Sex Pistols' music that separate it from standard rock and roll. British punk singers of various racial and ethnic backgrounds, including Steve Ignorant (Crass) and pioneering woman of color Poly Styrene (X-Ray Spex), exploited local-sounding vocal styles, highlighting working-class, regional, or otherwise identifiably

British accents, although it should be emphasized that these too were aesthetic stylizations.[43] The issue of syllable emphasis—one's literal *accent*—is of prime importance, and in music, it can be the primary signal when other aspects of one's voice are modified for singing. For one simple example, when Joe Strummer sings "back in the **ga**-rage with my bullshit detector," singing the strong first syllable of *garage* on the strong downbeat of the measure (just as he places the first syllable of ***ga**-rage* on strong beats throughout the song), one hears the British pronunciation of ***ga**-rage* as directly contrasted with the American pronunciation of *ga-**rage**.*[44]

The change in syllabic emphasis as a marker of British regionalism in rock goes back at least to Ray Davies of the Kinks. As a model for punk singers he self-consciously "had abandoned any attempt to Americanise my accent" by 1965.[45] Davies often did not take a blues-style *rhythmic* approach to his singing, even when he adopted a quasi-American tone. Instead, at key moments, he ignored the stress patterns of the syllables and avoided swing, evenly distributing the syllables in time with the beat. Treating the stress patterns equally yields an effect different from the syncopation in African American rhythm and blues, in which accented syllables fall on offbeats to generate rhythmic layering. Davies's approach is immediately apparent in the opening verse of "You Really Got Me." As shown in musical example 5.1, Davies holds and sneers the *n* of "doin'," finally adding a voweled *-na* on the upbeat of the next measure. A typical blues singer or a rock singer imitating a blues singer's approach would end the syllable in a more straightforward manner. Davies also shifts the typical rhythmic placement of the syllables in the ending line, "so I can't sleep at night." A blues singer would normally put at least the first stressed syllable, *I*, on the strong beat, and approximate the placement of the other strong syllables, *sleep* and *night*, on strong beats. Davies, instead, aligns the weak syllables—*so*, *can't*, and *at*—with beats 1 and 3, evenly performing the syllables in strict conformity to the guitar riff.

| | | 1 | | 2 | | 3 | | 4 | | |
|---|---|---|---|---|---|---|---|---|---|---|
| riff: | (x) | x | x | x | x | | | | x | | x |
| | | Girl_____ | | | | | | you | real- | ly |
| | | got | me | go- | ing, | | | you | got | me |
| | | **so** | I | don't | know | **what** | | I'm | do- | in- |
| | | **-na** | | | | | | | | |
| | | Yeah | | | | | | you | real- | ly |
| | | got | me | now, | | | | you | got | me |
| | | **so** | I | **can't** | sleep | **at** | | night | | |

Musical example 5.1. "You Really Got Me" vocal rhythm, Kinks, *Kinks*, 1964.

Compare "You Really Got Me" with Wire's "Three Girl Rhumba" from *Pink Flag* (1977). Like "You Really Got Me," "Three Girl Rhumba" is based on a nearly identical whole-step, barre-chord riff. However, unlike "You Really Got Me," "Three Girl Rhumba" stays almost completely on this riff, without moving to other harmonic centers in the manner of a three-part blues as "You Really Got Me" does, and the turnaround appears infrequently. The lyrics also lack the first-person subjectivity that is so characteristic of the blues and found in the raw power songs of the Stooges. Perhaps most importantly, singer Colin Newman extends Ray Davies's approach, avoiding an imitation of a blues voice in favor of a pronounced English accent, and without aligning strong syllables and strong beats. As shown in musical example 5.2, like Davies, Newman mostly divides the syllables evenly, and he places weak syllables (*-ber* instead of *num-*, *by* instead of *two*) on strong beats. The accent is enough to obscure this song from being heard as blues, despite the strong blues-based riff. If Newman had sung with a blues timbre and placed strong accents like *num-* on or near strong beats, there would seem to be little question about the song's blues foundation.

|        | 1     |      |     | 2    |  3    |  4   |      |
|--------|-------|------|-----|------|-------|------|------|
| riff:  | x     |      |     | x    | x     | x    |      |
|        | Think | of   | a   | num- | **ber** |      | di-  |
|        | vide  | it   | by  | two  |       |      |      |
|        | some- | thin | is  | no-  | **thin** |      |      |
|        | no-   | thin | is  | no-  | **thin** |      |      |

Musical example 5.2. "Three Girl Rhumba" vocal rhythm, Wire, *Pink Flag*, Harvest, 1977.

The shift to British accents was not immediate, demonstrating the back-and-forth of imitation and rejection between the US and UK that was essential to the formation of punk. While Johnny Rotten, Joe Strummer, Jimmy Pursey (Sham 69), Poly Styrene, and Howard Devoto (who sang on *Spiral Scratch*, before Pete Shelley became the main voice of Buzzcocks) emphasized British accents, other British singers still used American models. Many of the early British punks who had carried over from the rhythm and blues scene, such as Slaughter and the Dogs (Wayne Barrett) and Johnny Moped, continued to sing in an American style and generally over more traditional song structures, and some younger singers such as Billy Idol also used American accents at times. Stewart Home attributed the "insistence on singing in British regional accents" to the success of *The Clash*, and specifically, Strummer's accent combined with the "anti-Americanism" of "I'm So Bored with the U.S.A."[46] While "anti-Americanism" is much too strong of a word for what the Clash were up to, especially given their well-documented love for American music, *The Clash* and *Never Mind the Bollocks* (with its flippant "New York") certainly helped establish a new model for punk singers in the UK, and comparing singers after 1977 to earlier UK punk singers supports Home's claim.

British punks also disassociated punk from its American sources by applying the Ramones blueprint to longer song forms, reversing the trend among American punk musicians toward shorter cycles. Instead of the medium-length AAB, twenty-four-bar, and sixteen-bar cycles heard in pure rock and roll American punk, British punks used AABA forms and multiple contrasting sections, evocative of early Tin Pan Alley. Furthermore, the recordings produced by British punk bands in 1977, and which had the most impact among American punk bands at the time, tended to avoid the raw power style, which was still more connected to the blues.

The closed-form pure rock and roll structures favored by the Ramones had already been in wide circulation among American bands such as the New York Dolls and Blondie, and British R&B (or "pub rock") bands such as the 101ers. These songs rarely featured any extended vamps, and British punk bands mostly sang major melodies rather than the minor pentatonic melodies supported by one- and two-chord riff-based blues songs. Some groups picked up on extended patterns in the Velvet Underground style, including standard I–IV or I–IV–V rock cycles, but some of these groups, such as Siouxsie and the Banshees (e.g., on early songs such as "Carcass," with its ending V–IV–I vamp) and Throbbing Gristle ("Zyklon B Zombie" was based on "I Heard Her Call My Name") mostly moved away from the kind of punk described in this book. And although some British punk songs such as the Sex Pistols' "Submission" used minor pentatonic patterns played with barre chords in a Ramones style, and some songs such as X-Ray Spex's "Let's Submerge" (1978) and Chelsea's "Right to Work" (1977) used minor riffs in a Stooges style, minor riffs were often balanced with major sections. For example, the early Siouxsie and the Banshees song "Bad Shape," heard in Don Letts's *Punk Rock Movie*, is an AAB form with an A section following a I–IV–I–V short cycle, and the B section uses the minor pentatonic I–IV–♭III–I–V.[47]

The major tonality of the chorus of the Clash's "White Riot," which also begins the song (a standard option in verse-chorus forms), is a quintessential example of early British punk following a pure rock and roll approach:

Musical example 5.3. "White Riot," Clash, *The Clash*, 1977. Transcription by the author.

"White Riot" also uses a mi-fa-mi-do melody evocative of the types of melodies associated with the passamezzo moderno (e.g., "Pills" or "Bile Them Cabbage Down"), and the chorus is an eight-bar phrase divided into two equal halves, the I chord returning at regular intervals in strong positions and the second half ending on the I chord after increased harmonic movement.

Most archetypal British punk songs, such as the Clash's "Janie Jones" and "Career Opportunities," the Sex Pistols' "God Save the Queen" and "Anarchy in the UK," and Generation X's "Ready Steady Go" used similar combinations of I, IV, and V chords supporting major melodies and arranged with the I chords in strong positions. However, British punk bands also began diverging from the shorter cycle forms (AB, AAB) found in American rock and roll and early American punk in favor of longer cycles, and they used eight-bar blocks more freely to support original compositions. While some songs such as the Clash's "London's Burning" use short harmonic cycles (I–♭VII–IV–V) and a consistent AB or verse-chorus alternation, British punk musicians tended to use longer cycles, including the proper AABA type, as well as more bridges, middle eights, guitar solos, and other ways of expanding the song form. At the time, these longer cycles, including Tin Pan Alley forms such as the true AABA, signaled European rather than African American models—as well as, perhaps ironically, the white middle- and upper-class audience for pre–rock and roll Tin Pan Alley popular music, as opposed to the black and rural working-class white audiences for country and blues.[48]

Like the relative emphasis of beats two and four in drumming styles, changes in form are subtle but have a significant impact on the listener. As I argue in chapter 4, "AABA," "thirty-two-bar," and "Tin Pan Alley" are often used too generally when it comes to rock structures, and pure rock and roll musicians in the rhythm and blues vein often played shorter AB or AAB cycles. For example, the verses of "Blitzkrieg Bop" very noticeably return to the beginning of the cycle after the B section (twenty-four bars), although the song is often wrongly described as an AABA form.[49] These shorter cycles make the Real Kids, Blondie, Modern Lovers, the Ramones, and other American groups sound like earlier rock and roll or rhythm and blues, as rock and roll groups of the 1950s and early 1960s also tended to prefer shorter cycles. In contrast, British punk musicians gravitated toward longer forms. As shown in musical example 5.4, for the first time in punk's stylistic history we regularly start to hear actual AABA thirty-two-bar forms in songs such as "God Save the Queen":

| | 1 | 2 | 3 | 4 | 5 | 6 | 7 | 8 |
|---|---|---|---|---|---|---|---|---|
| A | I | IV-III-IV | I | IV-III-IV | I | IV-III-IV | I | |
| A | I | IV-III-IV | I | IV-III-IV | I | IV-III-IV | I | |
| B | V II* | V | V II | V | V II | V | V II | V |
| A' | I | IV-III-IV | I | IV-III-IV | I | IV-III-IV | I | |

(* the II chord in the B section is more accurately described as V of V)

Musical example 5.4. "God Save the Queen" chords, Sex Pistols, *Never Mind the Bollocks Here's the Sex Pistols*, 1977.

The I–V–I turnaround at the end of the cycle (bars 29 to 32), supported by a drum break, clearly marks the return to the beginning of the AABA form. Each "A" line also begins with "God save the queen," underscoring the form. "B" in this context operates as a bridge in a thirty-two-bar AABA form, not as an interlude between self-contained cycles. The guitar solo (over VI–II–VI–II–VI–II–VI–V) instead serves as a short eight-bar interlude before returning to A'. The outro ("no future") is not a familiar short-cycle or one- or two-chord vamp, such as would be used by the Stooges; rather, it is a coda of the Tin Pan Alley variety. "Anarchy in the UK" follows a similar AABA form. The AABA' verses are interrupted with sixteen-bar instrumental sections, but the AABA' cycle is supported harmonically and lyrically. And as with "God Save the Queen," the last A (A') serves as a coda, repeated twice.

Another classic song in this type is Buzzcocks' "Breakdown," also a major melody sung in a heavily emphasized British accent with equal syllabic treatment (what Jon Savage called "mickey-mouse, fake Cockney"), and with verses, refrains, bridges, and choruses, in an AABC form played twice:[50]

Intro, 4 mm.

A        Verse, with refrain (2x), 12 mm.

A        Verse, with refrain (2x), 12 mm.

B        Bridge (starts on IV), 8 mm.

C        Chorus, using refrain (I–IV alternation), 8 mm.

[the AABC form repeats]

Outro, 4 mm.

Musical example 5.5. "Boredom" form, Buzzcocks, *Spiral Scratch*, 1977.

Ambitious groups such as the Clash and Buzzcocks introduced bridges, middle eights, and guitar solos, and moved to unpredictable harmonic areas. Even songs with shorter alternations tended to be expanded with multiple sections. For example, "White Riot" goes through a fairly complex series of sections, more typical of British punk than American punk of the mid-1970s, with the first verse in a new key (down one whole step) and two guitar solos over the V chord.

Overall these British punk bands continued what the Ramones started by expanding cycle lengths, freely using structural blocks, and focusing on major-mode, equally divided "non-blues" pure rock and roll schemes. While perhaps not immediately apparent, the effect of playing longer cycles with more varied sections was certainly felt when compared with the trend toward shorter cycles, which was more typical of American bands. The overall trajectory is similar to what one hears when comparing early Beatles (short-cycle R&B tunes such as

"She Loves You," "Love Me Do") with mid- or late Beatles (consider the more varied structures of "While My Guitar Gently Weeps" and boldly non-blues songs like "Mother Nature's Son" and "Honey Pie"). The use of these "non-blues" harmonic schemes and longer forms helped categorize the music of the Clash and their contemporaries as connected to British musical traditions. These overtly European styles could also be connected to the British, Scottish, and Irish musical traditions in the United States, rather than black American traditions. A pronounced example of this path is XTC, who started in a punk mode (*White Music*, 1978) and increasingly adopted strong markers of English heritage.

Vamps, one-chord structures, and minor melodies as fundamental bases of songs often appear in early British punk as limited signifiers of blackness and black music styles such as reggae, funk, and soul, played against the mostly major-tonality, tightly-structured punk songs. Examples of these include the whole-step vamp which ends the Clash's version of Junior Murvin's "Police and Thieves," the minor melody of the Slits' version of "I Heard It Through the Grapevine," or the Clash's later forays into funk-infused music, such as "The Magnificent Seven" (1981) and "This is Radio Clash" (1981). These stylistic aspects took on increased associations with blackness in the late 1970s and early 1980s as reggae and then funk became the leading choices of black musics to explicitly incorporate into the punk aesthetic (e.g., Gang of Four, the Pop Group). However, as was the case with blues sources, the integration of these black musical styles into punk, either as stylistic elements or as repertoire, created a binary that served to recast the emerging standard punk style as white.

While the Sex Pistols and the Clash eventually had the most visibility, of the early British punk bands, the Damned ("The Beatles of Punk," according to Jeff Nelson of Minor Threat) had a particularly significant and immediate structural impact on American punk.[51] The Damned are especially notable for the ways in which they brought together the blues-based raw power approach of the Stooges and the pure rock and roll innovations of the Ramones into a distinctive sound. In retrospect, these two currents make sense as the main musical tributaries of punk, but in 1976 this was not the case. Although the Stooges were a common reference point for punk groups, the Ramones' music and the pure rock and roll approach had largely overshadowed the blues-based music of the Stooges, and when using blues elements, punk groups in the US and the UK tended to use the more ambiguous approaches favored by the Ramones. The Damned, on the other hand, helped bring the Stooges and their style back to punk's center, along with the music of similar blues-based bands such as the MC5. At the same time, subsumed under the main style of British punk, the raw power style became seriously removed from its original meanings.

The Damned's approach was not unprecedented—Chelsea, for example, had explored similar techniques—and soon many more groups would be inspirational to American bands, such as UK Subs, Sham 69, or the Raincoats, whose music opened up a tremendous amount of fresh approaches and possibilities especially for female punk musicians in the 1990s.[52] However, the Damned combined these styles in a particularly effective way, and they had a strong and early impact in the United States. They were the first British group to tour the US, where they played in the burgeoning new punk scenes of New York and Los Angeles. In LA in 1977, Pleasant Gehman recalled: "The Damned had usurped the Clash as our favorite English band. For weeks you could walk into any apartment at the Canterbury at any hour of the day or night and hear 'New Rose' or 'Fan Club' playing. In fact, The Damned album was always blaring so loudly, you didn't even have to be *in* the building—the sound carried out the open windows and you could hear it all the way down on Hollywood Boulevard."[53] While the fashion-centric Sex Pistols and the righteous Clash alienated many of the active American bands, the Damned's music resonated, drawing as it did on American sources in overt and compelling ways. They also shared a goofy sense of humor with many early American punk bands.

Several aspects of the Damned's music are indebted to the Stooges and other American bands, especially before Brian James left and the group reformed (*Machine Gun Etiquette*). At first Dave Vanian modeled his singing style after Iggy Pop, avoiding the British accents that had quickly become standard among British punk bands, and which he himself later cultivated. Vanian also invoked other American singers: "New Rose" (produced by American music enthusiast Nick Lowe) begins with a reference to the Shangri-Las' "Leader of the Pack": "Is she really going out with him?" Vanian's voice on "Born to Kill" and "Feel the Pain" could easily be mistaken for David Johansen or Wayne County, and lyrics such as those on "So Messed Up" are right out of the Stooges or New York Dolls catalog. Brian James played Stooges-esque blues-based guitar solos on songs such as "I Fall" and "1 of the 2," and his riff-based songs "Alone" and "You Know" on *Music for Pleasure* are based on the Stooges' style, including the open-ended sax solo (by Lol Coxhill) on "You Know." They covered "1970" ("I Feel Alright," *Damned Damned Damned*) one of the most quintessential blues-based Stooges songs, and later on *Machine Gun Etiquette*, the MC5's "Looking at You."

Brian James's "Neat Neat Neat," the opening track on *Damned Damned Damned*, demonstrates the Damned's approach to combining "raw power" and "pure rock and roll." As shown in musical example 5.6a, the verses exploit a classic raw power one-chord blues riff played by Captain Sensible on the bass, supported by Brian James's blues soloing around the tonic (F$\sharp$), with a riff that noticeably accents the syncopated "and of 2" in every second measure, underscoring Vanian's American-style singing. Similar to the Stooges, Vanian doubles the melodic riff, although here he sings a fifth above (harmonically the closest interval) rather than in unison or octaves. Also in the Stooges vein, the riff answers the verse in each break. During the verse Rat Scabies plays more of a backbeat than is typical of British punk (not represented in the music notation).

Musical example 5.6a and 5.6b. "Neat Neat Neat" riff and verse, Damned, *Damned Damned Damned*, 1997. Transcription by the author.

After the verse, the chorus shifts to a pure rock and roll style in the relative major key of A. The lyric is sung in a major mode, using mostly stepwise scalar motion, supported by a IV–I harmonic pattern. Although this combination of minor verse melodies and major choruses can be found in many mainstream pop songs of that era and earlier (e.g., the Lovin' Spoonful's "Summer in the City"), such forms are much less typical in the punk genealogy and have the effect of combining two distinct approaches. The contrast is underscored by the shift from a riff to chords. Musical example 5.6c shows the major melody and IV–I harmony of the chorus:

Musical example 5.6c. "Neat Neat Neat," Damned, *Damned Damned Damned*, 1997.

The two styles are meshed: the pure rock and roll chorus aligns with the verse by keeping the syncopated rhythm emphasizing the "and of 2" (here in every first measure of two), while the raw power verse fits with the chorus by being adjusted into a closed-form verse-chorus AAB format of eight-bar phrases, common to Ramones songs. And as shown in musical example 5.6d, in the expanded style of British punk, the AAB cycle is couched within a larger overall form that includes an intro, a guitar solo, a breakdown, and a short coda:

Bass riff, f♯ minor pentatonic (4 mm.)

Bass riff + guitar solo, f♯ minor pentatonic (8 mm.)

A       Verse, f♯ minor pentatonic (8 mm.)

A       Verse, f♯ minor pentatonic (8 mm.)

B       Chorus, A major (8 mm. + 2/4 bar)

        [repeat AAB]

Guitar solo, f# minor pentatonic (16 mm.)

drum breakdown, backbeat heavy (8 mm.)

A       Verse, f♯ minor pentatonic (8 mm.)

A       Verse, f♯ minor pentatonic (8 mm.)

B       Chorus, A major (8 mm.)

B       Coda: Chorus, A major (8 mm.)

Musical example 5.6d. "Neat Neat Neat," Damned, *Damned Damned Damned*, 1977.

Structurally speaking, the Damned's merging of raw power and pure rock and roll styles of punk rock established a synthesized model for punk, which also recontextualized the American source material and separated it from the social context from which it emerged. Two more elements, reggae and fashion, were also crucial to the ostensible break between early American punk and the more fully formed style of punk that became so well known after 1976.

### Reggae and Ska

In 1977 Lester Bangs called Burning Spear "utterly hypnotic, a slow vortex of spiraling rhythms, tidal horns, and sedimentary piano over which Rupert

Willington and Delroy [Hines] wave sad, brooding harmonies that sway like looming kelp behind Winston Rodney's sinuous, plaintive, hauntingly primitive chants which alternately telegraph or painfully cry out tribal philippics, painting stark images of slave ships and shackles around the legs," and he wrote, "Today you can hear the entire history of black music coming out of that little island below Cuba. . . ."[54] With widespread white appropriation of the blues and with rock becoming increasingly understood simply as white by the late 1970s, white musicians looked for new signifiers of blackness to give their music soul, meaning, authenticity, and tension. Jamaican music broadly came to fill a major role in punk as a black musical "other," especially as immigration from Jamaica increased in the UK and the US. For white musicians at the time, reggae could be seen as a more contemporary version of the blues—a symbol of society's outsiders, extremely black, hypnotic, spiritual, and ganja-addled.

British punks are consistently credited with the innovation of drawing on reggae for inspiration, and for introducing reggae and ska into the punk vocabulary. Hebdige devoted a great deal of *Subculture* to analyzing reggae and its distinctive relationship to the British punk subculture.[55] However, as with other white Atlantic phenomena, the reality of punk's relationship to reggae and ska is a product of typically complex exchange and parallel histories. More than has been properly appreciated, the use of reggae in early American punk preceded or paralleled the same types of use by punks in Great Britain. However, the British punks were more vocal and explicit about their interest in reggae and other Jamaican styles, and the British uses of reggae were especially instrumental in the white Atlantic processes that turned punk into something whiter and less American.

Without a doubt, the "punk–dread alliance," as Joe Strummer described it, was a factor in 1970s England.[56] Great Britain had become the major site of immigration for Jamaicans, as Commonwealth citizens leaving behind high levels of unemployment between 1950 and 1968.[57] Reggae in Britain played a crucial role as a newly "discovered" black roots music that could replace blues, the latter having become too associated with white rock musicians at this point to have the same powerful affect it used to have. Reggae had already been somewhat mainstream among white people in England since Desmond Dekker's "Israelites" hit #1 in 1969, and the movie and soundtrack to *The Harder They Come* (1972) was instrumental in further raising reggae's profile in the United Kingdom.

Punks in the United Kingdom went deep into reggae. Joe Strummer was introduced to dub around 1973 or 1974 through black acquaintances in South Wales.[58] Junior Murvin's "Police and Thieves" (1976) was famously covered by the Clash soon after its release (1977), heard by Strummer in the reggae clubs he and other punks frequented, such as the 4 Aces in Dalston.[59] Don Letts, one of the most prominent black figures in the London punk scene, came to Rastafarianism and reggae music after seeing *The Harder They Come* as a teenager, and as the DJ at the Roxy in 1977 he almost exclusively played dub and reggae for the punk clientele, which had a significant impact on the popularity of reggae in that scene. In 1978 he and John Lydon traveled to Jamaica to find artists for Virgin Records.[60] The Clash was not only one of the most prominent punk groups in the world, but reggae was a cornerstone of their style; they used reggae to bolster their political message, including songs about race such as "The Guns of Brixton" and "White Man in Hammersmith Palais," which also included some of Strummer's reflections about his own interest in the reggae scene. The Clash collaborated with Mikey Dread and Lee Perry, and they explored dub techniques, for example releasing Mikey Dread's "versions" of their cover of Willie Williams's "Armagideon Time" (like "Police and Thieves," released only slightly after Williams's single). The Slits heavily based their style on reggae, incorporating syncopated guitar patterns, heavy bass lines, and the "one drop" rhythm (leaving empty—"dropping"—a drumstroke marking the first beat of the measure) popularized by Carlton Barrett, Bob Marley's drummer, on songs such as "Newtown" from the Dennis Bovell–produced album *Cut*.

However, the relationship between American punk and reggae paralleled these developments in the UK, and in many cases was separate from the circumstances that led to reggae and ska's impact on British punk. In 1969 Britain closed off immigration from former colonies, increasing emigration to North America.[61] Mainstream reggae hits were similarly known among white rock listeners in the United States: "Israelites" hit #9 in the US, and Bob Marley was touring the US as early as 1973, the same year he started playing the UK. In 1964, several years before "Israelites," Millie Small's version of "My Boy Lollipop" reached #1 in the UK and #2 in the US; Johnny Nash had the first US reggae hit recorded in Jamaica, "Hold Me Tight," in 1968 (although he was American); Jimmy Cliff's "Wonderful World, Beautiful People" was a US hit in 1969.[62] In 1972 Nash charted with Bob Marley's "Stir It Up" on *I Can See Clearly Now* and Paul Simon had a hit with his reggae-infused single, "Mother and Child Reunion." *Rastaman Vibration* was a sensation in 1976, cracking the US Top 10, the same year Stevie Wonder met Third World. The impact of reggae on hip-hop, such as Jamaican DJ Kool Herc's adaptation of the reggae sound system for Bronx house parties, is well documented.[63] Because British and American punks had parallel interests in reggae, the style became an important social meeting point across the Atlantic; musicians such as Chrissie Hynde and Lenny Kaye connected with British punk musicians at reggae shows in England.[64] Patti Smith met Tappa Zukie in England through Don Letts in 1975.[65]

White people moderating the discussions over reggae's relationship to punk, following early discourse about blues, often misrepresented or underplayed the African diasporic exchanges and dynamic history that created the music and its sound. Of course, Jamaican reggae did not develop in isolation only to be "discovered" by white people in New York or London; rather, it was one style among many African diasporic styles in the Caribbean, Americas, and Europe that drew upon the same melodic and harmonic resources as jazz, blues, and rock.[66] Rock steady, precursor to reggae and ska, was modeled on American rhythm and blues. And much of the music that had a major effect on rock musicians, such as Bob Marley's recordings, were themselves commercial, hybrid creations: Catch a Fire (1973) was released on Island Records (the label run by Chris Blackwell, an English and Irish Sephardic Jew from a colonist family in Jamaica, and who spent much of his childhood in Jamaica) with songs written with the Houston-born Johnny Nash and guitar work by the Muscle Shoals session player Wayne Perkins.[67] These transatlantic and international networks were complicated by political issues, such as the strained relationships between the US and Jamaica under Prime Minister Michael Manley (1972–80) as he attempted to take greater control over the bauxite industry (historically controlled almost entirely by four North American companies) and aligned with Cuba.[68] But despite political obstacles and language separating reggae from rock, blues, jazz, and rhythm and blues—Hebdige, for example, wrote "the differences between rock and reggae should be sufficiently obvious"—the stylistic connections have been clear to musicians, who made productive use of these shared resources through the 1960s, 1970s, and 1980s, and continued with other developments in the family tree, such as dance music and hip-hop.[69]

Specifically regarding punk's history, Patti Smith introduced reggae to the vocabulary with "Redondo Beach" on Horses. But Patti Smith was much more committed to reggae than this one song suggests, and biographers and punk historians tend to mischaracterize and minimize her interests in reggae, for example describing the music of "Redondo Beach" as an "upbeat reggae beat and style" "juxtaposed" against "the truly horrible theme behind the lyrics."[70] Reggae was deeply serious for Smith, not an upbeat evocation of a carefree island vacation. As early as 1975, the Patti Smith Band was performing Lloyd Parks's "Mafia," released the same year, and by March 1976 they were regularly playing Burning Spear's "Slavery Days" (1975).[71] The reggae-inspired "Ain't It Strange" was in their repertoire in 1975 as well. On a TV interview preceding her October 3, 1976, concert in Stockholm, Patti Smith began by saying, "I like Bob Marley. Bob Marley I think is real sexy. I like Blue Öyster Cult, Television, I like Leo Fender for inventing the Fender guitar."[72] And considering Ari Up and Palmolive's initial idea for the Slits came at Patti Smith's 1976 show, Smith's use of reggae probably also had a direct impact on the Slits' reggae-based style.[73]

Smith connected to reggae as part of the overall affinity she was attempting to establish between all people "outside of society," including artists such as herself in search of absolute freedom. In an interview with Lee Paris, Smith explained:

I think our band has a connection with all people, like underdogs with a sense of vision. All these people whether Rastafarians [*sic*] or new wave kids. I couldn't call our band anything—we're not a punk rock band, we're not a reggae band, we're not even an outer space band. We're a band that strives for communication with all people. We've always existed as ROCK N ROLL NIGGER says—outside society. We've always tried to champion the underdog.[74]

Songs in Smith's repertoire, such as Burning Spear's "Slavery Days," were the epitome of serious roots reggae. For Smith, "slavery" was a metaphor for the enslaved artistic spirit that needed to be set free: "in the past the artist has existed within society in two disguises . . . the slave or the exiled."[75] In many ways, Patti Smith's interest in reggae paralleled that of Joe Strummer, John Lydon, and Ari Up. They each saw Rastafarians in particular as marginalized in ways that went beyond race, as Rastafarians were also on the fringes of black society.

Patti Smith's reggae and reggae-infused repertoire reflected a broader interest in reggae in New York. Sire Records, home to Patti Smith, Talking Heads, Richard Hell, and Dead Boys, was also the home of Martha Velez, the New York–based singer produced by Bob Marley and Lee "Scratch" Perry (*Escape from Babylon*, 1976). The 1978 compilation *The Sire Machine Turns You Up* shows the network of New York reggae and punk, featuring Velez next to Smith and Hell. Reggae had an outsize impact among rock audiences in New York through the efforts of Michael "Eppy" Epstein, the owner of My Father's Place in Roslyn, Long Island, and Denis McNamara, program director of WLIR, a small station that had an immense impact throughout the entire New York area.[76] My Father's Place opened in 1971 and began broadcasting concerts on WLIR in 1972, reaching a wide and varied New York listenership. Not only was My Father's Place a major venue for early punk bands—the Stooges, New York Dolls, Patti Smith, and Ramones all played early gigs there—but Epstein also booked some of the earliest concerts by reggae performers. Epstein visited Jamaica beginning in 1972, where he heard U-Roy, Big Youth, and others at the Chela Bay Hotel; he began booking reggae at My Father's Place in 1973, and Monday became a regular reggae night (he later also managed Burning Spear and hosted "Punky Reggae Party" on WLIR).[77] My Father's Place attracted diverse audiences for its lineups, and the punk rock, folk, blues, country, and reggae audiences would often overlap. Some of the earliest tapes in the collection of James Brawley, who attempted to record every show by Patti Smith as well as many more punk bands at CBGB, are reggae nights at My Father's Place in 1977 (e.g., U-Roy, September 12, 1977); his collection also includes Bob Marley at the Beacon Theater (1976), Peter Tosh at the Beacon (1976), and Max Romeo at NYU (1977).[78] These concerts are contemporaneous with the flowering of the British punk scene and its impact on New York.

In the UK, the use of reggae by punk musicians was more widespread, and punk and reggae were seen as styles that together represented black and white people living in similar circumstances as neighbors. But a by-product of incorporating reggae styles such as syncopated guitar and drum patterns into punk, or punks playing reggae repertoire, was more racialization.[79] These were heard *as* combinations, with "punk" increasingly inscribed as the "white" opposite to "black" reggae, and in this binary, black American styles such as the blues were no longer understood as a factor in punk. A song like Bob Marley's "Punky Reggae Party" (1977), while celebratory, implicitly presented the two as separate entities that could be combined as a hybrid, and Marley's mention of only British groups (the Damned, the Jam, the Clash, and Dr. Feelgood) further characterized punk as a British phenomenon. As Don Letts explained: ". . . the reggae thing and the punk thing . . . it's the same fuckin' thing. Just the black version and the white version."[80]

Some of the most intensive treatments of Jamaican popular music styles on the British punk scene were interracial reggae and ska groups, including the Specials, the Selecter, and the Beat (a/k/a the English Beat). These groups organized around the term *two-tone*, their record label and a reference to the movement's self-conscious efforts to unify black and white people.[81] These groups in particular were notable because they had black musicians, unlike the Clash, the Slits, and other early British punk groups interested in reggae, and because their musical foundation was reggae and ska, not punk as it was becoming understood. The Selecter was especially unusual in that they featured Pauline Black, a woman of color, and had only one white person in the seven-piece group. (Unsurprisingly, given the lucrative history of white appropriation, the most successful group to eventually come out of this scene was the all-white Madness.)[82]

Two-tone was the most racially integrated branch of the British punk scene, but by its emergence in the late 1970s punk had become primarily associated with British white people. Although two-tone groups played punk venues and were part of the scene, musically two-tone groups were committed to reggae and ska, underscoring the notion that reggae and ska were ideal musical formats for integrated groups, and that punk was a separate style implicitly associated with white British youth.

In the US, reggae followed a similar route, but with less intensity. American punk musicians continued to draw on reggae and ska, from limited uses (Circle Jerks' "Back Against the Wall") to groups based on reggae and ska models, such as the Offs in San Francisco and later Operation Ivy and Rancid out of Berkeley. Interracial bands in the two-tone mode formed in the US soon after they did in the UK, such as the Mighty Mighty Bosstones (formed in 1983), but without a parallel named "two-tone" movement and more separately from the broader punk scene. Reggae's symbolic relation to blackness in the late 1970s and early

1980s, strengthened by British punks' treatments of Jamaican music, may indicate why the most serious early efforts to combine punk and reggae came in the US in the early 1980s from the two major all–African American punk bands, Bad Brains and Fishbone. Reggae in Bad Brains' repertoire especially went well beyond borrowing or imitations of British punk, traced to H.R. and Earl Hudson's childhood period in Jamaica, formative experiences such as the band seeing Bob Marley at the Capitol Centre outside Landover (Maryland) in 1978, and the band's interest and eventual adoption of Rastafarianism—a path similar to that taken by Don Letts in England about six years earlier. However, Bad Brains' claiming of reggae did not change the racial associations that solidified in the late 1970s, in large part due to white Atlantic processes, of reggae serving as a black complement to punk, which had already been taken for granted as white and which was now also understood as British—"the black version and the white version." Hebdige already recognized the contradiction that "at one level, the punks openly acknowledged the significance of contact and exchange [with reggae], and on occasion even elevated the cultural connection into a political commitment. . . . But at another, deeper level, the association seems to have been repressed, displaced on the part of the punks into the construction of a music which was emphatically white and even more emphatically British."[83] The early- to mid-1970s intimations of similar energy around punk and reggae in the United States were mostly obscured or forgotten as part of the punk narrative, much in the same way that the language of the white Atlantic placed British rock musicians as the discoverers of American blues who reintroduced the music to Americans. Underlying the whole phenomenon of (white) punk uses of (black) reggae is that, repeating the phenomenon of (white) rock uses of (black) blues, reggae has had a mostly white audience in the United States.[84]

## Punk Fashion and Class

Punk's relationship to fashion and "packaging," not music, became the major area of contention between the US and the UK as well as the older and newer styles. Early American punk bands such as the Ramones often rejected or resented the success of the British punk that followed them, seeing it as media-created and too focused on selling clothes. They were especially critical of what they saw as a new conformity in Britain connected to fashion, while they considered American punk to be essentially and necessarily heterogeneous with respect to its looks, who could participate, and the way it sounded.

In the context of the UK, punk fashion became part of a lineage of subcultures linking dress codes to music, as well as racial attitudes, types of drugs, vehicles, and especially class divisions.[85] These subcultures also took American and West

Indian styles and transformed their uses and meanings. Such groups include the Teddy Boys, prominent since the 1950s, connected to American rock and roll, and who used Edwardian dress; the Rudy or Rude Boy style from Jamaica; and the scooter-riding short-haired Mods and motorcycle-riding bouffanted Rockers in the 1960s. The Doc Maarten–shod, suspenders-wearing Skinheads also emerged in the 1960s, their style also based on West Indian fashions. As Hebdige effectively argued decades ago, fashion codes were often an arena for youth to work out the tensions between "us" and "them" in situations where the groups lived in close proximity and had overlapping economic stresses as poor and working-class people.[86]

Punk fashion drew on all of these predecessors while breaking their attached norms and codes, just as punk music did. In one sense, punk was a new one of these social circles marked by dress, and in another sense it criss-crossed divisions. Dennis Anderson and Lois Kahlert remembered, "a band like the Jam the mods would embrace, then Motörhead the rockers would embrace . . . the Clash started as rockers."[87] As Hebdige writes, "Punk reproduced the entire sartorial history of post-war working-class fashion cultures in cut-up form, combining elements which had originally belonged to completely different epochs."[88] Beyond the subcultural and class-specific codes, expressing oneself through clothes, fashion, and design was explicitly embraced as an important value in Britain, not something to deny or shrug off. The clothes one chooses from Vivienne Westwood and Malcolm McLaren's shop SEX "define you," in the words of Viv Albertine. "We all care a lot about style; everyone is united on that subject, even if we have different taste . . . how we look is extremely important and the nuances within the small scene are rigorously observed and judged."[89]

For American punk, all of these new codes established new rules, new associations, and new schisms. For one, British punk was becoming something "more self-consciously proletarian" than its American predecessor scenes, which were understood among its participants to be an expression of their almost completely middle-class, suburban backgrounds, as well as a rejection of such a background.[90] As Jerry Casale of DEVO understood it, punk "in the narrow sense of the word, where you had to play a certain way, sound a certain way on record, look a certain way" had more resonance in England because the people there were "A, much more fashion conscious, and B, poor," as opposed to the United States, where "kids have plenty of toys to play with and Daddy bankrolls you for anything you want."[91]

British punks in fact came from a wide range of backgrounds, but the style and its affectations became associated with the white working class—hence the modest controversy surrounding Joe Strummer's "public school" (the British term for private school) background and his "guttersnipe" persona.[92] Despite Britain's own entrenched racism, the lasting effects of blackface minstrelsy, the appropriation of black American music by British rock musicians, and the heavily racialized nature of British fashion cultures, the back-and-forth of the white Atlantic helped the discourse shift to one solely focused on "class"—an idea that, as discussed throughout this book, cannot be responsibly separated from race in the United States.[93] The shift to a class-oriented paradigm was not only discursive, as Britain was in a serious economic downturn during the 1970s, most dramatically represented by the dustmen's (garbagemen's) strike in 1979.[94] US cities were also suffering economic hardship, but by and large these problems did not impact white American punks, except by choice (as it did affect, for example, urban African American populations), as they were mostly from middle-class suburban backgrounds whose overall status remained intact. If anything, the economic problems troubling American cities helped the punk scene as white suburbanites moved into cheap apartments and lofts.

The earlier American punk bands, even when they were the main contributors to aspects of the style (e.g., the Ramones' leather jackets and jeans, or Richard Hell's ripped shirt and safety-pin look) rejected the working-class associations of the new punk style. They considered their own looks to be an aspect of freedom and personal expression, not tied to a costume of group identification, and certainly not a reflection of a working-class background or identity. And they resented the unapologetic coalescence of the scene around Sex and Acme Attractions, stores that sold clothes. As Dennis Anderson told me: "Music [was] the dominant factor [in New York punk]. Not the fashion, not the politics; kids came for the music. In Britain it was more, 'Oh, you got a safety pin, I got a safety pin, let's go and see Siouxsie and the Banshees.'"[95] Some of the early British punk bands felt the same way about the sartorial aspects of the scene, which had quickly become perceived as the dominant element in punk. As Brian James remembered, "when we got back from The Damned's first US tour [in 1976] Rat and I went down to The Rainbow to see The Clash. The Clash were up on stage in that clothing they had started to wear, which was their choice, but we looked at the audience and they were all wearing the same—bondage trousers, etc. I just thought, do these people want to be like sheep? Is this what it's all come to when you have a uniform that people feel they need to wear? I thought then that the Punk scene was all over."[96] Even Don Letts, who co-managed the clothes shop Acme Attractions with Jeannette Lee, was skeptical in a 1977 interview with Mark P.: ". . . all the kids that come into the shop, they put so much importance in clothes. They're building up a force identity." Mark P. added: "I mean, safty-pins [sic] and all that game is OK but it's getting stupid. . . . no-one's done anything by worrying about clothes. Don said in his interview that he was 'above clothes,' well, we should all strive for that feeling."[97]

The shocking symbols used in punk fashion, especially the swastika, and the "moral panic" over incidents such as the Sex Pistols' appearance on Bill Grundy's television show, were like catnip to tabloid newspapers and other media outlets, and record labels saw potential for profits.[98] From the American perspective it appeared to be a punk movement in England, quite unlike punk rock in the United States, which was musically, ideologically, and sartorially diverse, and even though punk had been spreading in the US it was still limited to small communities in a handful of American cities. Punks in the US also saw their music as connected to a broader tradition of American music rather than something separate. As Johnny Ramone explained:

> [The music industry] wanted to play up on the negative aspect of the whole punk thing, make it into a fashion thing and not play up the music part of it.
>
> . . . People started doing articles on punk rock, they would start talking about the English punk rock, we were not included. We were an American band. It was different; there was no punk rock movement in America. So we would just be totally separate.
>
> . . . We were Americans . . . we did not want to become part of a fashion movement like that. Fashions come and go. By the time middle America finds out about a fashion, it's already been played out, it's no longer in fashion. . . . I already had my leather jackets since 1966. We settled on an image that we felt that everyone can relate to, that would not come in and out with trends. Jeans and sneakers and leather jackets had always been in. And they're still in.[99]

The intense linking of fashion with punk music through the explosive popularity of the British bands beginning in 1977 "fixed [punk] into an international teenage archetype of obnoxious, confrontation, and the simple celebration of the present and the future," establishing a new paradigm for Americans and orienting the whole idea of punk to younger people.[100] Punk became more of an "identity" in terms of a reflection of personality, which could be purchased and adopted with a little help and the right guide. One of the most blatant examples of this transformation of British fashion in the United States is the short 1977 zine "Punk Rock, The New Wave of Sound and Style: 'How to Look Punk'" by "Marliz," a collection of photos of members of the LA punk scene with instructions.[101] The zine seems absurd given punk's ethos, and by all accounts LA punks didn't take it seriously, but it also captures an important element of punk style and the beginnings of how Americans interpreted British fashion. With the new British bands and their looks, as well as the concomitant disavowal of the term "punk" by the earlier American groups, young American punks could see 1976 or 1977 England as "Ground Zero"—even if the musical lineage and historical record told a different story of exchange, continuity, and American roots. Young American punks accepted working-class associations as a factor in punk, without fully understanding the codes of the skinheads, rockers, and mods, at least partially because—just as with the British Invasion narrative—this move continued to draw punk away from black American sources and toward white and British alternatives (and, as with musical style, the British fashion codes were almost entirely read as white even when they were black in origin). As I have shown throughout this chapter, white Americans have found endless possibilities and uses in replacing or obscuring black American musical heritage with a superficially white British heritage, whether or not they are consciously applying this logic. Finally, the idea of a new origin point with British punk reflected the generational tension that was becoming clear between baby boomers and Generation X. As Lenny Kaye put it, "sometimes I think of us [Patti Smith Band] as the last of the '60s bands."[102] In the United States, these musical, racial, and generational tensions played out most dramatically in Los Angeles.

# 6

## "Less Art and More Machine": The California Crucible

The scene had changed a lot by then, and not for the better, if you ask me.
Clubs were shutting down because of the violence caused by people we didn't
know, those new guys from Orange County. Punk had turned a corner. Less art
and more machine, punk wasn't dead; it had just become something else.
—Robert Lopez (El Vez)[1]

The music created in California at the end of the 1970s effectively defined American punk. In Los Angeles and San Francisco, the currents of earlier northeastern and midwestern punk rock, partly reshaped by the British punk movement, formed into named punk styles. California became the major site for debates over the meaning and authenticity of these punk styles, and about what American punk should sound like going forward. Californians wrestled with punk's relation to race, ethnicity, gender, sexuality, class, and other axes of identity formation, as well as social privileges and political freedoms. It was also in California where punk rock as the last music of the sixties generation morphed into punk as a voice for Generation X heading into the eighties.

The familiar story of California's punk scene centers on the transformation from the Hollywood punk scene of the mid-1970s to the hardcore scene of the late 1970s and early 1980s associated with the Los Angeles suburbs.[2] The musicians often grouped together as the Hollywood punk scene, including X, the Screamers, the Go-Go's, the Zeros, the Plugz, the Dickies, the Flesh Eaters, the Deadbeats, the Bags, the Gun Club, the Germs, Black Randy, and the Alley Cats were characterized by a wide range of musical approaches, matching the diversity of the scene's participants. San Francisco's scene intersected with Los Angeles's, sometimes foregrounding social and political engagement following the city's deep involvement with the sixties counterculture. Proportionally, Hollywood punk was heavily queer, female, and Latinx, in many ways running parallel to the slightly earlier New York punk scene represented by groups such as Blondie, the Mumps, the Fast, Jayne County, and the Sic Fucks. Bands with female members included X, the Bags, the Avengers, the Nuns, Nervous Gender, the Germs, the Eyes, the Controllers, the Alley Cats, U.X.A., and a significant number of all-female bands, e.g., the Go-Go's, the Urge, and the Runaways (and Vs. in San Francisco). In LA, the groups with macho posturing, such as Fear and the Angry Samoans, were exceptions to the overall scene, and their ironic and confrontational music should be considered in relation to the lack of typical "cock rock" bands and fans. But by the early 1980s, Los Angeles's punk scene seemed to be dominated by the hardcore bands of young straight white males formed in semi-autonomous suburbs such as Hermosa Beach, Manhattan Beach, Huntington Beach, and Fullerton, beginning with the Middle Class and Black Flag, and other bands that formed early on, such as the Descendents, Vicious Circle/T.S.O.L., and Adolescents. A similar transformation was said to occur later in DC, as a scene with strong female representation changed "by mid-1981, [when] the punks' 'letting go' had effectively barred most women from both the dance floor and the stage."[3]

In actuality the LA Hollywood and hardcore scenes overlapped, or could be considered as one. Groups such as the Middle Class and Black Flag were widely appreciated when they came on the scene.[4] *Flipside* covered the wide range of LA punk early on, encouraging readers, "Who could imagine that out of a sedate beach community like Redondo Beach, a band like Black Flag could emerge. . . . If you have any balls you'd go see Black Flag and see what made the punk scene great in L.A. in the first place. Another point for the suburbs."[5] Women continued to be represented in LA punk bands, including hardcore bands such as Red Cross (with Tracy Lea and Janet Housden) and Black Flag (Kira Roessler, who had already played in Twisted Roots, Waxx, the Visitors, the Monsters, and DC3 before she joined Black Flag in 1983), as well as bands in other punk styles such as Suburban Lawns (fronted by Sue Tissue) and the all-female Bangs (who became the Bangles).[6] Kira Roessler, who participated in the LA scene through this entire period, told me: "My sense of history is not that there was this point at which things went to hardcore. I think that's a complete fabrication."[7] She added that many of these bands would not call themselves "hardcore," just as bands steered away from the "punk" label: "I certainly don't think Greg [Ginn] would think of Black Flag as hardcore. I think those are just oversimplifications and the rules are made to be broken." However, the story of separate LA scenes started quickly, in zines such as *Flipside*, *Slash*, and *Slush*.[8]

The hardcore style that emerged by 1980 so completely defined or redefined punk for American listeners that groups performing in the earlier styles, with the exception of a few such as X, were either disregarded or retrospectively disinvited from the punk category. As John Doe succinctly said, "Once hardcore came in, then people defined punk rock as that."[9] Those affiliated with the earlier punk rock often gravitated to other scenes and styles, including what came to be known more generally as "new wave" and American roots rock. And the transition to a new generation of punk musicians was apparent as musicians such as Bill Stevenson and Milo Aukerman (Descendents) and Steve Soto (Adolescents), all born in 1963, were infants when the baby boomer generation of earlier punk rockers were having their tastes formed by watching the Beatles on Ed Sullivan, or in the case of Iggy Pop, already playing professionally. The musicians playing in earlier punk rock styles, such as X, Black Randy, and the Bags, were still part of the baby boomer generation. Most were born in the 1950s, while Billy Zoom (X) and Tomata du Plenty (Screamers) were born in 1948, the same year as Wayne Kramer and Johnny Ramone.

The generational difference was hardly total, as members of early hardcore or transitional bands such as the Germs, Black Flag, and Circle Jerks were also born in the 1950s. However, the transition was becoming germane as the tail end of the baby boomers began to form punk bands in high school. The trend of high schoolers forming punk bands moved the timeline quite a bit, since earlier punk bands were often formed by musicians in their late twenties, adding at least a ten-year gap. Some examples were more extreme: Steven McDonald was only eleven years old and Jeff McDonald only fifteen when they formed Red Cross and opened for Black Flag. The first Red Cross (soon to be Redd Kross) EP was released in 1980, the same year as the first X album (*Los Angeles*), when Billy Zoom was thirty-two. They were contemporaries, but with very different experiences.[10]

## Hollywood Punk

The Hollywood punk scene mirrored the New York scene but with some key differences. As in New York, the Hollywood scene was an extremely small and diverse cohort of individuals who at least partially came to escape postwar suburbia or small-town America in order to thrive in an alternative urban culture of poets, queer people, and artists. John Doe and Exene Cervenka, for example, both came from out of town—Doe from Baltimore, Cervenka from Illinois and then Florida—and met at a poetry workshop in 1976. De De Troit (Denise D. Semrau) came from Harrison Township, Michigan. Others came from around California but not Los Angeles itself, such as Black Randy, who grew up in San Francisco. Also like New York's scene, the early LA punk scene included many who hailed from the more suburban outer areas of the city, such as Paul and Kira Roessler, Darby Crash, and Pat Smear (West Los Angeles, the Roesslers arriving from New Haven via Curaçao as teenagers), and Los Angeles County and other LA suburbs, such as Belinda Carlisle (Burbank), Joan Jett (West Covina, after her family moved from Rockville, Maryland), and Tomata du Plenty (Montebello). These musicians grew up on sixties music such as the Beatles and the Rolling

Stones, and they found inspiration in American bands such as the Stooges, the Ramones, and Blondie as they formed their own bands around 1975 and 1976. Also like the New York scene, early Los Angeles punk bands were almost completely devoid of African Americans and Asian Americans, especially notable given the vibrant populations of both groups in LA. But unlike the New York scene, which was almost entirely made up of transplants from the suburbs or outer boroughs, the Hollywood scene also attracted some people who had grown up in the urban center of Los Angeles, especially among the mostly Mexican American or Chicano population centered in East LA. Both the early New York and Los Angeles punk scenes were inclusive of some groups but remained closed or unappealing to others, an issue that will be further explored in this chapter.

Several aspects of Los Angeles's history attracted certain people to the scene and shaped the music they created. Los Angeles held a special place in the formation of postwar whiteness, serving as a utopian site of beaches, sunshine, highways, and youth.[11] As Greg Shaw of *Bomp!* magazine put it in a letter to Judy Holland, a freelance editor, in a correspondence regarding his proposal for a book on the history of rock music in southern California: "Fantasy and image are essential to any discussion of any aspect of California. . . . California was mythologized, through rock and roll, as a teenage Utopia to the rest of America."[12] Los Angeles punk served as a response to, and rejection of, the culture that supported these myths as well as the slickly produced major label recordings made in LA's studios. Underneath it all was the unsparing segregation and wealth disparity formed in the postwar geography of suburbs functionally removed from the city of Los Angeles: "Southern California is one giant, sterile suburb."[13] Punk was never subtle about its critique of how the geography of LA and its suburbs played as a locus of white fantasy, capitalism, and privilege: take for example, the Eyes' "Disneyland": Disneyland "makes me a Communist . . . Blow up Disneyland!"[14]

The cliché of punk as a response to banal seventies pap produced by major labels had more resonance in Los Angeles than anywhere else, including New York, given the pervasiveness of the music industry in everyday life. People moved from all over the country to attempt to break into the world of the major labels, and seventies LA rock musicians such as the Eagles, Jackson Browne, Linda Ronstadt, and Loggins and Messina were a part of LA's local musical life, not only radio hitmakers or distant millionaire rock stars—although they were those as well. John Doe remembered that in 1976 "it was all people that were part of the mega-corporate rock 'n' roll system."[15] Damon Edge of Chrome said:

> We know what record companies ARE, right? But just to be antagonistic to it you have to be aware of it. So you've got to almost cut yourself loose from that level of being antagonistic, because you still have it in your mind as a *foundation* . . . I came

from L.A.—the brainwashing power they have, the magnificent billboards on Sunset—"you have to spend 80 grand to record an album, and it's got to be Joe Hotshot engineer with gold cokespoon"—that's all really SICK, the producers are sick—and the KIDS got a sick view of it. There's so many people just waiting for the pie in the sky—all these managers that keep you waiting for 6 months for this deal or that.[16]

Or as scenester and writer for *Back Door Man* D. D. Faye was quoted as saying: "We're tired of people thinking everyone in L.A. is lying around Laurel Canyon, playing tennis and snorting cocaine. Anyone who thinks that is ignorant. The Masque [the central venue of the Hollywood punk scene] gives us a chance to wipe out that idea."[17]

But Los Angeles punks had various attitudes toward LA's unusual demographics. The vision of an alternative LA did not run through the entire scene, as Stan Lee (the Dickies) remembered: "England had all the bands singing about how fucked everything was, and we were going on water slides, living in the Valley, in my parents' backyard. It was swimming pools and movie stars . . . It's kind of what made us laugh at the time."[18] Despite claims of "no local music scene" before punk—a characterization which one would have difficulty supporting in any location—Los Angeles's extant music scene was vibrant and extremely diverse.[19] LA had a deep and abiding tradition of "freak," avant-garde, or pessimistic musicians, including those who were part of the major label system such as Captain Beefheart, Frank Zappa, and the Doors (for more on avant-garde California, see chapter 3)—even *The United States of America* was released on Columbia.[20] The city also boasted students and aficionados of American music such as Canned Heat and the Rising Sons. And the major label music industry in LA actually also had a major effect on early LA punk. For example, John Doe came to LA to be a songwriter, the Doors alumnus and industry giant Ray Manzarek produced X's first recordings, Iggy and the Stooges relocated to LA to support *Raw Power* (Iggy staying at Manzarek's in Laurel Canyon) and DEVO moved to LA in 1978 as they joined the Warner Bros. roster.[21] Industry veteran Kim Fowley managed the Runaways, with allegations of the ways in which he wielded "Hollywood" power dynamics, including rape, recently coming to light.[22]

The complex segregation of Los Angeles and its suburbs also helped set the stage for LA punk. By the 1970s, the race and class segregation in Los Angeles was extreme, even more complete than in New York and other northeastern and midwestern cities such as Detroit and Cleveland. While in New York suburban development expanded from the outer boroughs to Long Island, Westchester, and New Jersey out of New York's older immigrant core, in Los Angeles the entire city was transformed in the postwar era, built up in tandem with the extremely white suburbs. Race and class segregation in Los Angeles was also enforced and supported by governmental and police structures more intensely than in other American metropolises.

The city of Los Angeles was a historical site of immigration for Mexican, Chinese, and Japanese people, which continued after World War II, and it was a major site for African American settlement for the Great Migration, especially for people from Texas, Arkansas, and Louisiana.[23] But Los Angeles "before and after 1945, was qualitatively and quantitatively two different cities. Not only did immigration reshape the city, but so did its economic position, political relevance, and an urban growth that was fueled by the expanding economic opportunities in the region. The prosperity was, unfortunately, not shared equally by the whole city. . . ."[24] By 1965 African American "Watts and Compton residents lived in stark segregation in a narrow corridor connecting downtown Los Angeles to the port of San Pedro. This corridor was bordered on its east and west sides by predominately white suburban neighborhoods."[25] After the Watts uprising in 1965, segregation between white and black Angelenos intensified, making LA the third most segregated city in the nation, after Chicago and Gary, although other (non–African American) minority groups such as Mexican Americans had established enclaves in and around the white suburbs.[26] To compound matters, by 1970 Los Angeles's "suburban islands" had become "semi-autonomous urban zones" as workers stayed out of the city instead of commuting in and out, creating "the city without a downtown," a "polycentric conurbation."[27] This left a geography where, in the mid-1970s, John Doe and others realized, "we can just take over the city and have a whole music scene, and that's kind of what we did," echoing the prevailing sentiments about New York punk's relationship to the Bowery.[28]

The Los Angeles scene was closely connected to San Francisco, with its many early punk bands including Crime, the Nuns, the Dils, the Avengers ("probably the most well-known punk band" of the early California punk scene, according to Exene Cervenka), Negative Trend, and the Sleepers, as well as the important venue Mabuhay Gardens and the seminal zine *Search and Destroy*.[29] San Francisco punks had a defined but complicated relationship to the city's arty, bohemian, hippie, intellectual, gay heritage.[30] For example, Vale Hamanaka, the creator of *Search and Destroy* and the later *Re/Search* publications, began his magazine while working at the famous City Lights Bookstore.[31] San Franciscans brought a political awareness and wry sense of humor to their music, most strongly associated with the Dead Kennedys. Carlsbad transplants the Dils were among the earliest explicitly "political" US punk bands, but they were uncharacteristically serious in their presentation. More typical were Crime, with their self-conscious performance art representation (such as a formal concert program they distributed at Mabuhay Gardens on December 17, 1977, including an intermission and a dedication to "no one"), or the Nuns, with their provocative satire (the song "Decadent Jew," a spread in *Search and Destroy*: "IF YA CAN'T TAKE A JOKE, PUNK YOU!"). Vancouver was another important city on this early West Coast punk axis, with D.O.A. and Subhumans (not to be confused with the British band), the latter often playing political events such as Rock Against Racism concerts and anti–nuclear war rallies.[32]

California punk was steeped in the state's bohemian history, but what distinctly characterized the punk scene was a resistance to expected or standard expressions of identity among bohemian, underground, and marginalized groups. For example, early California punk "was very gay in the beginning," in the words of Kid Congo Powers (Brian Tristan), but even more so, as José Esteban Muñoz writes, punk provided "venues and stages where [early LA punks] could realize their plurality."[33] Gay LA punk was part of a more general underground culture surrounding gay identity in the 1970s and, as with the gay punk scene in New York, connected to the city's historic status as a gay haven.[34] Arguably the LA scene's most important band, the Screamers, was "basically a bunch of homosexuals out in Hollywood who had read too much *New Musical Express*," in the words of original member Dave Brown.[35] Black Randy (John Morris), one of the main early LA punk figures despite his current obscurity, sang about the police brutalizing hustlers at the Gold Cup on Hollywood Boulevard in "Trouble at the Cup"; he himself worked as a male prostitute, including alongside Dee Dee Ramone while living in New York between 1971 and 1974.[36] But a common attitude to gay identity was "who cares?" as Don Vinil, the gay singer of San Francisco's Offs, put it: "I despise the gay scene—they think it's a club, that it's something special to be gay, and it's not. They're just as middle-class as their parents were, just as hung up. What difference does it make if someone in a band is gay or straight?"[37]

Similarly, early California punk included many Latinx participants (Mexican Americans specifically) who were ambivalent about, or resistant to, identity conformity. Punk provided alternatives based on individual freedom of expression. As Roberto Lopez (a/k/a El Vez) of the Zeros told David Ensminger:

> That was the nice thing about being in that period because it didn't break down
> into girl bands, guy bands, and Chicano bands. We felt a part of the scene, the music
> scene, punk rock in whatever forms it was, like the Deadbeats, Weirdos, or nongui-
> tar bands like the Screamers. You just felt part of a movement of the scene, rather
> than saying we're Chicanos and we feel this way, or those are girls, and they feel this
> way.... being Chicano wasn't even a focal point or focus of the band [the Zeros].[38]

Women speak about their prominent place in the diverse LA scene in much the same way. Jane Wiedlin remembered: "Everyone was welcome, girls included. It was even okay to be gay in the Hollywood punk scene. It was an inclusive scene, centered on art, creativity, and fun rebellion against grownups."[39] Exene Cervenka said even more strongly: "when the punk scene happened it was as if people had always been equal men and women. It was as if there was no history of women doing one thing and men doing another. Women immediately started picking up instruments and playing. From my point of view, I noticed no sexism in the punk scene."[40] Or photographer Jenny Lens: "There would not be a scene without the women. . . . Strip out the women, and there is not much left in L.A. . . . I can say, with total conviction, that L.A. women took command. We did whatever the hell we wanted, when we wanted, the way we wanted."[41]

This diverse, fun-oriented scene was inspired by similarly fun New York punk groups, such as the Ramones and Blondie, and the Damned from England, and the music of Hollywood punk bands can be clearly linked to the pure rock and roll and raw power models refined and combined by these bands.[42] Hollywood punk musicians drew on the emerging punk style, using it as a set of expressive resources around which this diverse assemblage of participants could converge. Songs such as the Weirdos' "We Got the Neutron Bomb" (1978) combined pure rock and roll and raw power styles in a manner reminiscent of the Damned's "Neat Neat Neat": mainly in an AAB form, with the verse in a minor pentatonic mode (V–♭VII) and the chorus using a I–IV oscillation, a V–IV–I pattern bridge in a style very reminiscent of the Sex Pistols, an ending vamp with blues guitar soloing, and like the British punk songs, a more expanded form than most of the earlier American punk.[43] Other songs that combined these styles in a similar way are the Bags' "Survive" (1978) and the Zeros' "Wild Weekend" (1978). Musicians also composed songs in either the established raw power or pure rock and roll modes; raw power songs include the Weirdos' "A Life of Crime" (1977) and the Controllers' "Neutron Bomb" (not the same as the Weirdos song), which is built almost entirely on a $\hat{1}$–$\hat{2}$–♭$\hat{3}$ riff supporting the melody and a minor-pentatonic blues guitar solo, and pure rock and roll songs include the Plugz' "Mindless Contentment," the Randoms' New York Dolls–style "A B C D" (1977), and the Zeros' "Don't Push Me Around" (1977), which featured the Ramones' approach of having barre chords, bass notes, and the vocal line all in unison, supported by a strong backbeat. Such artistic choices supported the overall unity around a punk scene and a punk identity, rather than a miscellany of expressions matching a patchwork of specific ethnicities. For example, Latinx members of groups such as the Plugz, Bags, and Zeros mainly worked in this general punk style early on, making music without an explicit connection to their Latinx backgrounds.

The LA punk bands also asserted punk as part of an American popular music tradition, in many ways reacting to the mushrooming presence of British punk and the notion of the UK as punk's place of origin, an idea that was quickly taking hold. Some of these choices also added to the perception of punk as a mostly white style of music, an impression that would soon increase and also be significantly challenged. LA punks used vocal style as a major area of differentiation among Hollywood punk bands, reasserting American accents in response to the sudden pervasiveness of British punk, even though—or perhaps because—an idea was emerging that "everyone in L.A. has an English accent now."[44] The Bags' "We Don't Need the English" (on the *Yes L.A.* compilation, 1979) answered back to British songs such as "I'm So Bored with the U.S.A." and "New York," representing a larger trend. Other distinctive vocal styles emerged in Los Angeles: Black Randy and Darby Crash advanced a strong anti-singing style that was more pronounced than previous punk voices, with the exception perhaps of Dave E. of the Electric Eels, while Leonard Graves Phillips of the Dickies created an affected hybrid of early American and British punk singers following Joey Ramone and Dave Vanian, both of whom had already created stylized hybrid American/British accents.

X presented the most striking example of musicians reasserting American-ness through vocal style. The Appalachian-style harmony of Exene Cervenka and John Doe exploited their natural voices and avoided any imitation of other punk singers, black American styles, or British singers.[45] Vocal harmony in general is rare in punk, and Cervenka's and Doe's approach was highly unusual, emphasizing unisons, octaves, fourths, and fifths; however, their approach is familiar to bluegrass and country music, and shape-note hymnody.[46] Although this particular kind of harmony stayed distinctly associated with X, their idiosyncratic embodiment of white "Americana" redirected attention back to the United States and had a broader resonance. The presence of country approaches in X's music comes from their long-standing interest in America's vernacular music heritage. Exene Cervenka recalled:

> We use to listen to Hank Williams and George Jones and all kinds of stuff—and Leadbelly—and my favorite thing to do when X first started was to go to a radio station, and they would say, "bring some records that you like" . . . and they thought we were going to play Siouxsie and the Banshees or something like that . . . one time we went KROQ and we brought all the old blues records and all the old country records we had that had the stuff that was being ripped off by Led Zeppelin and those people . . . we had a lot of friends who were at the time record collectors, Bob Hite from Canned Heat . . . Phil Alvin and a lot of other people who had been collecting 78s and they would play us the old, really obscure records from the twenties.[47]

Hollywood punks also established American genealogy through throwback rockabilly and Chuck Berry–style guitar, as played by Billy Zoom, the guitarist for X. Zoom embodied a pure rock and roll throwback to the 1950s and early 1960s in Los Angeles, including his interest in vintage cars. The Alley Cats

(Randy Stodola) and Dave Alvin (the Flesh Eaters, the Blasters) also cultivated a classic rock and roll guitar style. In Los Angeles, several members of the punk scene including X, the Gun Club, and the Blasters were heavily into American roots music, a tradition following musicians such as Canned Heat and the Rising Sons, and which continued with groups such as the Minutemen, Meat Puppets, and Social Distortion. Mike Ness reflected: "I can't speak for any of them, but Social Distortion has always had a connection to early Americana music, whether it was blues, country, bluegrass, jazz or whatever. It was very important for us to grab ahold of our American roots. Second, the heartfelt-ness and honesty of that music felt like a direct connection to punk music, being basically working-class music, singing about working-class issues."[48] One compelling development in LA punk was Los Lobos' participation in the scene after the Plugz's Tito Larriva asked them to play an acoustic set of Mexican music as a last-minute replacement opening act for Public Image Limited in 1980, and then more consequentially, opening for their friends the Blasters in 1981 and 1982.[49] Like the Blasters, Los Lobos presented an expansive vision of American music—over their long career they have explored "virtually the entire breadth of American vernacular music"—and in the context of the late 1970s and early 1980s, their music was fundamentally different from the early vision of punk in Great Britain.[50]

In retrospect, some of X's most significant musical contributions to punk involved their focus on highly original composition beyond the more prescribed work of their contemporaries, and their insistence on rock's Americanness in light of the explosion of British bands. As Billy Zoom said regarding the Rolling Stones, "they're foreigners and foreigners can't play rock and roll . . . they never could."[51] Other LA punk bands also drew on country and blues, reinforcing an American punk lineage that ran counter to the emerging Eurocentric narrative. In the case of country music or "Americana," these groups also introduced a white (and not just racially ambiguous) American roots lineage that had not yet really been explored in punk.

### From Ethnic Difference to Racial Sameness

Latinx experiences in Los Angeles punk serve as a microcosm of the general transition from what was perceived as an ethnically diverse scene to a racially homogenous one, and from an urban art scene to a suburban one. The shift also mirrored similar alleged transformations across identity categories: from gender diversity to mostly males, and from various sexualities to mostly straight. These were shifts in the ways in which participants in the scene viewed themselves. LA punks considered the original scene to be ethnically and culturally diverse, especially in terms of the participation of Latinos, whose racial status in the United States has been mutable and ambiguous.[52] Members of the early punk scene perceived a transition from ethnic diversity to racial homogeneity, defined by an influx of predominantly white boys from Orange County and other suburban areas. There are many complications to this simple story, including the perception of that newer suburban contingent, which was also ethnically diverse and also included women; the continual presence of Hollywood punks; and the suburban and out-of-town elements in Hollywood punk itself. However, the perceptual shift from ethnic diversity to racial sameness was facilitated by the obvious dearth of African Americans in both the Hollywood and hardcore punk scenes, leaving whiteness as an ambiguous category that could be used and leveraged in various ways. The demographics of the LA scene remain heavily open to interpretation, especially in terms of Latinx participation.

Latinx people were strongly represented in Los Angeles punk, from the Hollywood to the hardcore scenes, but the attitudes surrounding Latinx participation in punk changed. The intersection of terminology, identity categories, and formations of ethnicity and race continue to impact understandings and analyses of LA punk's demographics, especially regarding Latinx identity and the 1970s. First, looking back at LA punk with the broad contemporary category of Latinx may distort the fact that the idea of Latinx participation was based almost entirely on the involvement of Mexican Americans specifically, and the discourse at the time almost exclusively used the terms Chicano, Chicana, or Mexican, not Mexican American (e.g., "THE PLUGZ are one of the only Chicano punk bands").[53] Second, as mentioned above, Latinos in the Hollywood punk scene such Robert Lopez and Alice Bag tended to view themselves as part of a heterogenous gathering of unique individuals. Although they were open about their Latinx identities, they generally avoided having this identity define them either externally or internally. As Alice Bag wrote in her memoir, a large part of her attraction to the punk scene was its focus on individuality, and what she recognized as an opportunity to explore her complicated identity—including, but not limited to, being Chicana—without conforming to the growing pressures of politicized identity in organizations and movements such as MEChA (Movimiento Estudiantil Chicano de Aztlán), the Brown Berets, and the Chicano Moratorium, which had developed in connection with the civil rights and black liberation movements.[54] Similarly, Habell-Pallán writes, "[Robert] Lopez, like many other disaffected Chicano youth (myself included) who were experiencing alienation from both the dominant and Chicano culture, was drawn to this scene because it was a site where identities outside ethnic stereotypes could be embodied."[55]

The choices of early Latinx punk musicians mostly followed the precedent set by musicians such as Chris Montez, the Los Angeles County–born and raised

(Hawthorne, also the home of the Beach Boys and Redd Kross) singer of "Let's Dance" (1962), covered on *Ramones*, and Ritchie Valens, also from LA County (Pacoima). (Montez, Brian Wilson, and Al Jardine were all Hawthorne High School class of 1960.) During their heydays of the late 1950s and early 1960s, Montez and Valens largely performed standard rock and roll songs, while occasionally expressing Latin identity in standalone markers of difference, such as Montez's "Chiquitita Mia" (1963) or, most famously, Valens's "La Bamba" (1958).[56] These songs highlighted Valens's and Montez's ethnicity, but their careers by and large avoided audibly Latin styles in favor of generalized American rock and roll, and the performance of rock and roll songs like "Let's Dance" by stars such as Chris Montez helped reframe this black American music as unmarked or racially ambiguous.[57] Latinx racial ambiguity is hard-wired into the United States' racial system, in formal distinctions such as the Hispanic/non-Hispanic categories separate from race, and Latinx individuals identify across a wide racial spectrum, including black, white, and other. Although Latinx identity has become increasingly associated with an expansive nonwhite people of color category, and while many Latinx people identify or are identified as black in the United States (often qualified with hyphenated designations such as "Afro-Colombian"), according to Julie Dowling, "for three decades now, approximately half of the Latino population has selected 'white' for their race" on the US Census, and these identities are not typically or necessarily attached to skin color or cultural assimilation.[58] The variability of choices regarding Latinx styles and signifiers reflect the larger distinction that, despite persistent discrimination and mistreatment in the United States, Latinos have not been systematically segregated by governmental policies in the ways that African Americans have been.[59] The variable status of Mexican Americans and other Latinos, and the different historical experiences of Latinos and African Americans, is especially germane when looking back at LA punk.

Many Mexican Americans had successfully relocated beyond the East LA barrio into the white dominated suburbs by the late 1970s.[60] Meanwhile, East LA remained a center of Chicano life. The Los Angeles punk scene notably included Chicanos from East LA and the suburbs, outlying areas, or nearby towns, and the East LA Chicano punks were the first group of American punks to come directly from the urban environment with which they were associated. Their presence and "brownness" became a hallmark of the scene's diversity, often romanticized by white punks as a kind of validation: "Black hair, brown faces, black hair, brown faces—beautiful, sweaty, Mexican teenagers swimming in a sea of white suburban kids. . . . Seeing this new contingent of teenagers from the east side made us feel legit, gave us a feeling that we could communicate to more than people we knew. . . . In our minds these people had a direct connection to Ritchie Valens & the heart of Los Angeles," wrote John Doe.[61] However, it should be underscored that many of LA's Latino punks came *not* from East LA but from the suburbs of LA or of nearby cities. Robert Lopez of the Zeros, for example, came from Chula Vista, a suburb of San Diego which in the mid-1970s was a predominantly white area. (Similarly, Chris Montez was supposedly one of only two Mexican Americans in his high school class.[62]) Charlie Quintana and Tito Larriva of the Plugz were from El Paso, Texas (Tito was born in Mexico City), and they had no connection to the East LA community when they moved to LA and started performing in the punk scene. In 1978 Quintana told Vale, "I've been telling these guys that we should play in East L.A. schools for sure! . . . I mean, they're so close to us, really—I mean, they're ready for it!"[63] Alice Bag was raised in East LA, but she was part of the Hollywood punk scene, not the East LA punk scene.[64]

This diversity of geography, class, and race engendered an ongoing question of assimilation among Latinos as hardcore more visibly attached punk to white suburban male youth. Individuals in the hardcore scene with Latinx backgrounds or connections such as Ron Reyes, Dez Cadena, and Robo (Black Flag) were making music without explicit ethnic markers to distinguish their contributions from their white suburban friends, but so were many before them, such as Alice Bag. But as punk became more generally understood as white and suburban, some Chicano musicians emphasized their ethnic backgrounds through the Spanish language and signifiers of Mexican music. The Plugz early on covered "La Bamba" live (with a new refrain: "Surados capitalistas mas bien fascistas / yo no soy fascista soy anarquista!") but otherwise played a representative pure rock and roll style (e.g., *Electrify Me* [1979]); later they sang more in Spanish and used overt Mexican musical gestures including an opening grito on "El Clavo y La Cruz" from *Better Luck* (1981). Alice Bag "came to Chicana consciousness in the early 1990s," and has since created a wide variety of music, including songs in Spanish, as well as doing pathbreaking activism and directly connecting to younger feminist, Latinx, and conscious punk groups, such as Downtown Boys.[65] In the early 1980s Los Lobos also became marginally involved in the punk scene, their explicit presentation of East LA Chicano identity through music (they were originally *Los Lobos del Este de Los Angeles*) following the Chicano consciousness movements of the 1960s.

Latinx identity in the early LA punk scene was highly variable, and sometimes strikingly different from contemporary understandings, altering the ways in which the early punk scene is retrospectively analyzed. Ron Reyes, Robo, and Dez Cadena, for example, are now sometimes discussed as examples of Latinx participation in LA punk (beyond this book), but it is unlikely that they would have been united by such an identity in the contemporary sense, or that they would have strongly identified with broader meanings of contemporary terms such as people of color (which historically referred specifically to African Americans).[66] Reyes is Puerto Rican, part of the US and outside of the Chicano political movements that were so prominent in LA during the 1960s and 1970s; Robo was from Colombia; and Dez Cadena, son of producer and record man Ozzie Cadena, was of Mexican American descent but this aspect of his background is nonexistent in accounts of the period. Cadena also goes unidentified as a Mexican American in the *Diccionario de punk y hardcore (España y Latinoamérica)*, which otherwise identifies the Latino backgrounds of Black Flag members Ron Reyes, Robo, and Anthony Martinez.[67]

As discussed throughout *Damaged*, "identity" is ever-changing, personal, and nearly impossible to pin down, but race in America, and whiteness in particular, is a social formation inseparable from empirical questions of privilege, discrimination, housing, wealth, and education. Cadena, who grew up in Newark in the 1960s "young and separated from that [racial tension] mostly in my part of town," and who moved at thirteen in 1974 with his father to Hermosa Beach and attended school without any apparent issues surrounding his race or ethnicity, had a different experience from that of Alice Bag in East LA, and certainly unlike that of African Americans in the punk scene or LA generally.[68] These various senses of identity, ethnicity, and race are especially important to keep in mind given some retrospective analyses of the scene that imprecisely apply contemporary racial categories to that period. For example, even with Ron Reyes, Robo, and Dez Cadena as members, characterizing Black Flag as a "multiracial band" that "[stood] out within a mostly white scene," as one scholar has done, seriously obscures the ideas of whiteness surrounding hardcore's emergence and probably speaks mostly to the ways in which contemporary fans of the band may wish to view the group in hindsight.[69] As Stew put it, "No way in hell would anybody have ever in a million years though of Black Flag as a mixed band. Not by a long shot."[70]

Most significant was the emergence of a grassroots punk scene in East LA centered around the Vex, a performance space housed on the top floor of the building occupied by Self Help Graphics, the non-profit that promoted and exhibited original Chicano artists and that, along with San Francisco's Galería de la Raza, "introduced Día de los Muertos observance as a public event in the U.S." in 1972.[71] The Vex became a crucial venue for the East LA bands, as "a hint of racism" limited the performance opportunities for Latinx groups west of the LA River.[72] The bands who performed there, including Los Illegals and Thee Undertakers, ran the gamut from the pop stylings of the Brat to the hardcore sound of the Stains, but as a scene these groups shared an East LA identity and a commitment to the well-being of the local community.[73]

Hardcore's growing links with violence, whiteness, and the suburbs ended this incarnation of the Vex's run as a punk venue:

> The original incarnation of the Vex closed with a Black Flag show that ended in a riot of broken glass and vandalism. White Huntington Beach punks threw chairs

out the windows and into the parking lot, broke copiers and art equipment, and destroyed paintings and sculptures. "It was like when Manson struck and broke the whole hippie feel, says [Jesus] Velo [of Los Illegals], who still wears mariachi pants and a United Farm Workers band around his arm when he plays. "That show just broke what the Vex was all about. It was like having your friends come to your house and tear up your parents' furniture. It broke our hearts."[74]

Hardcore and its associations with suburban white boys revolved around the perception of violence, behavior with overt racial significance in Los Angeles. This Black Flag show at the end of the Vex's run (August 20, 1983) was interpreted by many East LA punks as more than a misunderstanding, and through actions (rather than questions of individual identity) this event demarcated opposing intentions behind punk and the ways in which whiteness and Latinidad related to communities and privilege. "Self Help was largely an art community center, and these guys broke into where they had the prints and destroyed these works of art that had been archived there for who knows how many years. It was such disrespect of that place and our community," said Teresa Covarrubias of the Brat.[75] White privilege exudes from accounts of this event, describing white punks who came in from the suburbs to see Black Flag treating violence and destruction as actions with no threat of serious repercussions, while the Chicano community was only too aware of the irreplaceable losses it caused— even more intense as the Vex was literally located at "Self Help," a center of East LA activists' work.

Furthermore, African Americans remained almost completely absent from Los Angeles punk during the 1970s and even into the beginning of the 1980s, with the exception of SST's engineer Spot (Glen Lockett), Karla "Mad Dog" Duplantier of the Controllers, Duplantier's cousin the artist Vaginal Creme Davis, Pat Smear (his mother was African American and American Indian), Chuck Mosley (later of Faith No More, he was African American, Jewish, and American Indian), some participants more on the fringes of the scene such as Stew, and some scenesters such as Marlon Whitfield (Fishbone was also forming at the very end of the decade, first playing around LA in 1983).[76] Stew explained that Spot was one of "maybe two black guys" that were fully in the scene.[77] Even well into the 1980s, inclusion of African Americans in fanzines focused on the individual's race and their exceptional relationship to the white scene, e.g., the 1983 interview with Marlon Whitfield in *No Magazine* unfortunately titled "Marlon Only Knows One Nigger Joke."[78] Whether or not participants in the punk scene regarded this segregation as *de facto* or *de jure*, it is mostly due to the persistent lack of representation of African Americans that the punk scene could be read as white or diverse depending on the circumstances and the subjectivity of those involved.

The transition to hardcore and the violence surrounding events such as Black Flag's 1983 show at the Vex, and the absence of African Americans, effectively solidified a new punk environment of "racial sameness" with hardcore—a sense that the entire scene had become white, suburban, and middle class. The idea of ethnic diversity centered almost entirely around Chicanos in LA punk, as African American participation remained extremely rare in early LA punk from the late 1970s to the early 1980s, mirroring LA's overall social and cultural landscape, and members of other minority groups also remained either extremely underrepresented, as with Asian Americans (Dianne Chai of the Alley Cats is a singular figure), or considered white, as with most Jewish Americans and many Latinos as well. The loss of the Vex, the most explicit center of Chicano punk life and a tie to East LA, captured a dramatic sense of losing the element that made the early LA punk scene ethnically heterogeneous, even though Latinos continued to participate in the younger hardcore scene more than has been generally acknowledged.

## Violence and Suburban Punk

It seems as though everyone who participated in the Los Angeles punk scene at the end of the 1970s has made a comment about the transformation of the scene from the city to the suburbs, centered on the concept of violence, whiteness, and toxic masculinity. Although some attribute the perception of hardcore's violence to sensationalistic media pieces by outsiders, members of the earlier scene have regularly commented on the phenomenon, and it was a point of concern in zines such as *Slash*.[79] The question of violence mostly concerns not music, but dance—specifically a shift from the pogo (jumping up and down) to slam dancing (crashing into each other, initially also called the "H.B. Strut" referring to the punks from Huntington Beach). "In 1979 . . . beach punks and Cromagnon-esque jocks from Orange County had begun to infiltrate our scene, and many of us, especially the women, were put off by it because of the violence in the slam pits," wrote Pleasant Gehman.[80] "I always remember when I started feeling like the scene had grown a little *too* much. When guys from Orange County started showing up, ready for a bit of the old ultra-violence. When it went from being female friendly and gay friendly to more testosterone driven," recalled Jane Wiedlin.[81] "As I looked out into the audience, I could see that the once quirky men and women artists who prized originality above all else were being replaced by a belligerent, male-dominated mob who became anonymous, camouflaged by their homogeneous appearance," remembered Alice Bag.[82] "They were more focused on violence and rebellion; we were more of an artists' scene," said Paul Roessler. Stew corroborated, saying, "It was always about gay people, and dressing up, and art school; it really wasn't about being a pissed-off white guy."[83] To some, the idea of punk extending to the boys from the beach seemed absolutely antithetical to what the scene was about:

> Friday night at the beach, and the kids flock to make the scene. A scene which at first, in the days of "The Masque rules OK" seemed like the unlikeliest direction the hard core sound would take. The beach bleached blond brats into punk? Come on!!! Even the blacks going punk was easier to imagine. Orange County and all that stretch of materialistic paradise was a fortress of time warped values and anybody with different tastes and priorities quickly moved out and stayed away.[84]

John Doe described how X stopped playing the anti-rape song "Johnny Hit and Run Paulene" because young men in the audience misunderstood it as an exhortation to violence, and Exene Cervenka explained, "the audiences went from being relatively intelligent and understanding people to scary young kids that liked to spit at the bands a lot . . . and beat up people . . . and it became kind of a war between what was and this new hardcore scene."[85] The gendered violence of hardcore needs to be seen with respect to the alarmingly high rate of violence by men against women in general, and the ways in which punk went from an empowering scene for women, including those who had experienced violence, to a scene that seemed to encourage or enable such violence.[86] And as I continually return to questions of age, generation, and "youth," the fact that so many in the punk scene were actually adults means, as Kira Roessler said, "you have these adult people combined with really young people, so you did have what would these days be considered statutory rape at best going on."[87] At the same time, some women who participated in hardcore pits also remember the experience in positive ways. Jamie Lurtz recalled: ". . . I took a boot to the face . . . It wasn't like they kicked me. It was like, 'Ah! A boot's coming.' I was like, 'That's cool! I've got my war wounds.' I don't remember any violence really pertaining to any of the shows . . . Everybody was pretty cool."[88]

The connections between violence, masculinity, and what came to be called "hardcore" have been repeatedly made since the 1980s. And although focusing on violence, identity, and the conceit of "self-marginalization" clouds the driving force behind the scene, which was the music—as Ian MacKaye remarked, "the story is not about the violence . . . [it is] the people who navigated that violence because they knew that the music was important enough"—the specific relationship of violence to whiteness calls for deeper investigation, especially given the specific history of Los Angeles.[89] Women and people of color continued to participate in hardcore punk, but the perception of punk as white came to dominate LA hardcore, and hardcore's whiteness—as a racial formation—is not merely a misconception that can be corrected by identifying nonwhite participants. Hardcore in many respects reflected a particular expression, ideology, and lived experience of whiteness based in Los Angeles' segregation, class differences among white suburbanites, increasing racial and ethnic diversity in the suburbs, and busing. The music of hardcore expressed ideas and realities of whiteness, alienating and attracting many new participants—and in turn the authenticity of hardcore's expression spoke to a wide variety of suburbanites, and not always who might be imagined.

Geographic, generational, and racial contrasts manifested in a shift from punk as more of a performance style to punk as a direct form of expression, in some ways cyclically revisiting the original impulse of punk. Yet the initial spark of hardcore violence came from the *performance* of violence in punk, as Black Randy predicted in the late 1970s: ". . . the Clash take a posture of violence, and what they got in return was authentic violence, and the same thing may well happen with the punk movement."[90] DJ Bonebrake said similarly, "people [in the Masque days were] pretending that they were violent but they were only playacting . . . when that happens you're eventually gonna have someone who comes along and says, 'Gee, guess what, I'm really violent. I'll show you how to really beat up someone.'"[91] Jack Grisham summed it up: "They said we were violent, that we ruined their scene and brought in an element of muscle-headed beach thuggery . . . Looking back, I find it amusing that those earlier punks considered us violent when their lives, their words, and their beliefs all influenced the way we behaved. It was their fault—not ours."[92]

The idea of violence in LA hardcore went beyond the slam dancing at venues such as the Cuckoo's Nest in Costa Mesa or the Fleetwood in Redondo Beach.[93] The most dramatic confrontations were between young white punks and the Los Angeles Police Department, frequently described but rarely analyzed with respect to the full scope of the history of institutional racism in Los Angeles.[94] "Violence came easily. There were undercover police at many of the shows, and frequently uniformed ones outside, waiting with video cameras to get shots of the people walking out of the club . . . Black Flag had a song called 'Police Story,' which has a lyric that sums up that relationship very well: 'They hate us, we hate them. We can't win. No way,'" wrote Henry Rollins.[95] To me, the hardcore–LAPD axis is a central locus for understanding hardcore as an expression of whiteness and its relationship to white privilege, as these run-ins with the LAPD came during a particularly tense period of the police department's war on African Americans.[96] "Police Story" and N.W.A's significantly later "Fuck Tha Police" may have come from the same general part of the US and may have the same object of rage, but they come from vastly different experiences and realities. It is a mistake, and in some ways a symptom of white privilege itself, to conflate the experiences of white, Latinx, and black Angelenos with respect to the LAPD, as many writers on the early punk era have done. For example, Carducci argued against what he perceived as unthinking laudatory descriptions of N.W.A's anti-police songs just because they were black, in contrast to unthinking denunciations of Black Flag's anti-police songs just because they were white (and it should be obvious that such discussions of Black Flag and punk as "white," in binary opposition to N.W.A and rap as "black," underscore the unlikelihood that Black Flag could be read as "multiracial" in the late 1970s and early 1980s).[97] According to one study, between 1974 and 1978, 55 percent of individuals shot by the LAPD were black, while an equal number of 22 percent each applied to white and Hispanic individuals.[98]

The circumstances surrounding the altercations between white punks and the LAPD are murky, but as opposed to the African American communities who were under continuous harassment and assault from the LAPD, white punks were known to enter into the confrontations of their own volition and sometimes did so seemingly only to exercise the limits of white privilege. "Most of us weren't there to hatch outlines for careers, college, or anything our parents had in mind for us. We were simply there to have fun and F.S.U.—fuck shit up. Destroying property was our random revenge on a society we hated," said Steve Humann of the Vandals.[99] Others attempted to organize and establish a different relationship between punks and the police, producing groups such as Youth Brigade and the Better Youth Organization, formed as a direct response to the police brutality at the Elk's Lodge concert on March 17, 1979, although this major moment of police brutality against punks was not a hardcore show.[100]

From the point of view of the police state, young white punks seemed as though they could destabilize the white supremacism that produced a segregated and unequal Los Angeles and which needed constant protection (in the postwar era, the LAPD had "operated as a de facto army of occupation meant to keep the African American community contained").[101] These young punks seemed to outwardly reject their inherited privilege, posing a potential threat to the societal order. As Paul Roessler explained:

ROESSLER: *Potential* is the key. Where is this going? We can see them on the street, we see them out there, they're openly violent and rebellious, is this gonna turn into a huge wave, or is it something we need to nip in the bud? It's interesting too because you have neo-Nazis and racists now, and they don't seem to be being nipped in the bud in the same way.

RAPPORT: Right, because they aren't a threat to white supremacist society.

ROESSLER: Well, was punk rock a threat to white supremacist society? Or hippies really? Potentially hippies and punks are still instruments of white supremacy, they're mainly white movements. But I think that maybe more what people are worried about is free thought, because you just never know where it's going to go. What can this develop into, let's not let it develop into anything, and conformity is very comfortable for power.[102]

Hardcore became an intense form of internal critique that used the privileges of whiteness to reject it, becoming simultaneously—and paradoxically—a genuine threat to whiteness as well an agent of it. In this sense, hardcore was squarely in a punk tradition, Generation X's version of the White Panther Party or the critiques of the Residents and other avant-gardists of the baby boomer generation (see chapter 3).

For suburban white youth, a punk identity could be a form of rebellion or considered "self-marginalization," a dubious concept in that marginalization, like disenfranchisement, is fundamentally something imposed upon people by others, and in that members of a dominant group, by definition, are not marginal.[103] The violence of hardcore could be an expression of rage, boredom, or fun, but a personal choice oriented around the rejection of cultureless, cookie-cutter suburban neighborhoods that were in fact created by racist policies. In other words, hardcore violence was often directed at symptoms of privilege, such as one's parents' house in the suburbs, by the beneficiaries of systematic inequalities. Joe Nolte (the Last) recalled: "By adopting this punk rock musical ethos, we deliberately disenfranchised ourselves—it was almost as if we'd turned black overnight. We deliberately placed ourselves outside of society; we had a choice, but we put targets on our shirts for the police by daring to look different."[104]

But of course, Nolte and his friends had not turned black overnight, nor had they really become disenfranchised or deprived of power. The stakes for a young African American, punk or not, and a white punk in a confrontation with the LAPD were starkly different. Stew and "us middle-class black guys who were privileged enough to not be going hungry or worrying about things that happen in the 'hood [were] still getting racially profiled every time we're in a car, you got stopped by the police on a regular basis. . . . I didn't know what 'racial profiling' was, and when someone told me, I was like, 'oh, that's like LA my whole life.'"[105] Or as Sacha Jenkins put it, "As for the punk youth of color, they were getting billy clubs about the head anyway. Because to the system, their very existence was an opposing force. In essence, when you're black, you're punk all the time. . . . When you're white, you can put those safety pins through your nose; but when the time comes to get a 'real' job and contribute to 'mainstream society,' one can simply remove the safety pin and start anew."[106] For many African Americans in LA, a crucial moment was January 3, 1979, when the thirty-nine-year-old housewife Eula Love ended up dead, shot eight times in her own home by LAPD officers Edward Hopson and Lloyd O'Callaghan over a $22 unpaid gas bill.[107] The tensions between the LAPD and LA's black communities culminated in the 1992 LA uprisings, demonstrating the continued significance of August 1965.[108] Unlike African Americans, white punks could retreat from this targeted "identity" whenever they wanted, and most did.

The complex differences in the relationships between white people and black people and the LAPD added to the segregation of the scene. Beyond potential altercations with the police, the beach scene south of LA already had a reputation among African Americans as being insular with an racist undercurrent. While some white interviewees explained to me that they felt African Americans simply did not relate to punk and that the lack of an African American presence was basically *de facto*, the reality for Stew as an African American and an early fan of LA punk was much more straightforward:

> I loved the Germs, I loved them. . . . I saw them once at Hong Kong Café [in 1979] and it was terrifying. . . . I was all the way in the back and I felt like I couldn't get anywhere close to that shit. Because it was not playtime. . . . Let's face it. No black person I know is going to really get ready for going in there [to a hardcore pit] because of two reasons. Most don't feel like making a game of violence, but also there's the extra added level that when you go in there, you're going in there among people that very well might really enjoy a little bit too much to inflict violence on you. So it's double-edged. . . . If the Bad Brains are on stage, then maybe, I don't know what that must have been like. I don't know what that means at all. . . . But I can just remember being so, whatever is going on here at this Germs show, I'm not connected to it. I *can't* be connected to it. . . . I told Don Bolles [the Germs' drummer] this story, and he's like, of course, I totally fucking get it, I mean, he was freaked out by this shit. . . .
>
> Long before punk, we knew if you go a little bit south, there'll be these white guys who aren't necessarily thrilled to have you around. So we always stuck to our Santa Monica, and we could go north to Malibu, those people might have an issue for another reason, but they're not gonna get violent. But we heard there are some white boys that would protect their territory so it wasn't a thought to go there [south]. It wasn't even a thought.[109]

D. H. Peligro (Dead Kennedys) spoke more generally to the same situation: "Being Black and being in Hardcore—I felt I had a fucked-up life and have more reason to be Hardcore than any of these fucking kids. I had it rough. I had two strikes against me every time I stepped out the door. . . . [at shows] Skinheads would be chasing me screaming, Ace of spades! which was one of their anthems. . . . A lot of people accepted me and a lot of people had their own twisted views of what I should or shouldn't be."[110]

In contemporary histories, white punks from the late-1970s and early-1980s punk scene in Los Angeles often look back on their altercations with the police with some confusion. David Markey (*We Got Power!* fanzine) remembered:

It seems odd that the LAPD were threatened by primarily young white boys. The only retaliation I ever witnessed was a hurled beer bottle or two. Furthermore, there were never enough punks rioting. Far too often the LAPD had all the fun, with batons swinging and bashing, while Macing and tear-gassing kids at these shows.

. . . They moved in formation, without provocation, striking people randomly. It wasn't a fair fight. Punks were not armed or prepared with gas masks. Many of the punks were younger than driving age, or female, clearly no match for the football-player-size cops.

The LAPD had had it in for the punk scene in Los Angeles since the late '70s. These punks were primarily middle-class white kids, and not typically a menace under any other circumstances.[111]

But from a broader historical perspective, the "white-on-white violence" of the LAPD's assaults on punks is not so odd. A parallel can be found in the white terrorism aimed at other whites who were sympathetic to, or at least complying with, busing and other court-ordered desegregation efforts in the 1970s.[112] From William H. Parker to Daryl Gates, the LAPD made it their mission to protect property and wealth over people, both connected to a particular form of whiteness located in the Los Angeles suburbs. "The South Bay cops, Redondo Beach, Hermosa Beach . . . it was a menace to these white people who wanted their nice little beach towns clean," said Kira Roessler.[113] And while African Americans made up a sliver of the police force, the LAPD were white punks' brothers, fathers, uncles, and cousins—"and here he was, the image of my father, wearing the dark blue uniform of the LA police," remembered Jack Grisham.[114] As late as 1994, the ACLU had determined that 83.1 percent of LA's police officers lived in white, suburban communities.[115] "For a counterculture to exist in law-and-order Orange County seemed unthinkable in Punk's early days," wrote Steven Blush.[116] Furthermore, white punks were ostensibly jeopardizing this dynamic at a time when the older generation of white people who had initially populated the Los Angeles suburbs very much felt their "world" broadly threatened by changing demographics. Despite revived geographical segregation following 1965 and persistent inequalities, the minority populations in the suburbs and their economic importance continued to grow (the non-Hispanic white population in LA County went from 71 percent in 1970 to 53 percent in 1980), accompanied by the backlash mocked (or documented, or expressed) in Black Flag's "White Minority."[117] But whereas punk's previous struggles over whiteness took place almost entirely in the realm of music and culture, hardcore added a threat of real violence. And considering the LAPD was made up of individuals—like punks, mostly white people from the suburbs—they had a particular stake in the threats posed by hardcore to a particular mode of whiteness.

The suburban youth of Los Angeles grew up in some of the most extreme manifestations of white privilege in the country. "All the white guys we knew were blond, and they were at the beach, and their shirts were off, and the world seemed designed for them, they weren't getting pulled over," said Stew.[118] Within this suburban environment, hardcore exposed the widening class divisions that shaped punk's emergence and development. Since the 1970s, Los Angeles, fueled by "a seemingly limitless pool of cheap immigrant labor," has grown "in an atmosphere of breathtaking social and economic inequality."[119] White people, including many of the baby boomer erstwhile hippies, reaped almost all of the benefits from this inequality, becoming the right-wing, Republican environment that sent Ronald Reagan to the White House and passed Proposition 13.[120] But this inequality also brought into relief the class differences in white suburbia, not necessarily between poor and rich, but between varying degrees of the middle class. Many white punks came from families that did not fully gain access to the privileges that others seemed to unfairly come by. They were also one of the least parented generations in recent history, latch-key kids regulating their own social environments, and they were able to sneak out of the house or come and go easily.[121] (One of the recurring themes of my interviews with black punks was the stricter limits placed on them by their parents.) Tony Cadena (Adolescents) commented: "If you look at a map of Orange County, it's a huge area. If you go west, there's this affluent beach community, but Fullerton was more of a working-class environment. Some of us came from very stable families, but there was also a lot of turmoil, a lot of divorce, a lot of kids literally running their households."[122] Mike Ness echoed, "Just because we live in a suburban setting, what? There isn't alcoholism in the home? There isn't child abuse? There isn't fucking abandonment? There isn't fucking addiction?"[123]

The question of violence in LA hardcore stood in for larger conflicts over whiteness with respect to privilege, wealth, suburbia, white flight, and segregation. The almost–Gen Xers who developed hardcore in Fullerton, Hermosa Beach, and Huntington Beach followed in the footsteps of their baby boomer antecedents by repudiating the counterculture, but the "counterculture" could now include baby boomer punks themselves, who like the hippies, they saw as "selling out" or out of touch. The baby boomers were also the ones who elected Reagan; those who made Orange County and the LA suburbs right-wing, Republican, segregated enclaves; and those who had become the "me generation." As Charles Homans wrote, "We know now that the real story wasn't the people at the protests and the concerts; it was all the people who weren't."[124] Gen Xers expressed little love or nostalgia for the suburbs and the music of their youth the way baby boomer punks did, especially since many of them were still teenagers, *creating* the music of their youth. Their new music reflected their different perspective, as they—like the baby boomer punks before them—emphasized some elements of the punk style, transformed some, and rejected others.

## The Musical Style of Hardcore Punk, Part One

Younger punks drew on aspects of the dominant Hollywood and British punk style while making bold amplifications and transformations aligning with their particular concerns in the mostly white suburban Southern California environment, and the wilder and more physical dance that was becoming the norm. As described in this section, the major changes in hardcore involved the move to a guitar-based musical system, which enabled faster performances and further distanced punk from its musical sources, and a breakneck-tempo drumming style driving the new compositions.

Yet the shift from Hollywood punk to hardcore was not clear-cut, and both styles overlapped and coexisted. Hollywood bands such as the Germs and Fear helped create the hardcore style, and Black Flag (as Panic) played their first gig in 1977.[125] Even T.S.O.L. "identified more with the Hollywood scene than with the beach scene 'cause that's what we admired when we were kids. I was really into the first-wave Hollywood bands. I fuckin' loved the Weirdos and the Germs, those were my favorites. I dug the Go-Go's, too."[126] Groups such as the Angry Samoans straddled the line between the two punk styles, their aggressive music undermined by irony.

Hardcore style can be initially linked to the baby boomer punks such the Angry Samoans and Fear who used raw power and pure rock and roll approaches, but who sped up the tempos and added lyrics designed to offend other punks along with the usual non-punk targets. The Angry Samoans were initially Gregg Turner, "Metal Mike" Saunders (born 1952), and Metal Mike's sibling Bonze Anne Rose Blayk (born 1956, formerly known as Kevin Saunders), the latter two Arkansas natives who relocated to LA after Mike's brief stint in New York. They explicitly modeled themselves on New York's Dictators, the goofy and offensive pure rock and roll group known for "Master Race Rock" and their cover of "California Sun." Turner later remembered the Dictators as "great comedy put to music . . . it was just dopey."[127] The original Samoans repertoire included "California Sun," the Dictators' "Cars and Girls," and the Ramones' "I Don't Care," and their named influences were typical early punk rock reference points such as the Stooges, the Velvet Underground, Blue Öyster Cult, Kiss, the Ramones, and Generation X (the band). Mike, already twenty-six years old when the Samoans were formed, was described by their manager Steve Besser as "a veteran of various mid-60's Arkansas garage bands who never got out of the garage, Mike thinks the Shadows of Knight are 'God.'"[128]

Much of the Angry Samoans' music followed the I–IV–V song models played by the Dictators and Shadows of Knight. For example, their cover of the Chambers Brothers' "Time Has Come Today" (also later covered by the Ramones) follows the I–IV–V rotation of I–♭VII–IV (D–C–G instead of G–C–D) used in Them's "Gloria." And like the Dictators, the Angry Samoans' lyrics aimed to be ironic and ridiculous, including controversial songs such as "Homo-Sexual," which attempted to mock the religious right and closeted hypocrites (as Gregg Turner said, ". . . there was a lot of gay baiting going on, so we did a song called 'Homosexual' and we thought no one's going to even think this is falling in line with all the other idiots, we'll credit it to J. Falwell. In addition I sent a copy of the record to the Moral Majority hoping he'd sue us"), "They Saved Hitler's Cock," and their primary claim to fame, "Get Off the Air," directed at Rodney Bingenheimer of the influential station KROQ.[129] Even so, the Angry Samoans, Fear, and the Germs were less inflammatory than some other groups internationally. Toronto's Viletones, fronted by Nazi Dog (Steven Leckie), embraced an overblown confrontational style, perhaps inspired by the Sex Pistols' success.

In hardcore, functional harmony and the use of I–IV–V types of rock and roll schemes were deemphasized in favor of a different kind of harmonic movement based on barre chords played in whole steps and fourths, the elements from blues-based rock most adaptable to breakneck tempos on the guitar. As discussed in chapter 4, this approach originally stemmed from Johnny and Dee Dee Ramone's unison pairings of barre chords and bass notes, what Ian MacKaye described as "the bass and the guitar [should] be like one thing. It would be like drawing a thick black marker, underscoring, a line."[130] The Angry Samoans adopted this technique for "You Stupid Asshole," taking the familiar "ice cream changes" cycle I–vi–IV–V in its second rotation and playing it only with barre chords: I–VI–♭VII–♭III (A–F–G–C instead of C–a–F–G). Fear used the same techniques in their similarly intentionally offensive music, placing often ridiculous lyrics over Ramones-style barre chord/bass note treatments of classic pure rock and roll cycles, such as "Beef Bologna" over I–IV or "I Don't Care about You" over ♭VII–IV–I. Fear and the Angry Samoans presented one extreme end of the Dictators and Ramones approach to punk, which in retrospect was still connected to the sixties baby boomer generation, but which also served as a bridge to the more defined hardcore style of Black Flag and Circle Jerks.[131] Black Flag also consistently used conventional rock and roll chord movement, such as the I–♭VII–IV verse ("Time Has Come Today," "Gloria") of "I've Had It," and blues riffs in "What I See," "Police Story," and "Depression." One of the strongest examples of Ginn's use of conventional forms is "Thirsty and Miserable," a twelve-bar blues (moving to ♭III instead of IV) that obscures its blues roots through speed and Rollins's screamed vocals.[132]

Hardcore musicians ultimately embraced a hybrid approach to harmony and melody, combining the whole-step oscillations of raw power rock and the movement in fourths used in pure rock and roll punk, but without necessitating functional harmony. In other words, these chords no longer sound like they must "go" anywhere or resolve in any particular way, although they may still sound inclined to resolve. With this fundamental change, hardcore fully broke away from older rock and roll models and the racial associations they were meant to evoke, a musical reflection of the younger Generation X musicians' distance from their baby boomer antecedents and contemporaries. Hardcore's approach to harmony borrowed the structural conceits of the Damned, the Weirdos, and other bands, who tended toward raw power–style verses and pure rock and roll–style choruses, and hardcore reintroduced blues-based raw power guitar solos. But in hardcore, following the Ramones, the voice, guitar, and bass usually moved in unison, and groups of harmonic movement were treated as blocks relatively independent from each other compared to standard rock and roll. Whole-step movement dominates hardcore, with and without fourths, and due to their increased speed, can be heard as "a single gesture."[133] The Germs' "Lexicon Devil" demonstrates one early approach, with a chorus of "II"–"V"–IV moving to I–IV–I and then a whole step down to ♭VII–I for the verse, the "II" and "V" really operating as I and IV alternating in a whole-step movement that organizes the entire song. This is the same harmonic model as Black Flag's "Nervous Breakdown": fourths alternating in whole-step oscillation, followed by another section which uses another chord a whole step below: B–E / A–D, and G–A–B.

At the same time, the functional resolution of fourths from earlier rock songs could be retained in hardcore, demonstrating some continuity with the punk rock styles linked to older common-stock schemes. For example, discussing the composition of Minor Threat's "Small Man, Big Mouth" (1981), Lyle Preslar explained that Ian MacKaye originally composed the song as E / B / C–G / C–G, and Brian Baker moved the first two chords to F and C. Preslar continued: "move it a half-step man, it sounds right. And it sounds more musical, it sounds *much* more musical. And it flows better. . . . The riff resolves itself properly. . . . Now it's a rock and roll song."[134] The familiar movement in fourths (I–IV, I–V, etc.) was especially important for hardcore groups who explicitly stayed true to the idea of punk rock as part of a long American music tradition. Social Distortion's early song "Mainliner" (1981), for example, is built almost entirely on I and V chords (not barre chords), with a major melody, classic American rock and roll AAB (not AABA) form, and equally divided phrases.

The utility of this concise punk harmony meant guitarists could play at extremely fast tempos, sometimes twice as fast as previous punk songs. Barre chords in fourths only require the guitarist to move, for example, from the same shape on strings 4, 5, and 6 to strings 3, 4, and 5, and whole step movement with barre chords is similarly straightforward, moving the same shape the distance of two frets. For hardcore guitarists, the new challenge was to move quickly through these shapes (and preferably using downstrokes, like Johnny Ramone), rather than using a vocabulary of memorized chord shapes. And to play faster tempos, hardcore drummers initially turned American rock and roll backbeat drumming into a fast oom-pah rhythm (the Germs' "Forming" is one example).[135] This new level of speed appropriately matched the new slam dancing and the environment of the pit, and reinforced notions of violence and teenage testosterone becoming attached to hardcore.

This approach opened the door for newly original compositions, since guitarists and bassists could immediately compose, even before learning basic I, IV, and V chords, which are unintuitive shapes on the guitar fretboard and which change from key to key. Hardcore guitarists also started regularly employing half-step movement in melodies, and not just between sections (e.g., Black Flag's "I've Had It," Fear's "New York's Alright If You Like Saxophones," Circle Jerks' "I Just Want Some Skank" and "World Up My Ass"), also suggested by the use of barre chord shapes. Hardcore songs often revolved around the whole steps and minor thirds suggested by the fret markers on guitars, the dots along the neck indicating frets 3, 5, 7, 9, and 12 (on the sixth string, open E–G–A–B–C♯–E)—what my former student Oscar Rodriguez astutely referred to as "dot theory."[136]

Hardcore punk, in fact, is a truly guitar-based music, with a theory based on the guitar's construction as opposed to that of keyboard instruments.[137] The shift to a guitar-based system helped speed up the music and created a stylistic schism from earlier punk's basis in standard rock models. Circle Jerks' "Back Against the Wall" is a good example, as what appears to be V–♭III–I–♭VII (B–G–E–D) in the verses is better understood in terms of "dot theory," two minor-third movements (instead of the more common whole step) separated by a fourth. Using a barre chord shape, the cycle simply follows a back and forth movement of fret 7 on the E string (B)—fret 10 on the A string (G)—fret 7 on the A string (E)—fret 10 on the E string (D). Besides the opening guitar melody, the entire song uses barre chords on frets 0, 3, 5, 7, and 10, very close to the intervals suggested by the fret markers.

The Circle Jerks' music illustrates the connections between the sentiments expressed by younger punks and their innovations in hardcore composition and musicianship. As captured on their first record *Group Sex* (1980) ("hugely influential" and "perfect" to Ian MacKaye), songs such as "Red Tape" flew by at 392 beats per minute (the beat operating as an extremely fast 4/4, not as the double-time of a slower beat), almost twice as fast as the even fastest classic punk songs, such as "Janie Jones," which hovers around 210 bpm.[138] Keith "Lucky" Lehrer, Circle Jerks' drummer and only sixteen at the time, developed a highly technical, melodic, and fluid style, in the same vein as D.O.A.'s drummer Chuck Biscuits. Lehrer played accent hits along with Keith Morris's words (e.g., "Beverly Hills"), and the group used sudden tempo changes ("Back Against the Wall") and breakdowns ("Beverly Hills"). *Group Sex* is so condensed that the entire album of fourteen songs lasts under sixteen minutes.

*Group Sex* captured the attitudes of white suburban Southern Californian kids with ambivalence, humor, and anger, using the hardcore approaches that would become more representative of the new music. Keith Morris's refined scream and surfer-dude accent set a certain standard for authenticity in hardcore, notably rejecting the widespread trend of imitating British punk singers and their accents. He and the band mocked rich Angelenos ("Beverly Hills," "Don't Care"), teased and celebrated the punk scene ("I Just Want Some Skank," "Wasted," "Room 13"), lashed out at institutions and police ("Deny Everything," "Red Tape," "Back Against the Wall," "World Up My Ass"), war ("Paid Vacation"), teenage boy-girl troubles ("What's Your Problem?"), and Gen X angst ("Live Fast Die Young"). One of the funniest and most incisive songs on the record is "Group Sex," somewhat reminiscent of Frank Zappa's parodies, where Morris reads a personal ad for swingers ("Wouldn't it be nice to have a party with couples that are friendly and mellow? A low-key atmosphere where you can explore your most sensual fantasies with other aware, sensitive couples?").

Other LA hardcore groups echoed the Circle Jerks' stance on their social environment and their original compositions that extended punk's uses of rock conventions. Contemporaneous hardcore bands with teenage members out of Orange County (Agent Orange, formed in Placentia in 1979; Adolescents, Fullerton 1980) and Los Angeles County (Descendents, Manhattan Beach 1977) played entirely original material with extreme speed, tempo changes, and odd meters, all three aspects represented in the Descendents' "Tonyage." These groups also explored harmonic movement that was not attached to standard functional rock cycles or progressions, mostly with half-step and minor scale barre chord riffs, heard in early songs such as "Bloodstains" (Agent Orange, 1980), "I Hate Children," and "L.A. Girl" (Adolescents, 1981). The straightforward "Bloodstains" demonstrates how half-step riffs could be combined with the traditional whole-step alternation in a typical AABA (2:1:1) ratio for each verse, within a broader AAB cycle for the entire song:

| instrumental: | F♯ – (E) – **G** | (4x = 4 mm.) |
|---|---|---|
| verse (A): | F♯ – (E) – **G** | (4x = 4 mm.) |
| | E – (D) – **F** | (2x = 2 mm.) |
| | F♯ – (E) – **G** | (2x = 2 mm.) |
| verse (A): | F♯ – (E) – **G** | (4x = 4 mm.) |
| | E – (D) – **F** | (2x = 2 mm.) |
| | F♯ – (E) – **G** | (2x = 2 mm.) |
| chorus (B): | E | (2 mm.) |
| | F♯ – (E) – **G** | (2x = 2 mm.) |
| | E | (2 mm.) |
| | F♯ (stop time) | (2 mm.) |

[cycle repeats]

Musical example 6.1. "Bloodstains" chords, Agent Orange, *Agent Orange* EP, 1980.

These Orange County and LA County hardcore groups used the expanded repertoire of musical gestures to support their lyrics about white suburban California. Their songs—"Creatures," "Parents," "Marriage," "L.A. Girl," "No Friends," "Kabuki Girl"—reinforced a notion that punk was music by and for young (teenage) suburban white boys. The songs were obvious in their expression: e.g., "Parents, why won't they shut up? Parents, they're so fucked up." Half-step movement and minor thirds often represented angst, anger, or humorous contempt toward suburban society, a technique already used by the Urinals in "I'm White and Middle Class." The Adolescents used half-step movement throughout their debut (the "blue album") to paint lyrics such as, "LA girl, LA world, don't tell us how to act." The ubiquity of this word painting led to some ironic interpretations, the most blatant being the Descendents' "Suburban Home." The lyrics are split: half-step and minor intervals (I–♭VI–V / I–♭VI–V–♭III) support "I want to be stereotyped, I want to be classified" while major intervals and authentic V–I cadences support the second half "I want to be a clone, suburban home." In the context of hardcore composition, the half-step and minor melodies grate against the seemingly sarcastic words about suburbia, ending in a mocking, happy-sounding major resolution.[139]

In reality the song was more complicated, as composer Tony Lombardo was significantly older than the others. Lombardo was over thirty when he joined the band, while the others were still teenagers, and he was expressing his genuine desire to thrive in suburbia.[140] Like other paradoxes at the heart of punk, such as achieving financial success as professional musicians while ostensibly rejecting the music industry, suburban hardcore belied a deep conflict. While expressing contempt for suburban society, hardcore lyrics sung by teenage white boys simultaneously conveyed a desire for girls, social popularity, money, and attention. Part of what made suburban hardcore so potent for others was this ambiguity about their environment; one never knew quite how seriously to take them. Listeners chuckled at the Ramones' "Beat on the Brat" (with a baseball bat) because of its early 1960s musical style, while they shuddered at the Adolescents "I Hate Children" ("shut your mouth you stupid little brat / what you need's a smack smack") because of its sneered lyrics, minor melody, and breakneck tempo, but the two songs express similar ideas. The Adolescents' use of the first person in this song added to the musical effect, asking listeners to think about who is singing the lyric and how seriously they subscribed to the song's sentiment.

At the center of this maelstrom of meaning was Dead Kennedys, the San Francisco group who raised irony, humor, and seriousness to new expressive levels in hardcore. For example, "I Kill Children" uses minor and half-step melodies and it is very fast (more Adolescents), but singer Jello Biafra's over-the-top vocal style undermined the lyric (more Ramones). Their music was the apex of a style that punks understood as ironic and that outsiders would misunderstand as degenerate and immoral, right down to their name.

Dead Kennedys are especially important for the history of musical style outlined in *Damaged* as they boldly reworked the avant-garde approaches— the "Ignorance of Your Culture" music discussed in chapter 3—for the developing approaches of hardcore. They were formed with this aesthetic in mind, with bassist Klaus Flouride asking guitarist East Bay Ray in 1978 in response to Ray's ad to form a "punk or new wave band," "Are you on the Ramones side or the DEVO side of New Wave?" (Biafra recalled Klaus was more DEVO than Ramones, and they also discussed the Residents as influences.)[141] With the relocation of DEVO to Los Angeles, the presence of Captain Beefheart and Frank Zappa, and recordings and performances by the Residents, Chrome, L.A.F.M.S., and other experimentalists such as Winston Tong and Tuxedomoon, California remained a center of American avant-garde rock.

Dead Kennedys musically indicated the ways in which this experimental tradition could be explored in hardcore punk. Their techniques involved parodies and dead-on adaptations of musical gestures with clear associations, Biafra's theatrical and variable vocal delivery, and Winston Smith's arresting visual collages directly descended from John Heartfield and other Dadaists.[142] In their anthemic "California Über Alles," for example, they combined unnerving hardcore barre-chord and single-note riffs based on half-steps and minor intervals ($\hat{1}-\flat\hat{2}-\flat\hat{3}-\flat\hat{2}$, descending $\hat{1}-\flat\hat{7}-\flat\hat{5}-\flat\hat{3}$), lyrics both biting ("You will jog for the master race / and always wear a happy face") and foreboding (Jerry Brown "will be Führer one day") lyrics, and on-the-nose musical gestures (the militaristic march at the end of the song). Dead Kennedys also incorporated covers such as "Viva Las Vegas" (on *Fresh Fruit for Rotting Vegetables*) and "Rawhide" (*In God We Trust, Inc.*), again connecting them to groups such as the Residents and DEVO.

Finally, hardcore's musical style matched the physical contact that came to be associated with the scene. The blisteringly fast tempos and new levels of virtuosity among hardcore bands constituted a major break with the more relaxed style of earlier punk rock. However, this style was not created in a vacuum. Hardcore bands developed their style in relation to their audience's behavior, as all popular musicians do. Although historically unusual, slam dancing constitutes a form of dance, and as popular musicians, hardcore bands saw which songs generated the most energetic and intense response from their audience. As mentioned, it was slam dancing that gave the hardcore scene its strongest associations with violence, whiteness, and aggressive masculinity. As Paul Roessler analyzed, some musicians sped up hardcore for the young men in the pit:

> In the very very early days, there was a new kind of movement in the audience where people began jumping up and down and then began jumping into each other. . . . So that was a real change. When you're on stage and you are playing music and you watch the crowd start to jump up and down, it's very validating. And so as a musician you begin to crave that. You begin to crave seeing, "wow they're jumping up and down, I want them to jump around more. Oh, they're bumping into each other, I want them to bump into each other more. Wow, they're swirling in a huge circle" . . . So the way you get them to do it is you go faster. You go faster. . . . Bands like Black Flag and the Circle Jerks, some of those bands, they wanted to get that pit going, and there was this natural feedback between the audience and the musicians.[143]

For other musicians, hardcore became faster as bands tried to keep up with each other's stylistic innovations, or because they were pushing their own already high-energy creative vision. As Kira Roessler mentioned, "a lot of bands were just trying to do their thing. . . . [probably the less creative bands] just came and did really fast songs. Those are probably guys that aren't playing music anymore too. They were having fun! I don't question their motives, it was fun."[144] For other musicians, the pit could become a liability toward musicianship and creativity. Lyle Preslar remarked, "There's a lot of testosterone going on, there's a lot of hormones going on, and this music seems to be somewhat suitable for it. . . . now you've got this recipe for, essentially, a rugby scrum with a backing track to it. In many places that's what it became. . . . It has nothing to do with going to see this band, you're not even slightly interested in them, as long as it gives you the beats per minute you need to carry out your activity you're going to be fine."[145]

## Another View of New Wave

Punk's musical resources remained shared among hardcore and non-hardcore bands, but treated with different emphasis. But as hardcore came to define punk more generally, much of the existing scene stopped sounding like "punk," and members of that scene stopped relating to what punk was becoming. For example, Black Flag's "Thirsty and Miserable" on *Damaged* (1981) is a treatment of a twelve-bar blues (with ♭III standing in for IV), but its speed, volume, and Rollins's vocal style read as hardcore punk; in contrast, X's contemporaneous "Year One" on *Wild Gift* (also 1981) is a twelve-bar blues, but the medium tempo, major tonality, handclaps, and Cervenka's vocal style make the song sound like a rockabilly throwback. These two songs capture the stylistic split that had come to characterize LA punk by the early 1980s. In 1978 Black Flag and X audibly shared a great deal of stylistic features, but over those three years they moved away from each other in opposite directions.

Some punk groups changed their style or emphasized aspects that were already there, such as country, American vernacular music, or pop elements. Until some journalists began using the unfortunate term "cowpunk" in the mid-1990s, groups exploring country elements, such as X, the Gun Club, the Minutemen, and Meat Puppets, were able to stay within the punk chalk circle. "Power pop" and other terms similarly separated musicians who were stylistically connected and personally networked. However, groups that leaned toward pop in particular became increasingly excluded by hardcore fans, and also the musicians were often alienated by hardcore to the point where they separated themselves. "New wave" as a separate genre often incorporated pop and the queer camp aesthetics directly drawn from punk's early iterations.[146]

Violence, or the perception of violence, played a role. Mike Patton (Middle Class) described playing with Vicious Circle (pre-T.S.O.L.): "I remember seeing people getting beaten and bloodied. We were just appalled . . . it was like, 'Somebody's gonna throw a bottle at me? Shit!' That's when Middle Class said, 'We're not part of this,' and we scurried off into our Echo and the Bunnymen period."[147] This split had already begun after British punk led to audiences spitting ("gobbing") and becoming more violent. That was a "really hard demarcation line for me," said Lisa Jane Persky, "[Gary Valentine and I] didn't want to get hit or spit on or anything, we were just like, 'This is crap. We're not punks.' So I think that was a real divide that split people up."[148] In many cases, these were groups with female musicians, reinforcing the growing correlation of hardcore with young white males.

The Go-Go's were one extreme example. Deeply enmeshed in the LA punk scene at the beginning and trailblazers as an all-female group, they are almost completely absent from punk history today. Jane Wiedlin remembered: ". . . finally we weren't part of the Hollywood scene at all anymore. The scene continued on without us, and the history books erase The Go-Go's from the chronicles of those days, because it is just too much work to try to imagine how we had ever been a part of it."[149] Their success with pure rock and roll punk recategorized their group as simply pop or "new wave," the genre category that absorbed these erstwhile punk rock groups with pop characteristics. In New York, Blondie and Talking Heads would experience similar recategorizations in the early 1980s, especially as they began playing music more explicitly connected to contemporaneous black music such as funk and hip hop, and collaborating with black musicians (e.g., Talking Heads' "expanded band" that started touring in 1980, with Bernie Worrell, Busta Jones, Steve Scales, Nona Hendryx, Dolette McDonald, and Adrian Belew). Blondie was as synonymous with punk in the mid-1970s CBGBs scene as the Ramones or the Dead Boys, and yet today people can be surprised to learn that they were even once considered punk at all.

The term "new wave" was used interchangeably with "punk" through the 1970s in both alternative and mainstream media, and the bands later separated into these two categories were generally grouped together. For example, a 1978 KNXT-TV special on punk featured Sex Pistols, Blondie, Boomtown Rats, Dead Boys, Talking Heads, Ramones, Elvis Costello, the Jam, and the Voidoids.[150] While the word "punk" had commercial success in the United Kingdom, it failed to translate as a marketing term in the United States. In fact, "punk" could be seen as a liability in the US, for example, "Joey [Ramone] hated the 'punk' thing because he thought that limited their audience."[151] Instead, "new wave" became a way to sell bands such as DEVO who were associated with punk venues and other punk bands, and who took similar approaches to blues and common-stock resources as many other bands in the scene, but who never embraced the punk label and who had a pop orientation.[152] But these are marketing terms with little relationship to the stylistic and personal networks of the late 1970s. Musically, early punk and new wave cannot strictly be considered separate genres, as quintessential early "new wave" songs, even overdone heavy rotation hits like the Knack's "My Sharona" (1979), share many features with the music of many early punk bands, and the same can actually be applied to much "heavy metal." Even the areas of instrumentation and dress are basically unhelpful in any true generic distinction between "punk" and "new wave." For example, keyboards are associated with new wave bands, yet the Screamers, the Stranglers, and Suicide all used keyboards, as did Pere Ubu and the Residents. And very few members of early American punk bands, including early hardcore bands, dressed in the British fashion style stereotypically associated with punk, such as mohawks and safety pins.

The commercial quality of new wave eventually became one of the key distinguishing factors from punk, but this was less about musical style than social environments and relationships. More than the financial rewards, "selling out" or becoming "new wave" meant a less intimate relationship between performer and audience and a return to the alienated social scenes of arenas and recordings purchased in a generic shopping center. This seems to be an unavoidable cycle for punk due to the fact that the culture still basically operates within capitalist music industry structures.

So during the late 1970s and early 1980s, "punk" became increasingly associated with hardcore, while bands playing other kinds of punk rock were more and more linked with other categorical terms, especially "new wave." Meanwhile, these bands often remained connected musically, continued to play the same venues, and were discussed in the same fanzines. Hardcore was only one manifestation of multiple punk rock impulses, but the discursive separation of hardcore from other styles created a path for a white male lineage of punk looking backward, as well as revisionist misreadings of the past, such as imagining early punk bands as being composed of teenagers rather than adults. But the idea of a white male hardcore lineage and revisionist history never fully took hold. Punk remained a contested space of race, gender, and class moving forward, in line with punk's legacy of diversity and nonconformity.

Finally, the perhaps unexpected effect of hardcore, even with its associations of violence, masculinity, and whiteness, was its resonance for many women and people of color. For Jennifer Precious Finch of L7, for example, "music was sort of this athletic sport at the same time that it was movement and performance and not a contained craftsmanship, but it was explosive and big feeling. I got that directly from Black Flag and the Circle Jerks and all these big, masculine boy bands."[153] Hardcore solidified punk as an extreme form of music to match the extreme qualities of punk culture, and so it was polarizing; while it alienated many, it also attracted many others. For people of color, though, hardcore most dramatically became a viable mode of expression once Bad Brains exploded onto the DC scene in 1979.

# 7

## "Decisions with Precisions":
## New Directions for Hardcore in Washington, DC

My first cassette was that Bad Brains ROIR tape. I was listening to it and I thought
they were some white boys playing punk rock. Then I saw the picture and was like,
"Wow! They're black just like me." I'll put it to you like this: the Bad Brains were the
first band that made me feel like it was okay to be black and play punk rock . . .
Before that I thought it was only for white people. They were really liberating.
—Angelo Moore (Fishbone)[1]

Hardcore musicians took the contradictions and tangled meanings of race, class, gender, and sexuality embedded in punk's transformations of blues resources, early rock and roll schemes, and parody and pastiche, and instead of playfully toying with these elements, they distilled them into a powerful, productive, and long-lasting style. The punk scene in and around Washington, DC, at the turn to the 1980s helped established hardcore as a versatile vocabulary that could speak to a wide range of experiences for members of Generation X and the social environments in which they found themselves. Two groups, Bad Brains and Minor Threat, were most responsible for reframing these new possibilities for hardcore. But the trajectories of these two groups also once again revealed the recurring paradoxes and limitations of punk, especially as a space for criticizing, rejecting, or engaging formations of American whiteness.

Besides the few bands and areas covered in *Damaged*, by 1980 punk bands and small punk scenes had been springing up for years around the United States, in northern and midwestern metropolitan regions such as Chicago, Minneapolis, and Pittsburgh, and with punk's increased availability on recordings and the emergence of hardcore, Austin, Reno, San Antonio, and soon everywhere else.[2] Hardcore eventually became a major form of expression among Generation Xers living in the changing suburbs, either as new residents or as children of the baby boomers who first populated the suburbs with their parents. In some places, such as New York, hardcore became an important expression for urban youth as well. But the social and musical impact of Bad Brains, Minor Threat, and the DC scene changed the direction of hardcore in fundamental ways.

The significance of Bad Brains, an all-black quartet from the DC suburbs, emerging as one of the most important original hardcore bands—if not *the* most important—cannot be overstated. Not only did they broadcast punk's relevance to people of color at a time when the style had become almost completely associated with white people, they also resisted the categories and emerging stylistic norms of "hardcore" and "punk," once again uncovering the tensions in punk between conformity and nonconformity. Bad Brains introduced a wide variety of personal and philosophical ideas, including some that directly conflicted with those of other punks, and they made crucial musical innovations that reshaped punk rock as a vehicle for expression. They spoke to a wide variety of people, and their music stressed virtuosity and multiple rhythmic approaches. They also committed to a deep engagement with reggae, they left DC, and they at times withdrew from the punk scene, crucial aspects of their biography that should not be downplayed with respect to their role in punk history.

Minor Threat redefined punk as a music that could speak to the concerns of frustrated young people cast into difficult social situations that they did not create, but that they also did not blindly accept. Their songs were complex, designed to make other punks think and reflect on their own lives. At a time when punk seemed to be increasingly conformist, Minor Threat reestablished punk as a style for freethinking individuals. But like the Bad Brains, they also quickly found themselves facing problems with the reception of their music, exposing the limitations of hardcore as a space for social critique.

### ~~White Minority~~ Black Majority

While there had been some notable interracial punk bands with African American members, Bad Brains were exceptional in that they were all black and that they were also widely popular and influential.[3] Without implying causation, the Washington, DC, area helped shape, establish, and support Bad Brains, but more to the point, the connections between Bad Brains and their environment reflected the changing circumstances for people living in American cities and suburbs during the late 1970s and early 1980s. The DC case study also reveals broader issues surrounding race and class throughout the United States, especially in superficially diverse metropolitan regions.

Punk in late-1970s and early-1980s DC developed alongside Los Angeles, with some major differences. Like Los Angeles, Washington was an extremely segregated city, divided between a black, mostly urban population and mostly white suburbs. And as in Los Angeles, segregation increased with the postwar establishment of suburbs and the uprisings of 1965 in Watts and 1968 in DC. However, unlike Los Angeles, African Americans had constituted the majority of the population in DC since around 1960. In 1980 DC was 70 percent black, while the black population of LA hovered at around 10 percent to 15 percent. Within DC's city limits, the white population lived almost exclusively in enclaves of Northwest. "Indeed, as far as Chocolate Cities go, there is no more extreme case than Washington, D.C., in the second half of the twentieth century," writes Natalie Hopkinson.[4]

Meanwhile, middle-class African Americans had been moving to the Maryland and Virginia suburbs in significant numbers throughout the 1970s, especially to Prince George's County, Maryland.[5] Columbia, Maryland, in Howard County (my hometown, and a model for my neighbor Aaron McGruder's comic strip *The Boondocks*) had become an important site for relocating middle-class black and interracial families, in part because James Rouse created the suburb on planned development principles that were explicitly "colorblind."[6] These suburbs were also major sites for new immigrants from Korea, China, and Latin America. The Virginia suburbs were also becoming more racially diverse, although the state could also hew closer to its past as the seat of the Confederacy and the home of the American Nazi Party. Dug Birzdell of Beefeater remembered growing up in Arlington: "there was this family named Hall, which was a slave owning family, and they had a big house up on a hill . . . and the neighborhood down the hill was called Hall's Hill and that's where all the black families lived. . . . There was a lot of fucking bigotry that I ran across in Arlington."[7] But despite the significant increase in suburban integration and Prince George's County's status as "the wealthiest jurisdiction in the United States with a majority-black population," white and black families remained divided and unequal with respect to wealth and opportunities.[8]

Throughout the 1970s schools were a principal battleground for integration, as they had been for decades. Met with the reality that the Civil Rights Act of 1964 and *Brown v. Board of Education* were not being implemented in practice, school districts across the country were being ordered by courts to rectify demographic imbalances. In the Washington area, as well as in other cities, busing and magnet schools attempted to solve persistent segregation. Upper-middle-class and rich white families fought these solutions and also began sending their children to private schools in large numbers, choosing not to participate in desegregation projects: "[White Americans] endorse school integration in the abstract, expect it to happen, and seem to be accepting contact with middle-class blacks in many social relationships. But when faced with potentially extensive contact with poor blacks, which arouses fear of schools and neighborhoods being 'invaded' or 'overrun' by the black underclass, then resistance skyrockets."[9] Furthermore, "integration" is an ambiguous term, as "African Americans define an integrated community as one in which 20 to 50 percent of residents are African American. Whites define it as one where they dominate—and in which only 10 percent of residents are African American."[10] In the end, a new mix of young people was left to negotiate America's racial problems and issues of identity in the schools, particularly germane to the kind of underlying, yet often unacknowledged, racism that has consistently plagued the American North and West Coast.

Beyond the Washington, DC, area, large numbers of African Americans in the 1970s were moving to the suburbs, and more African American students were attending suburban schools because they lived in the school district or because they were being bused. In this suburban environment, musical choices acted as self-conscious indicators of personal identity chosen from a menu of options; listening to R&B, rap music, rock, soul, disco, or punk reflected group affiliation, personality, culture, and priorities. In these increasingly integrated environments, some white and black students began exchanging music and culture, and some formed bands together. Also, many black suburban students described experiencing the complex alienation of the suburbs' lack of culture as well as a specific layering of a suburban "misfit" mentality formed both in relation to, and in opposition to, suburban environments explicitly designed as white, generally understood to be white, and often forcefully maintained as white. These black suburban kids describe a different experience from that of white kids, with an awareness of the suburbs' whiteness and a distance from the urban black culture that had come to be regarded as the "real" black experience, sometimes represented by fellow black students who were being bused to the school. Some young people of color describe feeling like outsiders, typical of those drawn to punk, but compounded in their mostly white surroundings. Bubba Dupree, for example, who is, in his own words, mixed (black and Filipino), moved from Haight-Ashbury to Wheaton, Maryland, at age six, "a really very white, straight, suburban neighborhood, and that was the beginning of me feeling very outside of everything."[11]

The members of Bad Brains had biographies with similarities to those of other early punk rockers, with experiences that they identified as making them feel apart from many of their schoolmates and neighbors. Darryl Jenifer lived in Southeast DC, while Paul Hudson (also known as H.R.), his brother Earl Hudson, and Gary Miller (also known as Dr. Know) lived in nearby Capitol Heights, in Prince George's County. The Hudsons had a multifaceted upbringing before landing in Washington, with their father Leon in the Air Force. Their father was from Alabama and their mother from Jamaica. H.R. was born in England, they lived for a while in Jamaica (where H.R. "heard [his] first reggae song" at the age of three), as well as Texas, New York, California, and Hawaii. Finally attending Central High School (1971–72) and then Potomac High School (1973–74), H.R. felt like an outsider: "I spoke differently, I looked different and I did not do what those kids did in DC."[12] Earl had been playing drums since the age of five, and in junior high school he met Gary Miller, who was already playing guitar and jamming with Darryl Jenifer. Like other contemporaneous punk bands in the late 1970s, Bad Brains put together their band, rehearsed in a friend's basement (in their case, "at the end of the ultimate cul-de-sac" in Forestville), and tried to find their original voice.[13] A similar situation between African American students in the city and surrounding suburbs of LA led to the formation of Fishbone, the other major all-black punk band of the period, beginning in 1979 when Norwood Fisher was bused to Hale Junior High in Woodland Hills, where he met Angelo Moore, who lived there.

As much as DC's punk scene abided by the prevailing logic of race, class, and gender, in some ways it flipped the usual patterns, according to the city's exceptional nature. The demographics of the early DC scene reflected the majority black population in DC and PG County and the significant black population in surrounding suburbs, symbolized by Bad Brains. While still a mostly white scene, DC had more racially integrated bands than other scenes, including the Enzymes (with Dave Byers); Scream (with Skeeter Thompson) from Bailey's Crossroads, Virginia; Void (with Bubba Dupree) from Columbia, Maryland; and Red C, whose bassist Toni Young was a black woman living in Northeast. Meanwhile, in another unusual situation, the white punks did not come just from the suburbs but also from Northwest DC, a mostly wealthy or economically comfortable white residential enclave within the city limits. These are the circumstances for the emergence of Bad Brains and the Washington, DC, scene, an extreme manifestation of the race and class issues at the heart of punk that would generally reshape the meanings and perceptions of punk and hardcore.

### The Musical Style of Hardcore Punk, Part Two

That's the birth of Bad Brains. They took all of that experience—the African-American middle-class experience in a city that not long ago was a segregated city, within their lifetime—and they are taking these musical influences and the skills that they developed from trying to play this complicated jazz fusion, and they are adding in the incredibly energy and antiestablishment fervor. That passion. That's punk rock. And what they created out of all of these pieces is something unprecedented.
—Mark Andersen[14]

Bad Brains developed their style independently from LA punk, hardcore or otherwise. Like Black Flag and other punk bands in the late 1970s, Bad Brains primarily created their sound after being exposed to the Ramones, the Dead Boys, the Sex Pistols, the Damned, and other 1977–era New York and England bands, in this case by their friend Sid McCray.[15] Their name was a direct nod to the Ramones' "Bad Brain," from *Road to Ruin*.[16] Bad Brains, like Circle Jerks and some of the other LA bands, aimed to play faster than the Ramones and to apply high levels of musicianship, originality, and precision to their music. Bad Brains also drew on jazz and jazz fusion as music requiring high levels of technique. For Bad Brains, the genesis of their music is based in their early attempts to play jazz fusion as a group called Mind Power, formed in 1977. While the proficiency and impact of Mind Power as a band seems to have been overstated (similar to the proto–Sex Pistols group the Strand, which basically never played out and exists mostly in storytelling, or Lucky Lehrer's reputation among punks as an exceptionally proficient jazz drummer while in high school), the lasting importance of the Mind Power story is that Bad Brains aspired to great technical ability and unabashedly professed admiration for jazz fusion. Even though groups like the Damned were already demonstrating punk's potential with very high levels of musicianship, the repeated punk "party line" was that punk music developed in *opposition* to such music in favor of three-chord rock that anyone could learn quickly and get up on stage to play.

It's a safe bet that no one in DC saw Bad Brains in 1979 and thought they could immediately go on stage and do what H.R., Dr. Know, Darryl, and Earl were doing, as inspired as they might be by what they witnessed. However, the idea of punk's accessibility remained. What followed was a recipe for innovation, as members of the underground rock scene in DC heard Bad Brains and aspired to that level of musicianship, regardless of their experience. As Bubba Dupree reflected, "thank God I wasn't technically good enough to do whatever I was aiming for, because probably no one would care about it if I had gotten it right."[17] Anyone could form a band and play a show, but with Bad Brains leading the way, that also meant the group should be well rehearsed, tight, and extraordinarily musical. The Bad Brains were also older than most in the young emerging DC scene—H.R. was twenty-three and Earl Hudson twenty-two when Bad Brains formed—and the younger teenagers forming bands looked up to them as musical role models.

The group that came closest to Bad Brains' level of musicianship was Minor Threat, Ian MacKaye's group formed after the Teen Idles. MacKaye and the few other early DC punks had already become interested in punk and formed bands in the classic "D.I.Y." spirit—for MacKaye the turning point was seeing the Cramps in February 1979: "When I saw the Cramps, I thought, 'I can be in a band.'"[18] The Teen Idles, Untouchables (Ian's younger brother Alec's first band), Government Issue, and S.O.A. (State of Alert, Henry Rollins [Garfield]'s first band) were making music in an early hardcore punk style that was rapidly becoming standard. After Teen Idles, MacKaye formed Minor Threat to play his new songs, and the group he put together with Lyle Preslar, Brian Baker, and Jeff Nelson was a technically proficient ensemble. Brian Baker in particular had a reputation as a musical prodigy of sorts, having joined Carlos Santana on stage when he was twelve years old and living in Michigan. Baker was the youngest of the group, only fifteen when Minor Threat formed (MacKaye and Nelson were eighteen, Preslar seventeen).

Minor Threat's musical proficiency was clearly inspired by Bad Brains, as Preslar told me: "if you wanted to point to one specific *this is the blueprint for what you do* it was Bad Brains. For us."[19] Ian MacKaye echoed Preslar: "They were supernaturally good and I think it's safe to say that Minor Threat was deeply inspired by Bad Brains. The message I got from the Bad Brains was *practice, practice, practice*, and be good, don't ever waste the stage. H.R. would scream 'Are you ready?!?' at the beginning of their shows and it was clear that they weren't getting up there to just shuffle around. The message was to fucking *bring it*, so we did."[20] Minor Threat was also inspired by the music coming from the West Coast, especially Black Flag, D.O.A., Dead Kennedys, and Circle Jerks. MacKaye had been to the West Coast and seen a number of bands on tour with the Teen Idles, the most transformative concert being a Flipper, Dead Kennedys, and Circle Jerks show in San Francisco on August 9, 1980.[21]

Bad Brains and Minor Threat together ended up being major inspirations for the local scene. As Chris Stover of Void told me:

[It was] basically Bad Brains first and foremost, and then Minor Threat. And I specifically point out those two bands because they were the tightest, they were like the crème de la crème for all of us because they were the musicians. And you could tell. And when they got up on stage, you know, the music started and music stopped. Unfortunately sometimes [for us] the music started, but then it stopped because John broke his leg or Bubba broke three guitar strings or my bass got cracked because of somebody thrashing . . . But anyway, regardless, we aspired to that. And that being said, because we aspired to that, there was I think throughout the scene in general, there was this uniformity to practice, and practice like a motherfucker. I think that that was what you alluded to earlier was this sense of competitiveness, and I think that was at least from my perspective was that when you came out on that stage you wanted to be as professional as possible . . . because those guys in Minor Threat and Bad Brains were *musicians* and they *played* and when you heard them you could distinctly hear each song and know each song and there was no messing around. At the end of the day they were professionals.[22]

In practice, this meant musical changes ranging from the subtle to the radical. Bad Brains and Minor Threat perfected the art of sudden starts and stops, tempo changes, breakdowns, and extremely fast tempos. As mentioned, it was not just the speed at which Bad Brains were playing that was inspiring, it was the accuracy and technique, "decisions with precisions" as in the line from their groundbreaking song "Pay to Cum." As Lyle Preslar remembered, "I bought 'Pay to Cum' by Bad Brains and I brought it home and I put it on my mother's stereo . . . and I literally thought, it's the wrong speed . . . I couldn't believe they were playing that fast with that kind of precision."[23]

Bad Brains' Dr. Know (Gary Miller) and Lyle Preslar helped extend hardcore guitar technique by performing these lightning-speed songs using full six-string barre chords, as opposed to the two- or three-string downstroke style that was often used. Preslar based his technique on that of Pete Townshend. Like the guitar playing of Johnny Ramone, the full barre chord approach of Preslar and Dr. Know is often misrepresented as two- or three-string power chords—many online tablature transcriptions of Minor Threat songs indicates two-string chords, for instance—but their full chord sound is essential for understanding the musicianship they applied to their music. They were not the only ones to avoid two-string downstrokes, as Preslar elaborated:

> Bands like the Damned didn't do that, bands like the Circle Jerks didn't do that, they recognized the different sounds that could be obtained if you didn't just play the top two strings. . . . some of us recognized fairly early on that just playing two strings in downstrokes really didn't have a lot of sonic value. . . . People like me and Brian [Baker] prided ourselves on being able to do these different things within the same fast structure . . . a lot of this we got from Dr. Know frankly, it's like we want to play with precision but we also want to throw in little things that indicated we knew more about that guitar than just playing those two strings on that barre chord.

East Bay Ray, the guitarist for Dead Kennedys, also used full triads.[24] In these skillful ensembles, Bad Brains and Minor Threat refined the structural approaches that were becoming the cornerstone of the hardcore punk style, such as movement in whole steps and fourths, riffs using minor-third and other blues-based melodic scaffolding, monophonic or unison relationships between bass and guitar, tightly constructed AB or AAB cycles (often with contrasting minor and major sections), and closed phrases based on alternating strong and weak elements.

The opening song on the first Minor Threat EP, "Filler" (1981), demonstrates the foundation of their approach to hardcore. Structurally the song consists only of two alternating eight-bar sections played at a blazingly fast speed of about 370 beats per minute (I believe these hardcore songs are counted appropriately as a very fast 4/4), an A section in F♯ minor and a B section in the relative A major (returning to the F♯ minor at the close). "I Don't Wanna Hear It," "Seeing Red," "Small Man, Big Mouth," and "Stand Up" are more examples of Minor Threat songs with AB (or AABB) forms. This short AB or AAB type of form is common with American punk and hardcore bands, a return to the shorter cycles played by the Ramones and continuing the overall trend by shortening the forms even more, as opposed to the tendency of many British punk bands to expand out into cycles that sound longer, such as the proper AABA form heard on "Anarchy in the UK" and "God Save the Queen."

Minor Threat also incorporated minor-pentatonic blues-type movement in songs such as "Straight Edge" and "Out of Step (With the World)." As shown in musical example 7.1, "Out of Step" demonstrates one way that the multiple elements of hardcore came together in a distilled form. It contains verses built on minor pentatonic patterns, a contrasting chorus outlining a major third, and an oscillating whole step alternation pattern serving as a basis for a guitar solo (or in the case of a later version, a monologue).[25] The verse uses the minor pentatonic scaffolding D–F–G–A and a I–IV alternation (D–G) from bar to bar, while the chorus outlines the A major chord (V of V), starting on E, with MacKaye's vocal line shifting from a straight-across scream to a major third on "with the world," perhaps musically representing his feelings of being at odds with society. The interlude and guitar solo combine minor-third patterns with whole step alternations:

| measure: | 1 | | 2 | | 3 | | 4 | | 5 | | 6 | | 7 | | 8 | | |
|---|---|---|---|---|---|---|---|---|---|---|---|---|---|---|---|---|---|
| A (verse): | D | F | D | F | G | G | A | G | D | F | D | F | G | G | A | G | (2x) |
| B (chorus): | E | | | | | | C♯ | | E | | | | A | | | | (2x) |
| C (interlude): | D | F | D | F | C | ♭E | C | ♭E | D | F | D | F | C | ♭E | C | ♭E | (8x) |
| B (chorus): | E | | | | | | C♯ | | E | | | | A | | | | (2x) |

Musical example 7.1. "Out of Step (With the World)" chords, Minor Threat, *In My Eyes* EP, 1981.

However, as part of a wholesale stylistic shift, these elements of "Out of Step" had become increasingly difficult to associate with rock's roots in the blues.

As Minor Threat solidified the hardcore foundation with these songs they also, like the Circle Jerks, began stretching the form. They coordinated tight starts and stops and tempo changes, especially breakdowns, on songs such as "Screaming at a Wall" and the later "Betray."[26] Starts and stops were another major shift from traditional rock music, except for the stop-times found at the end of some cycles. And unlike older punk songs, which still relied on familiar harmonic cycles—and in the case of songs such as "Blitzkrieg Bop" or "X-Offender," they were of course *meant* to be heard as familiar—these hardcore songs were often composed of separate parts that did not necessarily relate to each other harmonically. Songs made up of starkly different parts such as "Betray" are often that way because they are composed block by block, with different players contributing separate parts; one person might bring in a part and then the group collectively figures where the song can go next, trying out different parts they might have already worked out.[27] Often these different parts do not relate in traditional harmonic ways, but they do make sense on the guitar as an instrument, and even when hardcore songs are composed on other instruments they follow the guitar-based theory. Musical example 7.2, "Screaming at a Wall," is composed of three sections with little conventional tonal relationships to each other, but which all fit the guitar-based language of hardcore. Notice especially how in section B the half-step and fourth movement on the guitar creates a tonal loop, pivoting on A♯. The third section is in a slower tempo, but with coordinated hits with the guitar, bass, and drums the second time around. All of this melodic-harmonic movement takes place under the vocal line, which stays entirely on G for sections A and B. Songs such as "Screaming at a Wall" satisfied the need to play as fast as possible for hardcore dancers and the pressure to create original music. Furthermore, the song demonstrates the virtuosic sensibility of Minor Threat and Bad Brains, but a nonstandard virtuosity coming out of the guitar-based hardcore language.

Form:    A (instrumental) A  A  B  B

A (instrumental) A  A  B  B

C (instr) C (instr) C (vocal + hits) C (vocal + hits)

A (instrumental) A

Instrumental intro:

| Fret: | 5 | 7 | 8 | 8 | 3 | 3 | 3 | 3 | 5 | 7 | 8 | 8 | 10 | 10 | 10 | 10 |
|---|---|---|---|---|---|---|---|---|---|---|---|---|---|---|---|---|
| | D | B | F | C | G | | | | D | B | F | C | G (up 8va) | | | |

Verse (A, 2x):

| Fret: | 5 | 7 | 8 | 8 | 3 | 3 | 3 | 3 | 5 | 7 | 8 | 8 | 3 | 3 | 3 | 3 |
|---|---|---|---|---|---|---|---|---|---|---|---|---|---|---|---|---|
| | D | B | F | C | G | | | | D | B | F | C | G | | | |

Chorus (B, 2x):

| Fret: | 1 | 2 3 3 | | 4 | 5 6 6 | | 1 | 2 3 3 | | 4 | 5 6 6 | |
|---|---|---|---|---|---|---|---|---|---|---|---|---|
| | A♯ B C G | | | C♯ D D♯ A♯ | | | A♯ B C G | | | C♯ D D♯ A♯ | | |

Breakdown (C, 2x + 2x with hits, slower, standard hardcore pattern):

| Fret: | 7 | 7 | 5 | 5 | 7 | 7 | 5 | 5 |
|---|---|---|---|---|---|---|---|---|
| | B | E | D | A | B | E | D | A |

Musical example 7.2. "Screaming at a Wall" chords, Minor Threat, *Minor Threat* EP, 1981.

Bad Brains' "Pay to Cum" is another song with a quintessential American hardcore form, but which demonstrated some major stylistic changes over time. The instrumental intro and outro are based on the familiar whole step and fourth movement (D–E–A). The song proper is an AAB cycle, with the A section using another whole step motion, and the B section based on the relative minor (G–F♯–D–B). Each section emphasizes the call-and-response binary phrase division heard throughout the Ramones' catalog.

Multiple versions of "Pay to Cum" capture the ways in which the enigmatic and charismatic H.R. altered the expectations of what a punk vocalist could and should do, one of the most significant innovations in the music of Bad Brains. In the B sections, H.R. sang melodically, a proficiency he demonstrated on many different songs, including the breakdown of "Banned in D.C.," "The Big Takeover," "I," and reggae songs such as "I Luv I Jah" and the B-side of "Pay to Cum," the love song "Stay Close to Me."[28] And as shown in musical example 7.3, in the A sections, H.R. percussively aligned the strong syllables of the lyric with strong beats while keeping a steady "rat-a-tat" accurate eighth-note rhythm, in a display of vocal virtuosity. Earl Hudson emphasized the eighth-notes with staccato attacks on a cowbell. The equal division of syllables regardless of stress had become an important break with the blues and American music, following British singers (as demonstrated in chapter 5), and H.R.'s realigning of the syllables returned the rat-a-tat style to more of an American aesthetic.

| Beats: | 1 | | 2 | | 3 | | 4 | |
|---|---|---|---|---|---|---|---|---|
| | | I | **make** | de- | **ci-** | sions | **with** | pre- |
| | **ci-** | sions | **lost** | in- | **side** | this | **manned** | co- |
| | **lli-** | sion | **Just** | to | **see** | that | **what** | to |
| | **be** | is | **per-** | fect- | **ly** | my | **fan-** | ta- |
| | **sy!** | | | | | | | |

Musical example 7.3. "Pay to Cum" vocal rhythm, Bad Brains, 1980.

On the Bad Brains' 1979 demos, released in 1996 as *Black Dots*, one can clearly hear these syllables at the relatively comfortable tempo of 268 beats per minute. The 7-inch single (1980) is up to 300 beats per minute and the syllables become blurred together in many sections, including the opening lines, although H.R.'s rat-a-tat vocals can still be clearly heard on lyrics such as the last lines, "and so it's now we choose to fight to stick up for our bloody right the right to sing the right to dance the right is ours we'll take the chance." By the time of the most famous Bad Brains release, the ROIR cassette known colloquially as the "yellow tape" (1982), "Pay to Cum" had become an ultimate demonstration of Bad Brains' speed, topping out at 322 beats per minute.[29] At this point, H.R. simply emphasizes certain strong syllables to bring out the rhythm of the lyric.

H.R.'s virtuosity extended to the realm of movement. While singers such as Keith Morris and Ron Reyes displayed wild energy on stage, H.R. introduced tremendous physical exertions and acrobatics to the punk frontperson's role, adding another important rhythmic element to Bad Brains' musical aesthetic. Perhaps unsurprisingly, African American observers linked H.R.'s movement to the styles of other black bandleaders and dancers. Vernon Reid (Living Colour) remembered:

> We're watching a show and he's doing a song and he does a backflip and lands exactly at the end of the song, and it was like, "Game over!" I remember Corey [Glover] being in the audience, and we looked at each other like, *WHAT THE FUCK?!* . . . H.R. did a standing somersault, which is one of the most difficult things. No run up. Standing. *Boom!* The only thing to compare it to was James Brown, the hardest working man in showbiz. Someone that can move like that changes the physical dimensions of the room, changes everything.[30]

H.R.'s virtuosity established a definitive break between what the vocalist and the rest of the band were doing. In hardcore especially, the vocal line became dissociated from the underlying textures, both in terms of the treatment of the syllables and the vocal line. H.R. and Ian MacKaye also sang straight-across melodies while the band moved through different chords, as opposed to singing in unison or parallel with the guitar and bass. Other rock styles depend on a strong coordination of the vocal line with the underlying instrumental accompaniment, which is one reason why guitarists can often also be vocalists. Hardcore started to demand that the vocalist be a separate person from the guitarist or bassist, as it would be virtually impossible for a human being to play what Dr. Know was playing and sing what H.R. was singing. A side effect of this phenomenon, also due to the fact that hardcore is performed extremely loudly and with poor sound quality in venues, is that hardcore instrumentalists may not know what a vocalist is saying or doing. Bubba Dupree explained, "[the lyrics and the rest of the band] were two different entities."[31] Lyle Preslar admitted, "When you're on stage, in those days anyway, you couldn't hear anything. Most of the time I had no idea what Ian was saying. Even between songs I had no idea, because you can't hear anything, and because you're worried about your own thing."[32]

Bad Brains rewrote the script for punk, reframing it as part of a black music tradition even as they invoked ideas of racial transcendence. Musically this manifested in many ways, including the overall emphasis on musicianship, H.R.'s vocal approach of rhythmically aligning syllables with attention to strong and weak beats, H.R.'s melodic singing, blues riffs on songs such as "I," Dr. Know's soloing with blues-based and classic-rock flourishes on songs such as "Banned in D.C." and "I," and Earl Hudson's drumming, which moved away from the conventional oom-pah hardcore beat toward a backbeat—even a shuffle feel on "Right Brigade." These were all elements that had been minimized or eliminated in much hardcore punk at this point, but Bad Brains were able to use these stylistic aspects in creating their own style firmly within the hardcore aesthetic. Bad Brains also explored reggae beyond the covers and adaptations of Patti Smith, the Clash, or the Slits. H.R. in particular professed Rastafarian ideas; H.R. and Earl lived as children for a short time in Jamaica, and their commitment to reggae flourished after seeing Bob Marley perform at the Capitol Centre in 1978.[33] Blackness was front and center in their band and their aesthetic, and they addressed race and punk's whiteness head on. The insert to the original "Pay to Cum" single announced:

> **THE BAD BRAINS** ARE ONE OF THE MOST ORIGINAL BANDS TO BE FOUND ON THIS SIDE OF THE ATLANTIC AND THEIR HIGH-POWERED NEW ERA ROCK AND ROLL REFLECTS THE BEST OF MANIAC PUNK. THAT THEY ARE BLACK MUSICIANS IN A SEEMINGLY ALL-WHITE MUSIC SCENE, SEEMS TO MATTER LITTLE FOR AS WITH ALL TRULY ORIGINAL CREATIVE ARTISTS—THEY WOULD BE UNUSUAL NO MATTER WHAT THEY WERE INTO.

Bad Brains emphasized blackness even as they stressed their uniqueness and transcendence of racial categories, affecting the reception of their sound. Bubba Dupree used the word *soul*, explained as an ineffable quality not directly linked to race, but there nonetheless: Bad Brains "clearly have soul," and Dupree himself always had "the conscious desire to put soul into" his music, "and I think that definitely had a lot to do with why DC hardcore sounded different than other hardcores."[34]

### Returning to Hippie Idealism

Another important factor in the Washington, DC, punk scene was that there was no corporate entertainment industry infrastructure as there was in Los Angeles or New York, meaning that the scene was entirely homegrown. No one moved to DC for the purposes of a high-profile pop music career. No one in DC's early punk scene was like Lenny Kaye, a third-generation member of AFM Local 802 (the powerful New York musician's union). By creating an internationally relevant scene from virtually no rock music infrastructure, DC punks established a revised blueprint and paradigm for local punk scenes moving forward throughout the country.

The lack of a rock infrastructure in DC often created a strong relationship between the teenagers playing hardcore and the older underground rock bands. This differed from the situation in Los Angeles, which often seemed to take the form of a more antagonistic or dismissive relationship between older punk rockers and suburban hardcore kids. In DC the slightly older generation of bands such as the Slickee Boys welcomed the new bands, if for no other reason than groups like Minor Threat and Bad Brains drew larger audiences, and now shared bills would sell out the 9:30 Club and other venues.[35]

The first wave of DC hardcore bands also had a more sympathetic view of the 1960s and its hippie utopian goals than other scenes. This attitude could range from simply connecting to the music of one's parents—often, DC's punks had a strong bond with supportive baby boomer parents—to embracing and wanting to rekindle the communal ideals and potential of that period. Bubba Dupree of Void, for example, told me: "even though I was too young to be like a 'hippie,' I was definitely a child of the sixties. I was born in '66. My parents and I actually lived on Haight-Ashbury, '69, '68, to the early '70s, so I was exposed to a lot of Haight-Ashbury stuff kind of early on."[36] In my interviews with DC punks, more musicians spoke to me without prompting about the Grateful Dead, Funkadelic, and most of all, Jimi Hendrix, than they did the Clash, Ramones, or Sex Pistols.

The most prominent musicians of early DC hardcore punk were born mostly around the early to mid-1960s, e.g., Daryl Jennifer (1960), Henry Rollins (1961), Ian MacKaye (1962), Lyle Preslar (1963), and Brian Baker (1965). A parallel can be made with the early punk rockers roughly a decade older; Ian MacKaye's relationship to the music of Woodstock and the late 1960s is similar to the attitude Joey Ramone had to the music of the late 1950s. In the generational cycle of punk in the long 1970s, the watershed era of the 1960s had gone through musicians wrestling with, reflecting, and performing extreme manifestations of the period (the Stooges, the Velvet Underground); disillusionment and critique, but still a part of it (DEVO, the Residents); nostalgia for an earlier time (Ramones, Flamin' Groovies, Modern Lovers); more opposition to the counterculture's failures (Black Flag, Dead Kennedys); to finally returning to the period's potential (Minor Threat). A lot of this general attitude toward the sixties stemmed from the dominant personality in DC punk, Ian MacKaye, who connected the underground scene he encountered to the sixties counterculture and the agency enacted by young people during that time:

MACKAYE: But that show [the Cramps, Urban Verbs, Chumps at the Hall of Nations, Georgetown University, February 3, 1979] was mindblowing for me. Just mindblowing. I mean the Cramps were just incredible. And what happened at that show, what I saw there, the people I saw there, I just found the underground. I think growing up in the sixties, late sixties early seventies, I really *believed*, I mean I loved Woodstock, I saw that movie three times, I went through the album, I wore it out, I just recently read three more books about Woodstock. I'm just a student of that.

RAPPORT: What appeals to you about Woodstock?

MACKAYE: Well the myth of it appeals to me, because I believe in it. I think of music as like a fire—you can cook with it or you can destroy with it, or you can use it to gather around and warm people up. So it's an energy, and it's a point of gathering to some degree. You think about Woodstock, even the setting of it, the basin, the idea that on this stage there's this fire burning, and thousands of people are trying to figure out, "Who are we? What are we?" They've already seceded from mainstream society to some degree, by growing their hair out or wearing weird clothes. That was a serious cultural shift in the sixties, unlike any shift I think maybe ever, when youth culture became a reality.

In the return to the 1960s, MacKaye rejected the rejection he heard in much of the music of the 1970s, what he deemed "a soundtrack for self-destruction."[37] Also in the spirit of the 1960s, he worked to foster alternative living and working environments, including the still active, independent Dischord Records, which helped document the DC scene and provided the starting point for dozens of bands, and Dischord House, the group house in Arlington that housed the label for years.

The relationship between the older and younger underground rock scenes centered on Madam's Organ, a hippie commune located in Adams Morgan in Northwest DC.[38] D.O.A., the groundbreaking band from Vancouver, were an important spark to this relationship when they played Madam's Organ on tour in November 1979, taking advantage of the venue network of the Youth International Party (Yippies). On the tour D.O.A. also played a Yippie venue at New York's Studio 10 (10 Bleecker Street), the expansion of famed countercultural institution Number 9 (9 Bleecker).[39] Punks found renewed connections to sixties countercultural activists such as the Yippies, who were still active and like punks were "professional shit disturbers."[40] Eventually, the punk–Yippie connection would have its most prominent representative in Tim Yohannan (born 1945) and *Maximumrocknroll.*[41]

Hardcore was a "rebellion against a rebellion."[42] As many mid-1970s punk musicians expressed frustration with the "lame hippie stuff" of the 1960s, hardcore musicians exposed what they perceived as the flimsiness of baby boomer punk for the challenges of the early 1980s.[43] In responding to early punk's rejection of hippie idealism, many found themselves returning to the potential of the 1960s counterculture. Furthermore, these hardcore punks were themselves at the tail end of the baby boomer generation, and still very close to the Woodstock period. The shadow of the 1960s continued to loom over punk even as Gen X musicians transformed the music into hardcore.

## Straight Edge and Mental Health

Bad Brains and Minor Threat stressed independence and free thought, emphasizing resistance to the conformist pressures of youth culture as well as the herd mentality that consistently threatened to dominate punk culture. From the principle of independent thought came one of Minor Threat's enduring legacies, the introduction of "straight edge" ideas to punk. Ian MacKaye's personal declaration on the song "Straight Edge," "I'm a person just like you / But I've better things to do / Than sit around and fuck my head / Hang out with the living dead," was taken up by other punk kids looking for an alternative to the persistent culture of drugs surrounding underground music. The impact of the 1960s drug culture loomed large over straight edge, with drugs' historical attachment to bohemian life, the notion of drugs enhancing musical experiences, as well as the still painful drug-induced deaths of Jimi Hendrix and other 1960s musical icons at the beginning of the 1970s. Beyond music, drug culture permeated every aspect of social life and leisure time for vast numbers of kids in the 1970s, including everyday hanging out. Initially, at least with respect to the Minor Threat songs "Straight Edge" and "Out of Step (With the World)," straight edge was about average white suburban teenagers using drugs and alcohol, more than it was directed at other punks, as it is usually characterized. This seems clear when considering that when Ian MacKaye wrote "Straight Edge," the punk scene in DC, and in the United States in general, was extremely small.

Straight edge was never meant to be an ideology or more than a personal choice, although MacKaye did want to "raise the flag" for others who may have felt similarly.[44] Besides MacKaye, the other members of Minor Threat did not adhere to a "straight edge" code. Yet others, such as Al Barile of Boston's SS Decontrol, took it on as a sort of movement, and in some cases straight edge bands and punks urged others to embrace the philosophy.[45] At times, straight edge punks could be forceful, militant, or preachy.[46] In this sense, straight edge was one of the first major tests of punk's ideals of freedom and free expression, which were becoming well established by the early 1980s. The ostensible nonconformist principles of defining one's own identity clashed with the unfolding collective agreement of "this is what punk is about." As Jack Grisham said, "if someone says Punk Rock is 'this,' we're gonna say it's 'that.'"[47] As was the case time and again for punks, pressures to conform and resistance to conformity played against each other.

But as with the other trends and controversies described in this book, some unconventional insights can come to light if straight edge is considered within its broader social context. Straight edge was less an exceptional "movement" than it was an articulation of ideas that punks had been exploring for years, albeit in extreme ways. As discussed above, punk has typically been presented as a response to the banal music of the 1970s, but as I have aimed to demonstrate, punk was less in reaction to the music of popular 1970s rock bands than to the social situations surrounding those bands and the sense of alienation those situations engendered. During the late 1970s and 1980s in metropolitan regions such as Washington, DC, rock concert culture was the world of *Heavy Metal Parking Lot*: driving out to an arena, getting stoned and hammered, listening to the music (or not), and driving back to more suburbs.[48] The abandonment of city music venues through the era of white flight intensified after the racial uprisings of the 1960s, including the DC uprising of 1968, moving rock entertainment to isolated geographical sites such as the Capital Centre near Landover, Maryland (opened 1973); Nassau Coliseum near Uniondale, New York (opened 1972); and the Meadowlands Arena near Rutherford, New Jersey (opened 1981). These environments were the cultural flipside of the communal music festival experience culminating in Woodstock. Although one was surrounded by huge numbers of people, as Mark Jenkins remembered, ". . . most fans could really only see the show on the huge video screens above the stage. Going to a rock concert was virtually the same experience as watching late-night TV rock shows like *Midnight Special*."[49] Punk rejected this druggy suburban arena parking lot culture in favor of alternative circumstances for social interaction and intimate live music experiences returned to urban surroundings, and straight edge was partly a manifestation of this broader impulse.

Straight edge was also an extreme manifestation of other punk ideals. Rejecting beer and cigarettes not only meant clean living, it meant rejecting the hypercapitalist alcohol and tobacco industries, which, supported by advertising, were knowingly killing people and ruining lives for profit. Vegetarianism, often linked to straight edge, had a similar appeal among punks; it could be less about the moral dilemma of eating meat per se than the ways in which eating meat contributed to an unethical industry that was also worsening environmental crises.[50] Similarly, rejecting harder drug culture meant removing oneself from the toxic racial imbalance that sustained the illegal drug trade, as white flight, segregation, and inequality sustained and exacerbated the widespread drug problems affecting urban life in Washington, Baltimore, Cleveland, and other metropolitan areas. The drug economy of DC, for instance, depended on white suburban buyers but it had a massively disproportionate impact on the lives of people in the cities, and it was heavily maintained by young people. While this relationship was not new, it had historically been more limited, for example, the "white boy" hipster scoring drugs "uptown" as described in the Velvet Underground's "I'm Waiting for the Man." In the late 1970s and early 1980s the expanded illegal drug economy was causing enormous harm to the cities. In rejecting hard drugs, straight edge also spurned the broader context of the so-called war on drugs, which in DC and Baltimore had been used to criminalize black people, while suburban white kids could engage with drugs without suffering the same consequences. Some punks who were interested in repairing the situation caused by white flight chose not to participate in this obvious product of racial inequality. Even if this was not consciously articulated, the racialized war on drugs communicated the effects of white flight and geographic segregation in an unavoidable way.

Finally, the straight edge ideals of clear, drug-free thought spoke to the widespread mental health issues among youth in the 1970s and early 1980s. As with other aspects of straight edge, its relationship to mental health can shed more light on punk at the time. I suggest that punk's intense sensory environments, the social rewards of playing in bands and the creative rewards of composing, and the ideal of punk being a place for free personal expression no matter how nonconformist, were all aspects attracting those who might now be called "non-neurotypical" or "atypical" individuals to punk during a time of little understanding or support for neurodiversity and emotional sensitivity. For Dug Birdzell, "growing up I felt like fucking crazy and playing was how I could heal . . . [musicians] just feel shit more intensely . . . [you can] numb yourself somehow or you can change course and write your own script."[51] Terms such as weirdo and misfit, pejorative and then reclaimed in punk, can in essence refer to neurodiversity, and kids who might now be diagnosed with ADHD, autism, bipolar disorder, and schizoaffective disorder. And many people involved with punk in the 1970s and early 1980s were diagnosed later, including such prominent examples as H.R.'s schizophrenia.[52] In "Straight Edge," MacKaye declared "I know I can cope" with reality and the world around him. Bad Brains' philosophy of "P.M.A." (Positive Mental Attitude), adapted from Napoleon Hill's *Think and Grow Rich*, broadcast a similar perspective, in this case using optimism and mental strategies to live successfully.[53]

Concurrent with the period of early hardcore, doctors and parents in suburban and middle-class society began medicating their kids on a massive scale, supported by a for-profit pharmaceutical industry. Alcohol and drugs, including pharmaceuticals, have always been ways for people to "self-medicate" when faced with mental health issues, but in the early 1980s, similar to the rapid expansion of the illegal drug economy, prescription medications administered by parents to their children became much more widespread. Henry Rollins, for example, was one among many diagnosed with ADHD and put on Ritalin as a young person.[54] It is my belief that, while it may not have directly inspired MacKaye's songs, this acute upswing in prescribing youth fueled the intense response by others to straight edge as a philosophy or solution. For once, a peer was providing a model for staying engaged, creative, and alive instead of medicating oneself; even if medication was necessary, it often had a conformist or authoritarian quality in this atmosphere.

Earlier punk was in step with rock's general embrace of drugs, but in the early 1980s this attitude could seem more conformist than countercultural, and the parents of Gen X punks were the baby boomers who fully popularized drug use. The Ramones sang "Now I Wanna Sniff Some Glue" in response to suburban boredom, even if ironic and humorous; Dee Dee Ramone also wrote "Chinese Rocks" (the Heartbreakers song) and was known to have struggled with heroin addiction. In contrast, in "Straight Edge" MacKaye "laugh[ed] at the thought of sniffing glue." With drugs both legal and illegal becoming so widespread, straight edge provided a meaningful alternative, and this is one reason why "a lot of people thought Ian was speaking to them personally."[55]

At the same time, straight edge turned into its own source of conformist pressure. Lyle Preslar, for a long time, "would have preferred that straight edge wasn't there, but I made my peace with [it]."[56] In one interview, he elaborated:

> I went along with it and I thought it was good, the basic idea of it. I thought being in control of yourself was good. Very quickly people adopted it but it wasn't enough for them to adopt it, they had to proselytize and police the situation. We started backing away; mid–band existence we said, "we're not going to talk about it." Then people said, "Oh, they're rejecting it." No, just enough has been said. But a lot of people then thought they couldn't be a part of it because they wanted to get a drink. Couldn't be further from the truth. We didn't care.[57]

The ways in which straight edge played out in punk communities was yet another expression of the tensions that remain at the core of punk aesthetics and ideas. On one hand, straight edge provided a meaningful response to some of the societal problems and circumstances that Gen X youth were left to navigate for themselves, articulated through personal creative expression. On the other hand, the tendency toward group affiliation and the "us and them" mentality that drew so many to punk in the first place created a constant threat of conformity. But ultimately, straight edge had a tremendous legacy on punk simply because it established possibilities of new ideas and new points of view for hardcore, thus making it more available as a form of expression to more kinds of people.

### In It But Not Of It

At the turn to the 1980s, punk's whiteness, masculinity, and persistent middle-class milieu was catching up with some of its lofty ideals as a space for critique, revolution, and even anticolonial or anticapitalist stances. For the international punk community, tensions surrounding race were most evident in the rise of white nationalist uses of punk music and, to counter such racist developments, Rock Against Racism alliances and concerts. England ostensibly led the way both in punk's racism problems and its antiracist initiatives.[58] In the United States, punk was increasingly becoming understood as a useful style for expressing political and activist ideas, although groups such as Positive Force, originally founded in Reno but finding its most prominent place in the DC scene, were still several years away from making an impact.[59] Punks in the US began following the UK playbook, replacing Thatcher with Reagan.

In Washington, DC, Bad Brains saw an opportunity to forge new relationships and build bridges between punk and the city's black majority. The city was facing heightened difficulties, including homicides, poverty, and widespread drug problems.[60] As members of DC's black majority in a punk rock scene that was mostly white, they were keenly aware of the issues facing the area. At the same time, punk seemed mostly unconnected to the black people of Washington, who had their own extremely vibrant local music in go-go, along with an energetic funk and jazz scene, what Ian MacKaye referred to as the "true culture" of DC.[61]

H.R. was inspired by the massive outdoor Rock Against Racism events in London, but he wanted to create a different kind of event that would be relevant to the black people of Washington. He used the RAR heading for a local show at the Valley Green Housing Complex, public housing located on Wheeler Road in the almost entirely black area of Southeast DC.[62] Built in 1961, Valley Green had become an unfortunate symbol of the city's and the nation's neglect of its poor, black citizens. This show on September 9, 1979, by Bad Brains and Trenchmouth (the early DC band fronted by Charlie Danbury, not the later Chicago group with Damon Locks and Fred Armisen) was a truly extraordinary event. The show featured the all-black Bad Brains performing for an almost entirely black local DC audience that had little to no awareness of, or interest in, the nascent DC punk scene. H.R., as the instigator of this event, brought punk to the black-majority world of DC rather than trying to bring black people into white spaces, a strategy almost certainly doomed to fail in DC on any significant scale. The Valley Green event was "something more street-level direct than if hordes of same-thinking music consumers descended on a place and transformed it into a green-zone party for their own entertainment," in the words of Alec MacKaye, who was there as an observer.[63] Bad Brains played one more Rock Against Racism show at Valley Green with the Teen Idles and Untouchables on July 27, 1980. The Valley Green shows did not immediately spark a black underground punk scene in DC or lead directly to similar events, but the fact that these shows *did* happen demonstrates the exceptional nature of Bad Brains' position at the center of DC punk, as well as the group's early dissatisfaction with playing to mostly white punks in mostly white spaces. For Bad Brains in 1979, punk held

Figure 7.1. Bad Brains performing at Valley Green Housing Complex, September 9, 1979.
Photograph by Lucian Perkins.

tremendous potential for bringing together groups of people who, as is typical in American cities, live within close geographic proximity but who do not interact on any meaningful level.

Race also played a major role in the life and times of Minor Threat. In what became a focal point for the group, Ian MacKaye penned the controversial "Guilty of Being White" for the *In My Eyes* EP. "Guilty of Being White" expressed MacKaye's frustration and anger at being assaulted by black students at his junior high school because he was white. The discourse around "Guilty of Being White" has generally been about MacKaye's intentions and whether or not the song lyrics are racist. But focusing the energy on MacKaye's point of view misses the larger issues, and sidesteps the structural racism that led to MacKaye's experiences (and such misdirection can itself be a symptom of whiteness). One central approach of punk musicians has been the formulation of critiques of whiteness from a white subjectivity, and "Guilty of Being White" is an excellent example. It is also one that ultimately falls short, as MacKaye's target encompasses a broadly conceived racism that allowed whiteness to reassert its ideological dominance as others changed the song's context. What is often called taking the song "out of context" is really more of an active unwillingness to understand and confront a context, or an aggressive ignorance of a context, or a violent recasting of a context.

In "Guilty of Being White," MacKaye expressed his relationship to the extreme racial circumstances of Washington, DC. MacKaye's motivation was a defensive reaction to being assaulted, but he responded with a song about his inner emotions and ultimately, a song he intended to be a condemnation of all racism:

> What I saw was a sense of marginalization, living in DC there was a marginalization as a white kid, you know, when I wrote "Guilty of Being White," I was being serious. I felt like I grew up as a minority in this particular town. I understand in the larger world that obviously I'm not a minority, but the point of the song was, in this situation, I'm clearly a minority, and I'm being attacked for that by people who don't have my best interests in mind. You know, I was the minority and I suffered for that, so I wrote a song about why racism was wrong, using this as my perspective, any bigotry, that's the idea.[64]

The more significant concern, though, is neither MacKaye's individual emotions nor his response to them. Rather, it is the processes of American whiteness and the tremendous racial imbalances throughout the US caused by white flight and racist housing policies that left MacKaye and his fellow students to navigate this situation, violently or otherwise. Everyone in the DC area in the late 1970s and early 1980s understood DC to be, in the words of my interviewees, "black," "predominantly black," or "almost exclusively black," a very different situation from what is articulated by interviewees from other metropolitan areas. In a city such as Washington, DC, or other "cosmopolitan" and "diverse" cities, school segregation within city limits is mostly maintained by white families opting out of the school system and court-ordered desegregation. As a fourth grader, MacKaye noticed white parents started taking their children out of the public school system. MacKaye is a fifth-generation Washingtonian whose parents believed strongly in integration, moving to a majority black neighborhood on Capitol Hill in 1960, rather than out to a suburban enclave. He understood the overall situation when he was younger:

> I was a white kid waiting to go to college like every other white kid I knew, just trying to get out. When I was going to DCPS [DC Public Schools], in fourth grade, all my friends left to go to private school, because nobody [white wanted their children] to go to middle or high school with black kids. That was just the way it was. When I get to fourth grade . . . everybody just skedaddles 'cause they're scared about their kids going to public DC junior high or—just because, at that point, the elementary schools are still neighborhood [schools]—you had this sense that people were just going to leave. So when you were in high school—I stayed in DCPS, I went to Gordon Junior High and Wilson Senior High, but there's this period, there's this sense that people are just going to leave, they're just gonna leave town.[65]

Wilson High School in DC "went from being 99 percent white in 1955 to 17 percent white in 1980," when MacKaye would have been attending.[66] MacKaye's situation was unusual: an economically comfortable white kid living within city limits and attending a majority black public school. In comparison, Brian Baker and Lyle Preslar attended the private Georgetown Day School, which was integrated but among wealthy and upper-middle-class white and black families.[67] The climate of private schools in the center of US power was one of extreme privilege, the world that was exposed with Brett Kavanaugh's appointment to the Supreme Court during the writing of this book.

The reception of "Guilty of Being White" is plagued not by the song being taken out of context, but by an unwillingness to understand the broader history and context of segregation and racism in cities such as Washington. Instead, the structural problems of American racism are simply projected onto the standard bogeyman of the white rural redneck, attached to individual racists with evil motivations, or understood as the naïveté or ignorance of privileged white people. MacKaye's song, like so much punk, captures the complex dilemmas of the artist trying to create responsible music within an unequal society. However, MacKaye's teenage idealism and frustration ultimately proved to be ill-advised and no match for the privileges and processes of whiteness that engender ignorance and backlash. MacKaye and his song can become a target while structural racism continues.

The life of "Guilty of Being White" revealed the limits of using a style associated with whiteness to make a critique of racism. The song has been coopted in various ways, including shocking misappropriations of the song from its original context of DC and the point of view of MacKaye, who has demonstrated his antiracist beliefs through continuous activist work for decades. MacKaye told me about the song being used on a white power website, while Slayer's cover on *Undisputed Attitude* (1996), which ended "Guilty of being right!," continues to be debated with respect to how much it supports or rejects racist ideas. Reflecting back almost forty years after he wrote "Guilty," MacKaye believes his early songs were able to be taken and used in these ways because, ironically, "In an attempt to write songs that couldn't be misinterpreted, I kept things short and direct. What didn't occur to me at the time was that because I was essentially turning out finished ideas, that these ideas could be easily picked up by anyone and used for their own agenda. It was almost as if I was crafting something akin to uniforms that people could just slip on without having to really engage with the ideas behind the lyrics. This became clear to me by the mid-'80s, and by the time I was writing for Fugazi I was keenly aware that I should be writing lyrics more akin to solid fabric and hope that people will be able to construct something out of them."[68] And as Lyle Preslar said, reflecting on the life of the song, "The problem was that taken out of a context, it changes everything."[69]

The context of Washington, DC, in the late 1970s and early 1980s was that of a majority black city, black and integrated suburbs, and segregated white neighborhoods and enclaves. As seen throughout *Damaged*, members of the punk scenes tend to replicate the broader social environments in which they live, even if they outwardly reject them or feel "outside" of them, and DC was no different. As Dug Birdzell explained, while the scene had more musicians of color in it than did other scenes,

> [the DC scene was more integrated] than other scenes, but it was integrated like a black and white cookie. . . . I mean, there was like the go-go scene and then there was the punks. The punks were mostly white, except for Bad Brains. And then Bad Brains, you know, would hang with Rastas, and some of the like white Rastas would hang with them, so there would be that. That little intermix there. But on the upside is, we're all on the same cookie, and you know, there's the place that they meet. And we do meet. . . . I sense more of that willingness to come together in DC . . . there is a separation, but there was a sense of being open to other kinds of lives and experiences than just what punk rockers were into. I don't know, maybe just living in a city where we [white people] were the minority, we could just fucking look around and see. And it makes it different than other parts of the States.[70]

Or as Lyle Preslar commented, "We had an appreciation that there were these other things happening. And that's why go-go was such a big deal. . . . And yet, at the same time, there was such an enormous divide. . . . While there was some integration, if you will, I'd still say it's pretty small. But when you went to Boston it was *zero*. It was *zero*. It was *zero*."[71]

The limitations of punk's conflicting ideals were drawn into sharp focus around issues of race, which have remained an "enormous divide" in American society. Another intense example of these crossed wires is the controversy surrounding a Bad Brains show in Austin in 1982, when the Bad Brains' interpretations of Rastafarian ideas conflicted with the Big Boys, the hardcore band from Austin known for their use of funk, and whose singer, the late Randy "Biscuit" Turner, was gay.[72] To this day, insults and arguments rage over exactly what happened, but it is generally accepted that the Bad Brains (except Earl Hudson) responded to learning about Biscuit's sexuality with religious homophobic vitriol.[73] The controversy is so significant that Tim Kerr of the Big Boys wrote he has "had to tell the Bad Brains/Big Boys story at least once every 5 or 6 months for the last 30 years."[74] Why is this particular incident still so inflammatory and central to punk discourse?

The persistence of arguments over this incident seem to revolve around the relationship of punk to race and sexuality. In one recent article, Bad Brains' "gaggle of pathetically-adoring and mostly white male fans" "gave them a pass for homophobia," while for Darryl Jenifer, despite the band's commitment to unity and positivity, the conflict over homosexuality was "one struggle within ourselves and the struggle within the band's self that stuck with us. I'm telling you: This is all simple, stupid shit, and that to me is racist, because if the Dead Kennedys would have came and done the same thing, that shit would not have stuck on and stigmatized them. If Black Flag would have come through there and called them dudes fags and took their weed, Mugger or somebody, that shit would not stigmatize them as homophobes and carry on throughout their careers."[75] Jenifer has admitted they were "over-zealous" at the beginning of learning about Rastafarianism, which can condemn homosexuality in quite disturbing terms, and "in short, no one in the Bad Brains hates gays, we love all God's children."[76]

While it is not clear how much this incident really has stigmatized Bad Brains (they were nominated, but not inducted, for the Rock and Roll Hall of Fame in 2017), Jenifer is not speaking purely hypothetically. Rather, like "Guilty of Being White," the long-lasting controversy surrounding this event speaks to wider issues, demonstrating some of the ways in which whiteness, race, masculinity, and homophobia intersect in rock. Punk history and rock history (and music history in general) is littered with homophobic, sexist, racist, and otherwise irresponsible and hateful comments that have been forgotten, dismissed, or ignored. It is easy to find examples: Eric Clapton's racist rant sparked Rock Against Racism in the UK, and Clapton has been inducted into the Rock and Roll Hall of Fame a record three times, and he has been named a Commander of the Most Excellent Order of the British Empire.[77] The *Adolescents* LP features lyrics such as "I could care less about the queers—they suck / The chicks are hot and full of cheers—pleasers / They say 'no' so I jerk white tears—teasers."[78] David Ensminger accounted homophobic slurs or comments from Brendan Mullen, Lee Ving, Operation Ivy, Sid Vicious, Johnny Rotten, Johnny Thunders, Handsome Dick Manitoba, Lemmy Kilmister, Government Issue, Ben Weasel, Casey Royer, Descendents, Black Flag, Iron Cross, and others.[79] Arguably, for white men, the processes of white privilege attribute such comments to part of punk's willfully offensive essence, the fault of drugs or alcohol, or "boys will be boys" youthful indiscretion, while none of these excuses or privileges extend to African Americans. Given the response at the time to boycott Bad Brains and the story's persistent attachment to their legacy, compared with the minimal repercussions for the prevalent homophobia among white male punks, it is strange—although rather indicative—that the overarching sentiment seems to be that the punk community has been *too* forgiving of Bad Brains because they are black: as Eric Weiss wrote (quoted by Ensminger), "could it be that we as individuals in a predominantly white music culture that nonetheless prides itself on its diversity . . . are afraid of being labeled racist by our own peers should we criticize the Bad Brains? . . . If the Bad Brains were Caucasian would their intolerant views about homosexuality have been more widely condemned?"[80]

The contradictions pile higher when considering the widespread appropria-tion of superficial elements of the Rastafarian religion by white people, such as dreadlocks and reggae music, without an attempt to follow Rastafarian religious principles, as the Bad Brains did.

One more event sheds light on these many issues and the distinctive con-text of the DC scene. Minor Threat played their last show on September 23, 1983, at the Lansburgh Center in Northwest DC with DC's go-go icons Trouble Funk and Austin's Big Boys (a show co-promoted by *American Hardcore* author Steven Blush while he was a college student at GWU).[81] The show attempted to bring together "white" and "black" elements of DC's musical life, with fli-ers directed at both punk and go-go audiences—Onam Emmet's hand-drawn punk flier with a dead dog on the ground and a circle-A anarchy symbol, and one made by Baltimore's Globe Poster Company, famous for advertisements of black music performances—and while the two groups did not necessarily unify, the musicians were interested in each other's approaches. This limited but "more than *zero*" interaction between black and white DC revealed both the potential and limitations of hardcore as a style for social critique. Preslar remembered: "There were two audiences there. And the white kids got into Trouble Funk, but the black kids didn't understand the Big Boys and us at all, they couldn't relate to it. . . . we ended up doing a Howard University radio broadcast together, but it was like that weird meeting of worlds. . . . I don't think either of us understood why we were doing what we were doing."[82]

The ideals and utopian trajectory of the DC scene became more entrenched through the growth of Positive Force, Dischord Records, and the "Revolution Summer" of 1985—a renewal of political engagement spurred by Amy Picker-ing and centering on anti-apartheid protests. However, tensions remained in the early hardcore scene surrounding race, ebbing and flowing in intensity.[83] Echoing the disillusionment following 1960s idealism, the promise of punk fell short for many who were initially drawn to the DC hardcore scene, and many members of the DC scene—as with other punk scenes—earnestly par-ticipated only for short periods of time. This seems to have been especially true for women and people of color. Bad Brains, for example, became Rastafarians and ended up leaving DC soon after their eruption on the punk scene, continu-ing to play in the District but fully relocating to New York by 1981, where they helped spark the hardcore scene.[84] Preslar considered: "The Bad Brains stepped out of their world and into our world, and I think it irritated them at a certain point, playing to this all-white audience. And trying to figure out, 'who are we speaking to?'"[85] Experiments in reaching larger segments of DC's black popula-tion, such as the Valley Green Housing Project shows or the Lansburgh Center show with Trouble Funk, often ended as studies in frustration or as anomalies despite good intentions.

As some of these individuals have expressed, they were drawn to the punk scene because they felt out of place in their more homogenous and conformist environments, only to find that the punk scene was also homogenous and conformist, problematically revolving around suburban middle-class whiteness and masculinity, and that they did not fit in there as well. The outward rebellion of punk often belied conventional or conservative subjectivities; for example, as Lyle Preslar remembered, "even though we [Minor Threat] were this punk band, we weren't 'cock rockers,' but still the gender roles were pretty much the same."[86] Similarly, with respect to the early LA punk scene, Kira Roessler remembered, "we were judgmental . . . I'm sure anyone who looked or felt different or in any way felt excluded would have to be awfully bold to face it and continue facing it enough to build up some friends and relationships."[87] Or as Bubba Dupree said, remembering his personal experience in the DC scene, "I was *in* all that but not really *of* it."[88]

The contradictions at punk's core never resolved. Punk promised a haven for nonconformists, but members of the scene exerted a tremendous amount of social pressure—explicit and implicit, physical and mental—toward group affiliation; nonconformity, by its very nature, creates a paradoxical tension within any group that attempts to organize in relation to it. Punk broadcast an open, multiracial and multigender ethos, yet the scene was continually put in tension with its consistent majority of white male participants, and debates about punk's authenticity revolved around its relationship to the intersections of whiteness, masculinity, heterosexuality, segregated schools and suburbs, and symptoms of privilege such as wealth. And despite a history of diverse participants, through the 1980s the idea of punk as predominantly white and male came to dominate narratives, and was only forcefully challenged in the 1990s and 2000s with grassroots movements such as Riot Grrrl and Afropunk. Mimi Thi Nguyen, for example, called for rejection and correcting of the "whitestraightboy hegemony [that] organizes punk," simultaneously underscoring punk's recurring problems with whiteness and masculinity.[89]

Bad Brains and Minor Threat pushed punk to include different ideas, both musically and ideologically, and I believe the boldest aspects of their approaches to hardcore came from the uniqueness of the Washington, DC, area at the end of the 1970s. Yet the new complexities these groups brought to understandings of race once again brought to the fore punk's intrinsic relationship to American formations of whiteness. Punk's critiques through the 1970s were simultaneously enabled and limited by its origins in such phenomena as white flight, nostalgia, and responses to changing stakes of musical appropriation. The recurring concerns with authenticity, independent thought, and nonconformity are manifestations or symptoms of the particular formations of American whiteness out of which punk emerged, in which authenticity is paradoxically based in the artifice of popular music and the appropriation of stereotyped blackness, and in which nonconformity is tied only to an individual sense of identity, allowing the empirical and structural differences of social formations to continue unchallenged. Although it revealed these tensions and paradoxes through expressive and meaningful music, punk never could or would dismantle or resolve those tensions, since they are so central to punk's expression and its meaning.

# 8

## Outro: A New Way to Pay Old Debts

Punk developed during the long 1970s in response to enormous changes in American society, especially with respect to race. Racial formations from the 1940s to the 1970s were inexorably tied to class and geography, as whiteness became essentially tied to the rapid growth and establishment of the American middle class and as white people physically segregated themselves in suburbs. Punk has been exceptionally useful and productive for those who wish to directly confront the problems of that period and its legacy, especially those young people who have inherited problems as well as privileges, who feel conflicted about how to address their reality, and who are craving fun and meaningful experiences.

One of the many misconceptions about punk is that it is ahistorical, a quality sometimes attached to whiteness and white privilege in general. A musical history of punk contradicts this evaluation, and in fact, punk musicians have been consistently engaged with sociohistorical questions. Punk was initially a product of questioning American culture, history, and society in the 1960s, and it has remained a vital tool for interrogating America's contradictions and paradoxes, such as ideals of freedom and free expression within an unequal and racist society.

The fundamental aspects of punk's musical style have remained remarkably consistent since the early 1980s, and with a few exceptions, they have remained tied to similar meanings and associations. Yet musicians have continued to innovate and respond to changing social realities using punk's techniques and practices. In this conclusion to *Damaged*, I look at some contemporary creative work by musicians who have continued to use punk approaches to address questions of race and American history, and who in doing so shed further light on the long 1970s and its present-day relevance.

## The Blues as Symptom

> I always thought [Harry Pussy] were playing blues music, in some sense. I don't know that I
> can really play anything other than the blues.... I just feel like if you're gonna play the blues
> you have to somehow address the fact that you're not Robert Johnson.... If you're playing
> any kind of folk music and you're not a member of that particular group, then it's problematic.
> —Bill Orcutt[1]

The axis of punk's musical style is also the source of its greatest tension: its relationship to the blues. In its original formulations, punk most directly expressed the world of white people who grew up in northern and West Coast suburbs during the postwar period of white flight and the Second Great Migration, and it captured the contradictions and paradoxes of a particular suburban white identity built on appropriations of, transformations of, and responses to black music. The complexities of whiteness's relationship to black music increase when we consider the full historical range of black American music, including the long tradition of white people attempting to shape ideas of black musical authenticity for themselves and their own audiences, and how black professional musicians often had to address those ideas for white audiences and within restrictive structures while simultaneously directing their music toward listeners in black communities. The blues, and particularly the blues' manifestations as rock music, was at the center of these racial dynamics during the twentieth century. Punk, as an extreme form of rock music, exposed the paradoxical notion of authenticity even as it contributed to it, and it has worked best when raising difficult questions and leaving them unanswered.

To unravel the blues' relationship to punk, the blues itself must be understood as constantly changing and extremely varied, not treated as something eternal and immutable. With respect to rock, particular notions of the blues' purity and authenticity as timeless, rural, and male (e.g., Robert Johnson but not Ethel Waters) are primarily something white men became invested in, and which they then used for their own purposes. Based on the ways in which rock musicians treated blues resources, rock music became a site of conversations, both musical and verbal, mostly by white men about whiteness. Questions of identity, musical authenticity, and rock aesthetics ultimately stood in for tougher questions about discrimination, segregation, and inequality, especially among white people in and around cities such as New York, Detroit, and Los Angeles.

"The blues as symptom" refers to the notes from Robert Musil's unpublished 1923 essay, "The German as Symptom," in which he rethought the concepts of race, nation, people, and culture as containing "questions and not answers: they are not sociological elements, but rather complex results. Nonetheless, people refer to them as if they were unities."[2] The blues too is referred to as if it is a unity and treated as an answer, as still are concepts of race and nation. "The blues as symptom" is also an attempt to add a third angle to the opening and closing chapters of Albert Murray's *Stomping the Blues*, "The Blues as Such" and "The Blues as Statement," both working toward defining the essence of the blues, which punk and rock musicians of all backgrounds wanted to access.[3] But like the concept of race, the blues is a symptom in that it indicates underlying processes, arguments, and realities of discrimination, migration, and inequality. In the case of rock, "the blues" was treated in various ways according to the changing stakes of performing black music and ideas of blackness in the 1960s and 1970s.

In punk, treatments of the blues are often explicit symptoms of white musicians' concerns with authenticity, American identity, questions of appropriation, and whiteness itself. Since the 1970s, the blues has become increasingly wrapped up with authenticity, but with added elements of reflexivity and intensified discourses surrounding white privilege and cultural appropriation. White musicians are still drawn to the power of the blues, with the mysterious layers of meaning it has acquired. African American musicians also continue to play blues-based music for its power, historical resonances, and meanings, while also navigating the cycles of appropriation and transformation by white people, which, at least since the mainstream spread of rock and roll, have consistently centered on blues resources.

Beginning with the raw power bands, the trajectory of punk aimed at treating the blues as a feeling or an essence rather than a twelve-bar form. Punk musicians wanted to emphasize the mysterious power of the blues in all of its manifestations and move it away from a simple formula that could be easily and unthoughtfully coopted. Joe Strummer said the blues "had become abused. You know, the twelve bar kind, people would be asleep before you hit the top chord . . . so it's not the form, but the feeling of something spiritual."[4] For those invested in the blues as the arcane roots of American music, the raw power emphasis on one-chord riffs and hypnotic short cycles has continued to be the blues style of choice. These musicians have also tended to become more intensely involved with the blues and its meanings over the course of their careers. Jonathan Kane, the original drummer for Swans, took a handful of riffs from Fred McDowell's "I Looked at the Sun" and turned them into a short-cycle meditation over a drone, gradually building and layering for over thirteen minutes. Peg Simone, who started in the Pittsburgh indie and punk bands Pleasure Head and Wormhole, and who is also a guitarist in Kane's group February, has similarly explored extended one-chord blues patterns, combining these blues styles with Southern gothic literature and poetry. Her exploration of "When the Levee Breaks" lasts over twenty-two minutes. As it is to other erstwhile punk and punk-influenced musicians, to Simone the blues is "visceral," "human," and "primal."[5]

Figure 8.1a and 8.1b. Bill Orcutt, from *Twenty-Five Songs*, "Strange Fruit" b/w "White Christmas." Reproduced with permission.

In the 1990s, Harry Pussy (the core duo of Bill Orcutt and Adris Hoyos) disassembled and dissembled the raw power blues-riff style, retaining hard blues melodies while pushing noise elements, screams, and jagged forms, and also sticking to tight condensed forms. On "No Hey . . . ," a Stooges-style monophonic minor-pentatonic riff and a rhythmically coordinated scream/ drum/guitar pattern are placed within a tight four-part form, repeated once, lasting under one minute. "Nazi USA" is another drone-based evocation of the blues, with a short move to the IV area. For Harry Pussy's version of Lightnin' Hopkins's "Black Ghost Blues," according to Orcutt, they used the first line for the lyrics and just one chord, which follows the punk approach of moving from multipart and multichord blues forms to riffs, drones, and one-chord blues.[6] But to me, the Harry Pussy interpretation is unrecognizable from the original and based mainly on impression and the title. Similarly, Orcutt's

later solo treatment of Hopkins's "Sad News from Korea" barely resembles the original composition, but it is consistent with other extreme extensions of the raw power approach in the way he circulates around one tonality with minor intervals—in this case alternating between the droning root, a fifth, and a flatted sixth.

Harry Pussy also harnessed the obscure references that have become a hallmark of Orcutt's style. Like Captain Beefheart, Orcutt draws liberally on American cultural history without direct explanation, including some of the most uncomfortable elements of music and popular culture. The obscurity of Orcutt's music and the visual elements, which are enigmatic, evocative, and referential, create a singular approach to the blues. In many ways, Orcutt's blues interpretations are contemporary solutions to the continual problem of a need to play the blues and to find a way to play them authentically, reflectively, and without direct imitation or appropriation of black musicians—to create what Lou Reed called "a legit, pure thing."[7]

Orcutt extended his purview of American music to include American minstrelsy and other historical repertoire, echoing other experimentalists such as Captain Beefheart and the Residents. In his most direct exploration of American musical history, Orcutt produced a box set of thirteen singles called "25 Songs" (the material also resurfaced on *A History of Every One* and *Bill Orcutt*). Each single contained a thought-provoking pairing, several of which were archetypal representations of "white" and "black" music, performed with varying degrees of abstraction and improvisation. For example, "Black Betty," from Lead Belly's *Negro Sinful Songs* (1939) is paired with the Harvard fight song "Ten Thousand Men of Harvard," and "Strange Fruit," the anti-lynching song by Abel Meeropol made famous by Billie Holiday, is backed by "White Christmas," by Irving Berlin and made famous by Bing Crosby. The collection also includes songs directly and uncomfortably linked to minstrelsy, such as "Zip Coon," "Zip-a-Dee-Doo-Dah," and Al Jolson's "My Mammy," which is intensely backed with Ornette Coleman's "Lonely Woman." As shown in figure 8.1, the artwork on the singles makes these connections both explicit and obscure, raising questions even as they expose complex dialectics. These pairings add up to an experimental vision of American musical history, culminating in the only song played twice, "The Star-Spangled Banner."

However, while Orcutt, Kane, and Simone have connections to punk styles, and while their approaches are indebted to punk treatments of the blues, ultimately their musical explorations of the blues became either too closely aligned with blues traditions (Kane and Simone) or too far removed from rock conventions (Orcutt) to make punk an effective vehicle for what they have wanted to express. But by exposing the limits of punk's connections to the blues, these musicians also illuminate the liminal sonic gray area where punk and the blues intersect, and how racial associations of musical gestures remain at punk's center.

Musicians zooming in on the sonic places where ideas of black and white music collide with ideas of race, identity, and American history have continued to use blues-based raw power punk for their purposes, although often with reflexivity and distance. Chain and the Gang, fronted by DC's Ian Svenonius (also of Nation of Ulysses, the Make-Up, and Weird War), delved into blues styles for their explorations of whiteness and white privilege, which they found located in the knowing appropriation of black music in rock.[8] This is a logical extension of the midwestern protopunk of the Stooges and MC5 but filtered through a critical theory lens, several self-consciously appropriative cycles away from the Rolling Stones and Them. Svenonius was already interested in historical references, for example, in Nation of Ulysses's song "Today I Met the Girl I'm Going to Marry," beginning with the New York Dolls' restatement of the Shangri-Las line, "when I say I'm in love, you best believe I'm in love, L.U.V." and Ulysses's parodies of 1960s designs such as Motown's "The Sound of Young America."

Svenonius, like Orcutt and the other musicians profiled in this section, moved away from more hardcore punk styles and toward more explicit uses of blues styles when exploring issues of race and society. Chain and the Gang songs such as "Detroit Music" are firmly in a blues-based style. A clear example of Chain and the Gang's reflexive music is "(I've Got) Privilege" on *Music's Not for Everyone* (2011), the cover of which shows Svenonius behind bars and in handcuffs in the recurring Svenonius-in-prison imagery of the band's releases; e.g., *Down with Liberty . . . Up with Chains!* has Svenonius in prison stripes, playing a guitar, with traces of the imagery of the Lomax prison recordings and the exceedingly uncomfortable 1935 *March of Time* newsreel of John A. Lomax recording Lead Belly.[9] On "(I've Got) Privilege," in a stripped-down minor R&B mode, Svenonius sings, "No matter what I say, it don't mean anything, you know why: the color of my skin, 'cause I've got privilege" and "No matter what I do, sacrifice it all for you, it don't mean nothin' at all, because my blood is blue, yeah I've got privilege." Privilege is "bearing down on me, makes it hard to see." Paired with the bluesy 7♯9 chords played on the organ and minor bass lines, Svenonius's lyrics can come off as alternately ironic, humorous, and earnest.

Although the lyrics are in the first person, Svenonius could be speaking from the point of view of someone else—in his words, one of the "blue-blooded heirs indulging an interim 'wild' phase before they settle into a career buying and selling currencies and countries" who make up today's rock bands.[10] At the same time, Svenonius implies his own privilege, both in lived experience and in artistic expression, a white man who grew up in the near suburbs of Washington, DC. With "(I've Got) Privilege," Svenonius seems to be speaking to other white people with backgrounds similar to his, in the tradition of rock musicians using black music resources to debate and discuss whiteness absent the voices or musical participation of black people. The unlikelihood of a white listener being spurred to self-reflection by "(I've Got) Privilege," or even recognizing himself or herself in the song, underscores the limitations of punks' use of the tools of whiteness to criticize or inveigh against whiteness. The most significant representation of white privilege is Svenonius dressing himself in prison garb for an album photo shoot, as opposed to someone like Lead Belly, who by most accounts resented being dressed in prison clothes and put on display. Svenonius wrestles with the "prison" of the mind he finds himself in while living in capitalist America, analogous to Patti Smith's earlier conception of the artist constrained by "slavery," while Lead Belly, who certainly did not have privilege, endured unsparing poverty and spent many years of his life in actual prison. Regardless of the sincerity or irony of Svenonius's prisoner drag and his blues-based music, he invites contrasts with the stark reality of African Americans' notorious overrepresentation in physical prisons (even though the gap is shrinking, in 2018 African Americans constituted 12 percent of the general US population but the highest rate of 33 percent of the US prison population).[11]

Svenonius's extensions of punk's conflicted approach to race and American society are also found in his writings, such as the manifesto-style handbook *The Psychic Soviet*. In a kind of refigured Gen X white-authored version of Baraka's *Blues People*, Svenonius theorizes, "rock's initial charisma stemmed from its ability to impart 'blackness' upon the adherent," and he explicitly offers his thoughts on the history of Lomax and Lead Belly, and the impact of white flight on punk.[12] In its manifesto style, ideas in *The Psychic Soviet* are presented without evidence, including many theories regarding race, class, and sexuality. Over nearly thirty years of playing music in a predominantly white scene and living in a majority black city, while playing blues-based music and regularly offering his theories on race, such one-way manifesto-style communications can be interpreted as a late expression of the "parallel but separate" approach of raw power groups such as the MC5.[13] This is one logical extension of punk's historical trajectory.

Given how mostly white punk scenes have historically functioned in urban environments, it is unsurprising that Svenonius's music and ideas have played out in mostly white spaces. Meanwhile, although DC punk remains mostly white, punk music and the DC punk scene also provide the forum for Rob Watson, the (black) singer of the DC hardcore band Pure Disgust, to directly confront white privilege and persistent inequality ("I.D.O.Y.S." [I Don't Owe You Shit], "The Oppressed," "White Silence"), and for the dance music–oriented Coup Sauvage and the Snips, featuring three black women—Kristina, Crystal, and Rain Sauvage—to address gentrification in DC and police brutality in their music.[14] Punk continues to be a productive arena for honest and open encounters with America's never-ending problems, even as those problems remain structural and embedded within punk. As Kristina Sauvage said, "D.C. is really good at mythologizing its punk and hardcore past . . . but let's not forget that as radical as it purports to be, it was hardly as inclusive as it could have been. There have always been people—especially women, queer people, and folks of color—who have felt alienated and been pushed to the margins in punk."[15] (Note "pushed to," not just "at," the margins.)

Raw power punk as played by groups with African American members can immediately evoke the questions located in punk's historical reliance on conflicting treatments of the blues, including cycles of appropriation and obfuscation, and decades of punk's associations with whiteness. If the blues in punk is a set of questions, not answers, these questions go straight to the heart of American formations of race and their musical expressions: why is punk continually characterized as "white," and can any rock music, being fundamentally based in the blues, ever be anything but "black"? Who has the power and platform to say what punk is, can be, or should be, and how are those power structures and platforms controlled and regulated?

This Moment in Black History is a racially diverse raw power–style punk group from Cleveland. Their music creatively uses punk's contradictory, paradoxical, and unsettled relationship to American history and race. Like most other contemporary raw power groups, they are steeped in references that hold a mirror up to the present. As shown in figure 8.2, for example, their album *It Takes a Nation of Assholes to Hold Us Back* visually replicates the Germs' *(GI)*, while the title references Public Enemy's *It Takes a Nation of Millions to Hold Us Back*. Other releases include *Raw Black Power*, directly speaking to the potential of the Stooges' approach for exploring ideas of freedom and black liberation, with the riff-based tribute "Obama (The Pres Is You, the Pres Is Me)."

For black punk musicians who grew up in the suburbs in the 1980s, such as This Moment in Black History's Lawrence Caswell ("I'm just a middle-class kid from the suburbs"), punk was another music in the air along with other rock and hip-hop. Chris Kulcsar, a white member of the group who grew up in the fairly successfully integrated suburb of Cleveland Heights, had a similarly eclectic attitude toward rap music, punk, and heavy metal.[16] In an interview, Caswell specifically connected punk to the Bomb Squad (Public Enemy's production team) and free jazz as described in the politically engaged book by Valerie Wilmer, *As Serious As Your Life.*[17] Discovering Bad Brains was a pivotal moment for Caswell, as he said, "It wasn't like I wasn't into rock, I was. . . . When you're a black kid, particularly in the suburbs, you don't even know if you're allowed to like it . . . Bad Brains blew me away. I knew at that moment, I'm allowed to do that, fuck the rest of y'all. . . . It gave me permission to do what I wanted."[18] The group keeps their multiple references ambiguous, which adds to their music's effect. This Moment in Black History's eclectic inclusion of multiple performance styles into their overall blues-based music demonstrates punk's effectiveness as a vehicle for free expression, plurality, and capturing layers of historical meanings.

Similar ideas of freedom punctuate the discourse of other black punk musicians. For Creature (Siddiq Booker), punk "feels like freedom" and "it feels like liberation."[19] For Stew in the 1970s, early British punk in particular was liberating, as groups such as the Sex Pistols and the Clash provided a model for unrestrained expression that he personally connected to the African American church, and because members of these bands also frequently named African American influences. He elaborated:

We were so fascinated by the idea of white guys being pissed off, because we didn't know that existed. . . . We just really wanted to know what they were pissed off

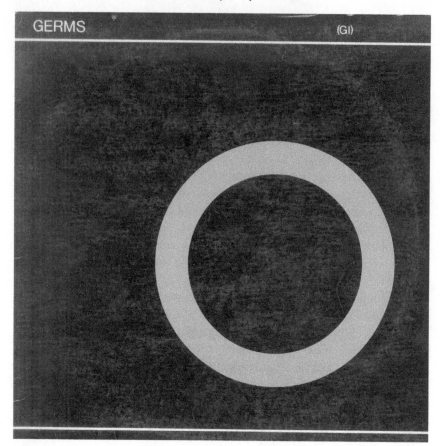

Figure 8.2a and 8.2b. Germs, *(GI)*. Courtesy of Rhino Entertainment Company. Reproduced with permission.

about. . . . It just didn't seem like they had the capacity for that. . . . [Punk was] this medium that black people actually said, ok, we're going to adopt [white people's] path, because actually our modes of protest have been restricted. We actually want to scream like you're screaming. We've actually wanted to do this for a while. . . . It was so sort of uncool to lose it in a punk rock kind of way. What we considered proper black aesthetics was to be on stage, the funk band is fucking tight as fuck, and we're just killing it. But we're all in control. And punk is so, to me, connected to black church . . . who knows what's going to happen.[20]

Following groups such as Bad Brains, who liberally drew on reggae and a wide range of rock styles, or Beefeater, who combined punk with funk elements after groups such as Funkadelic had explored the heaviest blends of funk and rock, black punk musicians freely incorporate and connect many styles. Punk

means a kind of freedom and resistance to the pressures of conformity, and these many music styles can also be brought together as having all descended from American black music roots. Caswell hears Bomb Squad productions as a kind of punk rock. Black Jack Johnson, Yasiin Bey (formerly known as Mos Def)'s group featuring Dr. Know, reclaims punk as rock, and thus blues, and thus black music.[21] Black Rock Coalition members likewise "recuperate rock as a black cultural form through the manifesto's unambiguous statement, 'Rock music is black music and we are its heirs. . . .'"[22] Sacha Jenkins, the writer, filmmaker, and member of the black punk group The 1865, explained, "We love the Stooges and The Ramones and the Sex Pistols and The Clash and Minor Threat. We also love Chuck Berry and James Brown and Sly & The Family Stone and Bad Brains. Erykah Badu too. . . . Music shifts, genres shift. The constant is who we are and how the art we create is a reflection of our environment—and a

Figure 8.2c and 8.2d. This Moment in Black History, *It Takes a Nation of Assholes to Hold Us Back.* Photography by Bryon Miller.

reaction to it as well. That is the blues. That is Jazz. That is R&B. That is Disco. That is hip-hop. That is house. That is punk. We are the music."[23]

From the musical history outlined in *Damaged*, it is intriguing that for all of these groups explicitly interested in punk as black music or as a vehicle for exploring American ideas of race, the raw power blues style is the most consistently used approach. The 1865, This Moment in Black History, and Black Jack Johnson all work with this style. Thus, the contemporary uses of the raw power style by all of these different groups help bring to light the ways in which groups such as the MC5 and the Stooges engaged with American racial formations in the social context of the late 1960s and early 1970s. The music of the Ramones or other pure rock and roll bands, and even the classic British punk approach, is less effective, reliant as it is on nostalgic attitudes toward the American suburbs of the 1950s or its rejection of the blues and its associations with blackness. While

the Stooges-style riffs of a group like This Moment in Black History are not intentionally meant to evoke blackness, when I asked Lawrence Caswell about his opinions regarding the racial associations of the Stooges and the Ramones, he responded in a lighthearted tone by contrasting Cleveland's West and East Sides, which have been historically segregated, with African Americans concentrated on the East Side.[24] Demonstrating the continuing resonance of these two bands with continuing racial and geographic separation, he said, "I'll say I'm much more into the Stooges than I am into the Ramones. I mean I like the Ramones, but, in Cleveland, that's 'West Side punk shit.' The West Side punks were the ones who dressed up as punks and did the stereotypical punk things, East Side's a little different.'" Stylistically as well, the noisy hip hop production of the Bomb Squad aligns with the Stooges' raw power style, both stemming from the same short-cycle blues materials and limited harmonic movement following the innovations of James Brown. The raw power style works for a multifaceted engagement with race—American ideas and experiences of blackness and whiteness specifically—because it comes from layers of appropriation and transformation, followed by obfuscation, and rediscovery and reclaiming.

### Fotos y Recuerdos

One of the most important developments in punk music since the 1980s was the explosion of punk and hardcore bands in the 1990s organized around the banner of Riot Grrrl, which included political action and zine making as part of a third-wave feminist movement.[25] In addition to spurring the creation of countless punk bands made up of mostly women, Riot Grrrl generally presented a strong vision of punk as a voice of resistance for disenfranchised and marginalized people, and proffered leftist and progressive standpoints as an expected, although not automatic, position for punk bands. The punk scene around Riot Grrrl focused intensely on dialogue regarding the potential of punk for social change and political action. As Carrie Brownstein remembered: "we wanted to protect one another, to be inoffensive, inclusive, aware of our own shortcomings and faults, to improve and evolve, to make radical changes. Yet there was so much pressure on this single indie and punk movement, one that clearly couldn't address all forms of personhood or inequality."[26]

In response to the male-dominated and sexist hardcore scene they experienced during the 1980s—with the exception of some politically conscious groundswells such as the punk protests in Washington, DC, generated by Amy Pickering in 1985 ("Revolution Summer")—Riot Grrrl moved anti-patriarchal principles to the center of conversations about punk in the 1990s, and also refocused the historical lens of punk on the many women who participated in the scene before hardcore came to dominate punk's narrative. The ideas of punk's straight white maleness have problematically persisted, and Riot Grrrl itself wrestled with issues of racism, but overall Riot Grrrl helped amplify the voices of women, people of color, and LGBTQ people with respect to punk culture on the whole. Riot Grrrl looked both forward and backward, engaging with punk's history as well as the ways in which progressive ideals could best be a part of punk in the future. In many ways, Riot Grrrl was the first major attempt to broadly recast punk and punk history as something other than a music and culture mostly for and by white, male, straight youth. The impact of Riot Grrrl in the 1990s was widespread, reaching across multiple punk styles and scenes and effectively changing the standard narrative of punk. The sounds and ideas of Riot Grrrl had international repercussions far beyond the US and UK, culminating most dramatically in Pussy Riot's music and political actions protesting

Putin's regime, which eventually led to the imprisonment of core members of the collective.[27]

Many Riot Grrrl bands drew on blues-based raw power approaches, which have consistently proven to be effective for bands drawn to sociopolitical issues. The music of Bikini Kill, the best known of the bands associated with Riot Grrrl, is mainly based on blues riffs and whole-step alternations, combined with the mutability of Kathleen Hanna's voice, which could go from guttural blues styles to clear projection to sing-songy to breathy all in the course of one song. Hanna and many other singers who came to prominence during the 1990s followed the path of hardcore singers who sang straight across instrumental melodic and harmonic movement, while adding the melodic elements heard in singers such as Poly Styrene (although Hanna explained to me that she did not hear Poly Styrene until after she started singing in Bikini Kill). The blues-based style of punk is also heavily represented in the music of Heavens to Betsy, the British band Huggy Bear, and Bratmobile—whose reinterpretation of the Runaways' raw power "Cherry Bomb" especially elicits a tangled web of associations.

While raw power–style punk was perhaps the most common approach for Riot Grrrl bands, they arguably made their boldest and most effective musical statements drawing on different models that musically supported their ideas in original and compelling ways. The tangled meanings of raw power blues materials, like the "girls to the front" strategy of creating a female-centered hardcore punk experience, made for a powerful rebuke of punk's sexism but also stylistically reinforced the broader underlying aspects of the genre, recycling the paradoxes at the core of so many punk critiques. But Riot Grrrl also reached back to the music of Crass, the anarchist British band who created such boldly feminist albums as *Penis Envy*; Crass's fellow travelers Poison Girls; and X-Ray Spex, whose mixed-race frontwoman Poly Styrene led the way for women of color in punk. Perhaps most of all, Riot Grrrl bands helped reinstate the music of the Raincoats and the Zurich-based LiLiPUT (originally Kleenex) into punk's stylistic repertoire. These two bands created singular musical aesthetics based on approaches outside of the typical rock models of most bands, including punk bands, although their music was accepted in the diverse punk scenes of their time.[28] A letter to V. Vale from Jean Caffeine (from the all-girl San Francisco punk band the Urge) after a Raincoats show in 1977 reflects a typical response to the way bands were accepted at face value, without measuring how "punk" they were: "Good new band, the Raincoats—with 3 girls Ana, Gina + Jeremy sharing vocal and guitar chores—with Richard (ex 101ers) on drums. Raincoats shouting strings of poetic lyrics over their own untidy noise."[29]

However, as punk musicians coalesced around certain approaches, and as those making music outside of those approaches started participating in other scenes, the ideal that punk could and should accommodate any musical approach increasingly became harder to support with on-the-ground reality. Certainly by the 1990s, the resurgence of interest in the Raincoats and LiLiPUT represented a dramatic break with punk's assumed sound, as well as a counter to the reinforcing of punk as a white male phenomenon by rock journalists, the general media, and many punks themselves. The Raincoats' unique music and their independence from punk rock conventions made them especially important to the scene in Olympia, Washington.[30] The Raincoats' sound was very explicitly outside of blues-based rock: "Rock'n'roll is based on black music. And it's based *in* the exclusion of women and the ghettoization of blacks. Which is why we want to put a bit of distance between what we do and the rock'n'roll tradition."[31] The opening salvo on the first *Kill Rock Stars* compilation, Bratmobile's low-fidelity "Girl Germs," set the stage for a renewed diversity of musical approaches, clearly inspired by the Raincoats' harnessing of punk's ideals to create a new sound and a different narrative.

The formal characteristics of the Raincoats' music was in a sympathetic rather than an oppositional or paradoxical relationship to the messages they conveyed, and when punk bands drew on their example they escaped some of the limitations of punk's conventional approaches. These are not alternative perspectives to a taken-for-granted straight, white, male standard but rather part of broader or intersecting lineages. Other bands have expanded and pushed this liberatory method, performing a complete narrative, aesthetic, and style that stands within its own tradition.

For considering the continued significance of repertoire and the power of invoking multiple traditions and genealogies, Downtown Boys is a particularly compelling group. They have a radical activist political orientation; the group is multigender and ethnically diverse; and the lead singer, Victoria Ruiz, identifies as Chicana and Latinx and often sings in Spanish.[32] However, the group does not present as conforming to one identity or point of view, besides perhaps an underlying pro-labor, pro–working class, activist perspective. They are deeply aware of the relationships between the past, present, and future, with their first song on *Full Communism* (2015) announcing their "riding in on a wave of history." Their music, notably augmented with the sound of the tenor saxophone, often harnesses major modes in addition to raw power–style hardcore, and their music has become progressively bolder with the use of major tonalities. Anthemic songs such as "Monstro," with the chorus of "she's brown, she's smart" is based on a major melody played on the saxophone (two saxes on the recording). The instrumentation of the band, specifically the use of saxophone, already evokes an unusual, but hardly unprecedented, approach to punk. To me, the instrumentation and their approach evokes various Los Angeles bands of the late 1970s, such as the Flesh Eaters and the Deadbeats, as well as Bruce Springsteen's E Street Band and Los Lobos.

Since 2015, Downtown Boys have included in their repertoire Bruce Springsteen's "Dancing in the Dark" and Selena's "Fotos y Recuerdos," her recasting of
the Pretenders' "Back on the Chain Gang."[33] Continuing in this mode of expansive repertoire, Downtown Boys also plays Buffy Sainte-Marie's "Little Wheel
Spin and Spin." These covers are especially interesting in the lineages and traditions they implicitly and unironically communicate. "Dancing in the Dark" is an
upbeat, major-tonality song, resonating with Downtown Boys' other work. And
although "Dancing in the Dark" is not an explicitly political song, the Springsteen song directly invokes rock music generally as an expression of the working class and as a vehicle for messages of social justice. In fact, Wayne Kramer
told me that he considered Springsteen, not any punk rock musicians, to be the
true torch-bearer of the MC5's mission of unity and social activism, pointing
to their shared guidance by Jon Landau as well as Springsteen's long-standing
work to connect with his audience and raise political awareness.[34] Downtown
Boys itself takes its name from a Springsteen lyric from "It's Hard to Be a Saint
in the City" (*Greetings from Asbury Park, N.J.*, 1973): "and them downtown boys
sure talk gritty."[35] When Amy Goodman asked Ruiz in an interview about her
influences, she responded by listing her grandmother, Los Crudos, Selena Quin-
tanilla, M.I.A., and "Bruce Springsteen, I mean, there's really no one like Bruce
Springsteen. And he's so punk. . . . he's talking about the working class. He's talking about love."[36]

Comparably, Downtown Boys' adaptation of the Selena song "Fotos y Recuerdos" establishes a female and Latinx lineage intersecting or parallel to taken-for-
granted punk narratives, not solely in opposition to them. Another song with
major melodies, "Fotos y Recuerdos" is a non-standard punk cover, and beyond
the love-song lyrics, it is itself a song about memory and narrative. Our histories
are the sum totals of our experiences and the remnants and artifacts (the photos) that evoke the past (the memories). The Selena song additionally conjures
memories for those who remember her massive stardom, and beyond that, it
refers back to the Pretenders' song "Back on the Chain Gang," of which "Fotos
y Recuerdos" is an adaptation. Like Springsteen, the Pretenders have a deeper
connection to punk history than is generally acknowledged. Chrissie Hynde
was a key figure in the transatlantic exchanges of early punk, and the Pretenders' work straddles conventional punk styles and a whole range of approaches,
much like Downtown Boys' music. Downtown Boys–Selena–Hynde/Pretenders
is a definitive lineage, but also one that forces inclusive, expansive, and reconsidered conceptions of "punk."

These many facets of Downtown Boys' music may seem to contradict each
other, but they operate as "different tentacles that people can latch on to, and be
drawn in to, much like the way folk music casts a broad net."[37] Presented as a
musical synthesis, these contradictions turn the punk paradox into a working

out of the tensions between ideals and reality: "our utopian vision of the world" and "the way everyone's living it," in the words of saxophonist Joe DeGeorge.[38] The musical qualities of this repertoire—the loveliness of "Fotos y Recuerdos" and the wistful melody of "Dancing in the Dark"—create an irresistible effect in relation to Downtown Boys' urge for social change. As Victoria Ruiz told me, "It would be a hell of a lot easier to be like, 'yup, fuck it, fuck the system, fuck the status quo,' but yet, we also try to bring out the most beautiful or grace-ful moments that we can feel."[39] Hearing DeGeorge's mention of utopia in our group interview, Ruiz continued:

> The Selena-Pretenders thing is a beautiful and tangible example of that utopia, because so many fans either think of it as a Selena cover, or think of it as a Pretend-ers cover. But there are a few people who see it as both. And it is both! The reality is that it is both. And it just shows how quickly we call a side, when in fact the world we're trying to build is going to have these beautiful coming-togethers of realities that [are never] put together. Of things that have been running parallel for so long. They are going to have to finally intersect.[40]

## Punk's Undead

Ever since the 1970s, those invested in punk have argued about its viability. Crass famously announced "punk is dead" in 1978 on their album *The Feed-ing of the 5000*, as they spelled out the unresolvable contradictions of rock stars such as the Clash and the Sex Pistols singing about "revolution, anarchy, and change" while generating profits for major labels, and as they castigated "punks" who wear punk fashions while being uncommitted to real social jus-tice (a battle dating back to the Motherfuckers' criticisms of the MC5 a decade earlier).[41] Responding to Crass, the Exploited titled their first album *Punk's Not Dead* (1981). Since then punk has been called dead and not dead count-less times.

Punk continues to exist in a Schrödinger's Cat unresolved state between life and death as it expresses the ultimate conflicts of freedom and the state (the deepest American contradiction being ideals of freedom and human rights espoused by slaveholders), anarchy or socialism and the capitalist music indus-try, whiteness and anti-racism, and other unresolvable ideas and paradoxes that human beings navigate every day. In the forty years since *The Feeding of the 5000*, punk's liminal undead state has manifested in many ways, including now an active reissue industry and collector's market, reunion tours, and archiving, as well as punk music that is steadily becoming unmoored from, or coming to terms with, its own entanglements.

The historical orientation of punk has steadily become more and more directed at punk itself, intensifying dramatically with the creation of punk archives, museum exhibits, reissued recordings, documentary films, expensive coffee-table volumes, memoirs, college classes, and analytical books such as this one. Despite rhetoric describing punk as ephemeral and unconcerned with either the future or the past, the archival and documentary impulse in punk was immediately apparent with fanzines, bootlegs, and countless independent recordings, and now punk has been undeniably revealed as a historical mode for self-understanding.

Initially, white American suburban baby boomers used punk to understand their youth, reject the choices of their parents, and fashion their own physical and emotional experiences. But as serious as early punk's critiques of suburbia, conformity, and American society were, punk also reflected a strong attachment to privilege and an idealized notion of "America" that sidestepped segregation and inequality, the actual sources of the white, middle-class, suburban world that punk ostensibly repudiated. In punk's early manifestations, these impulses were mostly expressed through a nostalgia for a fantasy of the early days of rock and roll, and such nostalgia has become more layered with each iteration of punk. So-called "grunge," for example, was a version of punk that reimagined earlier punk and an idealized fantasy of those days, and also like early punk it played out in a mostly white space. Lyle Preslar commented: "I went out [to Seattle] to one of the Ultra Lame Fests that Sub Pop put on. That would've been maybe '92. I even said to the guy from Sub Pop, 'I don't see *anyone* in this crowd that is not white.'"[42]

The first Harry Pussy album (1993) addressed the nostalgia for punk's early days during the period of grunge, although they did it in their typically mysterious fashion, as Orcutt explained:

It was coming from reading Lester Bangs's "The White Noise Supremacists" [which discusses racism in the early New York punk scene]. When we started [Harry Pussy], grunge was just happening and there was a lot of nostalgia around punk, and I was like, what are you nostalgic about exactly? It was my way of saying, on the one hand, yeah, great energy, but what else is going on there? . . . But I don't know that many people understood. . . .

The first album has the . . . collage—it's not much of a collage because it's just two elements—but one of them is the hardcore slam dance photo and the other is that quote from [Clinton Heylin's] *Velvets to the Voidoids*, with the joke about the toilet at CBGBs. . . .

A lot of people . . . at that time were at the age where looking back at the '80s was their youth, and it was a literal nostalgia for when they were younger. They just weren't thinking about the unpleasant aspects of this thing. You know, they weren't

Figure 8.3. Harry Pussy, *Harry Pussy*, 1993. Reproduced with permission.

thinking about sexism. They weren't thinking about racism. They were just, you know, it was like literal nostalgia where you're ignoring all the unpleasantness.[43]

As shown in figure 8.3, the offensive excerpt from Heylin's book featured on *Harry Pussy* is "A: In an emergency you can shit on a Puerto Rican whore," the answer to "As the contemporary joke went: Q: What's the difference between the toilets at CBGBs and a Puerto Rican whore?"[44] Not only did such aspects of the CBGB scene go ignored with grunge's nostalgic orientation, true to the cycle of punk's recuperation into the mainstream and even elite society, the actual CBGB toilets ended up recreated in the Metropolitan Museum of Art as part of the 2013 exhibit "Punk: Chaos to Couture."[45]

The nostalgia Orcutt described is supported by the respectful treatment of repertoire in most punk or punk-adjacent covers. Sonic Youth's version of the Stooges' "I Wanna Be Your Dog" is noisier and with female vocals by Kim Gordon, but otherwise retains the musical qualities of the original. The concert at

New York's Bowery Ballroom celebrating the ten-year anniversary of *Our Band Could Be Your Life*, Michael Azerrad's book profiling thirteen punk and indie rock bands of the 1980s, consisted mostly of similarly well-done and closely hewn covers, such as Delicate Steve playing the Minutemen, St. Vincent playing Big Black, and in one especially striking example, Ted Leo channeling Ian MacKaye as he sang Minor Threat songs along with a backing track.[46] Imaginative interpretations such as Tune-Yards' rendition of Sonic Youth's "The Burning Spear" on that same *Our Concert Could Be Your Life* show; Dirty Projectors' creative *Rise Above*, a memorial exercise recreating Black Flag's *Damaged* in a completely different style after not hearing the album for fifteen years; and Soft Pink Truth's (Drew Daniel's) electronic reconceptions of Minor Threat's "Out of Step," Angry Samoans' "Homo-Sexual," and other songs on the album *Do You Want New Wave or Do You Want the Soft Pink Truth*, represent less common but vitally important attempts to reclaim the punk of these artists' childhoods and punk's imagined heydays without nostalgia. The ending of *Do You Want New Wave or Do You Want the Soft Pink Truth* directly engages the question of nostalgia. The last track starts with Gladys Knight's introduction to "The Way We Were," famously sampled by Wu-Tang Clan for "Can It All Be So Simple": "Hey, you know, everybody's talking about the good old days, right?" before an eerily phased version of "Lookin' Back," sung by Carol Channing in the musical *Lorelei*: "It's nice lookin' back, lookin' back on the past / When you've a past full of mem'ries that last / Sweet souvenirs of a life that was fast / And full of fun / But now it's done."

Early punk has also become a major area for reissues and record collectors, with new vinyl pressings, and massive remastering and recovery projects (such as *Savage Young Dü*, dedicated to the early recordings of Hüsker Dü). The substantial art and coffee-table books, such as the reissues of the *Destroy All Monsters* magazines ($100), Johan Kugelberg and Jon Savage's *Punk: An Aesthetic* ($100), and Spot's photographs ($50), are similar products. These commodities are probably directed at those members of Generation X, now middle aged, who may have disposable income and "look back on a past full of memories that last."

One of the most complicated aspects of the phenomena of reissues and record collecting, specifically with respect to issues of race and the story outlined in *Damaged*, is the discovery and eventual reissue of the recordings made in the mid-1970s by Death, an all–African American trio of brothers from Detroit. As documented in *A Band Called Death*, the Hackney brothers Bobby, Dannis, and David—the visionary of the group who passed away in 2000—recorded a number of demos in 1975 that resulted in one self-released single produced in a run of 500: "Politicians in My Eyes" b/w "Keep on Knocking" on Tryangle.[47] Once the single surfaced in the early 2000s, it became known among some record collectors and a copy sold for $800, eventually leading to the release of the demo recordings on Drag City as ... *For the Whole World to See.* Death and these 1975 recordings became a phenomenon on their considerable strength as music but also on the exciting narrative of this fascinating and creative family, who have reformed and are now performing again as Death after having a long career as the Burlington, Vermont, reggae band Lambsbread.

The Death recordings are inventive originals in a Detroit garage or hard rock style, with some unusual vocal styles, such as the almost hardcore rat-a-tat singing on "Politicians in My Eyes." The trio was certainly distinctive among all-black groups at the time with their uncompromising band name. However, the style they played was not uncommon for the Detroit area, and white and black people in 1960s and early 1970s Detroit were fortunate enough to hear a tremendous variety of musical styles on the radio and in local venues. African Americans playing hard rock music had become somewhat less common in the early 1970s than in the 1960s, but it was still not as unusual as it would become after the 1980s. This is the same environment that hosted the eclectic rock music of Funkadelic, the band who recorded the psychedelic *Maggot Brain* at United Sound Systems only a few years before Death recorded there. As explained in *A Band Called Death,* Brian Spears and Don Davis of Groovesville Productions were enthusiastic about Death's music, and a record contract with Clive Davis fell through only because of the group's unwillingness to change what was thought to be an unmarketable band name. The members of Death themselves attest to their music's inherent relationship to their environment, growing up on the Beatles, Jimi Hendrix, the Who, and Motown. "We were just trying to be like the groups of the day that we loved, like the MC5 and Alice Cooper, and all those great rock and roll bands of the seventies. We were really just spring-boarding off of the sound that they were laying down, we were just doing it harder, faster, and louder," said Bobby Hackney in a recent interview.[48] In this sense, Death was like many other bands of the early and mid-1970s, especially in the northern Midwest, such as Rocket from the Tombs.

The type of music Death played had not gone through the stages in the late 1970s and early 1980s that led to punk styles, and thus also retrospectively identified "protopunk" styles, being generally understood as "white." As Bobby Hackney explained, "We never really considered ourselves a punk band. I mean, back then, if you called somebody a punk, you got into a fight. We were playing what we conceived of as hard-driving Detroit rock and roll."[49] But from the vantage point of the early 2000s, given the history of punk since the mid-1970s and especially the reframing of British punk as the worldwide "big bang" for punk, the idea of African Americans playing heavy hard-driving rock music in the 1970s seems out of place. It is particularly intriguing that much of the discourse surrounding the reissue of the recordings has not attempted to place the band in context—as more "of their time" than they seem now, the way Bobby Hackney speaks about his own music—but rather to place them as unique protopunk pioneers. "This Band was Punk before Punk was Punk" ran the *New York Times* headline in 2009.[50]

More problematically, in Al Jazeera (AJ+)'s *The Very Black History of Punk Music* special, narrator Sana Saeed explains, "Now even though Death didn't go mainstream, their music was known underground and by the most diehard punk fans. Meaning, they had influence."[51] Despite the merits of Death's music and the appeal of their story, this is inaccurate. Death's music was not known underground, and they did not have "influence," at least until the reissue of their music in 2009. Unlike some of their counterparts who also released little to no music, such as Rocket from the Tombs, Death did not play live shows. "We basically honed our skills in our bedroom, and from the bedroom we took it to the garage. And from the garage we took it to the studio," said Dannis Hackney.[52] Before the appearance of "Keep on Knocking" on the itself-very-rare 2001 compilation *No One Left to Blame*, almost no one had heard of the band, and they certainly had not been heard by any of the musicians who created punk as we know it in the mid-1970s.[53] Death have been compared to Bad Brains because they were both rock bands with only African American personnel, but unlike Death, Bad Brains had a huge impact on multiple scenes and in fact, they were the central band in the initial DC punk scene and then New York hardcore. Underlying all of these retrospective characterizations is the fact that, if one disregards the British "big bang" theory, the mid-1970s is not a particularly early period for the development of punk.

Just as the act of making 1976 Great Britain the starting point for punk says more about white American fantasies in the late 1970s and early 1980s than it does about the actual way punk developed, revising history to place Death in this central historical position as "influencers" says more about punk in the 2000s and 2010s than it does about punk (or American music in general) in the mid-1970s. Punk has been associated almost entirely with white people since its beginnings, but since the 1980s it has had enormous resonance for massive numbers of people from tremendously diverse backgrounds. Since that time it has also become a critical site of social consciousness and radical politics, making the problematic connections to whiteness and the often seemingly gratuitous offensiveness of punk's early days difficult to embrace for many contemporary punks or fans of the music. Especially after Bad Brains' presence on the punk scene, African Americans and other people of color became increasingly attracted to punk culture and represented.[54]

Heightening the visibility of groups such as Death helps communicate that punk is for anyone who wants to be a part of it, and amplifying the stories of African Americans, women, people of color, and LGBTQ people in punk is an essential corrective to the patently false notion that punk has been only, or even primarily, for and by young white men. However, reframing punk as a music that was pioneered by groups such as Death and sidestepping the ways in which early punk was informed by the formations of postwar whiteness potentially creates a new set of problems. Given how punk's history has been misused over the decades, overstating the biography of Death in the punk narrative threatens to provide an escape route for those who want to ignore larger social processes such as white flight, suburban sprawl, and persistent segregation and inequality, and how punk has reflected these invidious aspects of American history. Racism continues to beset punk scenes (as well as other popular music styles that have come to be associated with white people, such as metal).[55] Revising punk history in this way also runs the risk of misrepresenting or downplaying the culture in which a group such as Bad Brains emerged (they referred to themselves as "all black musicians in a seemingly all-white music scene" in 1980), the challenges punks of color have faced for decades, or the context in which Riot Grrrl became so crucial. The reception of Bad Brains in the late 1970s and early 1980s, for example, depended a great deal on their relationship to white audiences' ideas of race and group affiliation. In the lyrics of Sick of It All's tribute to Bad Brains, "That Crazy White Boy Shit" (2018), "Always grooved on that crazy white boy shit / Looking for who played it best . . . / They [Bad Brains] wrote the book on that crazy white boy shit / No one could even come close."

Ideas of music as "black" or "white" have resonance and yield commercial successes because they mirror and support a society in which these racial categories continue to have meanings and associations, and because they are connected to the tenacious segregation of housing, schools, and social life in the United States. In situations where these categories have less meaning, music in general and punk in particular have been less dependent on the racial associations of musical style.

A contemporary New York hardcore group, Show Me the Body, makes music that looks back without nostalgia and incorporates gestures from a wide range of musical resources without self-conscious hybridization. Their music comes from a New York environment and a hardcore tradition that prioritizes authentic expression and views punk as a catalyst for communal experiences that go beyond the rational, what vocalist and banjo player Julian Cashwan termed "folk music," "ceremony," and a "possession state."[56] Their music is tied to the need for physical involvement and presence, following the appeal to habeas corpus, the literal translation of which is the group's name. The unifying aspect of New York music is "it has to make you want to dance." Obliquely tied to the "New York sound" is punk's potential as a form of expression that is "anti-society," but in the sense of the complexities such a stance generates: "Punk rock and hardcore culture gives people the opportunity to reinvent identity and do it in a way that doesn't change their identity, but it redefines how an identity can serve you."[57]

Show Me the Body's music is informed by New York hardcore exponents such as Youth of Today, Sick of It All, Madball, and Bad Brains, but also the "real New York sound" of salsa, such as Hector Lavoe, Willie Colon, and Bobby Valentin, as well as the Ghetto Brothers and hip-hop. Cashwan spoke to me about his experiences growing up in neighborhoods on the west side of Manhattan, spending time among outlaw bikers and gang members on the Lower East Side, and a complex Jewish identity informed by the Jews he met in New York's gangs; he described these many points of reference as simply part and parcel of an urban New York life.[58] At the same time, the sound of Show Me the Body avoids overt references to any styles as a form of fusion. For example, Cashwan's vocal style is rhythmic and syncopated, in the style of many other New York hardcore vocalists, but Cashwan's cadenced vocals and Show Me the Body's personal associations with the hip-hop group Ratking and the art collective Letter Racer has led more than a few music writers to categorize their music as fusing punk and hip-hop ("disharmony of hardcore punk, hip-hop and harsh noise, shoving its visceral poetry through an industrial blender piped in from the band's underground garbage matrix").[59] For Cashwan, if hip hop is heard in their music, it is only there as a product of their environment, compared to doo-wop in the Ramones music: "it's part of the cultural environment they were raised in, but they would never say 'we are punk rock doo-wop.'" He is also very clear about respecting the connections between musical style and social formations:

> It's there, because by definition, if it makes you dance, it has roots in that. . . . It's about making people dance. But I don't consider what we do hip hop music. Or any form of rap music, or anything like that. Not only because it's not, but also because that is not our identity and cultural story to tell. So like whenever anyone is like, "oh, but you kind of rap," it's like, "*no, I do not.*" It's part of a New York sound.[60]

Similarly, Cashwan's use of the banjo as the group's main melodic instrument is the deepest way Show Me the Body conjures multiple layers of race and American history without nostalgia or nods to "fusion." The speed at which the instrument can be played in open tunings mirroring barre chords makes it ideal for hardcore, but Cashwan also likes the limitless and unexpected connections it generates. The banjo is perhaps the instrument that best captures American musical history and all of its complexities, especially with respect to the history of white and black people, even before the establishment of the United States as an independent nation. The banjo is one of the most African instruments in American musical life, and yet also an instrument that became almost exclusively associated with white people after they adopted it through processes of exchange in Appalachia and other places.[61] Near the end of one conversation, Cashwan showed me a banjo from the 1800s that he had been given, which in the style of some early Civil War–era Boucher banjos is half-fretless and with an actual drum for its body. He told me:

> CASHWAN: This shows you perfectly that rock and roll could never be white. By nature.
> RAPPORT: Do you think of the banjo as a black instrument?
> CASHWAN: Absolutely. It's fretless [like similar West African instruments]. Absolutely.
> RAPPORT: It is a black instrument. It's African.
> CASHWAN: Absolutely.
> RAPPORT: But a lot of people don't know that.
> CASHWAN: And that's foolish and white-centric. And that's why we live in a racist country.
> RAPPORT: I mean the banjo is really associated with white people.
> CASHWAN: Absolutely. Absolutely. And that was my first association.
> RAPPORT: It's like one of the closest African instruments we have. . . . So you like the historical layers there?
> CASHWAN: Yes. Absolutely. I found this instrument, I was like, immediately amazed, because that's what I realized, and doing research on it, I was like wow, this whole thing used to not have frets. . . . seeing that banjo really just made me think of American music in a completely different way. And literally the banjo in a different way. And it made me think of it as a drum.[62]

The banjo is not ironic in Show Me the Body's music, and nor are other elements such as Cashwan's rhythmic singing style. A related example is the band's engagement with World War II and Holocaust imagery. The swastika, for example, is the most banal cliché of punk fashion, almost devoid of meaning except as an element of potential "shock value." When Show Me the Body was asked to play a music festival in Poland, they used the opportunity to visit Auschwitz and other camps and film their experiences. In a short film for their Corpus TV channel, "Work Sets You Free" (the translation of Arbeit Macht Frei, the message above the gates at Auschwitz), they juxtaposed images of Auschwitz with American prisons in a meditation on the similar purposes of the structures.[63] This is a far cry from the Sex Pistols' "Belsen Was a Gas."

Punk continues to be a productive style for people wrestling with expressions of freedom within a society perpetually bound to historical legacies placing restraints on freedom, and for musicians who wish to communicate lived contradictions and complexities. The musical genealogy of early punk as detailed in

Figure 8.4a and 8.4b. Show Me the Body, Ramones retrospective art opening, Queens Museum, April 10, 2016. Photographs by the author.

*Damaged* continues to give punk much of its power, forty to fifty years later. At the same time, many of today's young punk musicians have rejected the modes of punk's early critiques that have proven to be self-defeating, such as ironic rejections of privilege coming from a position of privilege. Some musicians from the early days of punk described in *Damaged* also continue to create with punk's energy and freedom but without the nostalgia of playing old repertoire, without the increasingly anachronistic approach of playing music born of the late 1970s and early 1980s, and without a nod-and-a-wink take on American whiteness. Kira Roessler and Mike Watt's bass duo group Dos, Ian MacKaye and Amy Farina's group the Evens, and the wide ranging styles of Alice Bag's and Viv

Albertine's recent projects are direct examples that often bear little resemblance to preconceived notions of "punk" and no relation to predetermined expectations of punk as a musical genre but that have everything to do with punk's soul.

In a final vignette, the tensions and the freedoms of punk's past and its present were on full display at the Queens Museum's Ramones retrospective in 2016, when Show Me the Body performed at the opening. A combination of New York City cultural elites and senior citizen leather-clad rockers were in attendance, along with younger fans, many dressed in one of the most prominent legacies of the group, Ramones tee shirts. To commemorate the occasion, contemporary punk inheritors of the Ramones' New York punk legacy played, first the Kaminos, and then Show Me the Body. Supporters and friends of Show Me the Body turned the area in front of the stage into a New York pit, visibly diverse in contrast to the older and whiter contingent at the museum, and the band attempting to create an atmosphere approaching a possession ceremony with the audience. Security increasingly monitored and policed the show as the valuable artifacts and the museum environment became threatened, and older punks decided whether to participate, leave, or intervene as tensions surfaced from these competing ideas of "punk." Is punk an archival form now, an accomplishment of the baby boomers and a relic of the 1970s, or a living form embodying self-expression and nonconformity, to be put to unforeseen uses by its contemporary players and participants? The contradictions of punk will not be resolved as long as the contradictions of American society and American musical life remain.

# APPENDIX

The chart in this appendix shows ages, first shows, debut recordings, and world events.

About this chart:

Along the x-axis, each musician is placed at the year in which they turned eighteen. I tried to pick a wide variety of representative musicians for this chart, avoiding too many extreme or outlier cases.

Along the y-axis, the age at which their first significant professional show is marked by a white bar, with a gray bar extending to the age at which their debut recording (relevant to this book) was released. The title of the specific recording is indicated in the white bar after the musician's name. A thin horizontal line also crosses at age eighteen.

**Light gray** bars indicate pre-punk recordings (discussed primarily in chapters 2 and 3); **medium gray bars** indicate punk recordings (discussed primarily in chapters 4, 5, and 6); and **dark gray bars** indicate hardcore recordings (discussed primarily in chapters 6 and 7).

At the top of the chart is a timeline indicating some of the major events occurring during those years. For example, Jonathan Richman turned eighteen in 1969, the year of Woodstock, and he began performing live that year. His debut recording for the purposes of this book, the pre-punk album *The Modern Lovers* (discussed mainly in chapter 2), was released in 1976, when Richman was twenty-five.

Note: the numbers are based on years, and not always exact months and days, which may account for some discrepancies of up to one number (e.g., if someone turned eighteen after an album was released, but during the same year, I use the number 18 and not 17).

The data in this chart quickly shows a number of key points made throughout *Damaged*:

- The medium gray and dark gray bars indicate a very clear downward slope, demonstrating the dramatic shift toward younger musicians as the timeline gets later and hardcore punk emerges.
- Punk (medium gray) musicians began performing live after their teenage years, many from twenty-three to twenty-five, and punk recordings were released almost entirely by musicians over eighteen, most aged twenty-five and over. The only exception on the chart is Pat Smear, who was eighteen when the Germs' single "Forming" was released.
- The formative events for most punk musicians, around the ages of eighteen to twenty, are 1960s events such as the Beatles on Ed Sullivan (1964) and the Monterey Pop Festival (1967). Almost all of these musicians were well over the age of eighteen in the year 1977.
- Almost all of the punk musicians are baby boomers, i.e., born between 1946 and 1964; on the x-axis of the chart the baby boomer generation is from the years 1964 (Patti Smith) to 1982 (after Bill Stevenson). The musicians born on or after 1960, 1978 (Bob Mould) on the x-axis, can be considered a transitional group between baby boomers and Generation X.
- For most punk (medium gray) musicians, there is a considerable time gap between first shows and first recordings. For hardcore musicians, the time gap is negligible.
- The ages of musicians making pre-punk or proto-punk recordings (light gray) skew slightly younger than the punk recordings.

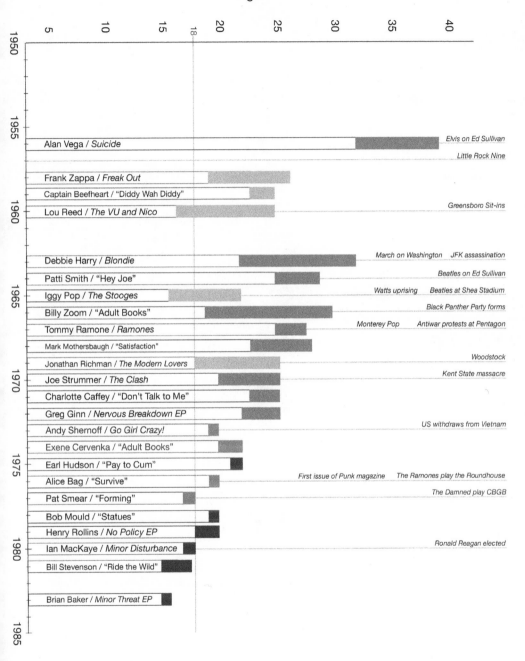

Age

1950

1955

Alan Vega / *Suicide*
*Elvis on Ed Sullivan*
*Little Rock Nine*

Frank Zappa / *Freak Out*
Captain Beefheart / "Diddy Wah Diddy"
*Greensboro Sit-ins*

1960

Lou Reed / *The VU and Nico*

Debbie Harry / *Blondie*
*March on Washington    JFK assassination*
Patti Smith / "Hey Joe"
*Beatles on Ed Sullivan*
Iggy Pop / *The Stooges*
*Watts uprising    Beatles at Shea Stadium*

1965

Billy Zoom / "Adult Books"
*Black Panther Party forms*
Tommy Ramone / *Ramones*
*Monterey Pop    Antiwar protests at Pentagon*
Mark Mothersbaugh / "Satisfaction"
Jonathan Richman / *The Modern Lovers*
*Woodstock*
Joe Strummer / *The Clash*
*Kent State massacre*

1970

Charlotte Caffey / "Don't Talk to Me"
Greg Ginn / *Nervous Breakdown EP*
Andy Shernoff / *Go Girl Crazy!*
*US withdraws from Vietnam*
Exene Cervenka / "Adult Books"
Earl Hudson / "Pay to Cum"
Alice Bag / "Survive"
*First issue of Punk magazine    The Ramones play the Roundhouse*

1975

Pat Smear / "Forming"
*The Damned play CBGB*
Bob Mould / "Statues"
Henry Rollins / *No Policy EP*
Ian MacKaye / *Minor Disturbance*
*Ronald Reagan elected*

1980

Bill Stevenson / "Ride the Wild"

Brian Baker / *Minor Threat EP*

1985

# NOTES

## Chapter 1: Intro: The Meanings of a Musical Style

1. Melissa Gomez, "Pro-Trump Fan of Social Distortion Says Lead Singer Punched Him at Concert," *New York Times*, August 16, 2018, https://www.nytimes.com/2018/08/16/us/social-distortion-singer-beating-trump.html.

2. By "long 1970s" I mean the late 1960s to the early 1980s, the period during which punk emerged as a distinct musical style. The era is bookended by such watershed events as the Tet Offensive and the assassinations of Martin Luther King Jr. and Robert Kennedy in 1968 and the beginning of Ronald Reagan's presidency in 1981. Musically, the same period is marked by the Stooges' first performances and the release of the Velvet Underground's *White Light/White Heat* in 1968, and the release of Black Flag's *Damaged* and Minor Threat's first two EPs in 1981.

3. Steven Blush, *American Hardcore: A Tribal History* (Los Angeles: Feral House, 2001), 88.

4. Colin Gunckel, "Defining Punk: Queerness and the LA Punk Scene, 1977–1981," *Journal of Popular Music Studies* 30/1–2 (March–June 2018): 155; Tavia Nyong'o, "Punk'd Theory," *Social Text* 84–85/23 (3–4).

5. Haki R. Madhubuti, *Why L.A. Happened: Implications of the '92 Los Angeles Rebellion* (Chicago: Third World Press, 1993), xiii.

6. Michael Omi and Howard Winant, *Racial Formation in the United States from the 1960s to the 1990s*, 2nd ed. (New York: Routledge, 1994), 95–112.

7. Omi and Winant, *Racial Formation*, 54–61; see also Cheryl I. Harris, "Whiteness as Property," *Harvard Law Review* 106/8 (June 1993): 1709–91.

8. Kimberlé Crenshaw, "Why Intersectionality Can't Wait," *Washington Post*, September 24, 2015; Kimberlé Crenshaw, "Demarginalizing the Intersection of Race and Sex: A Black Feminist Critique of Antidiscrimination Doctrine, Feminist Theory and Antiracist Politics," *University of Chicago Legal Forum* 1 (1989): 139–67.

9. Jack Hamilton, *Just Around Midnight: Rock and Roll and the Racial Imagination* (Cambridge: Harvard University Press, 2016); Jennifer Lynn Stoever, *The Sonic Color Line: Race and the Cultural Politics of Listening* (New York: New York University Press, 2016); Karl Hagstrom Miller, *Segregating Sound: Inventing Folk and Pop Music in the Age of Jim Crow* (Durham, NC: Duke University Press, 2010). Some earlier writings on race and American music with a major impact on my own work include Carol J. Oja, *Making Music Modern: New York in the 1920s* (New York: Oxford University Press, 2000); George E. Lewis, "Improvised Music after 1950: Afrological and Eurological Perspectives," *Black Music Research Journal* 16/1 (Spring 1996): 91–122; Charles Hiroshi Garrett, *Struggling to Define a Nation: American Music and the Twentieth Century* (Berkeley: University of California Press, 2008); and the essays in Ronald Radano and Philip V. Bohlman, eds., *Music and the Racial Imagination* (Chicago: University of Chicago Press, 2000).

10. See, for example, the writings collected in Stephen Duncombe and Maxwell Tremblay, eds., *White Riot: Punk Rock and the Politics of Race* (London: Verso, 2011).

11. Greil Marcus, *Lipstick Traces: A Secret History of the Twentieth Century* (Cambridge: Harvard University Press, 1989).

12. For a recent book devoted to women in punk, see Vivien Goldman, *Revenge of the She-Punks: A Feminist Music History from Poly Styrene to Pussy Riot* (Austin: University of Texas Press, 2019); and for an example of a recent corrective history accounting for many people of color, LGBTQ people, and Latinx people in punk, see David A. Ensminger, *Visual Vitriol: The Street Art and Subcultures of the Punk and Hardcore* (Jackson: University Press of Mississippi, 2011).

13. The most thorough report on African Americans in punk to date is James Porter and Jake Austen, "Black Punk Time: Blacks in Punk, New Wave, and Hardcore 1976–1984)," *Roctober* 32 (2002), updated on the internet beginning with www.roctober.com/roctober/black-punk1.html (accessed March 22, 2013). Unfortunately, this site is no longer active. See also Osa Atoe, *Shotgun Seamstress* (blog), http://shotgunseamstress.blogspot.com; Osa Atoe, *Shotgun Seamstress* (zines), accessed September 9, 2018, available online at https://issuu.com/shotgun seamstress (Toni Young is on the cover of issue 1); and https://www.blackwomeninrock.info/. Ensminger notes that "hardcore and punk provide a space for the likes of black lesbian female skater and drummer Mad Dog from the Controllers," and "Mad Dog was not a lone margin walker," but up until the 1980s I cannot find any examples to support this claim that Karla "Mad Dog" (who also once reportedly said she was "a white man trapped in a black woman's body") was one example among others ("the likes of"), and Ensminger does not name any specific individuals. Ensminger, *Visual Vitriol*, 246–47.

14. Sara Ahmed discusses many of these issues in *On Being Included,* such as the ways in which "diversity" and "antiracism" can protect or become an attribute of whiteness, and the potential for "solutions" to create problems "by concealing the problems in new ways." Sara Ahmed, *On Being Included: Racism and Diversity in Institutional Life* (Durham, NC: Duke University Press, 2012), 142.

15. Bill Owens, *Suburbia* (New York: Fotofolio, [1973] 1999), 5.

16. Owens, *Suburbia*, 5.

17. George Lipsitz, *The Possessive Investment in Whiteness: How White People Profit from Identity Politics*, rev. ed. (Philadelphia: Temple University Press, 2006), 7. See also Richard Rothstein, *The Color of Law: A Forgotten History of How Our Government Segregated America* (New York: Liveright, 2017); Robert Fogelson, *Bourgeois Nightmares: Suburbia, 1870–1930* (New Haven: Yale University Press, 2005); Robert Fishman, *Bourgeois Utopias: The Rise and Fall of Suburbia* (New York: Basic Books, 1987); Rachael A. Woldoff, *White Flight/Black Flight: The Dynamics of Racial Change in an American Neighborhood* (Ithaca, NY: Cornell University Press, 2011).

18. Nell Irvin Painter, *The History of White People* (New York: W.W. Norton, 2010), 371–72.

19. Lipsitz, *Possessive Investment*, 7.

20. Schomburg Center for Research in Black Culture, "The Second Great Migration," *In Motion: The African American Migration-Experience*, 2005, www.inmotionaame.org.

21. Campbell Robertson, "History of Lynchings in the South Documents Nearly 4,000 Names," *New York Times*, February 10, 2015, https://www.nytimes.com/2015/02/10/us/history -of-lynchings-in-the-south-documents-nearly-4000-names.html; Rothstein, *Color of Law*, 39–41.

22. Painter, *History of White People*, 371.

23. *Oxford English Dictionary*, s.v. "white flight."

24. Schomburg Center, "Second Great Migration."

25. Eric Avila, *Popular Culture in the Age of White Flight: Fear and Fantasy in Suburban Los Angeles* (Berkeley: University of California Press, 2004), 5.

26. Painter, *History of White People*, 370.

27. Lipsitz, *Possessive Investment*, 7. Also see Painter, *History of White People*, 359–82.

28. Rothstein, *Color of Law*, 25–34, 59–75, 93–99.

29. Matthew F. Delmont, *Why Busing Failed: Race, Media, and the National Resistance to School Desegregation* (Oakland: University of California Press, 2016), 6–9; Douglas S. Massey, "The Legacy of the 1968 Fair Housing Act," *Sociological Forum* 30/S1 (2015): 572.

30. Schomburg Center, "Second Great Migration"; Wayne Kramer, *The Hard Stuff: Dope, Crime, the MC5 and My Life of Impossibilities* (New York: Da Capo Press, 2018), 15, also 71–72; Mark Slobin, *Motor City Music: A Detroiter Looks Back* (New York: Oxford University Press, 2018), 5.

31. E.g., Avila, *Popular Culture*, 185–223, on streetcars and highways in Los Angeles.

32. Delmont, *Why Busing Failed*, 23–53.

33. Avila, *Popular Culture*, 2, 15, 145–84.

34. Dana Goldstein, "New York's Schools Chancellor Is Talking About Integration. Can He Make It Happen?" *New York Times*, September 3, 2018, https://www.nytimes.com/2018/09/03/nyregion/nyc-chancellor-school-segregation.html.

35. See, e.g., Ann Douglas, *Terrible Honesty: Mongrel Manhattan in the 1920s* (New York: Farrar, Straus, and Giroux, 1995); Oja, *Making Music Modern*; Harry Franqui-Rivera, "The Color Line: Afro-Puerto Ricans and the Harlem Hellfighters," *Centro Center for Puerto Rican Studies*, https://centropr.hunter.cuny.edu/digital-humanities/pr-military/color-line-afro-puerto -ricans-and-harlem-hellfighters.

36. Nadine Cohodas, *Spinning Blues into Gold: The Chess Brothers and the Legendary Chess Records* (New York: St. Martin's Griffin, 2000); Nelson George, *The Death of Rhythm and Blues* (New York: Plume, 1988), 26–29. One of the many common misconceptions of the blues is its age. The blues as a named style of music begins in the early twentieth century, and the style's national popularity can be traced to late 1910s and 1920s New York, with hits by James Reese Europe for Vernon and Irene Castle, and the massive successes of female blues singers in New York arriving during the Great Migration, such as Bessie Smith. The "country blues" of players such as Blind Lemon Jefferson, often described as "representing the roots of commercial stars such as Rainey and Handy" and the roots of rock and roll, emerged on recordings in the late 1920s, and "it is hard to say how accurately recordings made in the later 1920s reflect earlier traditions . . . they were tapping deep sources, but the rural bluesmen had grown up during the heyday of vaudeville blues and were clearly influenced by current trends." Elijah Wald, *The Blues: A Very Short Introduction* (New York: Oxford University Press, 2010), 11, 29, et passim.

37. Slobin, *Motor City Music*, 67–104; Dan Carlisle quoted in Steve Miller, *Detroit Rock City* (Boston: Da Capo Press, 2013), 3.

38. Richard A. Peterson, *Creating Country Music: Fabricating Authenticity* (Chicago: University of Chicago Press, 1997); Christopher A. Waterman, "Race Music: Bo Chatmon, 'Corrine Corrina,' and the Excluded Middle," in *Music and the Racial Imagination*, ed. Ronald Radano and Philip V. Bohlman, 167–205 (Chicago: University of Chicago Press, 2000). See also Patrick Huber, "Black Hillbillies: African American Musicians on Old-Time Records, 1924–1932," in *Hidden in the Mix: The African American Presence in Country Music*, ed. Diane Pecknold (Durham, NC: Duke University Press, 2013), 19–81; and Stephen Fox Lorenz, "Cosmopolitan Folk: The Cultural Politics of the North American Folk Music Revival in Washington, D.C." (PhD diss., George Washington University, 2014), 107–12, on the impact of Connie B. Gay in the early 1950s.

39. Lester Bangs, "Dead Lie the Velvets Underground R.I.P. Long Live Lou Reed," *Creem*, May 1971, reprinted in Johan Kugelberg, ed., *The Velvet Underground: New York Art* (New York: Rizzoli, 2009), 297.

40. "Leisure, mobility and privacy—it was the suburban myth transported to the Pacific Ocean, but rendered heroic." Jim Miller, "The Beach Boys," in *The Rolling Stone Illustrated History of Rock and Roll*, rev. ed., ed. Jim Miller (New York: Rolling Stone, 1980), 162 [162–68]. See also Ben Ratliff, "Looking for the Beach Boys," review of Brian Wilson, *I Am Brian Wilson: A Memoir*, and Mike Love with James S. Hirsch, *Good Vibrations: My Life as a Beach Boy*, *New York Review of Books*, October 26, 2016.

41. Michael Dimock, "Defining Generations: Where Millennials End and Post-Millennials Begin," *Pew Research Center*, March 1, 2018, http://www.pewresearch.org/fact-tank/2018/03/01/defining-generations-where-millennials-end-and-post-millennials-begin/.

42. In 1970 the average age in the US for a first marriage was twenty-three for men and twenty-one for women, making it quite a stretch to consider as part of a youth culture a group such as the Ramones, already aged twenty-three to twenty-six when they first formed in 1974.

43. E.g., Chrissie Hynde, *Reckless: My Life as a Pretender* (New York: Anchor Books, 2015).

44. Interview by the author, October 18, 2018; interview by the author, November 7, 2018.

45. Michael C. Heller, *Loft Jazz: Improvising New York in the 1970s* (Berkeley: University of California Press, 2016), 49–52.

46. Matt Riggle, Deedle LaCour, James Rayburn, and Justin Wilson, dirs. and eds., *Filmage: The Story of Descendents/All*, "The Lombardo Short" extra, 2013.

47. Ahmed, *On Being Included*, 3.

48. Lipsitz, *Possessive Investment*, 1.

49. Interview by the author, November 6, 2018.

50. See, e.g., Lipsitz, *Possessive Investment*, 105–17.

51. Interview by the author, September 30, 2016.

52. Marcus, *Lipstick Traces*, 82.

53. Dave Laing, *One Chord Wonders: Power and Meaning in Punk Rock* (Milton Keynes, UK: Open University Press, 1985), 12.

54. Tony Moon, *Sideburns* 1 (January 1977): 2.

55. John Doe with Tom DeSavia and friends, *Under the Big Black Sun: A Personal History of L.A. Punk* (Boston: Da Capo Press, 2016), 183–84.

56. Interview by the author, August 3, 2018.

57. Interview by the author, November 7, 2018.

58. Richard Hell, *HRR*; Steve Jones, *HRR*.

59. Interview by the author, November 6, 2018.

60. Paul Cook, *HRR*. The Pete Townshend quote is from a previous conversation between Cook's interviewer and Townshend.

61. For an example of music theory usefully applied to punk, see David B. Easley, "Riff Schemes, Form, and the Genre of Early American Hardcore Punk (1978–83)," *Music Theory Online* 21/1 (March 2015), http://www.mtosmt.org/issues/mto.15.21.1/mto.15.21.1.easley.html; and David B. Easley, "'It's Not My Imagination, I've Got a Gun on My Back': Style and Sound in Early American Hardcore Punk, 1978–1983" (PhD diss., Florida State University, 2011). Popular music analysis, while valuable, often depends on language limited to theorists and unfamiliar to most musicians, such as Everett's "SRDC" form (statement, restatement, departure, conclusion). Walter Everett, *The Foundations of Rock From "Blue Suede Shoes" to "Suite: Judy Blue Eyes"* (Oxford: Oxford University Press, 2009); Christopher Doll, *Hearing Harmony: Toward a Tonal Theory for the Rock Era* (Ann Arbor: University of Michigan Press, 2017).

62. Stephen Blum, "Rhythmic-Harmonic Cycles in Musical Idioms of the Black Atlantic," paper read at annual meeting of the American Musicological Society, November 13, 2004, 3.

https://www.academia.edu/7648658/Rhythmic-Harmonic_Cycles_Black_Atlantic_AMS_2004_.

63. Stewart Home, *Cranked Up Really High: Genre Theory and Punk Rock* (Hove, UK: Codex, 1995); Joe Carducci, *Rock and the Pop Narcotic: Testament for the Electric Church*, 2nd rev. ed. (Los Angeles: 2.13.61, 1994). Home and Carducci both avoid specific descriptions of musical style and, although critics and journalists are well represented, they rarely include musicians' voices.

64. See Blum, "Rhythmic-Harmonic Cycles"; Peter van der Merwe, *Origins of the Popular Style: The Antecedents of Twentieth-Century Popular Music* (Oxford: Clarendon Press, 1989), 198–204; Richard Middleton, *Studying Popular Music* (Milton Keynes, UK: Open University Press, 1990), 117–19; Tony Russell, *Blacks, Whites, and Blues* (New York: Stein and Day, 1970); Nicholas Stoia, "The Common Stock of Schemes in Early Blues and Country Music," *Music Theory Spectrum* 35/2 (Fall 2013): 194–234; John F. Szwed and Morton Marks, "The Afro-American Transformation of European Set Dances and Dance Suites," *Dance Research Journal* 20/1 (Summer 1988): 29–36.

65. On the transformation of these European dance forms, see Szwed and Marks, "Afro-American Transformation"; and Lawrence Gushee, *Pioneers of Jazz: The Story of the Creole Band* (New York: Oxford University Press, 2005), especially 4–7 on "Musical Exchanges between African and European Americans."

66. Interview by the author, October 28, 2018. To hear "The Ark," visit http://soundcloud.com/paul-roessler.

67. Greg Ginn "loved" the Grateful Dead (Blush, *American Hardcore*, 67), Lee Ranaldo of Sonic Youth "was more into the Grateful Dead kind of world" (Thurston Moore, interview by Charlie Bertsch, *We Owe You Nothing: Punk Planet, The Collected Interviews*, ed. Daniel Sinker [New York: Akashic Books, 2001], 53).

68. Allen Ravenstine, interview by Jason Gross, *Perfect Sound Forever*, accessed July 20, 2017, http://www.furious.com/perfect/allenravenstine3.html.

69. Hynde, *Reckless*, 22.

70. Ronald Radano, "Hot Fantasies: American Modernism and the Idea of Black Rhythm," in *Music and the Racial Imagination*, ed. Ronald Radano and Philip V. Bohlman (Chicago: University of Chicago Press, 2000), 464–65.

71. Lorenz, "Cosmopolitan Folk," 91–94; Jane Jacobs, *The Death and Life of Great American Cities* (New York: Random House, 1961).

72. Radio host Mary Cliff, interview by Stephen Lorenz, quoted in Lorenz, "Cosmopolitan Folk," 93.

73. On arena rock, see Steve Waksman, *This Ain't the Summer of Love: Conflict and Crossover in Heavy Metal and Punk* (Berkeley: University of California Press, 2009).

74. However, see also Michelle Habell-Pallán, *Loca Motion: The Travels of Chicana and Latina Popular Culture* (New York: New York University Press, 2005), 48–49, 150, 160, on the connection of DIY approaches to Chicana/o cultural practices.

75. William Tsitsos, "Rules of Rebellion: Slamdancing, Moshing, and the American Alternative Scene," *Popular Music* 18/3 (October 1999): 409.

76. José Esteban Muñoz, "'Gimme Gimme This . . . Gimme Gimme That': Annihilation and Innovation in the Punk Rock Commons," *Social Text* 31/3 (Fall 2013): 102.

77. Blush, *American Hardcore*, 24.

78. Joey Keithley, *I, Shithead: A Life in Punk* (Vancouver: Arsenal Pulp Press, 2003), 7.

79. Ryan Moore, "Postmodernism and Punk Subculture: Cultures of Authenticity and Deconstruction," *Communication Review* 7/3 (2004): 305–27.

80. Hamilton, *Just Around Midnight*, 18–19. See Jarek Paul Ervin, "New York Punk Rock: Genre as Mourning and Reconciliation (1967–1980)" (PhD diss., University of Virginia, 2017), 40–54, for one overview of rock criticism in relation to punk.

81. Elijah Wald, *How the Beatles Destroyed Rock 'n' Roll* (New York: Oxford University Press, 2009), 9.

82. Wald, *Beatles*, 8.

83. E.g., Legs McNeil and Gillian McCain, *Please Kill Me: The Uncensored Oral History of Punk* (New York: Grove Press, 1996). McNeil and McCain further complicate their roles by claiming "history is always cause and effect" (466), tracing one thing leading to another, which is generally understood by historians to be an important element of narrative but a misrepresentation of the complexities of historical processes (e.g., coincidences).

84. Bernard Gendron, *Between Montmartre and the Mudd Club: Popular Music and the Avant-Garde* (Chicago: University of Chicago Press, 2002).

85. Strummer, *HRR*. See chapter 5 for more on this quote.

86. Fred "Phast Phreddie" Patterson, "Sex Pistols: The Idiot Bastard Sons of Iggy Pop," *Back Door Man* 12 (July/August 1977), 5; Cramps, interview, *Slash* 1/12 (August 1978), 17.

87. The collections cited most frequently in *Damaged* are Greg Shaw's Bomp! Collection, James Brawley's tape collection, and the unedited archives for the *Time-Life History of Rock and Roll*, all located at the Rock and Roll Hall of Fame Library and Archives, and the V. Vale Search and Destroy collection at UCLA.

88. Ruth Finnegan, *The Hidden Musicians: Music Making in an English Town* (Middletown, CT: Wesleyan University Press, [1989] 2007), 6.

89. Interview by the author, November 7, 2018.

90. Don Letts, *HRR*.

91. McNeil and McCain, *Please Kill Me*; Johnny Ramone, *Commando* (New York: Abrams, 2012).

92. Ramone, *Commando*, 18–19.

93. Ramone, *Commando*, 19.

94. E.g., Stacy Russo, *We Were Going to Change the World: Interviews with Women from the 1970s and 1980s Southern California Punk Rock Scene* (Solana Beach, CA: Santa Monica Press, 2017); Viv Albertine, *Clothes, Clothes, Clothes. Music, Music, Music. Boys, Boys, Boys: A Memoir* (New York: St. Martin's Press, 2014); Cosey Fanni Tutti, *art sex music* (London: Faber & Faber, 2017); Alice Bag, *Violence Girl: East L.A. Rage to Hollywood Stage, A Chicana Punk Story* (Port Townsend, WA: Feral House, 2011).

95. Johan Kugelberg punk collection, Cornell University Library; The Riot Grrrl Collection at the Fales Library, New York University; The Sharon Cheslow Punk Flyers Collection, University of Maryland Libraries; *VV*; *BOMP*. On the Fales collection, see also Kate Eichhorn, *The Archival Turn in Feminism: Outrage in Order* (Philadelphia: Temple University Press, 2013).

96. See, e.g., Clinton Heylin, *Anarchy in the Year Zero: The Sex Pistols, the Clash, and the Class of '76* (Pontefract: Route, 2016).

97. For global perspectives on early punk, see, e.g., Caroline de Kergariou, *No future: Une histoire du punk* (Paris: Perrin, 2017); Luc Robène and Solveig Serre, eds., *La scène punk en France (1976–2016)*, special issue of *Volume! La revue des musique populaires* 13/1 (2016); Zona de Obras, ed., *Diccionario de punk y hardcore (España y Latinoamérica)* (Madrid: Fundación Autor, 2011); Jonathan Lukinovic, *La canción punk de los 80 en Chile* (Santiago: Ediciones Oxímoron, 2015); Fréderic Cisnal, *Berlin avant la techno: Du post-punk à la chute du mur* (Marseille: Le Mot et le Reste, 2015); John Greene, "Never Mind the Sex Pistols: Here's French Punk or Why Didn't *le punk français* Go Global?" *Journal of Popular Music Studies* 29 (December

2017), https://doi.org/10.1111/jpms.12241; Christian Eudeline, *Los années punk: 1972–1978* (Paris: Denoël, 2002); Silvio Essinger, *Punk: Anarquia planetária e a cena brasileira* (São Paulo: Editora 34, 1999); Ulrike Groos, Peter Gorschlüter, and Jürgen Teipel, eds., *Zurück zum Beton: Die Anfänge von Punk und New Wave in Deutschland 1977–82* (Köln: Verlag der Buchhandlung Walther König, 2002); Ronald Galenza, "Zwischen Plan und Planlos: Punk in Deutschland," in Barbara Hammerschmitt and Bernd Lindner, eds., *Rock! Jugend und Musik in Deutschland* (Berlin: Links, 2005); Il'ya Stogov, Aleksei Viktorovich Rubin, and Vladimir Tikhomirov, *Anarkhiya v RF: Pervaya polnaya istoriya russkogo panka* (Saint Petersburg: Amfora, 2007); and Jarkko Kuivanen, *Suomipunk 1977–1998* (Helsinki, 1999).

## Part One: *punk (adj.)*

1. Delmont, *Why Busing Failed*, 52, 227n115.

2. The FHA and VA created color-coded maps to determine eligibility for federally insured home loans, with African American neighborhoods or those determined in risk of becoming so colored red, meaning they were ineligible for such loans. See Massey, "Legacy of the 1968 Fair Housing Act," 573–74.

3. Massey, "Legacy of the 1968 Fair Housing Act"; Richard Rothstein, "The Supreme Court's Challenge to Housing Segregation," *American Prospect*, July 5, 2015, https://prospect.org/article/supreme-courts-challenge-housing-segregation.

4. Painter, *History of White People*, 359–73.

5. Ray Suarez, *The Old Neighborhood: What We Lost in the Great Suburban Migration, 1966–1999* (New York: Free Press, 1999), 122.

6. Maureen Mahon, *Right to Rock: The Black Rock Coalition and the Cultural Politics of Race* (New York: New York University Press, 2004), 92, 204–5.

7. James Brown, *HRR*.

8. Evan Rapport, "Hearing Punk as Blues," *Popular Music* 33/1 (January 2014): 39–67.

9. Jerry Leiber and Mike Stoller are prominent and straightforward examples, penning "Hound Dog" (1953) for "Big Mama" Thornton (and later one of Elvis Presley's biggest hits), "Yakety Yak" (1958) for the Coasters, and "Jailhouse Rock" (1957) for Presley.

10. Various artists, *Anthology of American Folk Music, Vol. 1: Ballads*, Folkways FP 251, 1952; *Vol. 2: Social Music*, Folkways FP 252, 1952; *Vol. 3: Songs*, Folkways FP 253, 1952; Lorenz, "Cosmopolitan Folk," 100–102.

11. Kramer, *The Hard Stuff*, 88.

12. Mahon, *Right to Rock*, 249; Tammy L. Kernodle, "'I Wish I Knew How It Would Feel to Be Free': Nina Simone and the Redefining of the Freedom Song of the 1960s," *Journal of the Society for American Music* 2/3 (August 2008): 295–317.

13. Ann Larabee and Mathew Bartkowiak, "Interview with John Sinclair," *Journal for the Study of Radicalism* 1/2 (Spring 2007): 131; Kramer, *The Hard Stuff*, 88. See also Mahon, *Right to Rock*, 28.

14. Mathew Bartkowiak, "Motor City Burning: Rock and Rebellion in the WPP and the MC5," *Journal for the Study of Radicalism* 1/2 (Spring 2007): 55–76; Larabee and Bartkowiak, "Interview with John Sinclair," 129–40. See also Slobin, *Motor City Music*, 160, on the Artists' Workshop.

15. He would have been about eighteen years old at the time. Bill Harkleroad, *Lunar Notes: Zoot Horn Rollo's Captain Beefheart Experience* (London: SAF Publishing, 1998), 20.

16. Kramer, *The Hard Stuff*, 77.

17. See also Suarez, *The Old Neighborhood*, 8–12.

18. Interview by the author, August 30, 2012.

19. Beginning in 1868, the Cuyahoga has caught fire thirteen times, the most damaging incident occurring November 3, 1952. Nonetheless, the fire of 1969 received the most media coverage and retains the most symbolic value for most people. *Ohio History Central*, http:// www.ohiohistorycentral.org/w/Cuyahoga_River_Fire.

20. Charlotte Pressler, "Those Were Different Times: A Memoir of Cleveland Life: 1967–1973 (Part One)," *CLE* 3A (1978).

21. Ravenstine, interview by Gross.

22. Gerald F. Goodwin, "Black and White in Vietnam," *New York Times*, July 18, 2017, https:// www.nytimes.com/2017/07/18/opinion/racism-vietnam-war.html.

23. Iggy Pop, *I Need More* (Los Angeles: 2.13.61 Publications, 1997), 47.

24. Interview by the author, October 25, 2018.

25. Hynde, *Reckless*, 80–82.

26. Casale, *HRR*.

27. Hynde, *Reckless*, 93.


## Chapter 2: "Raw Power": Protopunk Transformations of the Blues

1. Alan Suicide [Vega], interview by Edit De Ak, *No Magazine* 3 (Summer 1979): 8.

2. Sasha Frere-Jones, "Terra Cognita: Savages Carefully Reinvents the Wheel," *New Yorker*, May 6, 2013; Theo Cateforis, *Are We Not New Wave? Modern Pop at the Turn of the 1980s* (Ann Arbor: University of Michigan Press, 2011), 201.

3. On the "punk paradox," see Steven Taylor, *False Prophet: Field Notes from the Punk Underground* (Middletown, CT: Wesleyan University Press, 2003).

4. Elijah Wald, *Escaping the Delta: Robert Johnson and the Invention of the Blues* (New York: HarperCollins, 2004), 233–49; Paul Oliver, *Blues Fell This Morning: Meaning in the Blues* (London: Cassel, 1960); Miller, *Segregating Sound*; Sam Charters, *The Country Blues* (New York: Rinehart, 1959). See also Charles Keil, *Urban Blues* (Chicago: University of Chicago Press, 1966); Amiri Baraka, *Black Music* (New York: William Morrow, 1967); and John Gennari, *Blowin' Hot and Cool: Jazz and Its Critics* (Chicago: University of Chicago Press, 2006), 251–98.

5. Lorenz, "Cosmopolitan Folk," 190–318.

6. Mezz Mezzrow and Bernard Wolfe, *Really the Blues* (New York: Signet, [1946] 1964).

7. Norman Mailer, "The White Negro," *Dissent*, Fall 1957; George, *Death of Rhythm and Blues*, 61–62; see also Eric Lott, *Love and Theft: Blackface Minstrelsy and the American Working Class* (New York: Oxford University Press, 1993), 49–55, for nineteenth-century precedents.

8. Mailer, "White Negro"; Mezzrow and Wolfe, *Really the Blues*, 251–57.

9. Schomburg Center, "Second Great Migration."

10. Interview by the author, August 30, 2012.

11. Slobin, *Motor City Music*, 162–72.

12. See also Jon Stratton, *Jews, Race, and Popular Music* (Surrey: Ashgate, 2009), 79–103.

13. Pop, *HRR*.

14. Interview by the author, August 30, 2012. See Slobin, *Motor City Music*, 172–78, on Detroit radio.

15. Pop, *HRR*.

16. Hynde, *Reckless*, 32–33.

17. Dave Marsh, *Zig Zag* (December 1970), reprinted in Carrie Kania, ed., and Ed Caraeff, photographs, *Iggy & the Stooges: One Night at the Whisky 1970* (Woodbridge, UK: ACC Art Books, 2017), 186. Robert Sheff ("Blue" Gene Tyranny) was the keyboardist in the group.

18. Pop, *I Need More*, 47.

19. Mahon, *Right to Rock*, 205.

20. Lorenz, "Cosmopolitan Folk," 195; Iggy Pop, "Times Talks: Iggy Pop," interview by Ben Ratliff, New York Public Library, June 24, 2009; Wald, *Escaping the Delta*, 82.

21. Keil, *Urban Blues*, 34–35.

22. Hamilton, *Just Around Midnight*, 67–68.

23. See, for example, Lynn Abbott and Doug Seroff, "'They Cert'ly Sound Good to Me': Sheet Music, Southern Vaudeville, and the Commercial Ascendancy of the Blues," in *Ramblin' on My Mind: New Perspectives on the Blues*, ed. David Evans (Urbana: University of Illinois Press, 2008), 49–104.

24. Miller, *Segregating Sound*, 72–73.

25. Wald, *Escaping the Delta*, 58–59.

26. Cohodas, *Spinning Blues*; Wald, *Escaping the Delta*, 245.

27. Lorenz, "Cosmopolitan Folk," 192.

28. See Lorenz, "Cosmopolitan Folk," 201–5, for more on Charters.

29. Amiri Baraka [LeRoi Jones], *Blues People: The Negro Experience in White America and the Music That Developed from It* (New York: William Morrow, 1963).

30. Baraka, *Blues People*, 90, 176.

31. Baraka, *Blues People*, 122–41. See also Ralph Ellison, "The Blues" (Review of *Blues People*), *New York Review of Books*, February 6, 1964, reprinted in *Shadow and Act* (New York: Vintage, 1995), 252; and Mahon, *Right to Rock*, 10–12.

32. Ellison, "The Blues," 253.

33. Baraka, *Black Music*, 205.

34. Wald, *Escaping the Delta*, 243–49; George, *Death of Rhythm and Blues*, 107–8; Cohodas, *Spinning Blues into Gold*, 241–44; Dave Headlam, "Blues Transformations in the Music of Cream," in *Understanding Rock*, ed. John Covach and Graeme M. Boone, 59–92 (New York: Oxford University Press, 1997); Roberta Freund Schwartz, *How Britain Got the Blues: The Transmission and Reception of American Blues Style in the United Kingdom* (Aldershot: Ashgate, 2007); Ulrich Adelt, *Blues Music in the Sixties: A Story in Black and White* (New Brunswick: Rutgers University Press, 2010).

35. George, *Rhythm and Blues*, 77–108; Wald, *How the Beatles Destroyed Rock 'n' Roll*, 243–47.

36. Spottswood quoted in Lorenz, "Cosmopolitan Folk," 248.

37. Rob Bowman, "The Stax Sound: A Musicological Analysis," *Popular Music* 14/3 (October 1995): 295; see also Baraka, *Black Music*, 185–86.

38. See also Kernodle, "'I Wish I Knew.'"

39. Steve Waksman, "Kick Out the Jams! The MC5 and the Politics of Noise," in *Mapping the Beat: Popular Music and Contemporary Theory*, ed. Thomas Swiss, John Sloop, and Andrew Herman (Malden, MA: Blackwell, 1998); Sheila Whiteley, "'Kick Out the Jams': Creative Anarchy and Noise in 1960s Rock," in *Resonances: Noise and Contemporary Music*, ed. Michael Goddard, Benjamin Halligan, and Nicola Spelman (New York: Bloomsbury, 2013), 13–23.

40. Hamilton, *Just Around Midnight*, 219.

41. Interview by the author, August 30, 2012.

42. Iggy Pop, "Times Talks."

43. Iggy Pop, "The 100 Greatest Singers of All Time. #10: James Brown," *Rolling Stone*, November 26, 2008.

44. Interview by the author, August 30, 2012.

45. The 1978 dates are according to Google's Ngram application (books.google.com/ngram). The *Oxford English Dictionary* dates the first citation of *protopunk* in 1973, in a reference to the Surfaris' "Surfer Joe" (1963). See also de Kergariou, *No Future*, 501–11, on issues surrounding *punk* and *postpunk*.

46. Jas Obrecht, "'See See Rider Blues'—Gertrude 'Ma' Rainey (1924)," Library of Congress website, accessed December 12, 2008, https://www.loc.gov/programs/static/national-recording -preservation-board/documents/Ma%20Rainey.pdf.

47. Gerhard Kubik, *Africa and the Blues* (Jackson: University Press of Mississippi, 1999), 42. See also Peter Muir, *Long Lost Blues: Popular Blues in America, 1850–1920* (Urbana: University of Illinois Press, 2010).

48. Compare also the genealogy of "Corrine Corrina," discussed in Waterman, "Race Music."

49. Iggy Pop, "Times Talks."

50. Eric Lott, "Back Door Man: Howlin' Wolf and the Sound of Jim Crow," *American Quarterly* 63/3 (September 2011): 702.

51. Tyler Wilcox, "Peter Laughner—Mr. Charlie 1969 / The Ann Arbor Tapes 1976," *Doom and Gloom from the Tomb* (blog), June 22, 2015, https://doomandgloomfromthetomb.tumblr .com/post/122172039577/peter-laughner-mr-charlie-1969-the-ann-arbor.

52. Tyler Wilcox, "Peter Laughner & The Original Wolverines—WMMS Coffee Break Concert, Cleveland, Ohio, September 20, 1972," *Doom and Gloom from the Tomb* (blog), June 22, 2016, https://doomandgloomfromthetomb.tumblr.com/post/146308495692/ peter-laughner-the-original-wolverines-wmms.

53. Hear also the MC5 version released in 1999 on *'66 Breakout!*, Total Energy NER 3023, [1966] 1999.

54. Iggy Pop, *HRR*.

55. Exene Cervenka, *HRR*.

56. Although "Foggy Notion" was not commercially released until 1985, it was a standard part of Velvet Underground concerts and known by fans of the group who had seen them live. Two live versions can be heard on *The Velvet Underground Bootleg Series, Volume 1: The Quine Tapes*, Universal 589 067, 2001.

57. Interview by the author, August 30, 2012.

58. See also Baraka, *Black Music*, 194–99; and Clinton Heylin, *From the Velvets to the Voidoids: The Birth of American Punk Rock* (Chicago: A Capella Books, [1993] 2005), 33. For more on the reception of John Coltrane, Albert Ayler, and others among white and black listeners during the 1960s, see Robert K. McMichael, "'We Insist—Freedom Now!' Black Moral Authority, Jazz, and the Changeable Shape of Whiteness," *American Music* 16/4 (Winter 1998): 375–416.

59. Bangs, "Dead Lie the Velvets," 291.

60. Heylin, *From the Velvets*, 95.

61. John Lydon, with Keith and Kent Zimmerman, *Rotten: No Irish, No Blacks, No Dogs* (New York: Picador USA, 1994), 228.

62. Iggy Pop, *HRR*.

63. Lester Bangs, *Psychotic Reactions and Carburetor Dung*, ed. Greil Marcus (New York: Vintage Books, [1970] 1988), 43.

64. Lenny Kaye, review of Velvet Underground's *Loaded*, *Rolling Stone*, December 14, 1970, https://www.rollingstone.com/music/music-album-reviews/loaded-111308/.

65. Kugelberg, *The Velvet Underground*, 16.

66. David Carson, *Grit, Noise, and Revolution: The Birth of Detroit Rock 'n' Roll* (Ann Arbor: University of Michigan Press, 2006), 265.

67. The Modern Lovers' "Foggy Notion" can be heard on *Precise Modern Lovers Order*, Rounder CD 9042, 1994. As mentioned, "Foggy Notion" was known from live performances although unreleased; Jonathan Richman introduced the tune to the Berkeley, California, audience with: "Now the first one is one that we didn't write, it's one that the Velvet Underground wrote and never released, so you've never heard this one before. We like to do this as a tribute to the Velvet Underground. We all saw them a lot back east."

68. Benjamin Piekut, *Experimentalism Otherwise: The New York Avant-Garde and Its Limits* (Berkeley: University of California Press, 2011), 189–93.

69. Alan Licht, "The Hum of the City: La Monte Young and the Birth of NYC Drone," *Red Bull Music Academy Daily*, May 1, 2013, http://daily.redbullmusicacademy.com/2013/05/the-hum-of-the-city-la-monte-young.

70. Jeremy Grimshaw, *Draw a Straight Line and Follow It: The Music and Mysticism of La Monte Young* (New York: Oxford University Press, 2011), 23–24; see also Piekut, *Experimentalism Otherwise*, 72–73, and chapter 2 generally about Young's associate Henry Flynt, who had an intense and unsettled relationship with the ideas of black music and American folk music.

71. Grimshaw, *Draw a Straight Line*, 24.

72. La Monte Young, "The Forever Bad Blues Band," in liner notes to *Just Stompin'*, 7, quoted in Grimshaw, *Draw a Straight Line*, 24, 197n19.

73. Grimshaw, *Draw a Straight Line*, 88.

74. The recordings released as *The Modern Lovers* in 1976 were recorded in 1971 and 1972. Suicide billed themselves as "Punk Music By Suicide" in 1970. Johan Kugelberg and Jon Savage, eds., *Punk: An Aesthetic* (New York: Rizzoli, 2012), 48–50.

75. Although I have been unable to find any recordings of Suicide before *The First Rehearsal Tapes* from 1975, their sound is notably consistent from 1975 through the debut album on Red Star. As reported by Simon Reynolds, "Cheree" and "Ghost Rider" were their first songs. I believe I can safely infer that the approach heard on their recordings from 1975 is at least partially representative of their sound from 1970 to 1974. Simon Reynolds, *Rip it Up and Start Again: Postpunk 1978–1984* (New York: Penguin, 2006), 143.

76. Feelies, live at CBGB, September 18, 1977, *JBC*.

77. Walter Everett, "Making Sense of Rock's Tonal Systems," *Music Theory Online* 10/4 (December 2004), http://www.mtosmt.org/issues/mto.04.10.4/mto.04.10.4.w_everett.html.

78. See Robert Walser, *Running with the Devil: Power, Gender, and Madness in Heavy Metal Music* (Middletown, CT: Wesleyan University Press, 1993), 8–9 ("A heavy metal genealogy ought to trace the music back to African-American blues, but this is seldom done," 8); and Kevin Fellezs, "Black Metal Soul Music: Stone Vengeance and the Aesthetics of Race in Heavy Metal," in *Hardcore, Punk, and Other Junk: Aggressive Sounds in Contemporary Music*, ed. Eric James Abbey and Colin Helb (Lanham, MD: Lexington Books, 2014), 121–37. On the intertwined history of punk and heavy metal, see Waksman, *This Ain't the Summer of Love*.

79. Velvet Underground, interview by David Fricke, New York Public Library, December 8, 2009.

80. Velvet Underground, interview by Fricke.

81. Alexander Stewart, "'Funky Drummer': New Orleans, James Brown and the Rhythmic Transformation of American Popular Music," *Popular Music* 19/3 (October 2000): 296.

82. Alexander Stewart, "Make It Funky: Fela Kuti, James Brown and the Invention of Afrobeat," *American Studies* 52/4 (2013): 99–118.

83. Alan Licht, "Notes on Robert Quine," *Perfect Sound Forever*, accessed August 12, 2012, http://www.furious.com/perfect/quine/licht.html.

84. Angela Y. Davis, *Blues Legacies and Black Feminism: Gertrude "Ma" Rainey, Bessie Smith, and Billie Holiday* (New York: Pantheon, 1998).

85. Waksman, "Kick Out the Jams," 59.

86. Iggy Pop, "Times Talks"; David Nobakht, *Suicide: No Compromise* (London: SAF Publishing, 2004), 21.

87. Throughout *Damaged* I use the spellings as employed by the individuals under discussion. Patti Smith's spelling and pronunciation of "nigger" with the *-er* ending are essential elements of her particular usages. Altering the spelling—in this case, to "Rock N Roll Nigga," as is common on the internet—reflects a complete misunderstanding of Smith's song and does a huge disservice to the historical record.

88. Patti Smith setlists, setlists.pattismith.logbook.info; "Nigger Book" live at the Bottom Line, New York, December 28, 1975. https://www.youtube.com/watch?v=welUa71V570.

89. https://www.youtube.com/watch?v=kzsKRbGwcKQ (accessed 19 June 2018); Patti Smith, liner notes to *Radio Ethiopia*, Arista AL4097, 1976.

90. Jeff Chang, *Who We Be: The Colorization of America* (New York: St. Martin's Press, 2014), 85; see also chapter 5, "Color Theory," which details the saga of Donald Newman's *The Nigger Drawings*, apparently inspired by the Patti Smith song.

91. Patti Smith, interview by Lee Paris, *Search and Destroy* 4 (1977), reprinted in *Search & Destroy #1–6: The Complete Reprint*, ed. V. Vale (San Francisco: V/Search Publications, 1996), 69.

92. Mahon, *Right to Rock*, 204.

93. Russell, *Blacks, Whites and Blues*; Wald, *The Blues*, 99–102.

94. Lott, *Love and Theft*.

95. Hasia R. Diner, "Trading Faces," *CommonQuest* 2/1 (Summer 1997): 40–44.

96. Velvet Underground, interview by Fricke.


## Chapter 3: "Ignorance of Your Culture Is Not Considered Cool": Reconsidering the Avant-Garde Impulse in American Punk

1. The question of whether or not these were "Klansmen" is discussed in more detail in this chapter.

2. Following the lead of the musicians themselves, I use *experimental* and *avant-garde* interchangeably. I agree with Piekut that "doing otherwise would naturalize a difference that has been discursively produced"; Piekut, *Experimentalism Otherwise*, 14. For the musicians in this chapter, *avant-garde* was most commonly used, but today *experimental* seems to better connote their techniques and attitudes.

3. Dave Warden, *The Cryptic Guide to the Residents* (San Francisco: Bach's Decay, 1986), Jim Clevo papers, Rock and Roll Hall of Fame Library and Archives. Very early Residents projects include their first group, the Delta Nudes, the long unreleased reel-to-reel tapes *Rusty Coathangers for the Doctor* (recorded June 1970), *The Ballad of Stuffed Trigger* (recorded August 1970), *The Warner Bros. Album* (recorded September 1970 to May 1971), and *Baby Sex* (recorded August to November 1971).

4. Mike Kelley and Dan Nadel, eds., *Return of the Repressed: Destroy All Monsters 1973–1977* (New York and Los Angeles: PictureBox and PRISM, 2011).

5. Benjamin Piekut, *Henry Cow: The World is a Problem* (Durham, NC: Duke University Press, 2019), 387.

6. Half Japanese, *1/2 Gentlemen/Not Beasts*, Armageddon A Box 1, 1980.

7. Albertine, *Clothes Clothes Clothes*, 36.

8. DEVO, interview (part 2), *Search and Destroy* 3 (1977), reprinted in *Search & Destroy #1–6: The Complete Reprint*, 53.

9. Casale, *HRR*; DEVO, *Hardcore DEVO Volume 1*, Rykodisc RCD 10188, 1990.

10. Captain Beefheart is endlessly invoked as a touchstone for punk, but rarely with specificity of how or why punk musicians expanded on his music. E.g., "... *Trout Mask Replica* embodied the punk aesthetic eight years before it exploded in the UK with the Sex Pistols." Kevin Courrier, *Trout Mask Replica* (New York: Continuum, 2007), 12.

11. Various artists, *Blorp Esette Vol. 1*, LAFMS 5, 1977, compiled by Ace Farren Ford, featured a Residents track ("Whoopy Snorp") and cover art by Don Van Vliet (Captain Beefheart); *Light Bulb Magazine 4 Emergency Cassette Vol. 1 and 2*, LAFMS, 1981, compiled by Fredrik Nilsen and Dennis Duck, contained tracks by Jad Fair, 45 Grave, Bpeople, Phranc, and Meat Puppets.

12. Letter from Jad Fair to V. Vale, postmarked November 25, 1978, *VV*; see also Mark Jenkins, "Half Japanese Yik Yak: White Boys Makin' White Noise," *Descenes* 1/4 (November 1979): 7–9.

13. Marcus, *Lipstick Traces*; Jon Savage, *England's Dreaming: Anarchy, Sex Pistols, Punk Rock, and Beyond* (London: Faber and Faber, 1991), 27–36 et passim; Neil Nehring, *Flowers in the Dustbin: Culture, Anarchy, and Postwar England* (Ann Arbor: University of Michigan Press, 1993). See de Kergariou, *No Future*, 28–31, for a brief but trenchant critique of references to Situationist ideas in Marcus and Savage.

14. Marcus, *Lipstick Traces*, 6.

15. Marcus, *Lipstick Traces*, 16–22, 77–78, 87; also "[t]he question of ancestry in culture is spurious" (19) and "[r]eal mysteries cannot be solved, but they can be turned into better mysteries" (22).

16. See, e.g., Bradford D. Martin, *The Theater Is in the Street: Politics and Public Performance in Sixties America* (Amherst: University of Massachusetts Press, 2004), on the Living Theatre (NY).

17. See also Neil Nehring, "The Situationist Internationale in American Hardcore Punk, 1982–2002," *Popular Music and Society* 29/5 (December 2006): 519–30.

18. "Le liens tant conscients qu'inconscients entre situationnisme et punk semblent donc bien ténus, bien plus en tout cas qu'ils ne sont présentés dans la littérature anglo-saxonne...."; de Kergariou, *No Future*, 31. Translation by the author.

19. Recordings of DEVO dating back to 1974 can be heard on DEVO, *Hardcore DEVO Volume 1*, Rykodisc RCD 10188, 1990, and *Hardcore DEVO Volume 2*, Rykodisc 20208, 1991.

20. Pere Ubu, interview by Julene and David Deluca, *Search and Destroy* 6 (1978), reprinted in *Search & Destroy #1–6: The Complete Reprint*, 134.

21. Jello Biafra, interview by Peter Belsito, *Notes from the Pop Underground* (Berkeley: Last Gasp of San Francisco, 1985), 116.

22. Matthew Worley, *No Future: Punk, Politics and British Youth Culture, 1976–1984* (Cambridge: Cambridge University Press, 2017), 111–38.

23. Captain Beefheart gave all of his band members new names. The players on *Trout Mask Replica* were Bill Harkleroad (Zoot Horn Rollo), guitar; Mark Boston (Rockette Morton), bass; Jeff Cotton (Antennae Jimmy Semens), guitar and vocals; and John French (Drumbo), drums; with some contributions by Beefheart's cousin, Victor Hayden (The Mascara Snake).

24. Harkleroad, *Lunar Notes*, 38.

25. Martin, *Theater Is in the Street*, 86–124; Tim Hodgdon, *Manhood in the Age of Aquarius: Masculinity in Two Countercultural Communities, 1965–83* (New York: Columbia University Press, 2008), 7.

26. Martin, *Theater Is in the Street*, 87. See also Kugelberg and Savage, *Punk*, 76–77.

27. Martin, *Theater Is in the Street*, 94.

28. Ben Morea and Ron Hahne, *Black Mask and Up Against the Wall Motherfucker* (Oakland, CA: PM Press, 2011); Home, *Cranked Up Really High*, 26–27; Kramer, *The Hard Stuff*, 96–102.

29. Martin, *Theater Is in the Street*, 70.

30. Pressler, *Those Were Different Times*.

31. Liner notes to *Terminal Drive*, Smog Veil Records, SV133, 2017; Ravenstine, interview by Gross.

32. Greil Marcus, liner notes to reissue of *Anthology of American Folk Music*, Smithsonian Folkways SFW40090, 1997, 5; Lorenz, "Cosmopolitan Folk," 101.

33. Lorenz, "Cosmopolitan Folk," 199–200. See Miller, *Segregating Sound*, on the broader history of the racialization of common-stock repertoires and the recasting of popular music recordings as folk music.

34. John Encarnacao, *Punk Aesthetics and New Folk: Way Down the Old Plank Road* (Surrey: Ashgate, 2013), 59–74.

35. Marcus, liner notes to *Anthology*, 7. See also Encarnacao, *Punk Aesthetics*, 62.

36. Hamilton, *Just Around Midnight*, 61, 67–68.

37. Harkleroad, *Lunar Notes*, 21. Hear, e.g., Captain Beefheart, "Diddy Wah Diddy" single; "Plastic Factory," *Safe as Milk*; "Gimme Dat Harp Boy," *Strictly Personal*, Blue Thumb BTS1, 1968.

38. Langdon Winner, "I'm Not Even Here I Just Stick Around For My Friends: The Odyssey of Captain Beefheart," *Rolling Stone* 58, May 14, 1970.

39. Harkleroad, *Lunar Notes*, 35–36.

40. Elaine Shepherd, prod. and dir., *The Artist Formerly Known as Captain Beefheart*, BBC, 1997.

41. X_X, "A" (1979) and "Approaching the Minimal with Spray Guns" (1980); John D. Morton, *the eyeball of hell (annotated), or How One Single Man's Expectation of Self Becomes the Hopes and Dreams of the Lumpen Prole*, accessed July 20, 2017, http://www.pukekos.org/2013/01/electric-eels.html (site discontinued).

42. Mike Barnes, *Captain Beefheart: The Biography*, rev. ed. (London: Omnibus, 2011), 89.

43. Partch had been back living in California since 1962, and in 1970 his *Genesis of a Music* was republished by Da Capo Press.

44. Richard M. Kassel, "The Evolution of Harry Partch's Monophony" (PhD diss., City University of New York, 1996), 2.

45. Harry Partch was also living in the similar-sounding Encinitas, California, from 1969 until his death in 1974.

46. Lott, *Love and Theft*, 4.

47. Lorenz, "Cosmopolitan Folk," 212.

48. Lloyd Whitesell, "White Noise: Race and Erasure in the Cultural Avant-Garde," *American Music* 19/2 (Summer 2001): 168–89; Reich made *Come Out* with access to the testimonies, granted after he made a tape collage of them for a fundraising event to raise money for a retrial of the Harlem Six. Thanks to Derek Baron for their clarification of the history of *Come Out*.

49. Encarnacao, *Punk Aesthetics*, 106.

50. Samuel Andrew Granade II, "'I Was a Bum Once Myself': Harry Partch, *U.S. Highball*, and the Dust Bowl in the American Imagination" (PhD diss., University of Illinois, Urbana-Champaign, 2005), 69.

51. Library of Congress, *Voices from the Dust Bowl: The Charles L. Todd and Robert Sonkin Migrant Worker Collection, 1940 to 1941*, accessed December 21, 2018, http://memory.loc.gov/ammem/afctshtml/tshome.html.

52. Various artists, *Anthology of American Folk Music*; Various artists, *Goodbye, Babylon*, Dust-to-Digital DTD-01, 2003.

53. Barnes, *Captain Beefheart*, 92. In the revised edition of his Captain Beefheart biography, Mike Barnes added to the "Ella Guru" paragraph: "high yellow" as "a phrase, now thankfully

out of commission, to describe a person of a particular racial mix." This type of bowdleriza-
tion seems to come from discomfort with the term and an admirer's desire to paint Beefheart
favorably and avoid indications of racism, misogyny, or ignorance. However, it may undermine
the complexity of Beefheart's reference and the discomfort that I believe Beefheart intended to
generate in the first place.

54. Lott, *Love and Theft*, 159–68.

55. Lott, *Love and Theft*, 159.

56. Barnes, *Beefheart*, 99–100.

57. Krystyn R. Moon, *Yellowface: Creating the Chinese in American Popular Music and Performance, 1850s–1920s* (New Brunswick, NJ: Rutgers University Press, 2005).

58. Moon, *Yellowface*, 34–38, 42–52.

59. Zack Ruskin, "What the World Needs Now is Devo," *SF Weekly*, June 28, 2018.

60. Liner notes to Residents, *Meet the Residents*.

61. Ian Shirley, *Meet the Residents: America's Most Eccentric Band!* (Wembley, UK: SAF
Publishing, 1998), 45.

62. Chris Cutler, *File Under Popular* (Brooklyn: Autonomedia, 1993), 81.

63. The film *Vileness Fats* was shot in the early 1970s and never completed and released
until 1984, when the Residents edited and released a cut from the existing footage as *Whatever
Happened to Vileness Fats?* The blackface character is played by their friend Schwump (Barry
Schwam). Paulie, "Mole Interview," Barry Schwam & Schwump.com, accessed July 17, 2019,
http://pickleparade.tripod.com/id18.html.

64. Albums released in connection with *The Mole Trilogy* were *Mark of the Mole* (1981), *The
Tunes of Two Cities* (1982), *Intermission* (1982), and *The Big Bubble* (1985), along with the live
*Mole Show* (1983), originally a bootleg.

65. Matt Groening, "The True Story of the Residents: A Brief Summary of Known Facts,
Top Secrets, Hazy Details, Veiled Hints, and Blatant Lies," in *The Cryptic Guide to the Residents*,
ed. Dave Warden (San Francisco: Bach's Decay, 1986). Jim Clevo papers, Rock and Roll Hall
of Fame Archives and Museum. Originally published in *The Official W.E.I.R.D. Book of the
Residents* (1979).

66. Groening, "True Story."

67. Cryptic Corporation, "Third Reich 'n Roll (1976)," Residents.com, accessed January 6,
2018, http://www.residents.com/historical/?page=thirdreichandroll.

68. Ralph Records catalog #2, August 1977, *VV*.

69. Cary Levine, "Worried Man," in *Mark Mothersbaugh: Myopia*, ed. Adam Lerner (New
York: Princeton Architectural Press, 2014), 99. See also Cateforis, *Are We Not New Wave?*,
101–4.

70. RoseLee Goldberg, *Performance Art: From Futurism to the Present*, rev. and exp. ed.
(New York: Thames & Hudson, 2001), 76.

71. Goldberg, *Performance Art*, 55–66. Hugo Ball's sound poem, "gadji beri bimba" would be
adapted by Talking Heads for "I Zimbra," *Fear of Music*, Sire SRK 6076, 1979. See also Gendron,
*Between Montmartre*, 30–31, 72–79.

72. Jade Dellinger and David Giffels, *Are We Not Men? We Are Devo!* (London: SAF Publishing, 2003).

73. Adam Lerner, "Formative Years," in *Mark Mothersbaugh: Myopia*, 58.

74. Maria Elena Buszek, "Punk Rock Futurist," in *Mark Mothersbaugh: Myopia*, , 77–89.

75. Casale, *HRR*.

76. Mark Mothersbaugh, interview by Adam Lerner, in *Mark Mothersbaugh: Myopia*, 32.

77. Lerner, "Formative Years," 65.

78. Buszek, "Punk Rock Futurist," 82.

79. Mothersbaugh, interview by Lerner, 40; John Heartfield, *Photomontages of the Nazi Period* (New York: Universe Books, 1977).

80. Mothersbaugh, interview by Lerner, 37.

81. Lerner, "Formative Years," 66.

82. Mothersbaugh, interview by Lerner, 33. B. H. Shadduck, *Jocko-Homo Heavenbound* (Rogers, OH: Jocko-Homo Publishing, 1925).

83. B. H. Shadduck, *Rastus Agustus Explains Evolution* (Rogers, OH: Homo Publishing, 1928).

84. Kelley and Nadel, *Return of the Repressed*; Destroy All Monsters, *Destroy All Monsters Magazine* (New York: Primary Information, 2011); Cary Loren, "a manifesto of ignorance; destroy all monsters," *Perfect Sound Forever*, May 1996, http://www.furious.com/perfect/dam.html.

85. Morton, *the eyeball of hell*.

86. Morton, *the eyeball of hell*.

87. Piekut, *Experimentalism Otherwise*, 177–93; Pop, *HRR*.

88. George E. Lewis, *A Power Stronger than Itself: The A.A.C.M. and American Experimental Music* (Chicago: University of Chicago Press, 2008); Paul Steinbeck, *Message to Our Folks: The Art Ensemble of Chicago* (Chicago: University of Chicago Press, 2017).

89. See also Jay Keister, "The Long Freak Out: Unfinished Music and Countercultural Madness in Avant-Garde Rock of the 1960s and 1970s," in *Countercultures and Popular Music*, ed. Sheila Whiteley and Jedediah Sklower (Surrey, UK: Ashgate, 2014), 141–56.

90. Marc Masters, *No Wave* (London: Black Dog Publishing, 2007), 72–104.

91. Music from these bands and others from the scene are available on *Punk 45: Extermination Nights in the Sixth City! Cleveland, Ohio: Punk and the Decline of the Mid West 1975–82*, Soul Jazz Records SJRCD300, 2015; and Pere Ubu, *Datapanik in the Year Zero*.

92. Casale, *HRR*.

93. Liner notes to *LAFMS: The Lowest Form of Music*, 5.

94. Liner notes to *LAFMS: The Lowest Form of Music*, 4.

95. Ravenstine is probably referring to Doris Day's LP *Doris Day's Sentimental Journey*, Columbia CL2360, 1965, which reprised her hit version of 1944 singing with the Les Brown Orchestra.

96. Ravenstine, interview by Gross.

97. *Terminal Drive* went unreleased until "Home Life" (the final section) was released on *Datapanik in the Year Zero* (1996). The entire composition was finally released on Smog Veil Records SV133, 2017.

98. Alan Suicide [Vega], *Art-Rite* 13, January 1977.

99. Snakefinger was Philip Lithman, one of the Residents' main collaborators. https://www.youtube.com/watch?v=Uxmo8IKY9ss. Thanks to "Pickle," who pointed out this segment in a lively internet discussion thread in 2004.

100. Don Hardy, dir., *Theory of Obscurity: A Film about the Residents*, DoF Media and KTF Films, 2015. Thanks to Travis Jackson for help with accessing this film.

101. https://www.moma.org/interactives/exhibitions/2008/lookingatmusic/index.html.

102. Lewis, "Improvised Music."

103. Lewis, "Improvised Music," 100–104, 109–11.

## Chapter 4: "Pure Rock and Roll with No Blues or Folk or Any of That Stuff in It"

1. Timothy White, "The Importance of Being a Ramone," *Rolling Stone*, February 8, 1979.

2. Ernie Santosuosso, "Punk Rock," *Boston Sunday Globe*, August 29, 1976.

3. Tommy Ramone, press release for the Ramones, viewed as part of Queens Museum exhibit; Kugelberg and Savage, *Punk*, 133–34. See also Johnny Ramone, *Commando*, 95.

4. John Felice, interview by Jonathan Perry, *RPM: Jonathan Perry's Life in Analog*, September 21, 2014, https://rpmlifeinanalog.com/2014/09/21/return-of-the-real-kids-part-ii-john -felice-on-rock-roll-resurrections-dont-call-it-punk-shaking-outta-control-and-living-past -thirty/. Emphasis in original transcription.

5. Joe Strummer, *HRR*.

6. Ben Sisario, "Johnny Ramone, Pioneer Punk Guitarist, Is Dead at 55," *New York Times*, September 17, 2004.

7. I have been unable to find any documentation of Johnny Ramone ever having said "pure white rock 'n' roll," and none of the published versions of the quote that I have seen offer an actual citation. David Fricke quoted the line in his liner notes to the anthology *Hey! Ho! Let's Go!*, without citing a publication or giving any specific indication that the quote is from a new interview. Because of the similarity to the quote written by White in *Rolling Stone*, I strongly believe this is a misquote of the *Rolling Stone* interview. But even if Johnny did say "pure, white rock 'n' roll," it remains telling that even though I was unable to find the direct citation through extensive research, this phrase in particular has risen to the position of one of the quotes most associated with him and its legitimacy has been unquestioned. This is a quote, in other words, that people believe should be associated with Johnny and that it was something he would have said. David Fricke, liner notes to Ramones, *Hey! Ho! Let's Go! The Anthology*, Rhino R2 75817, 1999, 26; Everett True, *Hey Ho Let's Go: The Story of the Ramones* (London: Omnibus Press, 2002), 22. I tried but was unable to reach Mr. Fricke for clarification.

8. Loraine Alterman, "Rock 'n' Roots," *New York Times*, November 21, 1971.

9. The later iteration of the Flamin' Groovies (*Shake Some Action*) featured the Waltham, Massachusetts–born Chris Wilson, who lived around the Boston area until he moved to California and replaced Roy Loney in 1971.

10. "Heart of Glass" was part of Blondie's repertoire as early as 1975, written as "Once I Had a Love (The Disco Song)" in response to the Hues Corporation's hit "Rock the Boat" (1974).

11. Willie Alexander, interview by Larry Azrin, unpublished manuscript, *BOMP*.

12. *JBC*; Steven Blush, *New York Rock: From the Rise of The Velvet Underground to the Fall of CBGB* (New York: St. Martin's Griffin, 2016); Gary Valentine, *New York Rocker: My Life in the Blank Generation with Blondie, Iggy Pop, and Others 1974–1981* (New York: Thunder's Mouth Press, 2002); Binky Philips, *My Life in the Ghost of Planets: The Story of a CBGB Almost-Was* (Rhino, 2012); James Isaacs, "Power Chords and Boom-Boom; Bye-Bye Boogie: Punk *Nouveau* Burgeons in Boston," *Boston Phoenix*, March 23, 1976. Blue Öyster Cult, for example, a New York–area band since 1967 ("even among insiders . . . an insider's group"), invited the Ramones to tour with them in 1977, and CBGB mainstay Helen Wheels (Helen Robbins) was an early associate of the band and co-wrote some of their songs. Greg Shaw, Alan Betrock, Ron Ross, and Lester Bangs, "New York's Beasty, Brutal Music Explosion: The N.Y. Dolls and Blue Öyster Cult Revive Manhattan," *Phonograph Record*, October 1973.

13. Jesse Henderson (drummer for the Ramrods), interview by Larry Azrin, handwritten manuscript, *BOMP*; Stephen Haag, "The Rockin' Ramrods," *Music Museum of New England* website, accessed July 14, 2017, http://mmone.org/the-rockin-ramrods/.

14. Jamie Kitman, "Talking and Rocking with Punk's Elder Statesmen," *Columbia Daily Spectator*, October 8, 1976.

15. *JBC*.

16. Valentine, *New York Rocker*, 114; Kembrew McLeod, *Parallel Lines* (New York: Bloomsbury, 2016), 78; Gendron, *Between Montmartre*, 262–64.

17. On suburbs and housing discrimination, see Rothstein, *The Color of Law*; Fogelson, *Bourgeois Nightmares*; Fishman, *Bourgeois Utopias*; Woldoff, *White Flight/Black Flight*.

18. Lisa Jane Persky, for example, grew up Greenwich Village, but her background was unusual for the CBGBs scene. Her parents, however, followed the model, moving from South Carolina to the Village "to be bohemian." Interview by the author, October 25, 2018.

19. Forest Hills Gardens and the other developments built by the Olmsteds (Guilford, Maryland; Great Neck Hills, New York; Colony Hills in Springfield, Massachusetts), and many other suburban communities throughout the United States enlisted "a host of highly onerous restrictions on how the owners could use their property," barring owners from selling and leasing to "non-Caucasians." In 1925 the Supreme Court upheld these racial covenants as constitutional and they were not overturned until the *Shelley v. Kraemer* decision in 1948. Fogelson, *Bourgeois Nightmares*, 4, et passim. Rothstein, *The Color of Law*, 77–91.

20. Interview by the author, June 26, 2018.

21. Dick Porter and Kris Needs, *Blondie: Parallel Lives* (London: Omnibus Press, 2012), 3, 6, 24.

22. "Interview with John Felice (1998)," Jojoblog, posted May 25, 2004, https://jojofiles.blogspot.com/2004/05/john-felices-interview-1998.html.

23. Interview by the author, July 19, 2018. See also Ellen Goldfarb, dir., *Dare to Be Different*, 2017.

24. Isaacs, "Power Chords."

25. Soon after hip hop's emergence in New York City, youth from black suburban neighborhoods, such as EPMD and Eric B. and Rakim from the Long Island suburbs, played a crucial role.

26. Kembrew McLeod, *The Downtown Pop Underground: New York City and the Literary Punks, Renegade Artists, DIY Filmmakers, Mad Playwrights, and Rock 'n' Roll Glitter Queens who Revolutionized Culture* (New York: Abrams Press, 2018), 40–42.

27. Legs McNeil, *HRR*.

28. Andy Shernoff, liner notes to *The Dictators Go Girl Crazy! (40th Anniversary Edition)*, 2015.

29. McLeod, *Parallel Lines*, 120.

30. Interview by the author, October 25, 2018.

31. McLeod, *Downtown Pop Underground*; Lisa Jane Persky, *X-Offenders: A Year in the Life of a Proto-Punk, 1976* (self-published, 2016); Lisa Jane Persky, interview by the author, October 25, 2018.

32. Heller, *Loft Jazz*; Robert Palmer, "New Life for the Bowery," *New York Times*, April 15, 1977.

33. McLeod, *Downtown Pop Underground*, 4, 300–301.

34. Interview by the author, October 25, 2018.

35. For overviews of the relationships between New York's gay and punk scenes, see McLeod, *Downtown Pop Underground*; Persky, *X-Offenders*; Ervin, "New York Punk Rock," 91–134.

36. Roberta Bayley quoted in McLeod, *Downtown Pop Underground*, 249; Lisa Jane Persky, interview by the author, October 25, 2018.

37. Lott, *Love and Theft*, 25–27, 159–68.

38. Lott, *Love and Theft*, 161.

39. Persky, *X-Offenders*.

40. Patti Smith, *Just Kids* (New York: HarperCollins, 2010); McLeod, *Downtown Pop Underground*, 199–202; however, see also Tavia Nyong'o, "Do You Want Queer Theory (or Do You Want the Truth)? Intersections of Punk and Queer in the 1970s," *Radical History Review* 100 (Winter 2008): 103–19, for a multivalent view of Smith's relationship to queerness, including her "utopian views on reproductive futurity" (105).

41. McLeod, *Parallel Lines*, 10.

42. Lisa Jane Persky, interview by the author, October 25, 2018.

43. Randal Doane, *Stealing All Transmissions: A Secret History of the Clash* (Oakland: PM Press, 2014), 24–25.

44. Painter, *History of White People*, 359–73.

45. E.g., Rogin's severe mischaracterizations of Jewish life in the beginning of the twentieth century in *Blackface, White Noise* (Berkeley: University of California Press, 1996), detailed by Hasia R. Diner in her review, "Trading Faces." For one example, Rogin draws false conclusions based on the idea that African American women were exploited as domestic workers in urban, Jewish households of the late nineteenth and early twentieth centuries, when in fact, such relationships were extremely rare at the time and not indicative of the economic station of the vast majority of American Jews: "[i]n 1911 more than half of all American Jews worked as poorly-paid laborers in garment factories; the rest were recent immigrants who eked out a living by hawking their hodge-podge of goods from pushcarts or owned tiny shops where wives and children of all ages clerked behind the counters." Diner, "Trading Faces," 41.

46. Eric K. Ward, "Skin in the Game: How Antisemitism Animates White Nationalism," *Public Eye* (Summer 2017), 9–15.

47. Stratton, *Jews, Race, and Popular Music*, 37–58, provides an overview of this context with respect to popular music, although I disagree overall with his extension of Michael Rogin's thesis of the Jewish uses of blackface.

48. "In the place of the rock frills was doo-wop, girl groups, bubblegum—they all loved the Bay City Rollers—and the surf rock of Brian Wilson and Jan and Dean, which informed many of the melodies, a tuneful undertow to the cacophony." Mikal Gilmore, "The Curse of the Ramones," *Rolling Stone*, May 19, 2016, http://www.rollingstone.com/music/features/the-curse-of-the-ramones-20160519.

49. McLeod, *Parallel Lines*, 19–20; McLeod, *Downtown Pop Underground*, 313–14. Although "bubblegum" is sometimes used in reference to the early 1960s, the term is more accurately connected to the late 1960s and early 1970s, concurrent with punk's earliest days, with songs such as the Archies' "Sugar Sugar" and the Ohio Express's "Yummy Yummy Yummy" (1969), Middle of the Road's version of "Chirpy Chirpy Cheep Cheep" (1970), and (the Ramones' named inspirations) Bay City Rollers' "Saturday Night" (1973).

50. Jimmy Page, interview by Felix Dennis, *OZ* (London) 20 (April 1969): 42.

51. On issues related to the associations of country with particular ideas of whiteness, see Nadine Hubbs, *Rednecks, Queers, and Country Music* (Berkeley: University of California Press, 2014) and Jocelyn R. Neal, "Dancing around the Subject: Race in Country Fan Culture," *The Musical Quarterly* 89/4 (Winter 2006): 555–79.

52. Ramone, *Commando*, 43.

53. Porter and Needs, *Blondie*, 68.

54. Ian Inglis, "'Some Kind of Wonderful': The Creative Legacy of the Brill Building," *American Music* 21/2 (Summer 2003), 218; Anthony J. Gribin and Matthew M. Schiff, *The Complete Book of Doo-Wop* (Iola, WI: Krause Publications, 2000), 97–110. Female harmony groups were a major presence in American popular music through the 1940s.

55. John Michael Runowicz, *Forever Doo-Wop: Race, Nostalgia, and Vocal Harmony* (Amherst: University of Massachusetts Press, 2010); see also Stuart L. Goosman, *Group Harmony: The Black Urban Roots of Rhythm & Blues* (Philadelphia: University of Pennsylvania Press, 2005).

56. Mary E. Rohlfing, "'Don't Say Nothin' Bad About My Baby': A Re-Evaluation of Women's Roles in the Brill Building Era of Early Rock 'n' Roll," *Critical Studies in Mass Communication* 13/2 (June 1996): 93–114; Inglis, "'Some Kind of Wonderful.'"

57. Gribin and Schiff, *Complete Book of Doo-Wop*, 7, 55–56.

58. Santosuosso, "Punk Rock."

59. Jonathan Richman, interview by Janice Long from 1985, transcribed and posted on Jojoblog, posted November 11, 2006, https://jojofiles.blogspot.com/2006/11/favourite-child hood-songs-part-2.html. Similarly, on "Parties in the U.S.A." (1992), Richman explains, "I'm from the sixties, the time of 'Louie, Louie,' 'Little Latin Lupe Lu,' and I know we can't have those times back again, but we can have parties like there were then." The Kingsmen's famous version of "Louie, Louie" was released in 1963 and the Righteous Brothers' "Little Latin Lupe Lu" in 1962.

60. Lenny Kaye, *HRR*.

61. Porter and Needs, *Blondie*, 11, 47.

62. Interview by the author, November 6, 2018.

63. Interview by the author, July 10, 2018.

64. Inglis, "'Some Kind of Wonderful,'" 230–32; George, *Death of Rhythm and Blues*.

65. Lois Kahlert and Dennis Anderson, interview by the author, July 10, 2018.

66. Ramone, *Commando*, 18.

67. Porter and Needs, *Blondie*, 11.

68. Lois Kahlert and Dennis Anderson, interview by the author, July 10, 2018.

69. Mark Lisheron, "Rhythm-and-Jews: The Story of the Blacks and Jews who Worked Together to Create the Music of R&B," *CommonQuest* 2/1 (Summer 1997): 20–33; George, *Death of Rhythm and Blues*.

70. Waksman, *This Ain't the Summer of Love*, 322n26. See Tommy James with Martin Fitzpatrick, *Me, the Mob, and the Music: One Helluva Ride with Tommy James and the Shondells* (New York: Simon and Schuster, 2010).

71. Interview by the author, November 6, 2018.

72. Interview by the author, June 26, 2018.

73. Gribin and Schiff, *Complete Book of Doo-Wop*, 7, 55–56.

74. Inglis, "'Some Kind of Wonderful,'" 223–26.

75. Gribin and Schiff, *Complete Book of Doo-Wop*, 75.

76. Porter and Needs, *Blondie*, 13–15; McLeod, *Parallel Lines*, 16.

77. *VV*, notes of interview with Judy Nylon.

78. Various artists, *Oldies But Goodies in Hi-Fi*, Original Sound OSR-LP-5001, 1959. On nostalgia and doo-wop, see Runowicz, *Forever Doo-Wop*, 12–18, et passim.

79. Ramone, *Commando*, 18–19. New Cassel was founded in the mid-1700s by free people who were formerly enslaved, and black families moved there in the twentieth century when they were systematically denied mortgages in other nearby neighborhoods. Marcelle S. Fischler, "A Hamlet on the Long Road to Renewal," *New York Times*, November 24, 2010; Vivian S. Toy, "New Cassel, First for a Change," *New York Times*, April 4, 2004. See also Rothstein, *The Color of Law*, 69–73, 140–43. Up to 1970, 75 percent of all Westbury's black population lived in New Cassel, while the 1970 census reported tracts such as one in Westbury with only *nineteen* black people out of 3,986, the three tracts in neighboring Mineola with 101 black people out of 21,845 (0.46 percent), and one tract containing a mere *five* black people out of 7,345 (0.068 percent). These dramatic numbers demonstrate how segregated and unequal the geography was for Long Island and most other suburban developments throughout the United States, and how skewed memories of that period can be. See the Long Island Mapping Projects at the CUNY Center for Urban Research: historiccensus.longislandindexmaps.org and www .longislandindexmaps.org.

80. Runowicz, *Forever Doo-Wop*, 76–80; Gribin and Schiff, *Complete Book of Doo-Wop*, 200–202; Waksman, *This Ain't the Summer of Love*, 113; Cateforis, *Are We Not New Wave*,

123–24, 132–33; Raj Tawney, "'Rock 'n' Roll High' at 40: How the Ramones and a Rebellious Female Lead Invaded Theaters," *Variety*, August 5, 2019. For *American Graffiti* as an example of "nostalgia film," see Frederic Jameson, "Postmodernism and Consumer Society," in *The Anti-Aesthetic: Essays on Postmodern Culture*, ed. Hal Foster (New York: New Press, [1983] 2002), 133–34. On this nostalgia in Great Britain, see also Dick Hebdige, *Subculture: The Meaning of Style* (London: Routledge, [1979] 2001), 82.

81. Porter and Needs, *Blondie*, 97.

82. Jon Savage, *The England's Dreaming Tapes: The Essential Companion to England's Dreaming, The Seminal History of Punk* (Minneapolis: University of Minnesota Press, 2012), 123, quoted in McLeod, *Parallel Lines*, 118.

83. McNeil and McCain, *Please Kill Me*, 300.

84. Isaacs, "Power Chords and Boom-Boom."

85. Stoia, "Common Stock," 216.

86. On the passamezzo moderno pattern in American popular music see Otto Gombosi, "Stephen Foster and 'Gregory Walker,'" *Musical Quarterly* 30/2 (April 1944): 133–46; John M. Ward, "The *Buffons* Family of Tune Families: Variations on a Theme of Otto Gombosi's," in *Themes and Variations: Writings on Music in Honor of Rulan Chao Pian*, ed. Bell Yung and Joseph S. C. Lam (Cambridge, MA: Harvard University Department of Music, 1994), 291; van der Merwe, *Origins of the Popular Style*; Stoia, "Common Stock"; Blum, "Rhythmic-Harmonic Cycles"; and Middleton, *Studying Popular Music*, 117–19. Van der Merwe and Middleton theorize the twelve-bar blues as based on the passamezzo moderno, but I share Blum's and Stoia's disagreement with this opinion.

87. Gombosi, "Stephen Foster." According to Ward, "Gregory Walker" properly refers to a longer version of the passamezzo moderno, "a two-strain pattern of sixteen bars and a ripresa of eight" (Ward, 291). Van der Merwe, like Gombosi, uses "Gregory Walker" as a synonym for the passamezzo moderno. Although *passamezzo moderno* is awkwardly applied to these American popular music schemes, referring as it does to a sixteenth-century Italian dance, because the musicians themselves did not develop a working terminology for the pattern, and because many popular music scholars (including Richard Middleton in his widely read *Analysing Popular Music*) have used the term, I also employ it here.

88. Much of the American popular style and common stock came from musicians reworking harmonic schemes and dances such as the country dance, quadrille, polka, square dance, and schottische. An excellent overview that includes the Caribbean can be found in Szwed and Marks, "The Afro-American Transformation." W. C. Handy reminisced about school days in Florence, Alabama: "[Jim Turner from Memphis] organized an orchestra and taught dancing. Those were the days of the quadrille, the lancers, the polka, the schottische, the mazurka, the york, the two-step, the gavotte, the minuet and the varsovienne. The waltz was popular, as was also the rye waltz, a combination of three-four and two-four tempos." See Russell, *Blacks, Whites, and Blues*; Stoia, "The Common Stock"; Gushee, *Pioneers of Jazz*; and Michael C. Scoggins, *The Scotch-Irish Influence on Country Music in the Carolinas: Border Ballads, Fiddle Tunes, and Sacred Songs* (Charleston: History Press, 2013).

89. Stoia, "The Common Stock."

90. Kip Lornell, liner notes to *Virginia Traditions: Non-Blues Secular Black Music*, BRI Records 001, 1978.

91. Blum, "Rhythmic-Harmonic Cycles," 3.

92. Stoia, "Common Stock," 194–95, 203, 232–33.

93. See Ralf von Appen and Markus Frei-Hauenschild, "AABA, Refrain, Chorus, Bridge, Prechorus—Song Forms and their Historical Development," *Online-Publikationen der Gesellschaft für Popularmusikforschung* 13 (2015), 22–23, 36–43.

94. Ramone, *Commando*, 43.

95. "Watch Rolling Stones Recall Writing 'Honky Tonk Women,'" *Rolling Stone*, November 10, 2016, http://www.rollingstone.com/music/videos/watch-rolling-stones-recall-writing-honky-tonk-women-w449172; and "Ask Keith Richards: 'Country Honk' to 'Honky Tonk Women,'" Keith Richards YouTube channel, February 9, 2017, https://www.youtube.com/watch?v=FGzGZX-V1Kk.

96. Like the Rolling Stones and many other musicians, the Beatles treated common stock and other schemes as increasingly racialized over the course of the 1960s. Compare "Twist and Shout," "I Saw Her Standing There" and "She Loves You" (1963) to "Yer Blues," "Why Don't We Do It in the Road," "Rocky Raccoon," and "Honey Pie" (1968).

97. Thanks to David Racanelli for pointing out the Anderson East cover of "Forever Young," http://www.rollingstone.com/country/news/hear-anderson-east-cover-bob-dylans-forever-young-w462023.

98. "Pills" was released as a B-side in 1961 and did not chart. It was rereleased on the 1966 compilation *The Originator*, which is probably where the New York Dolls encountered it. According to Sylvain Sylvain, by the time the Dolls saw Bo Diddley live in 1973 he had forgotten the song. Nina Antonia, *Too Much Too Soon* (London: Omnibus Press, 1998).

99. Robert Christgau, *Stranded: Rock and Roll for a Desert Island*, ed. Greil Marcus (New York: Da Capo Press, 2007), 137.

100. Morton, *the eyeball of hell*.

101. Stoia, "Common Stock," 223–24.

102. von Appen and Frei-Hauenschild, "AABA," 69–74.

103. The long AABA forms discussed by John Covach as the "dramatic AABA" form are fundamentally different from the AABA cycles found in Tin Pan Alley compositions such as "I Got Rhythm" or "Blue Skies," in which the four eight-bar sections are treated as one audible cycle. For example, in the Coasters' "Charlie Brown," what Covach considers the B section ("Who's always writing on the wall?") only appears once in the composition. While one can refer to "Charlie Brown" as an AABA form (24+24+16+24 mm. before more repetitions of A), the B section here operates more as an interlude amid repetitions of a twenty-four-bar (or twelve-bar) AAB blues, the most audible cyclical pattern. "Leiber and Stoller, the Coasters, and the 'Dramatic AABA' Form," in *Sounding Out Pop: Analytical Essays in Popular Music*, ed. Mark Spicer and John Covach (Ann Arbor: University of Michigan Press, 2010).

104. Stoia, "Common Stock," 195.

105. On "Ice Cream Changes," see Runowicz, *Forever Doo-Wop*, 51; also von Appen and Frei-Hauenschild, "AABA," 46.

106. W. C. Handy, *Father of the Blues* (New York: Macmillan, 1941), 76–77; also Blum, "Rhythmic-Harmonic Cycles." One of the most famous illustrations of this process is Jelly Roll Morton's explanation that the quadrille, as the last strain or dance in a set, was extracted and turned into the basis of "Tiger Rag." Jelly Roll Morton, *Kansas City Stomp: The Library of Congress Recordings*, Vol. 1, Rounder 1091, [1938] 1993.

107. Blondie, "Denis," Live at the Palladium 1978 (bootleg).

108. See also von Appen and Frei-Hauenschild, "AABA," 52–53.

109. Compare also Buddy Holly, "That'll Be the Day," which has an ABA form of eight-bar sections, with a twelve-bar blues guitar solo added in the middle.

110. Waksman, *This Ain't the Summer of Love*, 117; Gribin and Schiff, *Complete Book of Doo-Wop*, 116–21. Note also that "Babylon" is about the Long Island town, and not a metaphor for New York City.

111. Shernoff, liner notes to *Go Girl Crazy!* On the Dictators, the Ramones, and other New York–area bands' fascination with California beach culture, see Waksman, *This Ain't the Summer of Love*, 117–19.

112. Blum, "Rhythmic-Harmonic Cycles."

113. Hugh Thomson, prod. and dir., *Dancing in the Street: A Rock and Roll History*, "Episode 8: No Fun," BBC, 1995. Recut for US release on PBS.

114. The reissue on Rhino Records (R2 70091, 1989) indicates the songs on the original album were recorded in the spring of 1972 in California and produced, perhaps only nominally, by John Cale. In 1975 Warner Bros. sold those recordings to Beserkley, and *The Modern Lovers* contains those Cale recordings, with the exception of "Hospital," recorded in Boston.

115. Advertisement in Greg Shaw, ed., *Flamin Groovies Monthly Book* 1, July 1976, BOMP. Miriam Linna, who was the original drummer for the Cramps, once ran the Flamin' Groovies fan club. Kris Needs, liner notes to *Dirty Water: The Birth of Punk Attitude*, Year Zero YZTD0008, 2010.

116. Richie Unterberger, *White Light/White Heat: The Velvet Underground Day-By-Day* (London: Jawbone, 2009); Victor Bockris and Gerald Malanga, *Up-Tight: The Velvet Underground Story* (London: Omnibus Press, 1983).

117. McLeod, *Downtown Pop Underground*, 254.

118. Interview by the author, October 25, 2018.

119. Lisa Jane Persky, "Transactional Analysis at Town Hall," *New York Rocker* (December 1976). Audio from *JBC*. Thanks also to Jonathan Brink for help with this recording.

120. Blush, *American Hardcore*, 14.

121. Ramone, *Commando*, 28–32.

122. Mickey Leigh with Legs McNeil, *I Slept with Joey Ramone* (New York: Touchstone, 2010); True, *Hey Ho Let's Go*. True calls Forest Hills a "middle-class, mostly Jewish, neighbourhood." He links that description to the posh, exclusive Forest Hills Gardens, which he misleadingly calls "alternative housing for the cramped apartment dwellers of New York City," without discussing the racist circumstances under which these developments were originally built or the restrictions governing them. See also Richard F. Shepard, "Memories of My Queens," *New York Times*, September 3, 1995.

123. Richard Nadeau, Richard G. Nieme, and Jeffrey Levine, "Innumeracy about Minority Populations," *Public Opinion Quarterly* 57/3 (Autumn 1993): 332–47; Lee Sigelman and Richard G. Niemi, "Innumeracy about Minority Populations: African Americans and Whites Compared," *Public Opinion Quarterly* 65/1 (Spring 2001): 86–94. Typically the numbers of Jews, African Americans, Asian Americans, and Latinos in particular are highly overrepresented. According to one 1990 study, "close to 40 percent of the population say that at least one in five Americans is Jewish," despite the true figure being only 2.4 percent, a massive tenfold overestimate (Nadeau et al., "Innumeracy," 334).

124. Forest Hills, in 1943 *New York City Market Analysis*. The 1943 *New York City Market Analysis* is available through www.1940snewyork.com and CUNY's Center for Urban Research website, http:www.gc.cuny.edu/CUR. By 1960 the total Jewish population in Queens had increased to its highest number, about 30 percent of the borough.

125. Annie Polland and Daniel Soyer, *Emerging Metropolis: New York in the Age of Immigration, 1840–1920*, Vol. 2 of *City of Promises: A History of the Jews of New York*, edited by Deborah Dash Moore (New York: New York University Press, 2012), 103–36; Jeffrey S. Gurock, *Jews in Gotham: New York Jews in a Changing City, 1920–2010*, Vol. 3 of *City of Promises: A History of the Jews of New York*, 14–16; Hasia R. Diner, *Lower East Side Memories: A Jewish Place in*

*America* (Princeton: Princeton University Press, 2002); Hasia R. Diner, *The Jews of the United States, 1654 to 2000* (Berkeley: University of California Press, 2006).

126. Rothstein, *The Color of Law*.

127. Leigh, *I Slept with Joey Ramone*, 113.

128. Kugelberg and Savage, *Punk*, 134.

129. Interview by the author, October 28, 2018.

130. Douglas Noble, "Guitar Techniques—Play Like: The Ramones," *Guitar Magazine*, January 7, 2014.

131. Everett, "Making Sense of Rock's Tonal Systems," documents other ways rock musicians moved away from functional harmony.

132. Cramps, interview, *Slash* 1/12 (August 1978): 16.

133. Johnny Ramone, interview by Stereo Steve, KROQ, August 1981, *BOMP*.

134. Joey Ramone, *HRR*.

## Part Two: *punk (n.)*

1. Jello Biafra, interview by V. Vale, introduction to *Search & Destroy #1–6: The Complete Reprint*, iii.

2. E.g., in *No Future*, Worley introduces punk as a "teenage warning" and asks us to "take youth and youth culture seriously" (2).

3. Delmont, *Why Busing Failed*; Ronald P. Formisano, *Boston Against Busing: Race, Class, and Ethnicity in the 1960s and 1970s* (Chapel Hill: University of North Carolina Press, 1991); Mahon, *Right to Rock*, 42–44.

4. Stacy E. Seicshnaydre, "Is Disparate Impact Having Any Impact? An Appellate Analysis of Forty Years of Disparate Impact Claims under the Fair Housing Act," *American University Law Review* 63/2 (2013), http://ssrn.com/abstract=2336266; Joseph M. Pastore Jr., "In Yonkers We Trust," *New York Times*, May 20, 2007, https://www.nytimes.com/2007/05/20/opinion/nyregionopinions/20WEpastore.html.

5. Rothstein, *Color of Law*, 39.

6. Mahon, *Right to Rock*, 40–42.

7. Delmont, *Why Busing Failed*, 124.

8. Rothstein, *Color of Law*, 235.

9. Ryan Moore, "Break on Through: The Counterculture and the Climax of American Modernism," in *Countercultures and Popular Music*, ed. Sheila Whiteley and Jedediah Sklower (Surrey, UK: Ashgate, 2014), 39–40; Avila, *Popular Culture*, 136–37.

## Chapter 5: Punk and the White Atlantic

1. Paul Gilroy, *The Black Atlantic: Modernity and Double Consciousness* (Cambridge, MA: Harvard University Press, 1993); Hamilton, *Just Around Midnight*.

2. Hamilton, *Just Around Midnight*, 90.

3. Charles Hamm, *Yesterdays: Popular Song in America* (New York: W.W. Norton, [1979] 1983), 121; see also Jon Stratton, *When Music Migrates: Crossing British and European Racial Faultlines, 1945–2010* (Surrey, UK: Ashgate, 2014), 10–11.

4. Delmont, *Why Busing Failed*, 3, 118.

5. Hamilton, *Just Around Midnight*, 92, 120.

6. Hamilton, *Just Around Midnight*, 92.

7. Pop, "Times Talks." I was not able to find this Pete Townshend interview, so Iggy Pop may be misremembering the quote or its speaker.

8. Jann S. Wenner, "The Rolling Stone Interview: John Lennon, Part 1," *Rolling Stone*, January 21, 1971.

9. Strummer, *HRR*.

10. Lorenz, "Cosmopolitan Folk," 190–318.

11. ? and the Mysteriers were a Mexican American group from Michigan, an exception among these otherwise white groups.

12. Richard Hell, *HRR*. See also Savage, *England's Dreaming*, 81.

13. Wald, *How the Beatles Destroyed Rock 'n' Roll*, 243.

14. This quote has been widely recycled but without attribution (e.g., "as one member put it," "the band's self-description was"). I came across what I believe is the original quote: Jim Sohns, *Record Beat* 1/12, July 5, 1966.

15. Willie Alexander, interview by Larry Azrin, unpublished manuscript, *BOMP*.

16. See also Worley, *No Future*, 55.

17. Strummer, *HRR*.

18. Review in "Newsheet," 1977, *BOMP*, Scene Files, United Kingdom, punk.

19. Wald, *How the Beatles Destroyed Rock 'n' Roll*, 238–39.

20. Savage, *England's Dreaming*, 81; Strummer, *HRR*. Some of these groups can be heard on Various artists, *Punk 45: Sick on You! One Way Spit! After the Love & Before the Revolution. Vol 3: Proto-Punk 1970–77*, Soul Jazz SJRCD279, 2014.

21. Strummer, *HRR*.

22. Hebdige, *Subculture*, 25.

23. Dick Hebdige, *Cut 'n' Mix: Culture, Identity and Caribbean Music* (London: Methuen, 1987), 43.

24. Savage, *England's Dreaming*, 59, 86–88; Richard Hell, *HRR*.

25. Hynde, *Reckless*.

26. Ronstadt was interested in the burgeoning punk and new wave scene well before her 1980 release *Mad Love*. On Jim Brawley's bootleg tape of Television at CBGB, February 24, 1977, he wrote: "Note: Attended by L. Ronstadt who stole my table & left in the middle." *JBC*.

27. Strummer, *HRR*.

28. Jenn Pelly, *The Raincoats* (New York: Bloomsbury, 2017), 5–7.

29. Strummer, *HRR*; Johnny Ramone, *HRR*.

30. Johnny Ramone, interview with Stereo Steve, KROQ, August 1981, *BOMP*.

31. Interview by the author, June 26, 2018.

32. Chris Morris, "LA Punk," in *Forming: The Early Days of L.A. Punk* (Santa Monica, CA: Track 16 Gallery/Smart Art Press, 1999), 13.

33. The Clash also supported younger black groups, such as E.S.G., Bad Brains, and Grandmaster Flash and the Furious Five, all of whom opened for them during their weeklong residency at New York's Bond's International Casino in May–June 1981. *JBC*, mostly Box 30.

34. Strummer, *HRR*.

35. Binky Philips, "The Damned at CBGB: The Night Punk was Officially Born in the USA," November 2, 2010, updated May 25, 2011, *Huffpost*, https://www.huffingtonpost.com/binky-philips/the-damned-at-cbgb-the-ni_b_777706.html.

36. Quoted in Tony Rettman, *NYHC: New York Hardcore 1980–1990* (Brooklyn: Bazillion Points, 2014), 17.

37. For more comprehensive histories of British punk during this period, see Savage, *England's Dreaming*; Worley, *No Future*; and de Kergariou, *No Future*.

38. Albertine, *Clothes*, 79.

39. Needs, liner notes to *Dirty Water*.

40. Strummer, *HRR*. Kevin Seconds said a similar thing, quoted in Blush, *American Hardcore*, 14.

41. Michael Azerrad, *Our Band Could Be Your Life: Scenes from the American Indie Underground, 1981–1991* (Boston: Back Bay Books, 2001), 16–17.

42. Earlier documents include the Damned's "New Rose" b/w "Help," Stiff BUY 6, 1976 (produced by Nick Lowe), and the Sex Pistols' "Anarchy in the UK" b/w "I Wanna Be Me," EMI 2566, 1976.

43. E.g., Crass, *The Feeding of the Five Thousand*, Small Wonder Records WEENY 2, 1978; X-Ray Spex, *Germ Free Adolescents*, EMI INS-3023, 1978.

44. Clash, "Garageland," *The Clash*.

45. Doug Hinman, *The Kinks: All Day and All of the Night* (San Francisco: Backbeat Books, 2004), 61.

46. Home, *Cranked Up Really High*, 37–38.

47. Don Letts, dir., *The Punk Rock Movie*, 1978.

48. Hamm, *Yesterdays*, 404–5.

49. Appen and Frei-Hauenschild, "AABA," 74.

50. Savage, *England's Dreaming*, 297.

51. Quoted in Azerrad, *Our Band Could Be Your Life*, 146.

52. Pelly, *Raincoats*.

53. Gehman, in Doe with DeSavia, *Under the Big Black Sun*, 43.

54. Lester Bangs, "How to Learn to Love Reggae," *Stereo Review*, April 1977.

55. E.g., Hebdige, *Subculture*, 30–45, 62–70.

56. Strummer, *HRR*; see also Letts, *HRR*, and Worley, *No Future*, 146–47.

57. Sherry Keith and Robert Girling, "Bauxite Dependency: Roots of Crisis," NACLA, Sep. 25, 2007, https://nacla.org/article/bauxite-dependency-roots-crisis.

58. Strummer, *HRR*.

59. Strummer, *HRR*.

60. Lydon, *Rotten*, 268, 274–77.

61. Keith and Girling, "Bauxite Dependency."

62. Many thanks to Will Rigby for these additions.

63. Jeff Chang, *Can't Stop Won't Stop: A History of the Hip-Hop Generation* (New York: St. Martin's Press, 2005), 21–39, 67–85.

64. Kaye, *HRR*.

65. Tappa Zukie, interview by Angus Taylor, *United Reggae*, March 1, 2012, https://unitedreggae.com/articles/n892/030112/interview-tappa-zukie-part-2; Robin Murray, "Don Letts on Why Reggae Was the Real Sound of '77," *Clash*, January 6, 2017, https://www.clashmusic.com/features/don-letts-on-why-reggae-was-the-real-sound-of-77.

66. Szwed and Marks, "Afro-American Transformation."

67. For more on Blackwell, see Stratton, *When Music Migrates*, 37–58.

68. Michael "Eppy" Epstein, interview by the author, July 19, 2018; Jon Bradshaw, "The Reggae Way to 'Salvation,'" *New York Times*, August 14, 1977; Keith and Girling, "Bauxite Dependency."

69. Hebdige, *Subculture*, 30.

70. Eric Wendell, *Patti Smith: America's Punk Rock Rhapsodist* (Lanham, MD: Rowman & Littlefield, 2015).

71. Thanks to Walter Everett, who pointed out to me one of the performances of Smith covering "Mafia."

72. https://www.youtube.com/watch?v=kzsKRbGwcKQ. Smith's inclusion of Blue Öyster Cult captures their close association with the early punk scene in New York. Beyond Smith's own romantic relationship with Allen Lanier, the group was considered part of the New York vanguard in the early 1970s, along with the New York Dolls. See Shaw et al., "New York's Beasty, Brutal Music Explosion." Allen Lanier contributed to *Horses*, *Radio Ethiopia*, and the Clash's *Give 'Em Enough Rope*.

73. See also Ari Up, remembering Patti Smith at the Brooklyn Museum in 2010: https://www.youtube.com/watch?v=KRbvkh9ONzg.

74. Smith, interview by Paris, 69.

75. Patti Smith, liner notes to *Radio Ethiopia*, Arista AL4097, 1976.

76. Goldfarb, *Dare to Be Different*.

77. Steve Rosenfield with Michael "Eppy" Epstein, *Fun + Dangerous: Untold Stories, Unseen Photos, Unearthed Music from My Father's Place 1975–1980* (New York: Ardent Artists, 2010); Epstein, interview by the author, July 19, 2018.

78. *JBC*.

79. I wrote about a similar effect in "concert jazz" in "Bill Finegan's Gershwin Arrangements and the American Concept of Hybridity," *Journal of the Society for American Music* 2/4 (November 2008): 507–30.

80. Don Letts, interview by Mark P., *Sniffin' Glue* 7 (February 1977).

81. Hebdige, *Cut 'n' Mix*, 106–14. See also Stratton, *When Music Migrates*, 125–45, for an analysis of ska and two-tone noting the movement's nostalgia and failure to reach integrated audiences.

82. Marc Spitz, "The Oral History of 2-Tone," *Spin*, September 28, 2009, https://www.spin.com/2009/09/oral-history-2-tone/.

83. Hebdige, *Subculture*, 66.

84. See, e.g., Peter Tosh, interview, *Slash* 2/1 (September 1978): 14–15; Burning Spear (Winston Rodney), interview by Jeffrey Lea and Don Snowdon, *Slash* 3/2 (1980): 22–23.

85. The fashion elements in British punk have been a major area of scholarly inquiry since Hebdige's *Subculture: The Meaning of Style*, and here I limit my rehearsal of British punk fashion to the pertinent concerns for American punk rock in "white Atlantic" exchanges.

86. Hebdige, *Subculture*.

87. Interview by the author, July 10, 2018.

88. Hebdige, *Subculture*, 26.

89. Albertine, *Clothes*, 130.

90. Hebdige, *Subculture*, 27.

91. Casale, *HRR*.

92. Home, *Cranked Up Really High*, 32.

93. Worley, *No Future*, deals extensively with racism and anti-racism in Great Britain, including with respect to the Rock Against Racism movement; see also Ashley Dawson, "'Love Music, Hate Racism': The Cultural Politics of the Rock Against Racism Campaigns, 1976–1981," *Postmodern Culture* 16/1 (September 2005), doi: 10.1353/pmc.2006.0002.

94. Carlo McCormick, "Out of Bounds: Cultural Synaesthesia and Art in Unexpected Places," in *Panic Attack! Art in the Punk Years*, ed. Mark Sladen and Ariella Yedgar (New York: Merrell, 2007), 95.

95. Interview by the author, July 10, 2018.

96. Brian James, interview by Dave Jennings, June 16, 2016. https://louderthanwar.com/brian-james-interview.

97. Letts, interview by Mark P.

98. Worley, *No Future*, 6.

99. Johnny Ramone, *HRR*.

100. Savage, *England's Dreaming*, 437.

101. *VV*.

102. Kaye, *HRR*.

## Chapter 6: "Less Art and More Machine": The California Crucible

1. Doe with DeSavia, *Under the Big Black Sun*, 109.

2. Anna Margarete Landes, "Vom britischen Punk zum Hardcore Punk in Los Angeles: Dei Entstehungsgeschichte des Hardcore Punks mit einer interdisziplinären Analyse von Texten der Band Bad Religion aus der Reagan-Ära" (PhD diss., Alpen-Adria-Universität Klagenfurt, 2009), 162–71.

3. Mark Andersen and Mark Jenkins, *Dance of Days: Two Decades of Punk in the Nation's Capital* (Brooklyn: Akashic Books, 2009), 93.

4. Claude Bessy (Kick Boy), "Middle Class, Negative Trend, Weirdos and Dils at the Azteca," *Slash* 2/1 (September 1978): 19; Claude Bessy (Kick), "Black Flag EP," *Slash* 2/6 (June 1979): 35.

5. "Black Flag," *Los Angeles Flipside* 16 (1979): n.p.

6. Red Cross, interview by Mark Wheaton, and the Bangs, interview by Bruce Kalberg, *No Magazine* (1982): n.p.

7. Interview by the author, November 7, 2018.

8. Noelle, "Behind the Orange Curtain," *Flipside* 15 (1979); Mike Patton, "Orange County," *Los Angeles Flipside* 16 (1979): n.p.; "Is There, Isn't There Punk Rock Violence???????" *Slush* (September/October 1980): 8.

9. John Doe, interview by Bob Andelman, https://www.youtube.com/watch?v=hqUYq_nXMvM.

10. See also Blush, *American Hardcore*, 76–82.

11. Avila, *Popular Culture*.

12. *BOMP*.

13. Blush, *American Hardcore*, 74; see also Landes, "Vom britischen Punk zum Hardcore Punk in Los Angeles," 157–60.

14. Avila, *Popular Culture*, 113–44.

15. Doe, *HRR*.

16. Chrome (Damon Edge), interview by Vale, *Search & Destroy* 8 (1978), reprinted in *Search & Destroy #7–11: The Complete Reprint*, 41.

17. Robert Hilburn, "A Positive Perspective on Punk," *Los Angeles Times*, February 28, 1978.

18. Steve Knopper, "The Dickies Going Long, Going Strong," *Chicago Tribune*, November 9, 2016, http://www.chicagotribune.com/entertainment/music/ct-the-dickies-punk-ott-1111-2016 1108-story.html.

19. Doe, *HRR*.

20. Dave McBride, "Counterculture," in *A Companion to Los Angeles*, ed. William Deverell and Greg Hise (West Sussex, UK: Blackwell Publishing, 2010), 327–45.

21. Marc Spitz and Brendan Mullen, *We Got the Neutron Bomb: The Untold Story of L.A. Punk* (New York: Three Rivers, 2001), 21–29, 91–93.

22. Spitz and Mullen, *We Got the Neutron Bomb*, 44–56; Jason Cherkis, "The Lost Girls," *Huffington Post Highline*, July 8, 2015, https://highline.huffingtonpost.com/articles/en/the-lost-girls/.

23. Schomburg Center, *In Motion.*

24. Ali Modarres, introduction to *City of Promise: Race and Historical Change in Los Angeles*, ed. Martin Schiesl and Mark Morrall Dodge (Claremont, CA: Regina Books, 2006), 2.

25. Kamran Afary, *Performance and Activism: Grassroots Discourse after the Los Angeles Rebellion of 1992* (Lanham, MD: Lexington Books, 2009), 41.

26. David M. Grant, Melvin L. Oliver, and Angela D. James, "African Americans: Social and Economic Bifurcation," in *Ethnic Los Angeles*, ed. Roger Waldinger and Mehdi Bozorgmehr (New York: Russell Sage Foundation, 1996), 381; John H. M. Laslett, "Historical Perspectives: Immigration and the Rise of a Distinctive Urban Region, 1900–1970," in *Ethnic Los Angeles*, ed. Roger Waldinger and Mehdi Bozorgmehr (New York: Russell Sage Foundation, 1996), 60–61.

27. Laslett, "Historical Perspectives," 60. See also Mike Davis, *City of Quartz: Excavating the Future in Los Angeles* (London: Verso, 1990).

28. John Doe, interview by Bob Andelman.

29. Cervenka, *HRR*; Jack Boulware and Silke Tudor, *Gimme Something Better: The Profound, Progressive, and Occasionally Pointless History of Bay Area Punk from Dead Kennedys to Green Day* (New York: Penguin, 2009).

30. Gunckel, "Defining Punk," 161–62.

31. Boulware and Tudor, *Gimme Something Better*, 52–53.

32. David Spaner, "Subhumans: The Vancouver Sound," *Public Enemy* 7 (Summer 1979): 8–9.

33. Jhoni Jackson, "Punk was Always Gay: Kid Congo Powers on the Genre's Queer Beginnings," June 30, 2016, http://remezcla.com/features/music/kid-congo-powers-interview; Muñoz, "'Gimme Gimme This," 97. Tristan was also the head of an unofficial Ramones Fan Club based in Los Angeles.

34. On LA's gay history, see Daniel Hurewitz, *Bohemian Los Angeles and the Making of Modern Politics* (Berkeley: University of California Press, 2007). Gunckel, "Defining Punk," presents a multifaceted view of sexuality and queer identity in the early LA punk scene.

35. Dave Brown, interview by Tim Yohannan, *Maximumrocknroll* 99 (1991), posted on http://www.breakmyface.com/bands/dangerhouse1.html.

36. Black Randy interview, *VV*; Nyong'o "Do You Want Queer Theory," 107–8.

37. Offs (Don Vinil), interview by Vale, *Search & Destroy* 8 (1978), reprinted in *Search & Destroy #7–11: The Complete Reprint*, 52.

38. David A. Ensminger, *Left of the Dial: Conversations with Punk Icons* (Oakland, CA: PM Press, 2013), 62.

39. Doe with DeSavia, *Under the Big Black Sun*, 22.

40. Cervenka, *HRR.*

41. Russo, *We Were Going to Change the World*, 123.

42. The Damned were a very important British band in the musical development of American punk, as I discuss in chapter 5, and they were extremely popular in Los Angeles. Dave Vanian was on the iconic cover of the first issue of *Slash*, and the group was regularly featured in *Flipside* and other zines.

43. Many of the songs in this chapter are collected on Various artists, *Punk 45: Chaos in the City of Angels and Devils, Hollywood from X to Zero & Hardcore on the Beaches, Punk in Los Angeles 1977–81*, Soul Jazz Records SJRCD329, 2016.

44. Black Randy interview, *VV.*

45. John Doe, interview by Bob Andelman.

46. John Garst, "Man of Constant Sorrow: Antecedents and Tradition," in *Country Music Annual 2002*, ed. Charles K. Wolfe and Jame E. Akenson (Lexington: University Press of Kentucky, 2002), 26–53; David Warren Steele, "Shape-Note Hymnody," in *Grove Music Online*, 2013.

47. Cervenka, *HRR*.

48. Mike Ness, interview by Chris Parker, *Pittsburgh City Paper*, October 1, 2009, https://www.pghcitypaper.com/pittsburgh/a-conversation-with-mike-ness-of-social-distortion/Content?oid=1342602.

49. Chris Morris, *Los Lobos: Dream In Blue* (Austin: University of Texas Press, 2015), 44–47, 48–55; Ensminger, *Visual Vitriol*, 216–17.

50. Morris, *Los Lobos*, xv.

51. X (Exene Cervenka, John Doe, Billy Zoom), interview, *No Magazine* 1 (1978): 15.

52. Julie Dowling, *Mexican Americans and the Question of Race* (Austin: University of Texas Press, 2014); Rothstein, *Color of Law*, 233–36; Ana Gonzalez-Barrera and Mark Hugo Lopez, "Is Being Hispanic a Matter of Race, Ethnicity or Both?" *Pew Research Center*, June 15, 2015, http://www.pewresearch.org/fact-tank/2015/06/15/is-being-hispanic-a-matter-of-race-ethnicity-or-both/.

53. Plugz (Tito Larriva, Barry McBride, and Charlie Quintana), interview by Vale, *Search & Destroy* 10 (1978), reprinted in *Search & Destroy #7–11: The Complete Reprint*, 92.

54. Bag, *Violence Girl*.

55. Habell-Pallán, *Loca Motion*, 183.

56. The 1950s rhythmic arpeggiation style heard on "Chiquitita Mia" is also played by Billy Zoom on X's first single, "Adult Books." It is not accurately described as a "calypso" beat, as characterized by Kory Grow, "X Look Back on 40 Years of Punk Iconoclasm," *Rolling Stone*, September 5, 2017.

57. Although "La Bamba" charted (peaking at #22), its success at the time was much less than "Donna," the A-side, which peaked at #2.

58. Dowling, *Mexican Americans*, 5.

59. Judges "often deemed Mexicans Americans to be 'Caucasians' and not subject to exclusion by restrictive covenants," Rothstein, *Color of Law*, 235; and the postwar "enlargement of American whiteness" included Mexicans and Mexican Americans, e.g., "since the mid-1930s, federal and Texas state laws had defined Mexicans as white and allowed them to vote in Texas's white primary"; Painter, *History of White People*, 359–60. The Hispanic/non-Hispanic distinction has been reserved for ethnicity ("Spanish/Hispanic origin or descent" on the 1980 questionnaire) rather than race in the US census.

60. Vilma Ortiz, "The Mexican-Origin Population: Permanent Working Class or Emerging Middle Class," in *Ethnic Los Angeles*, ed. Roger Waldinger and Mehdi Bozorgmehr (New York: Russell Sage Foundation, 1996), 247–77; Laslett, "Historical Perspectives."

61. Doe, *Under the Big Black Sun*, 91–92.

62. Burt Kearns, "Chris Montez and Brian Wilson: A 50-Year High School Reunion," *Please Kill Me* (blog), April 25, 2018, https://pleasekillme.com/chris-montez-brian-wilson-50-year-high-school-reunion/.

63. Plugz, interview by Vale, 93.

64. "Over the years, I have been interviewed by students and academics who are researching the East L.A. or Chicano punk movement. I always have to point out that I do not consider myself or the Bags to be part of that scene. . . . I'm not able to speak about their experiences [groups such as Thee Undertakers, the Brat, and Los Illegals] because I assume that they were different from mine." Alice Bag, "Racism in the Early Punk Scene," *Diary of a Bad Housewife* (blog), April 17, 2005, http://alicebag.blogspot.com/2005/04/racism-in-early-punk-scene.html.

65. Habell-Pallán, *Loca Motion*, 160; https://soundcloud.com/alicebag; Downtown Boys (Joe DeFrancesco), interview by the author, December 21, 2018.

66. Kee Malesky, "The Journey from 'Colored' to 'Minorities' to 'People of Color,'" *NPR Code Switch* (blog), March 30, 2014, https://www.npr.org/sections/codeswitch/2014/03/30/295931070/the-journey-from-colored-to-minorities-to-people-of-color.

67. Zona de Obras, *Diccionario de punk*, 32.

68. Dez Cadena, interview by Tony Rettman, *Noisey*, September 3, 2015, https://noisey.vice.com/en_us/article/r3zpe8/dez-cadena-interview.

69. Shaun Cullen, "White Skin, Black Flag: Hardcore Punk, Racialization, and the Politics of Sound in Southern California," *Criticism* 58/1 (Winter 2016): 66. Cullen writes that Black Flag "always included black and Latino members" (62); I don't know of any black members of Black Flag, except maybe Spot, who rehearsed with the pre–Black Flag group Panic before Chuck Dukowski joined.

70. Email to the author, November 12, 2018.

71. Online Archive of California, "Finding Aid for the Self Help Graphics & Art Research Collection 1973–2007," 2014; Josh Kun, "Vex Populi," *Los Angeles Magazine*, March 2003; Doe, *Under the Big Black Sun*, 94; Habell-Pallán, *Loca Motion*, 152.

72. Teresa Covarrubias: "When I went to shows on the Westside I always got a sense that I was an outsider. There was always a hint of racism in the punk movement in Hollywood," quoted in Kun, "Vex Populi."

73. Kun, "Vex Populi."

74. Kun, "Vex Populi."

75. Covarrubias, in Doe with DeSavia, *Under the Big Black Sun*, 117.

76. Controllers (Take Two), interview, *Slash* 2/6 (June 1979): 18–19; Controllers, interview, *No Magazine* 1 (1978): 5–6. Pat Smear (Georg Ruthenberg)'s mother was African American and American Indian, and his father a German immigrant, but I did not encounter descriptions of him as black in fanzines at the time. Certainly he was not subject to the relentless front-and-center race characterizations that dominate the profiles of and interviews with Karla "Mad Dog."

77. Interview by the author, November 6, 2018.

78. Marlon Whitfield, interview by Bruce Kalberg, *No Magazine* (1983): n.p.

79. Joe Carducci compiled some of the media's negative portrayals in *Rock and the Pop Narcotic*, 174–86.

80. Doe with DeSavia, *Under the Big Black Sun*, 51.

81. Doe with DeSavia, *Under the Big Black Sun*, 28.

82. Bag, *Violence Girl*, 308–9.

83. Roessler, interview by the author, October 28, 2018; Stew, interview by the author, November 6, 2018.

84. Claude Bessy (Kick), "The Decedents [*sic*], the Screwz, Vicious Circle, the Chiefs, the Mau Mau's and Black Flag at the Fleetwood (Redondo Beach)," *Slash* 3/4 (1980), 29–30.

85. Doe, *HRR*; Cervenka, *HRR*.

86. See also Habell-Pallán, *Loca Motion*, 156.

87. Interview by the author, November 7, 2018.

88. Quoted in Russo, *We Were Going to Change the World*, 100.

89. Interview by the author, September 30, 2016. On "self-marginalization," see Daniel S. Traber, "'L.A.'s 'White Minority': Punk and the Contradictions of Self-Marginalization," *Cultural Critique* 48 (2001): 30–64.

90. Black Randy interview, *VV*.

91. Spitz and Mullen, *We Got the Neutron Bomb*, 223.

92. Doe with DeSavia, *Under the Big Black Sun*, 212.

93. Paul Young, dir., *Urban Struggle: The Battle of the Cuckoo's Nest*, 1981; Blush, *American Hardcore*, 22–23, 87.

94. Blush, *American Hardcore*, 39–41.

95. Henry Rollins, "Everything Was Heavy," in *We Got Power! Hardcore Punk Scenes from 1980s Southern California*, ed. David Markey and Jordan Schwartz (Brooklyn: Bazillion Points, 2012), 6.

96. Martin Schiesl, "Behind the Shield: Social Discontent and the Los Angeles Police since 1950," in *City of Promise: Race and Historical Change in Los Angeles*, ed. Martin Schiesl and Mark Morrall Dodge (Claremont, CA: Regina Books, 2006), 137–73.

97. Also, N.W.A's music comes from the late 1980s, a different time period. Carducci, *Rock and the Pop Narcotic*, 181–82. In this passage he misnames "Fuck tha Police" as ". . . . tha Cops."

98. Marshall W. Meyer, "Police Shootings at Minorities: The Case of Los Angeles," *Annals of the American Academy of Political and Social Science* 452 (November 1980): 98–100 [102].

99. Markey and Schwartz, *We Got Power!*, 130.

100. Laurie O'Connell, "Elk's Lodge '79," *Slash* 2/5 (May 1979): 12–13; Blush, *American Hardcore*, 83.

101. Max Felker-Kantor, *Policing Los Angeles: Race, Resistance, and the Rise of the LAPD* (Chapel Hill: University of North Carolina Press, 2018), 19.

102. Interview by the author, October 28, 2018.

103. Traber, "L.A.'s 'White Minority.'"

104. Spitz and Mullen, *Neutron Bomb*, 200.

105. Interview by the author, November 6, 2018.

106. Sacha Jenkins, "FAQ Afropunk!," accessed November 3, 2018, https://afropunk.com/2018/08/faq-afropunk-by-sacha-jenkins/.

107. Joe Domanick, "A Shooting Reminiscent of the LAPD's Worst Days," *Los Angeles Times*, June 6, 1999, http://articles.latimes.com/1999/jun/06/opinion/op-44648.

108. Grant, Oliver, and James, "African Americans," 379.

109. Interview by the author, November 6, 2018.

110. Blush, *American Hardcore*, 33.

111. Markey, *We Got Power!*, 186.

112. Formisano, *Boston Against Busing*, 8.

113. Interview by the author, November 7, 2018.

114. Doe with DeSavia, *Under the Big Black Sun*, 213.

115. Jim Newton, "ACLU Says 83 percent of Police Live Outside L.A." *Los Angeles Times*, March 29, 1994.

116. Blush, *American Hardcore*, 86.

117. Avila, *Popular Culture*, 224–42; Laslett, "Historical Perspectives," 63. Ginn has said the lyrics to "White Minority" were a parody, and many of Black Flag's songs were ironic, silly, or mocking ("Six Pack," "TV Party"), yet "White Minority" has always generated mixed reactions among listeners. None of my interviewees had a definitive interpretation of the song, and it is certainly possible that Ginn wanted the song to be ambiguous. See Cullen, "White Skin," and Traber, "L.A.'s 'White Minority'" for two opposing views of the song.

118. Interview by the author, November 6, 2018.

119. Afary, *Performance and Activism*, 46–47.

120. Avila, *Popular Culture*, 230–37.

121. Markey and Schwartz, *We Got Power!*, 43

122. Spitz and Mullen, *We Got the Neutron Bomb*, 258.

123. Spitz and Mullen, *We Got the Neutron Bomb*, 258.

124. Charles Homans, "Bob Dylan and the Myth of Boomer Idealism," *New York Times Magazine*, July 17, 2019, https://www.nytimes.com/2019/07/17/magazine/bob-dylan-and-the -myth-of-boomer-idealism.html.

125. Blush, *American Hardcore*, 15.

126. Jack Grisham, quoted in Spitz and Mullen, *We Got the Neutron Bomb*, 230.

127. Mike Saunders letter to Kevin Saunders, May 17, 1978, http://www.angrysamoans.com/ gif/Dictatorship.gif; Angry Samoans (Gregg Turner and Mike Saunders), interview, *Ink Disease* 14 (Fall 1988): 48.

128. Steve Besser, "The Angry Samoans," accessed July 27, 2018, http://www.angrysamoans .com/gif/big/PHMS.1.gif.

129. Angry Samoans, interview, 46.

130. Interview by the author, September 30, 2016.

131. Blush, *American Hardcore*, 14–15.

132. Black Flag, *Damaged*. Later, Ginn remarked that Anthony Ramirez was his favorite Black Flag drummer because "he was a good blues drummer." Black Flag, interview by David Grad, in Sinker, *We Owe You Nothing*, 82.

133. Easley, "Riff Schemes," paragraph 3.3.

134. Interview with the author, August 3, 2018.

135. See Easley, "'It's Not My Imagination,'" 25–45, for a detailed overview of hardcore drumming patterns.

136. See Easley, "'It's Not My Imagination,'" 46–61, for another analysis of hardcore guitar pitch movement.

137. See also Easley, "Riff Schemes," paragraph 1.2.

138. Interview by the author, September 30, 2016.

139. An elaborated reading of the song in this respect can be found in Konstantin Butz, "Rereading American Hardcore: Intersectional Privilege and the Lyrics of Early Californian Hardcore Punk," *as|peers* 1(2008): 131–58. However, several of Butz's conclusions are based on the incorrect notion that "Suburban Home" was written by the teenage Milo Aukerman rather than Lombardo, who was over thirty years old when he joined the Descendents and wrote the song.

140. Riggle et al., *Filmage*, Lombardo extra footage.

141. Biafra, interview by Belsito, 114; Alex Ogg, *Dead Kennedys: Fresh Fruit for Rotting Vegetables, The Early Years* (Oakland: PM Press, 2014), 19; Boulware and Tudor, *Gimme Something Better*, 65.

142. Winston Smith, interview by Josh Hooten, in Sinker, *We Owe You Nothing*, 157.

143. Interview by the author, October 28, 2018.

144. Interview by the author, November 7, 2018.

145. Interview by the author, October 27, 2016.

146. See Cateforis, *Are We Not New Wave?*, 107–22, for more on kitsch and camp in new wave.

147. Spitz and Mullen, *Neutron Bomb*, 225.

148. Interview by the author, October 25, 2018.

149. Doe with DeSavia, *Under the Big Black Sun*, 28–29.

150. "Punk Rock Seen on KNXT-TV," *Billboard*, March 11, 1978.

151. Dennis Anderson, interview by the author, July 10, 2018.

152. On the history of the term *new wave* see Cateforis, *Are We Not New Wave?*, 20–27.

153. Russo, *We Were Going to Change the World*, 109–10.

## Chapter 7: "Decisions with Precisions":
## New Directions for Hardcore in Washington, DC

1. Quoted in Howie Abrams and James Lathos, *Finding Joseph I: An Oral History of H.R. from Bad Brains* (New York: Lesser Gods, 2017), 102–3.

2. Blush, *American Hardcore*, 209–44. This also includes international scenes, such as Germany (including Big Balls and the Great White Idiot), and Australia (including Radio Birdman and the Saints).

3. Philadelphia's Pure Hell, another early all-black punk rock group, was less successful and influential than Bad Brains. Detroit's Death, discussed in chapter 8, is another all-black rock group that has become well known as a protopunk group, but they were unknown in their time.

4. Natalie Hopkinson, *Go-Go Live: The Musical Life and Death of a Chocolate City* (Durham, NC: Duke University Press, 2012), ix.

5. Hopkinson, *Go-Go Live*, 103.

6. DeNeen L. Brown, "A Haven for Interracial Love amid Relentless Racism: Columbia Turns 50," *Washington Post*, July 21, 2017. Columbia had a significant African American population in the 1980s, hovering around 15 to 20 percent, but not the place described by Jeff Chang when he referred to the Chicago-born, Columbia-raised McGruder as a product of "Maryland's Black suburbs . . . hemmed in by clueless white exurban America on one side and aimless mixed-up urban America on the other." Chang, *Who We Be*, 32. I'm not sure that description accurately depicts any part of Maryland in the 1970s and 1980s.

7. Interview by the author, September 30, 2016. Bazil Hall first rented and then sold the land that became Hall's Hill to the people he had formerly enslaved. When the white Woodlawn Village was built in the 1930s, a wall was built to separate African Americans, and this wall remained fully intact until 1966. John Liebertz, *A Guide to the African American Heritage of Arlington County, Virginia* (Arlington: Department of Community Planning, Housing and Development, Historic Preservation Program, 2016), https://projects.arlingtonva.us/wp-content/uploads/sites/31/2016/09/A-Guide-to-the-African-American-Heritage-of-Arlington-County-Virginia.pdf ; see also "Our History," accessed December 28, 2018, http://www.highviewpark.com/history/; "'The Wall' of Hall's Hill Dedication," accessed December 28, 2018, http://www.highviewpark.com/news/2017/2/10/the-wall.

8. Hopkinson, *Go-Go Live*, 103.

9. Formisano, *Boston Against Busing*,18.

10. Rothstein, *Color of Law*, 223.

11. Interview by the author, November 1, 2016. See also the interviews in Mahon, *Right to Rock*, 42–53.

12. Abrams and Lathos, *Finding Joseph I*, 43.

13. Dave Findley, "Do Brains Make Bad Fish Food?" *Descenes* 1/4 (November 1979): 10.

14. Mark Andersen, quoted in Abrams and Lathos, *Finding Joseph I*, 59.

15. Andersen and Jenkins, *Dance of Days*, 27–30; Blush, *American Hardcore*, 118.

16. Abrams and Lathos, *Finding Joseph I*, 56.

17. Interview by the author, November 1, 2016.

18. Interview by the author, September 30, 2016. See Andersen and Jenkins, *Dance of Days*, 35–36.

19. Interview by the author, October 27, 2016.

20. Interview by the author, September 30, 2016.

21. Andersen and Jenkins, *Dance of Days*, 65–66; phone conversation with the author, July 24, 2019.

22. Interview by the author, October 28, 2016.

23. Interview by the author, October 27, 2016.

24. Easley, "'It's Not My Imagination,'" 15.

25. The guitar solo by Lyle Preslar is heard on the version of "Out of Step" featured on the original *In My Eyes* EP (1981). The version on the *Out of Step* LP (Dischord 10, 1983) replaces the guitar solo with Ian MacKaye speaking over the alternation pattern played on the bass.

26. On the breakdown in hardcore, see Easley, "'It's Not My Imagination,'" 145–52.

27. Ian MacKaye wrote the first Minor Threat songs by himself, except for "Seeing Red" by Jeff Nelson. "Betray," and probably some other later songs, were written with more input from the other members. The group added Steve Hansgen on bass and moved Brian Baker to second guitar in order to play songs composed by MacKaye on piano. Lyle Preslar, interview by the author, October 27, 2016.

28. Bad Brains, *Bad Brains* [the "yellow tape"], ROIR A106, 1982; for earlier recordings of these songs, hear the 1979 demos collected on Bad Brains, *Black Dots*, Caroline CAR 7534, 1996.

29. Easley, "'It's Not My Imagination,'" 11–12.

30. Abrams and Lathos, *Finding Joseph I*, 30.

31. Interview by the author, November 1, 2016.

32. Interview by the author, August 3, 2018.

33. Blush, *American Hardcore*, 121; Andersen and Jenkins, *Dance of Days*, 67–69.

34. Interview by the author, November 1, 2016.

35. On the Slickee Boys and their contemporaries, see Andersen and Jenkins, *Dance of Days*, 1–17.

36. Interview by the author, November 1, 2016.

37. Interview by the author, September 30, 2016.

38. Andersen and Jenkins, *Dance of Days*, 42–43.

39. Randy Rampage (Randall Archibald) with Chris Walter, *I Survived D.O.A.* (Vancouver: GFY Press, 2016); Keithley, *I, Shithead*, 73. Number 9 was vacated in 2014 for new developers.

40. Keithley, *I, Shithead*, 73.

41. Blush, *American Hardcore*, 32–33.

42. Kelefa Sanneh, "United Blood," *New Yorker*, March 9, 2015.

43. Sanneh, "United Blood."

44. Phone conversation with the author, July 24, 2019.

45. Tony Rettman, *Straight Edge: A Clear-Headed Hardcore Punk History* (Brooklyn: Bazillion Points, 2017). On straight edge after the 1980s, see, e.g., Gabriel Kuhn, ed., *Sober Living for the Revolution: Hardcore Punk, Straight Edge, and Radical Politics* (Oakland: PM Press, 2010).

46. Blush, *American Hardcore*, 26–29; Andersen and Jenkins, *Dance of Days*, 102–4.

47. Blush, *American Hardcore*, 28.

48. Jeff Krulik and John Heyn, dirs., *Heavy Metal Parking Lot*, 1986.

49. Andersen and Jenkins, *Dance of Days*, 12.

50. Andersen and Jenkins, *Dance of Days*, 139.

51. Interview by the author, September 30, 2016.

52. Abrams and Lathos, *Finding Joseph I*, 250–52.

53. Napoleon Hill, *Think and Grow Rich*, rev. ed. (North Hollywood, CA: Wilshire Book, [1937] 1966).

54. Andersen and Jenkins, *Dance of Days*, 20.

55. Preslar, interview by the author, October 27, 2016.

56. Interview by the author, August 3, 2018.

57. Interview by the author, September 30, 2016.

58. Worley, *No Future*; Dawson, "'Love Music, Hate Racism'"; see also Travis A. Jackson, "Falling into Fancy Fragments: Punk, Protest, and Politics," in *The Routledge History of Social Protest in Popular Music*, ed. Jonathan C. Friedman (New York: Routledge, 2013), 157–70, for a more equivocal assessment of RAR and punk's overall attitude toward protest and political engagement.

59. Andersen and Jenkins, *Dance of Days*, 168–71.

60. Hopkinson, *Go-Go Live*, 19–21.

61. Interview by the author, September 30, 2016.

62. Lucian Perkins, *Hard Art DC 1979* (New York: Akashic Books, 2013); Andersen and Jenkins, *Dance of Days*, 44–46.

63. Perkins, *Hard Art*, 13.

64. Interview by the author, September 30, 2016.

65. Interview by the author, September 30, 2016.

66. Jay P. Childers, *The Evolving Citizen: American Youth and the Changing Norms of Democratic Engagement* (University Park: Pennsylvania State University Press, 2012), 48. See also Andersen and Jenkins, *Dance of Days*, 20.

67. Blush, *American Hardcore*, 137.

68. Conversation with the author, July 24, 2019.

69. Interview by the author, August 3, 2018.

70. Interview by the author, September 30, 2016.

71. Interview by the author, October 27, 2016.

72. Andersen and Jenkins, *Dance of Days*, 106–9; Ensminger, *Visual Vitriol*, 170–71.

73. E.g., Blush, *American Hardcore*, 125–28; Andersen and Jenkins, *Dance of Days*, 135–37.

74. Tim Kerr, "Frequently Asked Questions," accessed September 9, 2018, https://www .timkerr.net/faq.htm.

75. Anonymous contributor, "Bad Brains Enter 30th Year of Getting a Pass for Homophobia," https://thehardtimes.net/music/bad-brains-enter-30th-year-of-getting-a-pass-for -homophobia/; Darryl Jenifer, interview by Dave Maher, *Pitchfork*, August 7, 2007, https:// pitchfork.com/features/interview/6663-bad-brains/.

76. Darryl Jenifer, interview by Richard Verducci, Punknews.org, July 13, 2010, https://www .punknews.org/article/39041/interviews-daryl-jenifer-bad-brains; Sonia Sabelli, "'Dubbing Di Diaspora': Gender and Reggae Music Inna Babylon," *Social Identities* 17/1 (January 2011): 137–52.

77. Worley, *No Future*, 144–46.

78. David Barnett, "Loved the Music, Hated the Bigots," *Independent*, July 19, 2016, https:// www.independent.co.uk/arts-entertainment/music/features/loved-the-music-hated-the -bigots-7138621.html.

79. Ensminger, *Visual Vitriol*, 150–53. See also Blush, *American Hardcore*, 36–38.

80. Eric Weiss, "The Bad Brains," *Rumpshaker* 5 (2000), quoted in Ensminger, *Visual Vitriol*, 171.

81. Andersen and Jenkins, *Dance of Days*, 148–49; http://stevenblush.com/promo/dchc/.

82. Interview by the author, October 27, 2016. Preslar distinctly remembers doing the WHUR broadcast and Brian Baker has some memory of it, but Jeff Nelson and Ian MacKaye do not.

83. Andersen and Jenkins, *Dance of Days*, 173–99.

84. Blush, *American Hardcore*, 124; Rettman, *NYHC*, 39–45. Roger Miret explained, "once the Bad Brains hit the New York scene it was game over. We caught up fast. We identified with this new, young scene of raging vocals, furious riffs and speed-of-sound tempos." Roger Miret with Jon Wiederhorn, *My Riot: Agnostic Front, Grits, Guts & Glory* (New York: Lesser Gods, 2017), 106.

85. Interview by the author, October 27, 2016.

86. Interview by the author, August 3, 2018.

87. Interview by the author, November 7, 2018.

88. Interview by the author, November 1, 2016.

89. Mimi Thi Nguyen, "It's (Not) a White World: Looking for Race in Punk," in Duncombe and Tremblay, *White Riot: Punk Rock and the Politics of Race*, 257–68, originally published in *Punk Planet* 28 (November/December 1998); see also Mimi Thi Nguyen, *Evolution of a Race Riot*, August 1997, accessed September 9, 2018, available online at the POC Zine Project, https://issuu.com/poczineproject/docs/evolution-of-a-race-riot-issue-1.

## Chapter 8: Outro: A New Way to Pay Old Debts

1. Bill Orcutt, interview by David Keenan, *The Wire: Adventures in Modern Music* 332 (October 2011): 29–32.

2. Robert Musil, *Precision and Soul: Essays and Addresses*, ed. and trans. Burton Pike and David S. Luft (Chicago: University of Chicago Press, [1978] 1990), 160, originally published in volumes 8 and 9 of Musil's *Gesammelte Werke*, ed. Adolf Frisé (Reinbek bei Hamburg: Rowohlt Verlag, 1978–81).

3. Albert Murray, *Stomping the Blues* (New York: Vintage Books, [1976] 1982).

4. Strummer, *HRR*.

5. Interview by the author, August 6, 2018.

6. Email to the author, October 15, 2012.

7. Velvet Underground, interview by Fricke.

8. See also Theodore Matula, "Pow! to the People: The Make-Up's Reorganization of Punk Rhetoric," *Popular Music and Society* 30 (2007): 19–38, which explores similar issues of race and appropriation in Svenonious's music.

9. "Leadbelly," *March of Time*, Volume 1, Episode 2, 1935.

10. Ian F. Svenonius, *The Psychic Soviet* (Chicago: Drag City, 2006), 144.

11. John Gramlich, "The Gap between the Number of Blacks and Whites in Prison Is Shrinking," *Pew Research Center*, January 12, 2018, http://www.pewresearch.org/fact-tank/2018/01/12/shrinking-gap-between-number-of-blacks-and-whites-in-prison/ft_18-01-10_prisonrace gaps_2/.

12. Svenonius, *Psychic Soviet*, 69, 104, 143–44.

13. Due to rapid gentrification, as of 2017 DC is 47.1 percent black, the percentage having fallen below 50 percent in 2011 after fifty-one years above it. Sabrina Tavernise, "A Population Changes, Uneasily," *New York Times*, July 17, 2011.

14. Rob Watson, interview by Sean Gray, April 9, 2015, http://bandwidth.wamu.org/rob-watson-of-pure-disgust-interview/; https://puredisgustdc.bandcamp.com/; https://www.coupsauvage.com/.

15. Amanda Teuscher, "The Evolving Politics of Punk in the Nation's Capital," *American Prospect*, July 15, 2015, https://prospect.org/article/evolving-politics-punk-nations-capital.

16. Interview by the author, October 16, 2018. "Due to a dispersed pattern of homebuying, Cleveland Hts. developed a high percentage of racially integrated neighborhoods [in the 1960s and 1970s]," *Encyclopedia of Cleveland History*, s.v. "Cleveland Heights," accessed January 5, 2019, https://case.edu/ech/articles/c/cleveland-heights.

17. Valerie Wilmer, *As Serious As Your Life: John Coltrane and Beyond* (London: Serpent's Tail, [1977] 1992).

18. Interview by the author, October 18, 2018.

19. Nathan Leigh, "'WTF is Punk?': Afropunk Bands Fight for the Genre's Soul, and for Our Communities," August 27, 2017, http://afropunk.com/2017/08/wtf-punk-afropunk-bands-fight -genres-soul-communities/.

20. Interview by the author, November 6, 2018. Stew's analysis echoes Jayna Brown's discussion of anger, catharsis, and "the scream" in Poly Styrene and Annabella Lwin's music. Jayna Brown, "'Brown Girl in the Ring': Poly Styrene, Annabella Lwin, and the Politics of Anger," *Journal of Popular Music Studies* 23/4 (December 2011): 455–78.

21. Mos Def, *The New Danger*, Geffen B0003558, 2004. See also Mahon, *Right to Rock*, and Fellezs, "Black Metal Soul Music."

22. Mahon, *Right to Rock*, 91.

23. Sacha Jenkins, "FAQ Afropunk!," accessed November 3, 2018, https://afropunk. com/2018/08/faq-afropunk-by-sacha-jenkins/.

24. Interview by the author, October 18, 2018.

25. Sara Marcus, *Girls to the Front: The True Story of the Riot Grrrl Revolution* (New York: Harper, 2010); Andersen and Jenkins, *Dance of Days*, 307–38.

26. Carrie Brownstein, *Hunger Makes Me a Modern Girl* (New York: Riverhead, 2015), 61–62.

27. Feminist Press, *Pussy Riot! A Punk Prayer for Freedom: Letters from Prison, Songs, Poems, and Courtroom Statements, Plus Tributes to the Punk Band That Shook the World* (New York: Feminist Press at City University of New York, 2013).

28. Marcus, *Girls to the Front*, 48–49; Brown, "'Brown Girl in the Ring.'"

29. *VV.* This show was with Ana de Silva, Gina Birch, Jeremie Frank, and Richard Dudanski, before Palmolive and Vicky Aspinall joined the band. Hear Jean Caffeine's recent song about the early San Francisco punk scene, "Sadie Saturday Nite," at http://jeancaffeine.bandcamp.com/.

30. Pelly, *The Raincoats*, 19–23.

31. Quoted in Pelly, *The Raincoats*, xi.

32. Maria Sherman, "Downtown Boys' Victoria Ruiz on Writing Chicana Protest-Punk Anthems," *Rolling Stone*, September 20, 2017, https://www.rollingstone.com/music/music -features/downtown-boys-victoria-ruiz-on-writing-chicana-protest-punk-anthems-117084/; Victoria Ruiz, "Navigating Whiteness in Latinx Spaces: Downtown Boys' Victoria Ruiz Interviews Joey DeFrancesco," Remezcla, February 10, 2017, http://remezcla.com/features/music/ dowtown-boys-la-neve-interview/.

33. Downtown Boys, "Dancing in the Dark," https://downtownboys.bandcamp.com/ album/full-communism-3; Cheky, "Downtown Boys Reimagine Selena's 'Fotos y Recuerdos' with a Punk Edge," Remezcla, May 24, 2018, http://remezcla.com/releases/music/ downtown-boys-fotos-y-recuerdos-track/.

34. Interview by the author, August 30, 2012.

35. David Grossman, "Downtown Boys: Meet America's Most Exciting Punk Band," *Rolling Stone*, December 11, 2015.

36. Victoria Ruiz and Joey DeFrancesco, interview by Amy Goodman, "Downtown Boys: 'America's Most Exciting Punk Band' Performs and Discusses Making Change Through Music,'" *Democracy Now!* January 13, 2016, https://www.democracynow.org/2016/1/13/ downtown_boys_americas_most_exciting_punk.

37. Downtown Boys (Joe DeGeorge), interview by the author, December 21, 2018.

38. Downtown Boys (Joe DeGeorge), interview by the author, December 21, 2018.

39. Downtown Boys (Victoria Ruiz), interview by the author, December 21, 2018.

40. Downtown Boys (Victoria Ruiz), interview by the author, December 21, 2018.

41. Worley, *No Future*, 24–27; Kramer, *The Hard Stuff*, 96–102.

42. Interview by the author, October 27, 2016. This was probably April 4, 1992, at the Paramount Theater, with Mudhoney headlining.

43. Interview by the author, November 4, 2018; Bangs, *Psychotic Reactions*.

44. Heylin, *Velvets to the Voidoids*, 182.

45. Eric Wilson, "A Necessary Stop," *New York Times*, May 29, 2013, https://www.nytimes.com/2013/05/30/fashion/a-necessary-stop-at-re-creation-of-cbgb-restroom.html.

46. Listen at "Our Concert Could Be Your Life: Indie's New Guard Pays Tribute to '80s Icons," NPR.org, May 24, 2011, https://www.npr.org/2011/05/24/136503845/our-concert-could-be-your-life-indies-new-guard-pays-tribute-to-80s-icons.

47. Mark Covino and Jeff Howlett, dirs., *A Band Called Death*, Drafthouse Films, 2012.

48. "The Very Black History of Punk Music," AJ+ (Al Jazeera Media Network), https://www.youtube.com/watch?v=WgIWDZ1xxdM

49. "The Very Black History."

50. Mike Rubin, "This Band Was Punk Before Punk Was Punk," *New York Times*, March 12, 2009.

51. "The Very Black History."

52. Jenny Farajbeik, "The Band Called Death Plays Ann Arbor for the First Time," *Detroit Metro Times*, September 9, 2015, https://www.metrotimes.com/detroit/the-band-called-death-plays-ann-arbor-for-the-first-time/Content?oid=2366947.

53. Pioneer status has also been attached to Philadelphia's all-black hard rock band Pure Hell, who were better known and more active, but also more "of their time" in the mid- to late 1970s than has been acknowledged. Other bands remain obscure, such as Detroit's brazenly named Niggers, billed as "the first black punk act" in *Billboard* when they played CBGB in 1978 as part of the "Motor City Review" with the Traitors and the Pigs. *Billboard*, March 11, 1978, 73; a tape of this show is available in the *JBC* (Box 5, Tape 5). Franziska Pietschmann, "A Blacker and Browner Shade of Pale: Reconstructing Punk Rock History" (M.A. thesis, Technische Universität Dresden, 2010), contains a useful interview with Kenny Gordon of Pure Hell. See also de Kergariou, *No Future*, 58–59. Similar contemporary impulses have situated Mexican American, Michigan-based band ? and the Mysterians as the originators of punk, as well as the mid-1960s Peruvian band Los Saicos. Zona de Obras, *Diccionario de punk*, 5, 222–23, 239–40.

54. Porter and Austen, "Black Punk Time."

55. Eugene S. Robinson, "White Supremacy + Me," OZY, January 14, 2016, https://www.ozy.com/c-notes/white-supremacy-me/30970; Laina Dawes, *What are You Doing Here? A Black Woman's Life and Liberation in Heavy Metal* (Brooklyn: Bazillion Points, 2012).

56. Interview by the author, November 5, 2018.

57. Interview by the author, November 5, 2018.

58. E.g., Benjamin Melendez, the member of the Ghetto Brothers (gang and band) who brokered the Hoe Avenue peace treaty in 1971, was from a Sephardic crypto-Jewish family and later reclaimed his Jewish identity.

59. Alex Woodward, "Body Politics: Show Me the Body's Rage Against the Machine," *Gambit*, July 9, 2018, https://www.theadvocate.com/gambit/new_orleans/music/article_9dea43b2-813e-11e8-85d7-77ad3ea13376.html.

60. Interview by the author, November 5, 2018.

61. Tony Thomas, "Why Africans Put the Banjo Down," in *Hidden in the Mix: The African American Presence in Country Music*, ed. Diane Pecknold (Durham, NC: Duke University Press, 2013), 143–70.

62. Interview by the author, November 5, 2018.

63. "Work Sets You Free," Corpus TV, episode 8, accessed December 22, 2018, https://www.youtube.com/watch?v=rkHVutjQakE.

# BIBLIOGRAPHY

## Archival Collections

*BOMP*: Bomp! Collection, ARC-0036, including Greg Shaw's Scene Files, Rock and Roll Hall of Fame Library and Archives.

*HRR*: Unedited interviews for the *Time-Life History of Rock and Roll*, ARC-0314, Rock and Roll Hall of Fame Library and Archives. Interviews conducted ca. 1994.

*JBC*: James Brawley Collection, ARC-0045, Rock and Roll Hall of Fame Library and Archives.

*VV*: V. Vale Collection of Search and Destroy and Re/Search Publications, UCLA Library Special Collections.

## Books and Articles

Abbott, Lynn, and Doug Seroff. "'They Cert'ly Sound Good to Me': Sheet Music, Southern Vaudeville, and the Commercial Ascendancy of the Blues." In *Ramblin' on My Mind: New Perspectives on the Blues*, edited by David Evans, 49–104. Urbana: University of Illinois Press, 2008.

Abrams, Howie, and James Lathos. *Finding Joseph I: An Oral History of H.R. from Bad Brains*. New York: Lesser Gods, 2017.

Adelt, Ulrich. *Blues Music in the Sixties: A Story in Black and White*. New Brunswick, NJ: Rutgers University Press, 2010.

Afary, Kamran. *Performance and Activism: Grassroots Discourse after the Los Angeles Rebellion of 1992*. Lanham, MD: Lexington Books, 2009.

Ahmed, Sara. *On Being Included: Racism and Diversity in Institutional Life*. Durham, NC: Duke University Press, 2012.

Albertine, Viv. *Clothes, Clothes, Clothes. Music, Music, Music. Boys, Boys, Boys: A Memoir*. New York: St. Martin's Press, 2014.

Alterman, Loraine. "Rock 'n' Roots," *New York Times*, November 21, 1971.

Andersen, Mark, and Mark Jenkins. *Dance of Days: Two Decades of Punk in the Nation's Capital*. Brooklyn: Akashic Books, 2009.

Angry Samoans (Gregg Turner and Mike Saunders). Interview. *Ink Disease* 14 (Fall 1988): 42–52.

Antonia, Nina. *Too Much Too Soon*. London: Omnibus Press, 1998.

Atoe, Osa. *Shotgun Seamstress* (blog). http://shotgunseamstress.blogspot.com.

Atoe, Osa. *Shotgun Seamstress* (zines). Available online at https://issuu.com/shotgunseamstress.

Avila, Eric. *Popular Culture in the Age of White Flight: Fear and Fantasy in Suburban Los Angeles*. Berkeley: University of California Press, 2004.

Azerrad, Michael. *Our Band Could Be Your Life: Scenes from the American Indie Underground, 1981–1991*. Boston: Back Bay Books, 2001.

Bag, Alice. "Racism in the Early Punk Scene." *Diary of a Bad Housewife* (blog), April 17, 2005, http://alicebag.blogspot.com/2005/04/racism-in-early-punk-scene.html.

Bag, Alice. *Violence Girl: East L.A. Rage to Hollywood Stage, A Chicana Punk Story.* Port Townsend, WA: Feral House, 2011.

Bangs (Debbie [Peterson], Vicki [Peterson], Annette [Zilinskas], Susanna [Hoffs]). Interview by Bruce Kalberg. *No Magazine*, 1982.

Bangs, Lester. "Dead Lie the Velvets Underground R.I.P. Long Live Lou Reed." *Creem*, May 1971. Reprinted in *The Velvet Underground: New York Art*, edited by Johan Kugelberg, 290–97. New York: Rizzoli, 2009.

Bangs, Lester. "How to Learn to Love Reggae." *Stereo Review*, April 1977.

Bangs, Lester. *Psychotic Reactions and Carburetor Dung*, edited by Greil Marcus. New York: Vintage Books, 1988.

Baraka, Amiri. *Black Music*. New York: William Morrow, 1967.

Baraka, Amiri [LeRoi Jones]. *Blues People: The Negro Experience in White America and the Music That Developed from It*. New York: William Morrow, 1963.

Barnes, Mike. *Captain Beefheart*. Rev. ed. London: Omnibus Press, 2011.

Barnett, David. "Loved the Music, Hated the Bigots." *Independent.* July 19, 2016. https://www.independent.co.uk/arts-entertainment/music/features/loved-the-music-hated-the-bigots-7138621.html.

Bartkowiak, Mathew. "Motor City Burning: Rock and Rebellion in the WPP and the MC5." *Journal for the Study of Radicalism* 1/2 (Spring 2007): 55–76.

Bessy, Claude (Kick). "Black Flag EP." *Slash* 2/6 (November 1979): 35.

Bessy, Claude (Kick). "The Decedents [*sic*], the Screwz, Vicious Circle, the Chiefs, the Mau Mau's and Black Flag at the Fleetwood (Redondo Beach)." *Slash* 3/4 (1980): 29–30.

Bessy, Claude (Kick Boy). "Middle Class, Negative Trend, Weirdos and Dils at the Azteca." *Slash* 2/1 (September 1978): 19.

Biafra, Jello. Interview by Peter Belsito. *Notes from the Pop Underground*. Berkeley: Last Gasp of San Francisco, 1985.

Biafra, Jello. Interview by V. Vale. Introduction to *Search & Destroy #1–6: The Complete Reprint*, edited by V. Vale, iii–vi. San Francisco: V/Search Publications, 1996.

Black Flag (Greg Ginn, Keith Morris, Chuck Dukowski, Dez Cadena, Henry Rollins, Bill Stevenson, Kira Roessler). Interview by David Grad. In *We Owe You Nothing*, edited by Daniel Sinker, 77–93. New York: Akashic Books, 2001.

"Black Flag." *Los Angeles Flipside* 16 (1979).

Blum, Stephen. "Rhythmic-Harmonic Cycles in Musical Idioms of the Black Atlantic." Paper read at annual meeting of the American Musicological Society, November 13, 2004. https://www.academia.edu/7648658/Rhythmic-Harmonic_Cycles_Black_Atlantic_AMS_2004_.

Blush, Steven. *American Hardcore: A Tribal History*. Los Angeles: Feral House, 2001.

Blush, Steven. *New York Rock: From the Rise of The Velvet Underground to the Fall of CBGB*. New York: St. Martin's Griffin, 2016.

Bockris, Victor, and Gerald Malanga. *Up-Tight: The Velvet Underground Story*. London: Omnibus Press, 1983.

Boulware, Jack, and Silke Tudor. *Gimme Something Better: The Profound, Progressive, and Occasionally Pointless History of Bay Area Punk from Dead Kennedys to Green Day*. New York: Penguin, 2009.

Bowman, Rob. "The Stax Sound: A Musicological Analysis." *Popular Music* 14/3 (October 1995): 285–320.

Bradshaw, Jon. "The Reggae Way to 'Salvation.'" *New York Times*, August 14, 1977.

Brown, DeNeen L. "A Haven for Interracial Love amid Relentless Racism: Columbia Turns 50." *Washington Post*, July 21, 2017.

Brown, Jayna. "'Brown Girl in the Ring': Poly Styrene, Annabella Lwin, and the Politics of Anger." *Journal of Popular Music Studies* 23/4 (December 2011): 455–78.

Brownstein, Carrie. *Hunger Makes Me a Modern Girl*. New York: Riverhead, 2015.

Burning Spear (Winston Rodney). Interview by Jeffrey Lea and Don Snowdon. *Slash* 3/2 (1980): 22–23.

Buszek, Maria Elena. "Punk Rock Futurist." In *Mark Mothersbaugh: Myopia*, edited by Adam Lerner, 77–89. New York: Princeton Architectural Press, 2014.

Butz, Konstantin. "Rereading American Hardcore: Intersectional Privilege and the Lyrics of Early Californian Hardcore Punk." *as|peers* 1 (2008): 131–58.

Cadena, Dez. Interview by Tony Rettman. *Noisey*, September 3, 2015, https://noisey.vice.com/en_us/article/r3zpe8/dez-cadena-interview.

Carducci, Joe. *Rock and the Pop Narcotic: Testament for the Electric Church*. 2nd rev. ed. Los Angeles: 2.13.61, 1994.

Carson, David. *Grit, Noise, and Revolution: The Birth of Detroit Rock 'n' Roll*. Ann Arbor: University of Michigan Press, 2006.

Cateforis, Theo. *Are We Not New Wave? Modern Pop at the Turn of the 1980s*. Ann Arbor: University of Michigan Press, 2011.

Chang, Jeff. *Can't Stop Won't Stop: A History of the Hip-Hop Generation*. New York: St. Martin's Press, 2005.

Chang, Jeff. *Who We Be: The Colorization of America*. New York: St. Martin's Press, 2014.

Charters, Sam. *The Country Blues*. New York: Rinehart, 1959.

Cherkis, Jason. "The Lost Girls." *Huffington Post Highline*, July 8, 2015. https://highline.huffingtonpost.com/articles/en/the-lost-girls/.

Childers, Jay P. *The Evolving Citizen: American Youth and the Changing Norms of Democratic Engagement*. University Park: Pennsylvania State University Press, 2012.

Christgau, Robert. *Stranded: Rock and Roll for a Desert Island*, edited by Greil Marcus. New York: Da Capo Press, 2007.

Chrome (Damon Edge). Interview by Vale. *Search & Destroy* 8 (1978), reprinted in *Search & Destroy #7–11: The Complete Reprint*, edited by V. Vale, 41. San Francisco: V/Search Publications, 1996.

Cisnal, Fréderic. *Berlin avant la techno: Du post-punk à la chute du mur*. Marseille, France: Le Mot et le Reste, 2015.

Cohodas, Nadine. *Spinning Blues into Gold: The Chess Brothers and the Legendary Chess Records*. New York: St. Martin's Griffin, 2000.

Controllers (Karla "Mad Dog" Duplantier and Kidd Spike). Interview. *No Magazine* 1 (1978): 5–6.

Controllers (Kid Spike, Johnny Stingray, Karla Mad Dog). Interview. *Slash* 2/6 (June 1979): 18–19.

Courrier, Kevin. *Trout Mask Replica*. New York: Continuum, 2007.

Covach, John. "Leiber and Stoller, the Coasters, and the 'Dramatic AABA' Form." In *Sounding Out Pop: Analytical Essays in Popular Music*, edited by Mark Spicer and John Covach, 1–17. Ann Arbor: University of Michigan Press, 2010.

Cramps (Lux Interior, Ivy Rorschach, Bryan Gregory, and Nick Knox). Interview. *Slash* 1/12 (August 1978): 17–18.

Crenshaw, Kimberlé. "Demarginalizing the Intersection of Race and Sex: A Black Feminist Critique of Antidiscrimination Doctrine, Feminist Theory and Antiracist Politics." *University of Chicago Legal Forum* 1 (1989): 139–67.

Crenshaw, Kimberlé. "Why Intersectionality Can't Wait." *Washington Post*, September 24, 2015.

Cullen, Shaun. "White Skin, Black Flag: Hardcore Punk, Racialization, and the Politics of Sound in Southern California." *Criticism* 58/1 (Winter 2016): 59–85.

Cutler, Chris. *File Under Popular.* Brooklyn: Autonomedia, 1993.

Davis, Angela Y. *Blues Legacies and Black Feminism: Gertrude "Ma" Rainey, Bessie Smith, and Billie Holiday.* New York: Pantheon, 1998.

Davis, Mike. *City of Quartz: Excavating the Future in Los Angeles.* London: Verso, 1990.

Dawes, Laina. *What Are You Doing Here? A Black Woman's Life and Liberation in Heavy Metal.* Brooklyn: Bazillion Points, 2012.

Dawson, Ashley. "'Love Music, Hate Racism': The Cultural Politics of the Rock Against Racism Campaigns, 1976–1981." *Postmodern Culture* 16/1 (September 2005). DOI: 10.1353/pmc.2006.0002.

de Kergariou, Caroline. *No future: Une histoire du punk.* Paris: Perrin, 2017.

Dellinger, Jade, and David Giffels. *Are We Not Men? We Are Devo!* London: SAF Publishing, 2003.

Delmont, Matthew F. *Why Busing Failed: Race, Media, and the National Resistance to School Desegregation.* Oakland: University of California Press, 2016.

Destroy All Monsters. *Destroy All Monsters Magazine.* New York: Primary Information, 2011.

DEVO. Interview (part two). *Search and Destroy* 3 (1977), reprinted in *Search & Destroy #1–6: The Complete Reprint,* edited by V. Vale, 52–53. San Francisco: V/Search Publications, 1996.

Dimock, Michael. "Defining Generations: Where Millennials End and Post-Millennials Begin." *Pew Research Center,* March 1, 2018. http://www.pewresearch.org/fact-tank/2018/03/01/defining-generations-where-millennials-end-and-post-millennials-begin/.

Diner, Hasia R. *The Jews of the United States, 1654 to 2000.* Berkeley: University of California Press, 2006.

Diner, Hasia R. *Lower East Side Memories: A Jewish Place in America.* Princeton, NJ: Princeton University Press, 2002.

Diner, Hasia R. "Trading Faces." Review of *Blackface, White Noise,* by Michael Rogin. *CommonQuest* 2/1 (Summer 1997): 40–44.

Doane, Randal. *Stealing All Transmissions: A Secret History of the Clash.* Oakland: PM Press, 2014.

Doe, John, with Tom DeSavia and friends. *Under the Big Black Sun: A Personal History of L.A. Punk.* Boston: Da Capo Press, 2016.

Doll, Christopher. *Hearing Harmony: Toward a Tonal Theory for the Rock Era.* Ann Arbor: University of Michigan Press, 2017.

Domanick, Joe. "A Shooting Reminiscent of the LAPD's Worst Days." *Los Angeles Times,* June 6, 1999. http://articles.latimes.com/1999/jun/06/opinion/op-44648.

Douglas, Ann. *Terrible Honesty: Mongrel Manhattan in the 1920s.* New York: Farrar, Straus, and Giroux, 1995.

Dowling, Julie. *Mexican Americans and the Question of Race.* Austin: University of Texas Press, 2014.

Duncombe, Stephen and Maxwell Tremblay, eds. *White Riot: Punk Rock and the Politics of Race.* London: Verso, 2011.

Easley, David B. "'It's Not My Imagination, I've Got a Gun on My Back': Style and Sound in Early American Hardcore Punk, 1978–1983." PhD diss., Florida State University, 2011.

Easley, David B. "Riff Schemes, Form, and the Genre of Early American Hardcore Punk (1978–83)." *Music Theory Online* 21/1 (March 2015). http://www.mtosmt.org/issues/mto.15.21.1/mto.15.21.1.easley.html.

Eichhorn, Kate. *The Archival Turn in Feminism: Outrage in Order.* Philadelphia: Temple University Press: 2013.

Ellison, Ralph. "The Blues." Review of *Blues People,* by LeRoi Jones [Amiri Baraka]. *New York Review of Books,* February 6, 1964. Reprinted in *Shadow and Act.* New York: Vintage, 1995.

Encarnacao, John. *Punk Aesthetics and New Folk: Way Down the Old Plank Road.* Surrey: Ashgate, 2013.

Ensminger, David A. *Left of the Dial: Conversations with Punk Icons.* Oakland: PM Press, 2013.

Ensminger, David A. *Visual Vitriol: The Street Art and Subcultures of the Punk and Hardcore.* Jackson: University Press of Mississippi, 2011.

Ervin, Jarek Paul. "New York Punk Rock: Genre as Mourning and Reconciliation (1967–1980)." PhD diss., University of Virginia, 2017.

Essinger, Silvio. *Punk: Anarquia planetária e a cena brasileira.* São Paulo: Editora 34, 1999.

Eudeline, Christian. *Los années punk: 1972–1978.* Paris: Denoël, 2002.

Everett, Walter. *The Foundations of Rock from "Blue Suede Shoes" to "Suite: Judy Blue Eyes."* Oxford: Oxford University Press, 2009.

Everett, Walter. "Making Sense of Rock's Tonal Systems." *Music Theory Online* 10/4 (December 2004). http://www.mtosmt.org/issues/mto.04.10.4/mto.04.10.4.w_everett.html.

Felker-Kantor, Max. *Policing Los Angeles: Race, Resistance, and the Rise of the LAPD.* Chapel Hill: University of North Carolina Press, 2018.

Fellezs, Kevin. "Black Metal Soul Music: Stone Vengeance and the Aesthetics of Race in Heavy Metal." In *Hardcore, Punk, and Other Junk: Aggressive Sounds in Contemporary Music,* edited by Eric James Abbey and Colin Helb, 121–37. Lanham, MD: Lexington Books, 2014.

Feminist Press. *Pussy Riot! A Punk Prayer for Freedom: Letters from Prison, Songs, Poems, and Courtroom Statements, Plus Tributes to the Punk Band That Shook the World.* New York: Feminist Press at the City University of New York, 2013.

Findley, Dave. "Do Brains Make Bad Fish Food?" *Descenes* 1/4 (November 1979): 10.

Finnegan, Ruth. *The Hidden Musicians: Music Making in an English Town.* Middletown, CT: Wesleyan University Press, [1989] 2007.

Fischler, Marcelle S. "A Hamlet on the Long Road to Renewal." *New York Times,* November 24, 2010.

Fishman, Robert. *Bourgeois Utopias: The Rise and Fall of Suburbia.* New York: Basic Books, 1987.

Fogelson, Robert. *Bourgeois Nightmares: Suburbia, 1870–1930.* New Haven: Yale University Press, 2005.

Formisano, Ronald P. *Boston Against Busing: Race, Class, and Ethnicity in the 1960s and 1970s.* Chapel Hill: University of North Carolina Press, 1991.

Franqui-Rivera, Harry. "The Color Line: Afro-Puerto Ricans and the Harlem Hellfighters." Centro Center for Puerto Rican Studies. https://centropr.hunter.cuny.edu/digital-humanities/pr-military/color-line-afro-puerto-ricans-and-harlem-hellfighters.

Frere-Jones, Sasha. "Terra Cognita: Savages Carefully Reinvents the Wheel." *New Yorker,* May 6, 2013.

Fricke, David. Liner notes to Ramones, *Hey! Ho! Let's Go! The Anthology.* Rhino R2 75817, 1999.

Galenza, Ronald. "Zwischen Plan und Planlos: Punk in Deutschland." In *Rock! Jugend und Musik in Deutschland,* edited by Barbara Hammerschmitt and Bernd Lindner, 97–103. Berlin: Links, 2005.

Garrett, Charles Hiroshi. *Struggling to Define a Nation: American Music and the Twentieth Century.* Berkeley: University of California Press, 2008.

Garst, John. "Man of Constant Sorrow: Antecedents and Tradition." In *Country Music Annual 2002,* edited by Charles K. Wolfe and Jame E. Akenson, 26–53. Lexington: University Press of Kentucky, 2002.

Gendron, Bernard. *Between Montmartre and the Mudd Club: Popular Music and the Avant-Garde.* Chicago: University of Chicago Press, 2002.

Gennari, John. *Blowin' Hot and Cool: Jazz and Its Critics.* Chicago: University of Chicago Press, 2006.

George, Nelson. *The Death of Rhythm and Blues.* New York: Plume, 1988.

Gilmore, Mikal. "The Curse of the Ramones." *Rolling Stone*, May 19, 2016. http://www.rolling stone.com/music/features/the-curse-of-the-ramones-20160519.

Gilroy, Paul. *The Black Atlantic: Modernity and Double Consciousness.* Cambridge: Harvard University Press, 1993.

Goldberg, RoseLee. *Performance Art: From Futurism to the Present.* Rev. and exp. ed. New York: Thames & Hudson, 2001.

Goldman, Vivien. *Revenge of the She-Punks: A Feminist Music History from Poly Styrene to Pussy Riot.* Austin: University of Texas Press, 2019.

Goldstein, Dana. "New York's Schools Chancellor Is Talking About Integration. Can He Make It Happen?" *New York Times*, September 3, 2018. https://www.nytimes.com/2018/09/03/nyre gion/nyc-chancellor-school-segregation.html.

Gombosi, Otto. "Stephen Foster and 'Gregory Walker.'" *Musical Quarterly* 30/2 (April 1944): 133–46.

Gomez, Melissa. "Pro-Trump Fan of Social Distortion Says Lead Singer Punched Him at Concert." *New York Times*, August 16, 2018. https://www.nytimes.com/2018/08/16/us/social -distortion-singer-beating-trump.html.

Gonzalez-Barrera, Ana, and Mark Hugo Lopez. "Is Being Hispanic a Matter of Race, Ethnicity or Both?" *Pew Research Center*, June 15, 2015. http://www.pewresearch.org/fact-tank/2015/ 06/15/is-being-hispanic-a-matter-of-race-ethnicity-or-both/.

Goodwin, Gerald F. "Black and White in Vietnam." *New York Times*, July 18, 2017. https://www .nytimes.com/2017/07/18/opinion/racism-vietnam-war.html.

Goosman, Stuart L. *Group Harmony: The Black Urban Roots of Rhythm & Blues.* Philadelphia: University of Pennsylvania Press, 2005.

Gramlich, John. "The Gap between the Number of Blacks and Whites in Prison Is Shrinking." *Pew Research Center*, January 12, 2018. http://www.pewresearch.org/fact-tank/2018/01/12/ shrinking-gap-between-number-of-blacks-and-whites-in-prison/ft_18-01-10_prison racegaps_2/.

Granade, Samuel Andrew, II. "'I Was a Bum Once Myself': Harry Partch, *U.S. Highball*, and the Dust Bowl in the American Imagination." PhD diss., University of Illinois at Urbana-Champaign, 2005.

Grant, David M., Melvin L. Oliver, and Angela D. James. "African Americans: Social and Economic Bifurcation." In *Ethnic Los Angeles*, edited by Roger Waldinger and Mehdi Bozorg-mehr, 379–411. New York: Russell Sage Foundation, 1996.

Greene, John. "Never Mind the Sex Pistols: Here's French Punk or Why Didn't *le punk français* Go Global?" *Journal of Popular Music Studies* 29/4 (December 2017). https://doi.org/10.1111/ jpms.12241.

Gribin, Anthony J., and Matthew M. Schiff. *The Complete Book of Doo-Wop.* Iola, WI: Krause Publications, 2000.

Grimshaw, Jeremy. *Draw a Straight Line and Follow It: The Music and Mysticism of La Monte Young.* New York: Oxford University Press, 2011.

Groening, Matt. "The True Story of the Residents: A Brief Summary of Known Facts, Top Secrets, Hazy Details, Veiled Hints, and Blatant Lies." In *The Cryptic Guide to the Residents*, edited by Dave Warden. San Francisco: Bach's Decay, 1986.

Groos, Ulrike, Peter Gorschlüter, and Jürgen Teipel, eds. *Zurück zum Beton: Die Anfänge von Punk und New Wave in Deutschland 1977–82*. Köln: Verlag der Buchhandlung Walther König, 2002.

Grossman, David. "Downtown Boys: Meet America's Most Exciting Punk Band." *Rolling Stone*, December 11, 2015.

Grow, Kory. "X Look Back on 40 Years of Punk Iconoclasm." *Rolling Stone*, September 5, 2017.

Gunckel, Colin. "Defining Punk: Queerness and the LA Punk Scene, 1977–1981." *Journal of Popular Music Studies* 30/1–2 (March–June 2018): 155–70.

Gurock, Jeffrey S. *Jews in Gotham: New York Jews in a Changing City, 1920–2010*. Vol. 3 of *City of Promises: A History of the Jews of New York*, edited by Deborah Dash Moore. New York: New York University Press, 2012.

Gushee, Lawrence. *Pioneers of Jazz: The Story of the Creole Band*. New York: Oxford University Press, 2005.

Habell-Pallán, Michelle. *Loca Motion: The Travels of Chicana and Latina Popular Culture*. New York: New York University Press, 2005.

Hamilton, Jack. *Just Around Midnight: Rock and Roll and the Racial Imagination*. Cambridge: Harvard University Press, 2016.

Hamm, Charles. *Yesterdays: Popular Song in America*. New York: W.W. Norton, [1979] 1983.

Handy, W. C. *Father of the Blues*. New York: Macmillan, 1941.

Harkleroad, Bill. *Lunar Notes: Zoot Horn Rollo's Captain Beefheart Experience*. London: SAF Publishing, 1998.

Harris, Cheryl I. "Whiteness as Property." *Harvard Law Review* 106/8 (June 1993): 1709–91.

Headlam, Dave. "Blues Transformations in the Music of Cream." In *Understanding Rock*, edited by John Covach and Graeme M. Boone, 59–92. New York: Oxford University Press, 1997.

Heartfield, John. *Photomontages of the Nazi Period*. New York: Universe Books, 1977.

Hebdige, Dick. *Subculture: The Meaning of Style*. London: Routledge, [1979] 2001.

Heller, Michael C. *Loft Jazz: Improvising New York in the 1970s*. Berkeley: University of California Press, 2016.

Heylin, Clinton. *Anarchy in the Year Zero: The Sex Pistols, the Clash, and the Class of '76*. Pontefract: Route, 2016.

Heylin, Clinton. *From the Velvets to the Voidoids: The Birth of American Punk Rock*. Chicago: A Capella Books, [1993] 2005.

Hilburn, Robert. "A Positive Perspective on Punk." *Los Angeles Times*, February 28, 1978.

Hill, Napoleon. *Think and Grow Rich*. Rev. ed. North Hollywood, CA: Wilshire Book, [1937] 1966.

Hinman, Doug. *The Kinks: All Day and All of the Night*. San Francisco: Backbeat Books, 2004.

Hodgdon, Tim. *Manhood in the Age of Aquarius: Masculinity in Two Countercultural Communities, 1965–83*. New York: Columbia University Press, 2008.

Home, Stewart. *Cranked Up Really High: Genre Theory and Punk Rock*. Hove, UK: Codex, 1995.

Hopkinson, Natalie. *Go-Go Live: The Musical Life and Death of a Chocolate City*. Durham, NC: Duke University Press, 2012.

Hubbs, Nadine. *Rednecks, Queers, and Country Music*. Berkeley: University of California Press, 2014.

Huber, Patrick. "Black Hillbillies: African American Musicians on Old-Time Records, 1924–1932." In *Hidden in the Mix: The African American Presence in Country Music*, edited by Diane Pecknold, 19–81. Durham, NC: Duke University Press, 2013.

Hurewitz, Daniel. *Bohemian Los Angeles and the Making of Modern Politics*. Berkeley: University of California Press, 2007.

Hynde, Chrissie. *Reckless: My Life as a Pretender.* New York: Anchor Books, 2015.

Inglis, Ian. "'Some Kind of Wonderful': The Creative Legacy of the Brill Building." *American Music* 21/2 (Summer 2003): 214–35.

Isaacs, James. "Power Chords and Boom-Boom; Bye-Bye Boogie: Punk *Nouveau* Burgeons in Boston." *Boston Phoenix*, March 23, 1976.

"Is There, Isn't There Punk Rock Violence???????" *Slush* (September/October 1980): 8.

Jackson, Jhoni. "Punk Was Always Gay: Kid Congo Powers on the Genre's Queer Beginnings." *Remezcla.com*, June 30, 2016. http://remezcla.com/features/music/kid-congo-powers-interview.

Jackson, Travis A. "Falling into Fancy Fragments: Punk, Protest, and Politics." In *The Routledge History of Social Protest in Popular Music*, edited by Jonathan C. Friedman, 157–70. New York: Routledge, 2013.

Jacobs, Jane. *The Death and Life of Great American Cities.* New York: Random House, 1961.

James, Tommy, with Martin Fitzpatrick. *Me, the Mob, and the Music: One Helluva Ride with Tommy James and the Shondells.* New York: Simon and Schuster, 2010.

Jameson, Frederic. "Postmodernism and Consumer Society." In *The Anti-Aesthetic: Essays on Postmodern Culture*, edited by Hal Foster, 127–44. New York: New Press, [1983] 2002.

Jenifer, Darryl. Interview by Dave Maher. *Pitchfork*, August 7, 2007. https://pitchfork.com/features/interview/6663-bad-brains/.

Jenkins, Mark. "Half Japanese Yik Yak: White Boys Makin' White Noise." *Descenes* 1/4 (November 1979): 7–9.

Jenkins, Sacha. "FAQ Afropunk!" *Afropunk.com.* Accessed November 3, 2017. https://afropunk.com/2018/08/faq-afropunk-by-sacha-jenkins/.

Kania, Carrie, ed., and Ed Caraeff, photographs. *Iggy & the Stooges: One Night at the Whisky 1970.* Woodbridge, UK: ACC Art Books, 2017.

Kassel, Richard M. "The Evolution of Harry Partch's Monophony." PhD diss., City University of New York, 1996.

Keil, Charles. *Urban Blues.* Chicago: University of Chicago Press, 1966.

Keister, Jay. "The Long Freak Out: Unfinished Music and Countercultural Madness in Avant-Garde Rock of the 1960s and 1970s." In *Countercultures and Popular Music*, edited by Sheila Whiteley and Jedediah Sklower, 141–56. Surrey, UK: Ashgate, 2014.

Keith, Sherry, and Robert Girling. "Bauxite Dependency: Roots of Crisis." NACLA, September 25, 2007. https://nacla.org/article/bauxite-dependency-roots-crisis.

Keithley, Joey. *I, Shithead: A Life in Punk.* Vancouver: Arsenal Pulp Press, 2003.

Kelley, Mike, and Dan Nadel. *Return of the Repressed: Destroy All Monsters 1973–1977.* New York and Los Angeles: PictureBox and PRISM, 2011.

Kernodle, Tammy L. "'I Wish I Knew How It Would Feel to Be Free': Nina Simone and the Redefining of the Freedom Song of the 1960s." *Journal of the Society for American Music* 2/3 (August 2008): 295–317.

Kitman, Jamie. "Talking and Rocking with Punk's Elder Statesmen." *Columbia Daily Spectator*, October 8, 1976.

Knopper, Steve. "The Dickies Going Long, Going Strong." *Chicago Tribune*, November 9, 2016. http://www.chicagotribune.com/entertainment/music/ct-the-dickies-punk-ott-1111-2016 1108-story.html.

Kramer, Wayne. *The Hard Stuff: Dope, Crime, the MC5 and My Life of Impossibilities.* New York: Da Capo Press, 2018.

Kubik, Gerhard. *Africa and the Blues.* Jackson: University Press of Mississippi, 1999.

Kugelberg, Johan, ed. *The Velvet Underground: New York Art* (New York: Rizzoli, 2009), 16.

Kugelberg, Johan, and Jon Savage, eds. *Punk: An Aesthetic*. New York: Rizzoli, 2012.

Kuhn, Gabriel, ed. *Sober Living for the Revolution: Hardcore Punk, Straight Edge, and Radical Politics*. Oakland: PM Press, 2010.

Kuivanen, Jarkko. *Suomipunk 1977–1998*. Helsinki, 1999.

Kun, Josh. "Vex Populi." *Los Angeles Magazine*, March 2003.

Laing, Dave. *One Chord Wonders: Power and Meaning in Punk Rock*. Milton Keynes, UK: Open University Press, 1985.

Landes, Anna Margarete. "Vom britischen Punk zum Hardcore Punk in Los Angeles: Dei Entstehungsgeschichte des Hardcore Punks mit einer interdisziplinären Analyse von Texten der Band Bad Religion aus der Reagan-Ära." PhD diss., Alpen-Adria-Universität Klagenfurt, 2009.

Larabee, Ann, and Mathew Bartkowiak. "Interview with John Sinclair." *Journal for the Study of Radicalism* 1/2 (Spring 2007): 129–40.

Laslett, John H. M. "Historical Perspectives: Immigration and the Rise of a Distinctive Urban Region, 1900–1970." In *Ethnic Los Angeles*, edited by Roger Waldinger and Mehdi Bozorgmehr, 39–75. New York: Russell Sage Foundation, 1996.

Leigh, Mickey, with Legs McNeil. *I Slept with Joey Ramone*. New York: Touchstone, 2010.

Leigh, Nathan. "'WTF is Punk?': Afropunk Bands Fight for the Genre's Soul, and for Our Communities." Afropunk.com, August 27, 2017. http://afropunk.com/2017/08/wtf-punk-afropunk-bands-fight-genres-soul-communities/.

Lerner, Adam. "Formative Years." In *Mark Mothersbaugh: Myopia*, edited by Adam Lerner, 57–75. New York: Princeton Architectural Press, 2014.

Letts, Don. Interview by Mark P. *Sniffin' Glue* 7, February 1977.

Levine, Cary. "Worried Man." In *Mark Mothersbaugh: Myopia*, edited by Adam Lerner, 91–99. New York: Princeton Architectural Press, 2014.

Lewis, George E. "Improvised Music after 1950: Afrological and Eurological Perspectives." *Black Music Research Journal* 16/1 (Spring 1996): 91–122.

Lewis, George E. *A Power Stronger than Itself: The A.A.C.M. and American Experimental Music*. Chicago: University of Chicago Press, 2008.

Library of Congress. *Voices from the Dust Bowl: The Charles L. Todd and Robert Sonkin Migrant Worker Collection, 1940 to 1941*. Accessed December 21, 2018. http://memory.loc.gov/ammem/afctshtml/tshome.html.

Licht, Alan. "The Hum of the City: La Monte Young and the Birth of NYC Drone." *Red Bull Music Academy Daily*, May 1, 2013. http://daily.redbullmusicacademy.com/2013/05/the-hum-of-the-city-la-monte-young.

Licht, Alan. "Notes on Robert Quine." *Perfect Sound Forever*. Accessed August 12, 2012. http://www.furious.com/perfect/quine/licht.html.

Liebertz, John. *A Guide to the African American Heritage of Arlington County, Virginia*. Arlington: Department of Community Planning, Housing and Development, Historic Preservation Program, 2016. https://projects.arlingtonva.us/wp-content/uploads/sites/31/2016/09/A-Guide-to-the-African-American-Heritage-of-Arlington-County-Virginia.pdf.

Lipsitz, George. *The Possessive Investment in Whiteness: How White People Profit from Identity Politics*. Rev. ed. Philadelphia: Temple University Press, 2006.

Lisheron, Mark. "Rhythm-and-Jews: The Story of the Blacks and Jews Who Worked Together to Create the Music of R&B." *CommonQuest* 2/1 (Summer 1997): 20–33.

Loney, Roy. Interview by Jason Gross. *Perfect Sound Forever*, April 2005. http://www.furious.com/perfect/royloney.html.

Loren, Cary. "a manifesto of ignorance; destroy all monsters." *Perfect Sound Forever*, May 1996. http://www.furious.com/perfect/dam.html.

Lorenz, Stephen Fox. "Cosmopolitan Folk: The Cultural Politics of the North American Folk Music Revival in Washington, D.C." PhD diss., George Washington University, 2014.

Lornell, Kip. Liner notes to *Virginia Traditions: Non-Blues Secular Black Music*. BRI Records 001, 1978.

Lott, Eric. "Back Door Man: Howlin' Wolf and the Sound of Jim Crow." *American Quarterly* 63/3 (September 2011): 697–710.

Lott, Eric. *Love and Theft: Blackface Minstrelsy and the American Working Class*. New York, Oxford University Press, 1993.

Lukinovic, Jonathan. *La canción punk de los 80 en Chile*. Santiago: Ediciones Oxímoron, 2015.

Lydon, John, with Keith and Kent Zimmerman. *Rotten: No Irish, No Blacks, No Dogs*. New York: Picador USA, 1994.

Madhubuti, Haki R. *Why L.A. Happened: Implications of the '92 Los Angeles Rebellion*. Chicago: Third World Press, 1993.

Mahon, Maureen. *Right to Rock: The Black Rock Coalition and the Cultural Politics of Race*. New York: New York University Press, 2004.

Mailer, Norman. "The White Negro." *Dissent*, Fall 1957.

Malesky, Kee. "The Journey from 'Colored' to 'Minorities' to 'People of Color.'" *Code Switch* (blog), NPR, March 30, 2014. https://www.npr.org/sections/codeswitch/2014/03/30/295931070/the-journey-from-colored-to-minorities-to-people-of-color.

Marcus, Greil. Liner notes to reissue of *Anthology of American Folk Music*, compiled by Harry Smith. Smithsonian Folkways SFW 40090, 1997.

Marcus, Greil. *Lipstick Traces: A Secret History of the Twentieth Century*. Cambridge: Harvard University Press, 1989.

Marcus, Sara. *Girls to the Front: The True Story of the Riot Grrrl Revolution*. New York: Harper, 2010.

Markey, David, and Jordan Schwartz, eds. *We Got Power! Hardcore Punk Scenes from 1980s Southern California*. Brooklyn: Bazillion Points, 2012.

Martin, Bradford D. *The Theater Is in the Street: Politics and Public Performance in Sixties America*. Amherst: University of Massachusetts Press, 2004.

Massey, Douglas S. "The Legacy of the 1968 Fair Housing Act." *Sociological Forum* 30/S1 (June 2015): 571–88.

Masters, Marc. *No Wave*. London: Black Dog, 2007.

McBride, Dave. "Counterculture." In *A Companion to Los Angeles*, edited by William Deverell and Greg Hise, 327–45. West Sussex, UK: Blackwell, 2010.

McCormick, Carlo. "Out of Bounds: Cultural Synaesthesia and Art in Unexpected Places." In *Panic Attack! Art in the Punk Years*, edited by Mark Sladen and Ariella Yedgar, 94–99. New York: Merrell, 2007.

McLeod, Kembrew. *The Downtown Pop Underground: New York City and the Literary Punks, Renegade Artists, DIY Filmmakers, Mad Playwrights, and Rock 'n' Roll Glitter Queens who Revolutionized Culture*. New York: Abrams Press, 2018.

McLeod, Kembrew. *Parallel Lines*. New York: Bloomsbury, 2016.

McMichael, Robert K. "'We Insist—Freedom Now!' Black Moral Authority, Jazz, and the Changeable Shape of Whiteness." *American Music* 16/4 (Winter 1998): 375–416.

McNeil, Legs, and Gillian McCain. *Please Kill Me: The Uncensored Oral History of Punk*. New York: Grove Press, 1996.

Meyer, Marshall W. "Police Shootings at Minorities: The Case of Los Angeles." *Annals of the American Academy of Political and Social Science* 452 (November 1980): 98–102.

Mezzrow, Mezz, and Bernard Wolfe. *Really the Blues.* New York: Signet, [1946] 1964.

Middleton, Richard. *Studying Popular Music.* Milton Keynes, UK: Open University Press, 1990.

Miller, Jim. "The Beach Boys." In *The Rolling Stone Illustrated History of Rock and Roll,* rev. ed., edited by Jim Miller, 162–68. New York: Rolling Stone, 1980.

Miller, Karl Hagstrom. *Segregating Sound: Inventing Folk and Pop Music in the Age of Jim Crow.* Durham, NC: Duke University Press, 2010.

Miller, Steve. *Detroit Rock City.* Boston: Da Capo Press, 2013.

Miret, Roger, with Jon Wiederhorn. *My Riot: Agnostic Front, Grits, Guts & Glory.* New York: Lesser Gods, 2017.

Modarres, Ali. Introduction. *City of Promise: Race and Historical Change in Los Angeles,* edited by Martin Schiesl and Mark Morrall Dodge. Claremont, CA: Regina Books, 2006.

Moon, Krystyn R. *Yellowface: Creating the Chinese in American Popular Music and Performance, 1850s–1920s.* New Brunswick, NJ: Rutgers University Press, 2005.

Moon, Tony. *Sideburns* 1 (January 1977).

Moore, Ryan. "Break on Through: The Counterculture and the Climax of American Modernism." In *Countercultures and Popular Music,* edited by Sheila Whiteley and Jedediah Sklower, 29–43. Surrey, UK: Ashgate, 2014.

Moore, Ryan. "Postmodernism and Punk Subculture: Cultures of Authenticity and Deconstruction." *Communication Review* 7/3 (2004): 305–27.

Moore, Thurston. Interview by Charlie Bertsch. *We Owe You Nothing: Punk Planet, The Collected Interviews,* edited by Daniel Sinker, 49–57. New York: Akashic Books, 2001.

Morea, Ben, and Ron Hahne. *Black Mask and Up Against the Wall Motherfucker.* Oakland, CA: PM Press, 2011.

Morris, Chris. "LA Punk." In *Forming: The Early Days of L.A. Punk,* 12–24. Santa Monica: Track 16 Gallery/Smart Art Press, 1999.

Morton, John D. *the eyeball of hell (annotated), or How One Single Man's Expectation of Self Becomes the Hopes and Dreams of the Lumpen Prole.* Accessed July 20, 2017. http://www.pukekos.org/2013/01/electric-eels.html (site discontinued).

Mothersbaugh, Mark. Interview by Adam Lerner. In *Mark Mothersbaugh: Myopia,* edited by Adam Lerner, 31–52. New York: Princeton Architectural Press, 2014.

Muir, Peter. *Long Lost Blues: Popular Blues in America, 1850–1920.* Urbana: University of Illinois Press, 2010.

Muñoz, José Esteban. "'Gimme Gimme This . . . Gimme Gimme That': Annihilation and Innovation in the Punk Rock Commons." *Social Text* 31/3 (Fall 2013): 95–110.

Murray, Albert. *Stomping the Blues.* New York: Vintage Books, [1976] 1982.

Musil, Robert. *Precision and Soul: Essays and Addresses,* edited and translated by Burton Pike and David S. Luft. Chicago: University of Chicago Press, [1978] 1990. Originally published in volumes 8 and 9 of Musil's *Gesammelte Werke,* edited by Adolf Frisé. Reinbek bei Hamburg: Rowohlt Verlag, 1978–1981.

Nadeau, Richard, Richard G. Nieme, and Jeffrey Levine. "Innumeracy about Minority Populations." *Public Opinion Quarterly* 57/3 (Autumn 1993): 332–47.

Neal, Jocelyn R. "Dancing around the Subject: Race in Country Fan Culture." *Musical Quarterly* 89/4 (Winter 2006): 555–79.

Needs, Kris. Liner notes to *Dirty Water: The Birth of Punk Attitude.* Year Zero YZTD0008, 2010.

Nehring, Neil. *Flowers in the Dustbin: Culture, Anarchy, and Postwar England.* Ann Arbor: University of Michigan Press, 1993.

Nehring, Neil. "The Situationist Internationale in American Hardcore Punk, 1982–2002." *Popular Music and Society* 29/5 (December 2006): 519–30.

Ness, Mike. Interview by Chris Parker. *Pittsburgh City Paper*, October 1, 2009. https://www
.pghcitypaper.com/pittsburgh/a-conversation-with-mike-ness-of-social-distortion/
Content?oid=1342602.

Newton, Jim. "ACLU Says 83% of Police Live Outside L.A." *Los Angeles Times*, March 29, 1994.

Nguyen, Mimi Thi. *Evolution of a Race Riot*. August 1997. Available online at the POC Zine
Project, https://issuu.com/poczineproject/docs/evolution-of-a-race-riot-issue-1.

Nguyen, Mimi Thi. "It's (Not) a White World: Looking for Race in Punk." In *White Riot: Punk
Rock and the Politics of Race*, edited by Stephen Duncombe and Maxwell Tremblay, 257–68.
London: Verso, 2011. Originally published in *Punk Planet* 28 (November/December 1998).

Nobakht, David. *Suicide: No Compromise*. London: SAF Publishing, 2004.

Noble, Douglas. "Guitar Techniques—Play Like: The Ramones." *Guitar Magazine*, January 7,
2014.

Noelle. "Behind the Orange Curtain." *Flipside* 15 (1979).

Norman, Michael. "To Some, Call to Arms Is But an Echo." *New York Times*, May 31, 1982.

Nyong'o, Tavia. "Do You Want Queer Theory (or Do You Want the Truth)? Intersections of
Punk and Queer in the 1970s." *Radical History Review* 100 (Winter 2008): 102–19.

Nyong'o, Tavia. "Punk'd Theory." *Social Text* 23/3–4 (Fall–Winter 2005): 19–34.

O'Connell, Laurie. "Elk's Lodge '79." *Slash* 2/5 (May 1979): 12–13.

Offs (Don Vinil). Interview by Vale. *Search & Destroy* 8 (1978), reprinted in *Search & Destroy
#7–11: The Complete Reprint*, edited by V. Vale, 52. San Francisco: V/Search Publications,
1996.

Ogg, Alex. *Dead Kennedys: Fresh Fruit for Rotting Vegetables, The Early Years*. Oakland, CA: PM
Press, 2014.

Oja, Carol J. *Making Music Modern: New York in the 1920s*. New York: Oxford University Press,
2000.

Oliver, Paul. *Blues Fell This Morning: Meaning in the Blues*. London: Cassel, 1960.

Omi, Michael, and Howard Winant. *Racial Formation in the United States from the 1960s to the
1990s*. 2nd ed. New York: Routledge, 1994.

Online Archive of California. "Finding Aid for the Self Help Graphics & Art Research Collection 1973–2007." 2014. https://oac.cdlib.org/findaid/ark:/13030/kt6199r13m/?query=Self+Hel
p+Graphics+&+Art+Research+Collection+1973%E2%80%932007.

Orcutt, Bill. Interview by David Keenan. *The Wire: Adventures in Modern Music* 332 (October
2011): 29–32.

Ortiz, Vilma. "The Mexican-Origin Population: Permanent Working Class or Emerging Middle
Class?" In *Ethnic Los Angeles*, edited by Roger Waldinger and Mehdi Bozorgmehr, 247–77.
New York: Russell Sage Foundation, 1996.

Owens, Bill. *Suburbia*. New York: Fotofolio, [1973] 1999.

Page, Jimmy. Interview by Felix Dennis. *OZ* (London), April 1969.

Painter, Nell Irvin. *The History of White People*. New York: W.W. Norton, 2010.

Palmer, Robert. "New Life for the Bowery." *New York Times*, April 15, 1977.

Pastore, Joseph M., Jr. "In Yonkers We Trust." *New York Times*, May 20, 2007. https://www
.nytimes.com/2007/05/20/opinion/nyregionopinions/20WEpastore.html.

Patterson, Fred "Phast Phreddie." "Sex Pistols: The Idiot Bastard Sons of Iggy Pop." *Back Door
Man* 12 (July/August 1977): 5.

Patton, Mike. "Orange County." *Los Angeles Flipside* 16 (1979).

Pelly, Jenn. *The Raincoats*. New York: Bloomsbury, 2017.

Pere Ubu (David Thomas). Interview by Julene and David Deluca. *Search and Destroy* 6 (1978),
reprinted in *Search & Destroy #1–6: The Complete Reprint*, edited by V. Vale, 134. San Francisco: V/Search Publications, 1996.

Perkins, Lucian. *Hard Art DC 1979.* New York: Akashic Books, 2013.

Persky, Lisa Jane. "Transactional Analysis at Town Hall." *New York Rocker*, December 1976.

Persky, Lisa Jane. *X-Offenders: A Year in the Life of a Proto-Punk, 1976.* Self-published, 2016.

Peterson, Richard A. *Creating Country Music: Fabricating Authenticity.* Chicago: University of Chicago Press, 1997.

Philips, Binky. *My Life in the Ghost of Planets: The Story of a CBGB Almost-Was.* Rhino, 2012. Kindle.

Piekut, Benjamin. *Experimentalism Otherwise: The New York Avant-Garde and Its Limits.* Berkeley: University of California Press, 2011.

Piekut, Benjamin. *Henry Cow: The World Is a Problem.* Durham, NC: Duke University Press, 2019.

Pietschmann, Franziska. "A Blacker and Browner Shade of Pale: Reconstructing Punk Rock History." M.A. thesis, Technische Universität Dresden, 2010.

Plugz (Tito Larriva, Barry McBride, and Charlie Quintana). Interview by Vale, *Search & Destroy* 10 (1978), reprinted in *Search & Destroy #7–11: The Complete Reprint*, edited by V. Vale, 92–93. San Francisco: V/Search Publications, 1996.

Polland, Annie, and Daniel Soyer. *Emerging Metropolis: New York in the Age of Immigration, 1840–1920.* Vol. 2 of *City of Promises: A History of the Jews of New York*, edited by Deborah Dash Moore. New York: New York University Press, 2012.

Pop, Iggy. *I Need More.* Los Angeles: 2.13.61 Publications, 1997.

Pop, Iggy. "The 100 Greatest Singers of All Time. #10: James Brown." *Rolling Stone*, November 26, 2008.

Pop, Iggy. "Times Talks: Iggy Pop." Interview by Ben Ratliff. New York Public Library, June 24, 2009.

Porter, Dick, and Kris Needs. *Blondie: Parallel Lives.* London: Omnibus Press, 2012.

Porter, James, and Jake Austen. "Black Punk Time: Blacks in Punk, New Wave, and Hardcore 1976–1984)." *Roctober.* Accessed March 22, 2013. www.roctober.com/roctober/blackpunk1 .html (site discontinued). Originally published in *Roctober* 32 (2002).

Pressler, Charlotte. "Those Were Different Times: A Memoir of Cleveland Life: 1967–1973 (Part One)." *CLE* 3A (1978).

"Punk Rock Seen on KNXT-TV." *Billboard*, March 11, 1978.

Radano, Ronald. "Hot Fantasies: American Modernism and the Idea of Black Rhythm." In *Music and the Racial Imagination*, edited by Ronald Radano and Philip V. Bohlman, 459–80. Chicago: University of Chicago Press, 2000.

Radano, Ronald, and Philip V. Bohlman, eds. *Music and the Racial Imagination.* Chicago: University of Chicago Press, 2000.

Ramone, Johnny. *Commando.* New York: Abrams, 2012.

Rampage, Randy (Randall Archibald), with Chris Walter. *I Survived D.O.A.* Vancouver: GFY Press, 2016.

Rapport, Evan. "Bill Finegan's Gershwin Arrangements and the American Concept of Hybridity." *Journal of the Society for American Music* 2/4 (November 2008): 507–30.

Rapport, Evan. "Hearing Punk as Blues." *Popular Music* 33/1 (January 2014): 39–67.

Ratliff, Ben. "Looking for the Beach Boys." Review of Brian Wilson, *I Am Brian Wilson: A Memoir*, and Mike Love with James S. Hirsch, *Good Vibrations: My Life as a Beach Boy. New York Review of Books*, October 26, 2016.

Ravenstine, Allen. Interview by Jason Gross. *Perfect Sound Forever.* Accessed July 20, 2017. http://www.furious.com/perfect/allenravenstine3.html.

Red Cross (Janet Housden, Tracy Lea, Steve McDonald, and Jeff McDonald). Interview by Mark Wheaton. *No Magazine* (1982).

Rettman, Tony. *NYHC: New York Hardcore 1980–1990*. Brooklyn: Bazillion Points, 2014.

Reynolds, Simon. *Rip It Up and Start Again: Postpunk 1978–1984*. New York: Penguin, 2006.

Robène, Luc, and Solveig Serre, eds. *La scène punk en France (1976–2016)*. Special issue of *Volume! La revue des musique populaires* 13/1 (2016).

Robertson, Campbell. "History of Lynchings in the South Documents Nearly 4,000 Names." *New York Times*, February 10, 2015. https://www.nytimes.com/2015/02/10/us/history-of -lynchings-in-the-south-documents-nearly-4000-names.html.

Robinson, Eugene S. "White Supremacy + Me." *OZY*, January 14, 2016. https://www.ozy.com/ c-notes/white-supremacy-me/30970.

Rogin, Michael. *Blackface, White Noise*. Berkeley: University of California Press, 1996.

Rohlfing, Mary E. "'Don't Say Nothin' Bad About My Baby': A Re-Evaluation of Women's Roles in the Brill Building Era of Early Rock 'n' Roll." *Critical Studies in Mass Communication* 13/2 (June 1996): 93–114.

Rollins, Henry. "Everything Was Heavy." In *We Got Power! Hardcore Punk Scenes from 1980s Southern California*, edited by David Markey and Jordan Schwartz, 6–10. Brooklyn: Bazillion Points, 2012.

Rosenfield, Steve, with Michael "Eppy" Epstein. *Fun + Dangerous: Untold Stories, Unseen Photos, Unearthed Music from My Father's Place 1975–1980*. New York: Ardent Artists, 2010.

Rothstein, Richard. *The Color of Law: A Forgotten History of How Our Government Segregated America*. New York: Liveright, 2017.

Rothstein, Richard. "The Supreme Court's Challenge to Housing Segregation." *The American Prospect*, July 5, 2015. https://prospect.org/article/supreme-courts-challenge-housing -segregation.

Rubin, Mike. "This Band Was Punk Before Punk Was Punk." *New York Times*, March 12, 2009.

Ruiz, Victoria. "Navigating Whiteness in Latinx Spaces: Downtown Boys' Victoria Ruiz Interviews Joey DeFrancesco." *Remezcla*, February 10, 2017. http://remezcla.com/features/music/ dowtown-boys-la-neve-interview/.

Runowicz, John Michael. *Forever Doo-Wop: Race, Nostalgia, and Vocal Harmony*. Amherst: University of Massachusetts Press, 2010.

Russell, Tony. *Blacks, Whites, and Blues*. New York: Stein and Day, 1970.

Russo, Stacy. *We Were Going to Change the World: Interviews with Women from the 1970s and 1980s Southern California Punk Rock Scene*. Solana Beach, CA: Santa Monica Press, 2017.

Sabelli, Sonia. "'Dubbing Di Diaspora': Gender and Reggae Music Inna Babylon." *Social Identities* 17/1 (January 2011): 137–52.

Sanneh, Kelefa. "United Blood." *New Yorker*, March 9, 2015.

Santosuosso, Ernie. "Punk Rock." *Boston Sunday Globe*, August 29, 1976.

Savage, Jon. *England's Dreaming: Anarchy, Sex Pistols, Punk Rock, and Beyond*. London: Faber and Faber, 1991.

Savage, Jon. *The England's Dreaming Tapes: The Essential Companion to England's Dreaming, The Seminal History of Punk*. Minneapolis: University of Minnesota Press, 2012.

Schiesl, Martin. "Behind the Shield: Social Discontent and the Los Angeles Police since 1950." In *City of Promise: Race and Historical Change in Los Angeles*, edited by Martin Schiesl and Mark Morrall Dodge, 137–73. Claremont, CA: Regina Books, 2006.

Schomburg Center for Research in Black Culture. "The Second Great Migration." *In Motion: The African American Migration-Experience*. 2005. www.inmotionaame.org.

Schwartz, Roberta Freund. *How Britain Got the Blues: The Transmission and Reception of American Blues Style in the United Kingdom*. Aldershot: Ashgate, 2007.

Scoggins, Michael C. *The Scotch-Irish Influence on Country Music in the Carolinas: Border Ballads, Fiddle Tunes, and Sacred Songs.* Charleston, SC: History Press, 2013.

Seicshnaydre, Stacy E. "Is Disparate Impact Having Any Impact? An Appellate Analysis of Forty Years of Disparate Impact Claims under the Fair Housing Act." *American University Law Review* 63/2 (2013). http://ssrn.com/abstract=2336266.

Shadduck, B. H. *Jocko-Homo Heavenbound.* Rogers, OH: Jocko-Homo Publishing, 1925.

Shadduck, B. H. *Rastus Agustus Explains Evolution.* Rogers, OH: Homo Publishing, 1928.

Shaw, Greg, ed. *Flamin Groovies Monthly Book* 1, July 1976.

Shaw, Greg, Alan Betrock, Ron Ross, and Lester Bangs. "New York's Beasty, Brutal Music Explosion: The N.Y. Dolls and Blue Öyster Cult Revive Manhattan." *Phonograph Record*, October 1973.

Shepard, Richard F. "Memories of My Queens." *New York Times*, September 3, 1995.

Sherman, Maria. "Downtown Boys' Victoria Ruiz on Writing Chicana Protest-Punk Anthems." *Rolling Stone*, September 20, 2017. https://www.rollingstone.com/music/music-features/downtown-boys-victoria-ruiz-on-writing-chicana-protest-punk-anthems-117084/.

Shernoff, Andy. Liner notes to *The Dictators Go Girl Crazy! (40th Anniversary Edition)*, Real Gone Music RGM-0411, 2015.

Shirley, Ian. *Meet the Residents: America's Most Eccentric Band!* Wembley: SAF Publishing, 1998.

Sigelman, Lee, and Richard G. Niemi. "Innumeracy about Minority Populations: African Americans and Whites Compared." *Public Opinion Quarterly* 65/1 (Spring 2001): 86–94.

Sisario, Ben. "Johnny Ramone, Pioneer Punk Guitarist, Is Dead at 55." *New York Times*, September 17, 2004.

Slobin, Mark. *Motor City Music: A Detroiter Looks Back.* New York: Oxford University Press, 2018.

Smith, Patti. Interview by Lee Paris. *Search and Destroy* 4 (1977), reprinted in *Search & Destroy #1–6: The Complete Reprint*, edited by V. Vale, 69. San Francisco: V/Search Publications, 1996.

Smith, Patti. *Just Kids.* New York: HarperCollins, 2010.

Smith, Winston. Interview by Josh Hooten. In *We Owe You Nothing: Punk Planet, The Collected Interviews*, edited by Daniel Sinker, 155–63. New York: Akashic Books, 2001.

Spaner, David. "Subhumans: The Vancouver Sound." *Public Enemy* 7 (Summer 1979): 8–9.

Spitz, Marc. "The Oral History of 2-Tone." *Spin*, September 28, 2009. https://www.spin.com/2009/09/oral-history-2-tone/.

Spitz, Marc, and Brendan Mullen. *We Got the Neutron Bomb: The Untold Story of L.A. Punk.* New York: Three Rivers, 2001.

Steele, David Warren. "Shape-Note Hymnody." Grove Music Online, 2013.

Steinbeck, Paul. *Message to Our Folks: The Art Ensemble of Chicago.* Chicago: University of Chicago Press, 2017.

Stewart, Alexander. "'Funky Drummer': New Orleans, James Brown and the Rhythmic Transformation of American Popular Music." *Popular Music* 19/3 (October 2000): 293–318.

Stewart, Alexander. "Make It Funky: Fela Kuti, James Brown and the Invention of Afrobeat." *American Studies* 52/4 (2013): 99–118.

Stoever, Jennifer Lynn. *The Sonic Color Line: Race and the Cultural Politics of Listening.* New York: New York University Press, 2016.

Stogov, Il'ya, Aleksei Viktorovich Rubin, and Vladimir Tikhomirov. *Anarkhiya v RF: Pervaya polnaya istoriya russkogo panka.* Saint Petersburg, Russia: Amfora, 2007.

Stoia, Nicholas. "The Common Stock of Schemes in Early Blues and Country Music." *Music Theory Spectrum* 35/2 (Fall 2013): 194–234.

Stratton, Jon. *Jews, Race, and Popular Music.* Surrey, UK: Ashgate, 2009.

Stratton, Jon. *When Music Migrates: Crossing British and European Racial Faultlines, 1945–2010*. Surrey, UK: Ashgate, 2014.

Suarez, Ray. *The Old Neighborhood: What We Lost in the Great Suburban Migration, 1966–1999*. New York: Free Press, 1999.

Suicide [Vega], Alan. *Art-Rite* 13, January 1977.

Suicide [Vega], Alan. Interview by Edit De Ak. *No Magazine* 3 (Summer 1979): 6–10.

Svenonius, Ian F. *The Psychic Soviet*. Chicago: Drag City, 2006.

Szwed, John F., and Morton Marks. "The Afro-American Transformation of European Set Dances and Dance Suites." *Dance Research Journal* 20/1 (Summer 1988): 29–36.

Tavernise, Sabrina. "A Population Changes, Uneasily." *New York Times*, July 17, 2011.

Tawney, Raj. "'Rock 'n' Roll High' at 40: How the Ramones and a Rebellious Female Lead Invaded Theaters." *Variety*, August 5, 2019.

Taylor, Steven. *False Prophet: Field Notes from the Punk Underground*. Middletown, CT: Wesleyan University Press, 2003.

Teuscher, Amanda. "The Evolving Politics of Punk in the Nation's Capital." *American Prospect*, July 15, 2015. https://prospect.org/article/evolving-politics-punk-nations-capital.

Thomas, Tony. "Why Africans Put the Banjo Down." In *Hidden in the Mix: The African American Presence in Country Music*, edited by Diane Pecknold, 143–70. Durham, NC: Duke University Press, 2013.

Tosh, Peter. Interview. *Slash* 2/1 (September 1978): 14–15.

Toy, Vivian S. "New Cassel, First for a Change." *New York Times*, April 4, 2004.

Traber, Daniel S. "L.A.'s 'White Minority': Punk and the Contradictions of Self-Marginalization." *Cultural Critique* 48 (Spring 2001): 30–64.

True, Everett. *Hey Ho Let's Go: The Story of the Ramones*. London: Omnibus Press, 2002.

Tsitsos, William. "Rules of Rebellion: Slamdancing, Moshing, and the American Alternative Scene." *Popular Music* 18/3 (October 1999): 397–414.

Tutti, Cosey Fanni. *art sex music*. London: Faber & Faber, 2017.

Unterberger, Richie. *White Light/White Heat: The Velvet Underground Day-by-Day*. London: Jawbone, 2009.

Valentine, Gary. *New York Rocker: My Life in the Blank Generation with Blondie, Iggy Pop, and Others 1974–1981*. New York: Thunder's Mouth Press, 2002.

van der Merwe, Peter. *Origins of the Popular Style: The Antecedents of Twentieth-Century Popular Music*. Oxford: Clarendon Press, 1989.

Velvet Underground (Lou Reed, Maureen Tucker, and Doug Yule). Interview by David Fricke. New York Public Library, December 8, 2009.

von Appen, Ralf, and Markus Frei-Hauenschild. "AABA, Refrain, Chorus, Bridge, Prechorus—Song Forms and Their Historical Development." *Online-Publikationen der Gesellschaft für Popularmusikforschung* 13 (2015). http://geb.uni-giessen.de/geb/volltexte/2015/11421/pdf/Samples_13_appenfrei.pdf.

Waksman, Steve. "Kick Out the Jams! The MC5 and the Politics of Noise." In *Mapping the Beat: Popular Music and Contemporary Theory*, edited by Thomas Swiss, John Sloop, and Andrew Herman, 47–75. Malden, MA: Blackwell, 1998.

Waksman, Steve. *This Ain't the Summer of Love: Conflict and Crossover in Heavy Metal and Punk*. Berkeley: University of California Press, 2009.

Wald, Elijah. *The Blues: A Very Short Introduction*. New York: Oxford University Press, 2010.

Wald, Elijah. *Escaping the Delta: Robert Johnson and the Invention of the Blues*. New York: HarperCollins, 2004.

Wald, Elijah. *How the Beatles Destroyed Rock 'n' Roll*. New York: Oxford University Press, 2009.

Walser, Robert. *Running with the Devil: Power, Gender, and Madness in Heavy Metal Music.* Middletown, CT: Wesleyan University Press, 1993.

Ward, Eric K. "Skin in the Game: How Antisemitism Animates White Nationalism." *Public Eye* (Summer 2017): 9–15.

Ward, John M. "The *Buffons* Family of Tune Families: Variations on a Theme of Otto Gombosi's." In *Themes and Variations: Writings on Music in Honor of Rulan Chao Pian,* edited by Bell Yung and Joseph S. C. Lam, 290–351. Cambridge, MA: Harvard University Department of Music, 1994.

Waterman, Christopher A. "Race Music: Bo Chatmon, 'Corrine Corrina,' and the Excluded Middle." In *Music and the Racial Imagination,* edited by Ronald Radano and Philip V. Bohlman, 167–205. Chicago: University of Chicago Press, 2000.

Wendell, Eric. *Patti Smith: America's Punk Rock Rhapsodist.* Lanham, MD: Rowman & Littlefield, 2015.

Wenner, Jann S. "The Rolling Stone Interview: John Lennon, Part 1." *Rolling Stone,* January 21, 1971.

White, Timothy. "The Importance of Being a Ramone." *Rolling Stone,* February 8, 1979.

Whiteley, Sheila. "'Kick Out the Jams': Creative Anarchy and Noise in 1960s Rock." In *Resonances: Noise and Contemporary Music,* edited by Michael Goddard, Benjamin Halligan, and Nicola Spelman, 13–23. New York: Bloomsbury, 2013.

Whitesell, Lloyd. "White Noise: Race and Erasure in the Cultural Avant-Garde." *American Music* 19/2 (Summer 2001): 168–89.

Whitfield, Marlon. Interview by Bruce Kalberg. *No Magazine* (1983).

Wilmer, Valerie. *As Serious as Your Life: John Coltrane and Beyond.* London: Serpent's Tail, [1977] 1992.

Wilson, Eric. "A Necessary Stop." *New York Times,* May 29, 2013. https://www.nytimes.com/2013/05/30/fashion/a-necessary-stop-at-re-creation-of-cbgb-restroom.html.

Winner, Langdon. "I'm Not Even Here I Just Stick Around For My Friends: The Odyssey of Captain Beefheart." *Rolling Stone,* May 14, 1970.

Woldoff, Rachael A. *White Flight/Black Flight: The Dynamics of Racial Change in an American Neighborhood.* Ithaca, NY: Cornell University Press, 2011.

Woodward, Alex. "Body Politics: Show Me the Body's Rage Against the Machine." *Gambit,* July 9, 2018. https://www.theadvocate.com/gambit/new_orleans/music/article_9dea43b2–813e-11e8–85d7–77ad3ea13376.html.

Worley, Matthew. *No Future: Punk, Politics and British Youth Culture, 1976–1984.* Cambridge: Cambridge University Press, 2017.

X (Exene Cervenka, John Doe, and Billy Zoom). Interview. *No Magazine* 1 (1978).

Zona de Obras, ed. *Diccionario de punk y hardcore (España y Latinoamérica).* Madrid: Fundación Autor, 2011.

# DISCOGRAPHY

Adolescents. *Adolescents* ["blue album"]. Frontier FLP 1003, 1981.

Agent Orange. *Agent Orange* EP. Agent Orange Records 245-T-1, 1980.

Albertine, Viv. *The Vermilion Border*. Cadiz Music CADIZCD117, 2013.

Amboy Dukes. *The Amboy Dukes*. Mainstream 56104, 1967.

Angry Samoans. *Inside My Brain*. Bad Trip BT 201, 1980.

Bad Brains. *Bad Brains* ["yellow tape"]. ROIR A106, 1982.

Bad Brains. *Black Dots*. Caroline CAR 7534, 1996.

Bad Brains. "Pay to Cum" b/w "Stay Close to Me." Bad Brain Records BB001, 1980.

Bag, Alice. *Alice Bag*. Don Giovanni DG-116, 2016.

Bags. "Survive" b/w "Babylonian Gorgon." Dangerhouse BAG 199, 1978.

Baker, LaVern. "See See Rider" b/w "The Story of My Love." Atlantic 45–2167, 1962.

Beatles. *Please Please Me*. Parlophone PMC 1202, 1963.

Bikini Kill. *Pussy Whipped*. Kill Rock Stars KRS 218, 1993.

Black Flag. *Damaged*. SST 007, [1981] 1984. Contains "Depression," "Police Story," "Thirsty and Miserable," and "What I See."

Black Flag. *Jealous Again*. SST 003, 1980. Contains "White Minority."

Black Flag. *Nervous Breakdown* EP. SST 001, 1979. Contains "I've Had It" and "Nervous Breakdown."

Blondie. *Blondie*. Chrysalis 1165, 1976. Contains "X-Offender."

Blondie. *Plastic Letters*. Chrysalis CHS 1166, 1977. Contains "Denis."

Bo Diddley. "Call Me" b/w "Pills." Checker CK-985, 1961.

Bratmobile. *Potty Mouth*. Kill Rock Stars KRS-208, 1993.

Broonzy, Big Bill. *Vol. 3, 1934–1935*. Document DOCD-5052, 1991.

Brown, James. "I Can't Stand Myself (When You Touch Me)" b/w "There was a Time." King 45–6144, 1967.

Burdon, Eric, and the Animals. "See See Rider" b/w "She'll Return It." MGM K-13582, 1966.

Burning Spear. *Marcus Garvey*. Island ILPS 9377, 1975.

Buzzcocks. *Spiral Scratch* EP. New Hormones ORG 1, 1977.

Canned Heat. *Boogie with Canned Heat*. Liberty LST-7541, 1968.

Captain Beefheart and His Magic Band. "Diddy Wah Diddy" b/w "Who Do You Think You're Fooling." A&M 794, 1966.

Captain Beefheart and His Magic Band. *Safe as Milk*. Buddah 1001, 1967. Contains "Grown So Ugly."

Captain Beefheart and His Magic Band. *Strictly Personal*. Blue Thumb BTS1, 1968.

Captain Beefheart and His Magic Band. *Trout Mask Replica*. Straight STS 1053, 1969.

Chain and the Gang. *Down with Liberty . . . Up with Chains!* K KLP203, 2009.

Chain and the Gang. *Music's Not for Everyone*. K KLP220, 2011.

Chelsea. "Right to Work" b/w "The Loner." Step-Forward Records SF 2, 1977.

Chrome. *Alien Soundtracks*. Siren DE21–22, 1977.

Chrome. *Half Machine Lip Moves*. Siren DE-333-SEC, 1979.

Circle Jerks. *Group Sex*. Frontier FLP 1002, 1980.

Clash. *The Clash*. CBS 82000, 1977. Contains "Janie Jones," "London's Burning," "Police and Thieves," and "White Riot."

Clash. "I Fought the Law" b/w "White Man in Hammersmith Palais." Epic 9–50738, 1979.

Clash. *London Calling*. CBS CLASH 3, 1979. Contains "Brand New Cadillac" and "The Guns of Brixton."

Clash. "London Calling." 12" single. CBS 12–8087, 1979. Contains "Armagideon Time (Version)," "Justice Tonight (Version)," and "Kick It Over (Version)."

Clash. *Sandinista!* CBS FSLN 1, 1980. Contains "The Magnificent Seven."

Clash. "This is Radio Clash" b/w "Radio Clash." CBS A1797, 1981.

Clash. "White Man in Hammersmith Palais" b/w "The Prisoner." CBS 6383, 1978.

Controllers. "Neutron Bomb" b/w "Killer Queers." What Records? WHAT 04, 1978.

Crass. *The Feeding of the Five Thousand*. Small Wonder Records WEENY 2, 1978.

Damned. "New Rose" b/w "Help." Stiff BUY 6, 1976.

Damned. *Damned Damned Damned*. Stiff SEEZ1, 1977.

Damned. *Music for Pleasure*. Stiff SEEZ 5, 1977.

Damned. *Machine Gun Etiquette*. Chiswick CWK3011, 1979.

Dead Kennedys. *Fresh Fruit for Rotting Vegetables*. Cherry Red B RED 10, 1980.

Dead Kennedys. *In God We Trust, Inc.* Alternative Tentacles VIRUS 5, 1981.

Death. . . . *For the Whole World to See*. Drag City DC387, 2009.

Descendents. *Milo Goes to College*. New Alliance NAR-012, 1982.

Destroy All Monsters. *Destroy All Monsters 1974–1976*. Ecstatic Peace! E# 47, 1994.

DEVO. *Duty Now For the Future*. Warner Bros. BSK 3337, 1979. Contains "DEVO Corporate Anthem."

DEVO. *Freedom of Choice*. Warner Bros. BSK 3435, 1980. Contains "Whip It."

DEVO. *Hardcore DEVO Volume 1*. Rykodisc RCD 10188, 1990. Contains "Auto Modown," "Mechanical Man," and "Soo Bawls."

DEVO. *Hardcore DEVO Volume 2*. Rykodisc RCD 20208, 1991. Contains "Bamboo Bimbo."

DEVO. "(I Can't Get Me No) Satisfaction" b/w "Sloppy (I Saw My Baby Getting)." Booji Boy Records, 1977.

DEVO. *Recombo DNA*. Rhino Handmade RHM2 7718, 2000. Contains "Somewhere with DEVO."

Dictators. *Go Girl Crazy!* Epic KE 33348, 1975.

Dictators. *The Dictators Go Girl Crazy! (40th Anniversary Edition)*. Real Gone Music RGM-0411, 2015.

Dirty Projectors. *Rise Above*. Dead Oceans DOC001, 2007.

Doors. *The Doors*. Elektra EKL-4007, 1967.

Dos. *Dos y Dos*. Clenched Wrench Clenched002, 2011.

Downtown Boys. *Full Communism*. Don Giovanni DG-94, 2015.

8-Eyed Spy. *8-Eyed Spy*. Fetish FR2003, 1981.

Electric Eels. *God Says Fuck You*. Homestead HMS174–2, 1991.

Evens. *The Odds*. Dischord Dis180, 2012.

Fear. *The Record*. Slash SR-111, 1982.

Flamin' Groovies. *Shake Some Action*. Sire SASD-7521, 1976.

Flamin' Groovies. "Slow Death" b/w "Tallahassee Lassie." United Artists 35392, 1972.

Flamin' Groovies. *Teenage Head*. Kama Sutra KSBS 2031, 1971.

Flesh Eaters. *Disintegration Nation EP*. Upsetter UPSET 8, 1978.

Garland, Red. *Red in Bluesville*. Prestige PRST-7157, 1959.

Generation X. *Generation X*. Chrysalis CHR 1169, 1978.

Germs. *(GI)*. Slash SR-103, 1979.

Germs. *Lexicon Devil* EP. Slash Scam 101, 1978.

Half Japanese. *1/2 Gentlemen/Not Beasts*. Armageddon A Box 1, 1980.

Harry Pussy. "Black Ghost." Siltbreeze SB56, 1995.

Harry Pussy. *Harry Pussy*. Palilalia PAL-031, [1993] 2014.

Harry Pussy. "Please Don't Come Back from the Moon," "Nazi USA." Blackjack JACK 016, 1994.

Harry Pussy. *You'll Never Play this Town Again*. Load LOAD 121, 2008. Contains "No Hey . . ."

Heavens to Betsy. *Calculated*. Kill Rock Stars KRS-222, 1994.

Hopkins, Lightnin'. "Baby Please Don't Go" b/w "Death Bells." Gold Star 646, 1949.

Holly, Buddy. *Buddy Holly*. Coral CRL-57210, 1958.

Howlin' Wolf. *Howlin' Wolf*. Chess LP1469, 1962.

Huggy Bear. *Taking the Rough with the Smooch* EP. *Kill Rock Stars*, KRS-214, 1993.

Kane, Jonathan. *I Looked at the Sun*. Table of the Elements/Radium TOE-CD-803, 2006.

Kinks. *Kinks*. Reprise K-6143, 1964.

Knack. *Get the Knack*. Capitol SO-11948, 1979.

Lead Belly. *Leadbelly's Legacy Volume 3: Early Recordings*. Folkways FP 24, 1951.

Led Zeppelin. *Untitled (IV)*. Atlantic 2401012, 1971.

LiLiPUT. *Liliput*. Rough Trade, ROUGH 43, 1982.

LiLiPUT. *Some Songs*. Rough Trade RTD 15, 1983.

Marcels. *Blue Moon*. Colpix CP 416, 1961.

Marley, Bob. "Punky Reggae Party." Tuff Gong, 1977.

MC5. *Back in the USA*. Atlantic SD 8247, 1970.

MC5. *Kick Out the Jams*. Elektra EKS 74042, 1969.

MC5. *'66 Breakout!* Total Energy NER 3023, [1966] 1999.

Middle Class. *Out of Vogue* EP. Joke 09831, 1978.

Minor Threat. *In My Eyes* EP. Dischord 5, 1981. Contains "Guilty of Being White" and "Out of Step."

Minor Threat. *Minor Threat* EP. Dischord 3, 1981. Contains "Filler," "Screaming at a Wall," "Small Man, Big Mouth," and "Straight Edge."

Minor Threat. *Out of Step*. Dischord 10, 1983. Contains "Betray."

Modern Lovers. *Jonathan Richman and the Modern Lovers*. BZ-0048, 1976.

Modern Lovers. *The Modern Lovers*. Beserkley (Home of the Hits) HH-1910, 1976. Reissued on Rhino Records, R2 70091, 1989.

Modern Lovers. *Precise Modern Lovers Order*. Rounder CD 9042, 1994.

Montez, Chris. "Let's Dance" b/w "You're the One." Monogram MR-505, 1962.

Morton, Jelly Roll. *Kansas City Stomp: The Library of Congress Recordings, Vol. 1*. Rounder 1091, [1938] 1993.

Mos Def. *The New Danger*. Geffen B0003558, 2004.

Muddy Waters. "Rollin' and Tumblin'." Aristocrat 412, 1950.

Murvin, Junior. "Police and Thieves" b/w "Soldier and Police War." Island WIP 6539, 1979.

Nation of Ulysses. *13-Point Program to Destroy America*. Dischord DIS 57, 1991.

New York Dolls. *New York Dolls*. Mercury SRM-1-675, 1973.

Orcutt, Bill. *Bill Orcutt*. Palilalia PAL-048, 2017.

Orcutt, Bill. *A History of Every One*. Editions Mego EMEGO 173, 2013.

Orcutt, Bill. *A New Way to Pay Old Debts*. Palilalia PAL-002, 2009. Contains "Sad News from Korea."

Orcutt, Bill. *Twenty-Five Songs*. Palilalia PAL-025, 2013.

Parks, Lloyd. "Mafia" b/w Black Expression Band, "Parks." Parks LS 6105, 1975.

Pere Ubu. *The Modern Dance*. Mercury 9100 052, 1978.

Pere Ubu. *Datapanik in the Year Zero*. Geffen DGC5–24969, 1996.

Plugz. *Better Luck*. Fatima Recordz FTM80, 1981.

Plugz. *Electrify Me*. Plug Recordz PR001, 1979.

Plugz. *Move* EP. Slash SCAM 102, 1978. Contains "Mindless Contentment."

Presley, Elvis. *Elvis Presley*. RCA Victor, LPM-1254, 1956.

Raincoats. *Odyshape*. Rough Trade ROUGH 13, 1981.

Raincoats. *The Raincoats*. Rough Trade ROUGH 3, 1979.

Rainey, Ma. "Jealous Hearted Blues" b/w "See See Rider Blues." Paramount 12252, 1924.

Ramones. *End of the Century*. Sire SRK 6077, 1980. Contains "Do You Remember Rock 'n' Roll Radio?"

Ramones. *Leave Home*. Sire SA-7528, 1977. Contains "California Sun" and "Pinhead."

Ramones. *Ramones*. Sire SASD-7520, 1976.

Ramones. *Road to Ruin*. Sire SRK 6063, 1978.

Ramones. *Rocket to Russia*. Sire SR 6042, 1977.

Randoms. "A B C D" b/w "Let's Get Rid of New York." Dangerhouse PT-1, 1977.

Ravenstine, Allen. *Terminal Drive*. Smog Veil SV133, 2017.

Real Kids. *The Real Kids*. Red Star RS2, 1977.

Red Cross [Redd Kross]. *Red Cross* EP. Posh Boy PBS-1010, 1980.

Reich, Steve. *Early Works*. Elektra Nonesuch 79169, 1987.

Residents. *Babyfingers*. Ralph RR0377, 1979.

Residents. "The Beatles Play the Residents and the Residents Play the Beatles." Ralph RR0577, 1977.

Residents. *The Big Bubble*. Ralph RZ-8552, 1985.

Residents. *Daydream B Liver*. UWEB 005, 1991. Contains "King Kong."

Residents. *Duck Stab/Buster and Glen*. Ralph Records RR0278, 1978.

Residents. *Eskimo*. Ralph ESK7906, 1979.

Residents. *Fingerprince*. Ralph RR1276, 1976.

Residents. *George & James (American Composer Series—Volume 1)*. Ralph RZ-8402, 1984.

Residents. *Intermission*. Ralph RZ-8252, 1982.

Residents. *Mark of the Mole*. Ralph RZ-8152, 1981.

Residents. *Meet the Residents*. Ralph 0677, [1974] 1977.

Residents. *The Residents Present the Third Reich 'n Roll*. Ralph RR1075, [1975] 1979.

Residents. *Stars & Hank Forever (American Composer Series—Volume 2)*. Ralph RZ-8652, 1986.

Residents. *The Tunes of Two Cities*. Ralph RZ-8202, 1982.

Richman, Jonathan. *I, Jonathan*. Rounder 9036, 1992. Contains "Parties in the U.S.A."

Rivieras. "California Sun" b/w "H.B. Goose Step." Riviera R-1401, 1964.

Rocket from the Tombs. *The Day the Earth Met the Rocket from the Tombs*. Smog Veil SV37, 2002.

Rolling Stones. "Honky Tonk Women" b/w "You Can't Always Get What You Want." Decca F 12952, 1969.

Rolling Stones. *Let it Bleed*. Decca LK 5025, 1969.

Ronettes. "Be My Baby" b/w "Tedesco and Pitman." Phillies 116, 1963.

Roxy Music. *Roxy Music*. Island ILPS 9200, 1972.

Ryder, Mitch. *Detroit*. Paramount PAS-6010, 1971.

Sex Pistols. "Anarchy in the UK" b/w "I Wanna Be Me." EMI 2566, 1976.

Sex Pistols. *Never Mind the Bollocks Here's the Sex Pistols.* Virgin V 2086, 1977.

Show Me the Body. *Body War.* The Famous Letter Racer LVR00040, 2016.

Sick of It All. *Wake the Sleeping Dragon!* Fat Wreck Records FAT111, 2018.

Simone, Peg. *Secrets from the Storm.* Table of the Elements/Radium TOE-CD-820, 2010.

Siouxsie and the Banshees. *The Scream.* Polydor POLD 5009, 1978. Contains "Carcass."

Slits. *Cut.* Island ILPS 9573, 1979.

Slits. "Typical Girls" b/w "I Heard It through the Grapevine." Island WIP 6505, 1979.

Smith, Patti. *Easter.* Arista AB 4171, 1978.

Smith, Patti. *Horses.* Arista AL 4066, 1975.

Smith, Patti. *Radio Ethiopia.* Arista AL4097, 1976.

Social Distortion. "Playpen" b/w "Mainliner." Posh Boy PBS 11, 1981.

Soft Pink Truth. *Do You Want New Wave or Do You Want the Soft Pink Truth?* Soundslike SL 17
    CD, 2004.

Sonic Youth. *Confusion Is Sex.* Neutral 9, 1983.

Springsteen, Bruce. *Nebraska.* Columbia 38358, 1982.

Stooges. *Fun House.* Elektra EKS 74071, 1970.

Stooges. *Raw Power.* Columbia 32111, 1973.

Stooges. *The Stooges.* Elektra EKS 74051, 1969.

Suicide. *Suicide.* Red Star RS1, 1977.

Talking Heads. *Fear of Music.* Sire SRK 6076, 1979.

Them. *The "Angry" Young Them.* Decca LK 4700, 1965.

Them. "Baby Please Don't Go" b/w "Gloria." Decca F 12018, 1964.

This Moment In Black History. *It Take a Nation of Assholes to Hold Us Back.* X-Mist XM-094,
    2006.

This Moment In Black History. *Raw Black Power* EP. (iN)Sect Records IRS-0002, 2008.

Throbbing Gristle. "United" b/w "Zyklon B Zombie." Industrial IR0003, 1978.

United States of America. *The United States of America.* Columbia CS 9614, 1968.

Urinals. *Another EP.* Happy Squid HS002, 1979.

Various artists. *The Akron Compilation.* Stiff Records GET3, 1978.

Various artists. *Anthology of American Folk Music, Vol. 1: Ballads.* Folkways FP 251, 1952.

Various artists. *Anthology of American Folk Music, Vol. 2: Social Music.* Folkways FP 252, 1952.

Various artists. *Anthology of American Folk Music, Vol. 3: Songs.* Folkways FP 253, 1952.

Various artists. *Anthology of American Folk Music.* Reissue. Smithsonian Folkways SFW40090,
    1997.

Various artists. *Beserkley Chartbusters Volume 1.* Beserkley BZ-0044, 1975.

Various artists. *Blorp Esette Vol. 1.* LAFMS 5, 1977.

Various artists. *Dirty Water: The Birth of Punk Attitude.* Year Zero YZTD0008, 2010.

Various artists. *Flex Your Head.* Dischord 7, 1982.

Various artists. *Goodbye, Babylon.* Dust-to-Digital DTD-01, 2003.

Various artists. *Kill Rock Stars.* Kill Rock Stars KRS 201, 1991.

Various artists. *LAFMS: The Lowest Form of Music: The Los Angeles Free Music Society 1973–
    1994.* RRR-CD-17, 1996, 28.

Various artists. *Light Bulb Magazine 4 Emergency Cassette Vol. 1 and 2.* LAFMS, 1981.

Various artists. *Nuggets: Original Artyfacts from the First Psychedelic Era 1965–1968.* Elektra
    7E-2006, 1972.

Various artists. *Oldies But Goodies in Hi-Fi.* Original Sound OSR-LP-5001, 1959.

Various artists. *Punk 45: Chaos in the City of Angels and Devils, Hollywood from X to Zero &
    Hardcore on the Beaches, Punk in Los Angeles 1977–81.* Soul Jazz Records SJRCD329, 2016.

Various artists. *Punk 45: Extermination Nights in the Sixth City! Cleveland, Ohio: Punk and the Decline of the Mid West 1975–82*. Soul Jazz Records SJRCD300, 2015.

Various artists. *Punk 45: Sick on You! One Way Spit! After the Love & Before the Revolution. Vol 3: Proto-Punk 1970–77*. Soul Jazz SJRCD279, 2014.

Various artists. *The Sire Machine Turns You Up*. Sire SMP1, 1978.

Various artists. *Yes L.A.* Dangerhouse EW-79, 1979.

Velvet Underground. *Loaded*. Cotillion 9034, 1970. Contains "Rock and Roll" and "Sweet Jane."

Velvet Underground. *1969 Velvet Underground Live with Lou Reed*. Mercury SRM-2-7504, 1974.

Velvet Underground. *The Velvet Underground and Nico*. Verve V-5008, 1967. Contains "Heroin," "I'm Waiting for the Man," and "Venus in Furs."

Velvet Underground. *The Velvet Underground Bootleg Series, Volume 1: The Quine Tapes*. Universal 589 067, 2001.

Velvet Underground. *VU*. Verve 823 721, 1985. Contains "Foggy Notion."

Velvet Underground. *White Light/White Heat*. Verve V6-5046, 1968. Contains "The Gift" and "Sister Ray."

Violent Femmes. *Hallowed Ground*. Slash 25094, 1984.

Weirdos. *Destroy All Music* [EP]. Bomp! BOMP 112, 1977.

Weirdos. "We Got the Neutron Bomb" b/w "Solitary Confinement." Dangerhouse SP-1063, 1978.

Williams, Joe. "Baby Please Don't Go" b/w "Wild Cow Blues." Bluebird B-6200, 1935.

Williams, Robert Pete. *Free Again*. Prestige Bluesville 1026, 1961.

Wire. *Pink Flag*. Harvest ST-11757, 1977.

X. "Adult Books" b/w "We're Desperate." Dangerhouse D88, 1978.

X. *Los Angeles*. Slash SR-104, 1980.

X. *Wild Gift*. Slash SR-107, 1981.

X-Ray Spex. *Germ Free Adolescents*. EMI INS-3023, 1978.

X_X. "A" b/w "You're Full of Shit." Drome DR2, 1979.

X_X. "No Nonsense" b/w "Approaching the Minimal with Spray Guns." Drome DR8, 1980.

Young, La Monte. *La Monte Young & The Forever Bad Blues Band: Just Stompin'/Live at the Kitchen*. Gramavision 79487, 1993.

Zeros. "Beat Your Heart Out" b/w "Wild Weekend." Bomp! BOMP 118, 1978.

Zeros. "Don't Push Me Around" b/w "Wimp." Bomp! BOMP 110, 1977.

# FILMOGRAPHY

Covino, Mark, and Jeff Howlett, dirs., *A Band Called Death*, Drafthouse Films, 2012.

Goldfarb, Ellen, dir. *Dare to be Different*. 2017.

Hardy, Don, dir., *Theory of Obscurity: A Film about the Residents*. DoF Media and KTF Films, 2015.

Krulik, Jeff, and John Heyn, dirs. *Heavy Metal Parking Lot*. 1986.

Letts, Don, dir. *The Punk Rock Movie*. 1978.

Riggle, Matt, Deedle LaCour, James Rayburn, and Justin Wilson, dirs. and eds. *Filmage: The Story of Descendents/All*, 2013.

Shepherd, Elaine, prod. and dir. *The Artist Formerly Known as Captain Beefheart*. BBC, 1997.

Thomson, Hugh, prod. and dir. *Dancing in the Street: A Rock and Roll History*. "Episode 8: No Fun." BBC, 1995.

Young, Paul, dir. *Urban Struggle: The Battle of the Cuckoo's Nest*. 1981.

# CREDITS

Peter Laughner's personal notes to "Pete Laughner Sings the Blues Pt. II" courtesy the estate of Peter Laughner, the Peter Laughner archives at Smog Veil Records, and the Rock and Roll Hall of Fame Library and Archives.

Photograph of DEVO at Mabuhay Gardens copyright Richard Alden Peterson and reproduced with permission.

Photograph of Bad Brains performing at Valley Green Housing Complex copyright Lucian Perkins and reproduced with permission.

"No Fun," words and music by Dave Alexander, Scott Asheton, Ronald Asheton and Iggy Pop (James Osterberg). Copyright © 1969 BMG Bumblebee, Warner-Tamerlane Publishing Corp. and Stooge Staffel Music. Copyright Renewed. This arrangement Copyright © 2019 BMG Bumblebee, Warner-Tamerlane Publishing Corp. and Stooge Staffel Music. All rights for BMG Bumblebee administered by BMG Rights Management (US) LLC. All rights for Stooge Staffel Music administered by Warner-Tamerlane Publishing Corp. All rights reserved and used by permission. Reprinted by permission of Hal Leonard LLC and Alfred Music.

"Pills," words and music by Ellas McDaniel. Copyright © 1961 (Renewed) Arc Music Corp. (BMI). This arrangement Copyright © 2019 Arc Music Corp. (BMI). All rights administered by BMG Rights Management (US) LLC. International copyright secured. All rights reserved. Reprinted by permission of Hal Leonard LLC.

"White Riot," words and music by Joe Strummer and Mick Jones. Copyright © 1977 Nineden Ltd. Copyright renewed. This arrangement copyright © 2019 Nineden Ltd. All rights in the U.S. and Canada controlled and administered by Universal—Polygram International Publishing, Inc. All rights reserved. Used by permission. Reprinted by permission of Hal Leonard LLC.

"Neat Neat Neat," words and music by Brian James. Copyright © 1977 Imagem London Ltd. This arrangement © 2019 Imagem London Ltd. All rights for Imagem London Ltd. in the U.S. and Canada controlled and administered by Universal Music—Z Tunes LLC. All rights reserved. Used by permission. Reprinted by permission of Hal Leonard LLC.

Leaflet for the Residents W.E.I.R.D. fan club copyright © 1977 and reproduced with permission of the Cryptic Corporation.

Artwork for Chrome, *Alien Soundtracks*, copyright © 1977 and reproduced with permission.

Artwork for Harry Pussy, *Harry Pussy*, and Bill Orcutt, *Twenty-Five Songs* reproduced with permission.

Artwork for Flamin' Groovies, *Teenage Head*, reproduced with permission of Sony Music Entertainment.

Artwork for Flamin' Groovies, *Shake Some Action*, and Germs, *(GI)*, reproduced with permission of Rhino Entertainment Company, a Warner Music Group Company.

Artwork for This Moment in Black History, *It Takes a Nation of Assholes to Hold Us Back*, reproduced with permission. Photography by Bryon Miller.

Excerpts of Jason Gross interview with Allen Ravenstine copyright © Jason Gross and reproduced with permission.

Portions of chapter 2 appeared as "Hearing Punk as Blues," *Popular Music* 33/1 (2014), 39–67.

# INDEX

# ABOUT THE AUTHOR

Photo credit: Nathalie Moreno

Evan Rapport is associate professor of ethnomusicology at The New School in New York City. He is the author of *Greeted with Smiles: Bukharian Jewish Music and Musicians in New York* (Oxford University Press, 2014), as well as articles on arrangements of George Gershwin's concert works, settings of Persian poetry, and the idea of "ethnic music" in New York.

CPSIA information can be obtained
at www.ICGtesting.com
Printed in the USA
BVHW030736130921
616569BV00005B/121

9 781496 831224